MODERNITY AND ITS OTHER

MODERNITY AND ITS OTHER

The Encounter with North American Indians in the Eighteenth Century

ROBERT WOODS SAYRE

University of Nebraska Press
Lincoln and London

English-language edition © 2017 by the Board of Regents of
the University of Nebraska. Originally published in French
as *La modernité et son autre: Récits de la rencontre avec l'Indien
en Amérique du Nord au XVIIIe siècle* by Les Perséides, 2008.

All rights reserved
Manufactured in the United States of America

Library of Congress Cataloging-in-Publication Data
Names: Sayre, Robert, 1943– author.
Title: Modernity and its other: the encounter with North
American Indians in the eighteenth century / Robert
Woods Sayre; translated by Robert Woods Sayre.
Other titles: Modernité et son autre. English
Description: Lincoln: University of Nebraska Press,
2017. | Includes bibliographical references and index.
Identifiers: LCCN 2017030431 (print)
LCCN 2017035683 (ebook)
ISBN 9780803280977 (paperback: alk. paper)
ISBN 9781496204776 (epub)
ISBN 9781496204783 (mobi)
ISBN 9781496204790 (pdf)
Subjects: LCSH: Indians of North America—First
contact with Europeans. | Travelers' writings, European—
History and criticism. | Europeans—Travel—North
America—History—18th century. | Indians of North
America—History—18th century. | North America—
Discovery and exploration—European. | BISAC: SOCIAL
SCIENCE / Ethnic Studies / Native American Studies. |
HISTORY / United States / Colonial Period (1600–1775).
Classification: LCC E77 (ebook) | LCC E77 .S2913
2017 (print) | DDC 970.004/97—dc23
LC record available at https://lccn.loc.gov/2017030431

Set in Adobe Jenson by Rachel Gould.
Designed by N. Putens.

To my international family, who sustain me

CONTENTS

List of Illustrations *ix*

Preface *xi*

Acknowledgments *xv*

Introduction *1*

Part 1. Views of Modernity: Internal/External Discovery

1. Crèvecoeur: British America before and during the Revolutionary Upheaval *29*

2. Philip Freneau: After the Revolution *57*

3. Moreau de Saint-Méry: Fin de Siècle *81*

Part 2. Views of the Other: Travels in "Indian Territory"

4. The Zero Degree of the Other: Indian Violence and "Adventure" with Indians *101*

5. Accounts of Travel in New France: Lahontan and Charlevoix *131*

6. Anglo-American Travelers: John Lawson and Jonathan Carver *167*

7. Travels of William Bartram, Quaker Botanist   205

8. Fur Traders: Alexander Mackenzie and Jean-Baptiste Trudeau   235

   Epilogue: Into the Nineteenth Century—George Catlin   269

   Conclusion   295

   Appendix: Chronology of Historical Events, Travels, and Publications   307

   Notes   313

   Bibliography   369

   Index   397

ILLUSTRATIONS

Following page 98

1. *A New Map of North America from the Latest Discoveries,* 1763

2. *Tontine Coffee House, N.Y.C.,* by Francis Guy, ca. 1797

3. *Elijah Boardman,* by Ralph Earl, 1789

4. *Marinus Willett,* by Ralph Earl, ca. 1791

5. Title page, *Narratives of a Late Expedition against the Indians,* 1783

6. Portrait of Alexander Henry, frontispiece of *Travels and Adventures in Canada and the Indian Territories,* 1809

7. Title page of Henry's *Travels and Adventures in Canada and the Indian Territories*

8. Frontispiece of Lahontan's *Nouveaux voyages,* 1703

9. Indian hunting practices depicted in *Nouveaux voyages*

10. Map of the "Rivière longue" in *Nouveaux voyages*

11. Map by J.-N. Bellin illustrating Charlevoix's *Journal d'un voyage,* 1744

12. Title page of Lawson's *A New Voyage to Carolina*, 1709

13. Map of Carolina in *A New Voyage to Carolina*

14. Map of Great Lakes and upper Mississippi region in Carver's *Travels*, 1778.

15. *A Pipe of Peace*, etc. in Carver's *Travels*

16. *A Man and Woman of the Ottigaumies* in Carver's *Travels*

17. Frontispiece (Mico Chlucco) and title page of Bartram's *Travels*, 1791

18. Map of the Coast of East Florida from Bartram's *Travels* (London edition, 1792)

19. A page from Squier's edition of Bartram's "Observations on the Creek and Cherokee Indians, 1789," 1853

20. A View of *Alatchua Savanah*, map drawing by Bartram

21. Frontispiece of Catlin's *Letters and Notes on the Manners, Customs, and Condition of the North American Indians*, 1841

22. Buffalo's Back Fat, Blackfoot chief, in Catlin's *Letters and Notes*

23. One Horn, Miniconjou chief, in Catlin's *Letters and Notes*

24. Indian artifacts, in Catlin's *Letters and Notes*

25. "Wi-jun-jon, Pigeon's Egg Head, going to and returning from Washington," in Catlin's *Letters and Notes*

PREFACE

This book was first published in French, in 2008.[1] For the present edition I have translated, revised, and considerably expanded that publication. Sections added to the original work are chapter 3, on Moreau de Saint-Méry; chapter 8, on Alexander Mackenzie and Jean-Baptiste Trudeau; and the epilogue, on George Catlin. I am an American who, after university training and initial teaching in the United States, resettled in France, where I have spent the larger part of my career. My research interests and activities over that time have involved in almost equal part French and Anglo-American studies.

In preparing this new, revised edition destined for an American public, I have taken into account important developments and publications in early North American history and ethnohistory that have occurred since the writing of the original French work. I have also engaged with some crucial issues that are part of current American discussions and debates on Native American history. In this regard it seems important to situate my book in the context of these contemporary developments in North American scholarship and reflection.

In the past several decades extraordinarily rich and varied work has been done on all aspects of Native America, both present and historical. This period has seen the rise to prominence of significant numbers of Native American intellectuals and scholars, such as Gerald Vizenor, Robert Warrior, and Donald Fixico. In the ethnohistorical domain, a plethora of writings have appeared that make new departures in a number of respects, building on and in some cases diverging from the equally fruitful, groundbreaking productions of the several decades before that. A new generation of scholars, nonnative as well as native, has tended to shift the focus from Euro-American actions and representations to indigenous agency and perspective. Turning from the overarching narrative of dispossession, cultural and material destruction, and assimilation, these scholars have increasingly emphasized Indian power, persistence, and creative adaptation in the centuries following first contacts with Europeans. Change has also been apparent in the area of gender. Much more work than in the past has been done on Indian women and the roles they have played historically, and studies of them, as well as of other topics, have often been authored by women scholars—Theda Perdue, Susan Sleeper-Smith, Nancy Shoemaker, and many others. Many fundamental questions have been raised in this proliferation of publications since the 1990s: How should American Indian history be studied and written? How can native perspectives be retrieved? How did the fur trade function, and what were its consequences? How exactly did European and native religions interact? And there are other questions as well. This most recent period has opened the field, then, to many new discussions and new formulations of older ones—discussions that are by no means closed today.

In this context some explanation of my book's subject and aim is in order. It seems crucial from the outset to establish that this study is not a work of ethnohistory, nor am I an ethnohistorian. Although I draw extensively on materials from eighteenth-century Native American history, my book is not about eighteenth-century Native America per se. It is rather about the encounter of two types of society—both evolving, but which came into particularly sharp opposition and close interrelation, exemplary in larger, world-historical terms—at that particular time and place. As I conceive it—to be further elaborated in my introduction—this opposition involves the advent, in the colonial settler societies, of "modernity," defined as the overall civilization created by developing capitalist economic structures, and its confrontation with its "Other," the indigenous communities that persist and resist its incursion. The civilization of modernity achieves its purest form in the British colonies, and the French in North America constitute a kind of mediating factor in terms of the opposition I am studying.

I explore the encounter of modernity with its Other from *within*, that is, through the experience and perceptions of those who live within modernity. This means that the perspective, or perspectives—for they are highly diversified—I analyze are generally Euro-American, with Indian points of view appearing for the most part only indirectly or by refraction. I might add as well that by virtue of the fact that textual expression was largely dominated by men in the period concerned, the voices are also primarily male. I am aware that from the vantage point of contemporary Native American studies my approach may appear to some to be a limiting one, or worse, guilty of bias.

I would contend, however, not only that my focus is called for by the nature of my inquiry but also, importantly, that it in no way contradicts current efforts to foreground and highlight Indian consciousness and agency. In dealing with the history of early America, multiple angles of approach can and should be complementary rather than exclusive. Moreover it seems clear that in understanding the dynamics of the period, the testimony of significant Euro-American writers remains an important part of the overall picture. The native scholar Donald Fixico, although he strongly advocates the inclusion of Indians' own views in writing about them, acknowledges as much in his contribution to a collection of essays by Indian intellectuals and teachers, *Natives and Academics*. Historians of North America, Fixico asserts, must look at the "whole picture," which for him includes "the diverse perspectives of white American views" as well as those of indigenous peoples.[2]

Although the backbone of my work is thus the analysis of Euro-American texts, and through them exploring the collective "memory" of that group, I have contextualized them wherever possible from ethnohistorical sources and attempted to enrich apprehension of the encounters by bringing in a fuller understanding of native practices, beliefs, and situations than Euro-American witnesses and commentators might have had. In preparing this revised version of my book I have learned much from the multifaceted new materials I have delved into, and I hope that further layers of meaning have been added to the book in the process.

I hope at the same time that my work—coming as it does out of an international background—may make some specific contributions to the field, such as it is currently developing in the United States. In the first place, my divided French and Anglo-American training and research interests have allowed me to give a thoroughgoing comparative thrust to this study, focusing on the interface of two dominant colonial presences in eighteenth-century North America, the British and the French. Also, my extended participation in the European academic and intellectual milieu has informed the writing of the book, bringing to bear a somewhat different set of approaches and references that may be of interest to an American public.

In his presidential address to the 2008 annual meeting of the American Society for Ethnohistory, Colin Calloway, one of the finest ethnohistorians working today, spoke of his own peregrinations between his native Britain and various parts of the United States, where he has spent a large part of his professional life. He pointed out that "trying to understand other people's historical experience from the perspective of their own culture should not blind us to the possibilities offered for understanding our own histories with views from outside our own cultures." The Indian historical studies that he himself has written have come from "all over the place," as he put it, "and that may not be all bad. Indian history, in addition to being rooted in place, should be all over the place."[3] Calloway, then, calls for recognition of the potential of viewpoints coming from *without* as well as from within and celebrates plurality of perspective. This statement of principle might apply in two ways to my book. Like Calloway's own, my vantage point comes partially from without and from "all over the place," that is, from a diversity of locations. But beyond that the same thing can be said of the writers who are the principal subjects in my book.

Later in his address Calloway makes a forceful plea for internationalizing Indian and early American history, connecting it not only with "Atlantic" or "continental" but also with "global history." In the examples of global connections that he puts forward, the world market, with the early development of capitalism in interrelated ways in different countries, figures prominently. World history, it would seem, is inescapably economic history. I share this conception or project of historical and cultural understanding, and in writing *Modernity and Its Other* I hope I have laid a stone on that edifice.

ACKNOWLEDGMENTS

This book, in its revised, translated form, has been a very long time in the making—more than twenty-five years if you count from my first discovery of and research on some of its main themes and authors. I am grateful to many people and institutions for their help along the way.

The University of Paris-Est Marne-la-Vallée, where I taught for the last ten years before my retirement, granted me an extended leave of absence for research on and writing of the original French version of the work. Through the research unit to which I was attached, the university also provided generous financial support for its publication. For several years I taught a graduate seminar on the theme of the book, and I gave a pair of lectures on it, open to the broader university community. The feedback I received from these helped me in the earlier stages of my work.

Through its rich, varied program of seminars and talks the European Early American Studies Association, to which I belong, has brought me much food for thought and contextual points of reference in my work. In addition the discussion of the French version of my book at one of its annual "Recent Publications" colloquia was extremely encouraging and helpful in preparing the expanded, English edition. The comments, then and on other occasions, of two senior scholars in the group, Marie-Jeanne Rossignol and Elise Marienstras, were particularly valuable. Conversations and exchanges with two younger researchers whose doctoral work intersected with my interests, Anne-Marie Libério and Felicity Donohoe (from an affiliated British research group), also provided much stimulation.

I also have gained much through my membership in the French Society for the Study of Travel Writing in English, which holds regular colloquia, at a number of which I have presented work related to my book. In addition I have greatly profited from participation in a series of international conferences on travel writing entitled "Borders and Crossings," held in various European venues. Comments on papers I delivered, as well as discussions on areas and issues peripheral to mine, were extremely stimulating as I worked on the book at different stages.

In a more general way I am indebted to the ongoing seminar on North American Indians organized by Marie Mauzé and Joëlle Rostkovski at the Ecole des Hautes Etudes en Sciences Sociales in Paris, which provides a fascinating forum for talks and discussions on a wide range of topics involving Native Americans, both historical and contemporary.

During preparation of both the original and the present edition of the book, I have been fortunate to spend extended periods of time using the extraordinary resources of the British Library and the Harvard Libraries, not least important their manuscript and rare books departments. The librarians of both institutions whom I consulted were unfailingly knowledgeable and eager to be of help. I am also grateful to have been able to consult the Bartram Papers at the Pennsylvania Historical Society.

Early versions of or materials for parts of chapters of the book have appeared in the following journals and collective works:

CHAPTER 1: "L'expérience et l'interprétation de la crise chez Crèvecoeur," *Revue Française d'Études Américaines* 64 (May 1995): 279–87.

CHAPTER 2: "'Romantisme anti-capitaliste' et révolution chez Freneau," *Revue Française d'Etudes Américaines* 40 (April 1989): 175–86; "Philip Freneau, poète et journaliste, ou la lutte contre l'oubli," *Études Anglaises* 48, no. 1 (1995): 12–24.

CHAPTER 3: "A French Creole Émigré in Late Eighteenth-Century Philadelphia: Moreau de Saint-Méry," in *La France en Amérique: Mémoires d'une conquête*, edited by Susanne Berthier-Fogler, 207–16 (Chambéry, France: Presses de l'Université de Savoie, 2009); "Moreau de Saint-Méry's Voyage: Transatlantic Crossing as Prefiguration of a Discovery of the Early United States (1793–98)," in *Riding/Writing across Borders in North American Travelogues and Fiction*, edited by Waldemar Zacharasiewicz, 35–44 (Vienna: Verlag der Österreichischen Akademie der Wissenschaften, 2011).

CHAPTER 4: "La Violence guerrière des Indiens: Représentations et réactions anglo-américaines au XVIIIᵉ siècle," *XVII–XVIII: Bulletin de la société d'études anglo-américaines des XVIIᵉ et XVIIIᵉ siècles* 44 (June 1997): 61–72.

CHAPTER 6: "Domestication and Recognition of the Other in John Lawson's *A New Voyage to Carolina* (1709)," in *British Narratives of Exploration: Case Studies of the Self and Other*, edited by Frederic Regard, 63–70 (London: Pickering & Chatto, 2009); "From Journal to 'Travels': Jonathan Carver's 18th-Century Voyage into Indian Country," in *Seuils et Traverses: Enjeux de l'écriture du voyage*, Acts of a colloquium in Brest (July 2000), edited by Jan Borm and Jean-Yves Le Disez, 2:239–47 (Brest: Presses de l'Université de Bretagne Occidentale, 2002).

CHAPTER 7: "William Bartram and Environmentalism," *American Studies Journal* 54, no. 1 (2015): 67–87.

CHAPTER 8: "Alexander Mackenzie's Search for the Northwest Passage: The Commercial Imperative (1789–93)," in *The Quest for the Northwest Passage: Knowledge, Nation and Empire, 1576–1806*, edited by Frederic Regard, 121–37 (London: Pickering & Chatto, 2013); "An Eighteenth-Century Narrative of Encounter in the Trans-Mississippi West: Jean-Baptiste Trudeau on the Missouri River," in *Before the West Was West: Critical Essays on Pre-1800 Literature of the American Frontiers*, edited by Amy T. Hamilton and Tom J. Hillard, 291–312 (Lincoln: University of Nebraska Press, 2014).

EPILOGUE: "The Romantic Indian Commodified: Text and Image in George Catlin's *Letters and Notes* (1841)," in *Transatlantic Romanticism: British and American Art and Literature, 1790–1860*, edited by Andrew Hemingway and Alan Wallach, 259–84 (Amherst: University of Massachusetts Press, 2015).

In preparing the present edition of this work I have been greatly aided by my editor at the University of Nebraska Press, Matthew Bokovoy, and by the comments and suggestions of the readers of the manuscript. Their input has been truly crucial in the process of preparing a revised, updated version of the original French work and, I hope, substantially improving it thereby.

I would like to thank Mary Campbell and Gordon Sayre (a remote relative; his branch of the Sayre family separated from mine in the seventeenth century). Both read the French version of my book, and their comments on it—in view of their own work in related areas—were especially useful to me in making the revised English edition.

In a broader sense this work owes a great deal to Michael Löwy, with whom I have collaborated, starting even before my interest in the eighteenth-century North American encounter began to take shape, on a series of books and articles. Taking off from an original idea of his, we have attempted to elaborate and illustrate an interpretation of romanticism as a many-faceted revolt against capitalist modernity. This conception is one important underpinning of my study of the confrontation of cultures in the book. Michael's comments on my work as it has developed have been extremely helpful, but his contribution in the larger sense goes far beyond them.

Finally, the contribution to this work of my companion, Ilana, has been considerable. Through the entire process she has read most of its versions, bringing to bear her critical acumen while at the same time being consistently encouraging. I can only hope that I have been half as helpful a reader of her work as she has been of mine.

It goes without saying that any failings this book may have are my responsibility alone.

MODERNITY AND ITS OTHER

Introduction

In eighteenth-century North America the early civilization of "modernity" in the colonies—especially the British—clashed radically with the "premodern" Native American cultures with which it was in close contact. This study proposes a new perspective on that decisive historical moment, drawing on two fields that are not often brought together—the socioeconomic history of the European colonies and the ethnohistory of indigenous peoples—but approaching the subject through examination of writings from the period itself. The analysis focuses on texts—narratives and personal testimonies, imaginative and realistic depictions, representations of ways of looking at and responding to the social, historical, and cultural situation under consideration.

My point of departure is the observation that two fundamental and interrelated developments characterize early American history, from first colonization to the beginning of the nineteenth century: the unfolding confrontation between European and indigenous societies and the coming of modernity in the social fabric of the former. By *modernity* I mean the overall mode of civilization that accompanied the rise of capitalist economic structures.

MODERNITY

Modernity is a highly polysemic term that has been used to refer to an exceedingly wide range of phenomena—from innovation in legal and governmental theories and practices to new forms of art and literature—and to different time spans, starting anywhere from the Renaissance to the periods following World Wars I or II. Consequently it is important to clarify how I will be using the term and the concept. My conception is social and historical in the broadest sense and follows that of a number of theoreticians and practitioners of social and economic history. According to this usage of the term, the coming of modernity constituted an unprecedented upheaval, on a global scale, one that was brilliantly analyzed by Karl Polanyi, the Austro-Hungarian economist and historian, in *The Great Transformation* (1944). In a pivotal metamorphosis of societies and cultures that first occurred in western Europe and North America, the economic dimension of society—in the form of a self-regulating market—took on an ever-increasing autonomy and power, and finally effected a reversal of values that "subordinat[ed] the substance of society itself to the laws of the market."[1] In this reversal traditional, qualitative values gave way to quantitative ones, that is, to exchange value.

In *The Protestant Ethic and the Spirit of Capitalism*, Max Weber similarly sees the coming of capitalism as the historical moment at which "economic acquisition is no longer subordinated to man as the means for the satisfaction of his material needs," but rather "man is dominated by the making of money, by acquisition as the ultimate purpose of his life." In this way, according to Weber, a "reversal of what we should call the natural relationship" becomes a "leading principle of capitalism." Another, more recent historian and theoretician of this crucial change is Immanuel Wallerstein, who defines its essence as the "commodification of everything."[2] The basic shift is accompanied by many ancillary developments, such as the progressive weakening and dissolution of traditional social bonds and the growing predominance of possessive individualism, social and economic competitiveness, and calculating rationalism. The germination of the phenomenon is of course long and complex, and its origins reach back to the decay of feudalism in Europe.

Historians have long agreed that England was at the forefront of the transformation that led traditional societies toward a capitalist organization of socioeconomic relations, and more generally toward modernity. This clearly advanced position of the English caused some historians to conclude that capitalism existed in the British colonies of North America from the start, or that, to use Carl Degler's expression, capitalism "came in the first ships."[3] According to this view, the New World was a sort of tabula rasa that allowed for an accelerated development of modern tendencies by eliminating the necessity of overcoming traditions that persisted in Europe and England, thereby putting a brake on their evolution. This perspective, which predominated after the Second World War, was contested in the 1960s and thereafter by a rising generation of historians associated with the "new social history." For these scholars, North America was to be seen more as an arena of struggle between the new social forces and older currents of thought, feeling, and behavior. In this view precapitalist mentalities were also brought over in the first ships.

A very fruitful debate developed within this historiographic tendency concerning the nature and specific manifestations of the changes that took place in the society of British America. Broadly speaking, two approaches were put forward. On the one hand, a "consumer revolution" was discovered to have occurred during the eighteenth century, an early manifestation of the "consumer society" in a period that preceded the Industrial Revolution.[4] On the other hand, there was an attempt to trace the origins and stages of a "transition to capitalism." While the "new historians" generally rejected the notion of European capitalism being transported to the New World in the first ships, they also refused to accept the other extreme in periodization: the identification of the advent of capitalism in North America with nineteenth-century industrialization. Though they diverge on some points—the rhythm of change, the most fundamental factors in the process, and so on—they generally agree that the eighteenth century, especially in its second half, was the locus of a crucial social reconfiguration, the coming of a society fully dominated by the market.[5] For James Henretta, one of the foremost economic historians of the period, after a slow initial preparation during the first half of the century the qualitative leap to a "full-fledged capitalist economic system" occurs in the second half, especially in the period between 1770 and 1800.[6] In spite of substantial differences of analysis among several contemporary trends in historiography, a broad consensus does seem to have emerged regarding the general phenomenon and its timing.[7]

In the British colonies of North America, then, the eighteenth century is a watershed, the key moment in a process of evolution toward capitalism and modernity.[8] Though their seeds were doubtless already sown in the seventeenth-century colonies,[9] only in the following century did they fully take root and fructify. Toward the middle of the eighteenth century commercialization was already well under way. One historian quotes, for example, a Rhode Island sea captain who in 1748 declared, "A man who has money here, no matter how he came by it, he is everything, and wanting that he's a mere nothing, let his conduct be ever so irreproachable."[10] Another quotes Cadwallader Colden, an administrator of the province of New York, who complained in the same year that "the only principle of life propagated among the young people is to get money, and men are only esteemed according to what they are worth—that is, the money they are possessed of."[11]

This growing predominance of a mercantile mentality, although it was only partially adopted by the rural populations, prepared the way for later developments. According to James Henretta, "the market, along with private property, wage labor, and sophisticated financial instruments, constituted the institutional core of early modern capitalism. In the short space of the fifty years between 1750 and 1800, the ingredients of a capitalist order had risen in prominence as the traditional limitations on economic development in America . . . had been overcome."[12] During this period the American Revolution constituted the key event that triggered a leap forward in the process. Gordon Wood, eminent historian of the Revolution, shares this point of view with Henretta: "In the 1780s we can actually sense the shift from a premodern traditional society to a modern one in which business interests and consumer tastes of ordinary people were coming to dominate."[13]

THE ENCOUNTER WITH INDIANS

The eighteenth century, and more particularly the revolutionary period, were equally critical in the confrontation between North American Indians and Europeans, and near the end of the century the balance of power shifted decisively in favor of the colonists. This development was closely linked to the advent of modernity, since the new market society was firmly rooted in agriculture, which depended on the expropriation of Indian lands. In conjunction with this trait, scholars have increasingly drawn on the concept of "settler colonialism," a process and condition that characterized some but not all colonial situations elsewhere in the world, as a way of understanding the development of British America.[14] Over the course of the eighteenth century an acceleration of the process of British territorial expansion took place, and the Revolution and its aftermath marked a decisive turning point in the struggle between Indians and colonists.[15] For Neil Salisbury, an ethnohistorian specializing in this period, "the new nation constituted a political force in which the landholding and commercial aspirations long held by most British colonists had been elevated to national purpose. This self-proclaimed, American-based 'empire of liberty' represented a more sinister threat to Native existence than any that had originated in Europe during the preceding three centuries."[16]

The consequences were indeed disastrous for the Indians. Throughout the century Amerindians had continued in large measure to be independent of the Europeans, to exercise de facto control over most of the land east as well as west of the Mississippi, and to constitute a formidable political power in the country. As the colonial historian Alan Taylor summarizes the situation, into the 1790s "most of North America remained Indian country."[17] A number of important recent studies have demonstrated the extent and the kinds of power exercised by native groups in different regions.[18] But by the end of the century, and especially after the War of 1812, indigenous peoples east of the Mississippi had been almost entirely vanquished and reduced to severe dependency.[19] Indians continued to dominate areas of the trans-Mississippi West, however, for a good part of the nineteenth century.[20]

The eighteenth century in British America was, finally, the moment at which the contrast between an "advanced" European civilization and a "primitive" colonized culture sharpened into radical opposition. In other colonial situations the dichotomy might be less stark, insofar as colonizing groups continued to retain significant elements of traditional European culture. The mentalities of aristocrats and priests in New France and even of Puritans in the early New England settlements were in some ways analogous to that of the Indians. The aristocrats shared with them a code of honor and the cult of war and hunting as a way of life, whereas pious Christians often posited the presence of the supernatural in the natural world.[21] But as the British colonies became more and more penetrated with the mercantile ethos, the neighboring Indian cultures became more profoundly alien (which is not to deny that mutual adaptation played an important role in the period as well).

OTHERNESS

The term *Other* is fashionable today in academic discourse and is sometimes overused. It has also given rise to considerable critical discussion that problematizes the concept.[22] Yet in the case of the two cultures facing off in eighteenth-century North America, the notion has particular pertinence and is to be taken in the strongest sense as radical alterity. Here one finds, juxtaposed in close proximity, two modes of living that were not only different but polar opposites. What Wilcomb Washburn called the "clash of morality" in colonial North America and James Axtell called the "contest of cultures" reached its culminating point in the eighteenth century.[23] The attributes of the civilization of modernity that accompanied the new capitalist economy were in total contradiction with the lifeways of the Amerindians.[24]

There were, of course, considerable differences among Native American nations in that period, from one region to another and often within a region, in terms of specific kinship systems, social structures, beliefs, rituals, practices, and customs. This diversity has indeed caused many contemporary Native American scholars to emphasize that American Indian history is multiple rather than unitary, and to call for the study of "tribal histories" in the plural.[25] That emphasis constitutes an important insight and direction of study in recent developments in the field. Yet at the same time it seems clear—a consideration that is particularly relevant in the context of the present study—that the most fundamental traits of the cultures of Indians in the East, and even beyond, were sufficiently similar, especially when compared with the civilization of modernity, that one can meaningfully speak of an Amerindian culture in the singular.[26] At the heart of this cultural difference one finds the opposition between, on the one hand, traditional, premodern societies founded on qualitative values such as honor, the sacred, and community solidarities, and in which the "economy" has no autonomous existence but is entirely integrated into institutions that reflect these values, and on the other, modernity, ruled by exchange value and motivated by economic individualism and the commercial bent of mind, with its calculation of profits and losses.[27]

In regard to human relations, then, Indians were powerfully incorporated within clans, tribes, and nations. In spite of differences in the definition and structuring of these bonds, they were generally cemented by the systematic practice of sharing and gift-giving, and their strength has been widely recognized.[28] Even beyond the limits of their local groupings, Native Americans were also bound by broad principles of hospitality. By contrast the European individual in the eighteenth century, most markedly in the British colonies, had a growing tendency to display egocentric and competitive behaviors, even toward members of his own community, including members of the immediate family (which remained nonetheless the locus of an intense identification).[29]

The contrast is equally sharp if one looks at the relationship with the natural environment in the two cultures. In the case of Native Americans, one finds an all-pervasive and many-faceted intimacy with the natural world, a utilization of resources for daily needs, and a tendency to establish patterns of relative ecological equilibrium, although this was not necessarily the result of conscious policy, grounded in scientifically "correct" knowledge, or even based on a concept of nature.[30]

Since the 1990s a number of scholarly books and articles have questioned the stereotype of the "ecological Indian."[31] While they have been beneficial in combating oversimplifications and providing a welcome corrective to the notion that Indians were passive "children of nature" who never actively molded their environment to their purposes, many of the claims made and arguments developed remain speculative and controversial. Many of the issues they have raised are the subject of ongoing debate, and they have not provided any conclusive demonstration that Indian practices, at least before the presence of Europeans began to influence their behavior, produced significantly harmful or self-defeating effects on their environment.[32] William Cronon, an authoritative source on the question as regards colonial New England, asserts on the contrary that Indian practices in that region, which included mobility of settlement, the intermingling of several kinds of crops, a particular method of field preparation, and the periodic burning of woods, were well adapted to the maintenance of a stable and sustained relationship between Indian communities and their natural surroundings.[33] In the English colonies, on the other hand, increasingly over the course of the eighteenth century one finds the exploitation of nature as a source of profit, promoting a tendency toward continual expansion and waste. English methods of grazing and farming, applied with a view to "improving" the land, required large surface areas and tended to exhaust the soil.[34]

These different practices of Indians and colonists went hand in hand with opposed attitudes toward the land. The former considered it to be inalienable common ground, dividing it only into customary tribal or hunting territories and, in some cases, into plots for use by families. In both cases it was a matter of usufructuary rights, not of private property in the European sense. For North American Indians land was always ultimately held in common, allocated for use that was dictated by need.[35] In eighteenth-century Anglo-American society, on the other hand, one finds institutions and conceptions that treated land as alienable private property, "real estate" translatable into money, and valued as such. It was the property of individuals (or associations of individuals), and these individuals often attempted to create profits from it through speculation, extending their ownership in land far beyond their capacity personally to occupy, use, or enjoy it, for the purpose of financial gain. The desire for acquisition of land by individuals was in principle unlimited. Consequently, as Cronon indicates, in colonial New England villages that originally were centered on common land (commons) soon came to be divided into private lots. When this process was completed, "more than anything else, it was the treatment of land and property as commodities traded at market that distinguished English conceptions of ownership from Indian ones."[36]

A final contrast between the two overall worldviews should be mentioned. That of American Indians included the marvelous and the supernatural, peopling the natural world with occult, mythical, magical presences and meanings, whereas the Anglo-American civilization of the eighteenth century—rationalistic and scientific, utilitarian and mercantile, deistic and "methodist"—tended increasingly to banish those elements. Indeed, according to Max Weber, a fundamental characteristic of modernity is constituted by this lack: the "disenchantment of the world" (*Entzauberung der Welt*).[37] The wonder of the supernatural was in particular susceptible to being frozen and drowned in the "icy water of egotistical calculation," to use a famous phrase,[38] and that spirit of calculation was well disseminated in British colonial society.

These two portraits are to be taken as "ideal types" in the Weberian sense. Concrete realities are always complex and include much diversity and ambiguity. In the context I am dealing with, however, these types are especially relevant. In eighteenth-century North America, in spite of earlier contacts with Europeans, Indians continued to preserve to a large degree the integrity of their traditional cultures—as they had evolved, of course, through the precontact histories of their interactions among themselves—while British America had already created the groundwork of modernity in the full sense. Recent studies of the period have often focused on the areas of interchange and mixing between the two types of society—the creation of a "middle ground," the role played by "go-betweens" and mixed-birth individuals, the development of "métis" cultures, and so on—and these unstable, intermediary realities are of prime importance in my study as well. Yet mixture and crossover necessarily imply a dichotomy, and my contention is that this dichotomy can best be defined in terms of the radical opposition I have traced.

To return to my point of departure, the coming of modernity and the encounter of divergent cultures—of colonizer and of colonized—coincide in eighteenth-century North America. These are crucial historical processes on a global scale and can be found in many other historical conjunctures. What makes the context I am examining particularly interesting is that the development of a modern capitalist society occurs in immediate proximity to the encounter with a colonized, dominated Other. Most often these phenomena, though interrelated, are largely separated in spatial terms, divided between metropole and colony. The core of each process is *elsewhere* in relation to the other. But here, since the two historical processes have the same locus, are fully superimposed, we can perceive with particular clarity the relationship that constitutes the book's subject and title.

It is striking, however, that the historiographic trends that have reshaped the study of these two phenomena rarely come together. The historians of the "transition to capitalism" and of the "consumer revolution" have not often considered possible links between their objects of study and the Amerindian world, while the ethnohistorians generally do not attempt to bring into their work any in-depth analysis of the society and economy of the colonists. A few have nonetheless become aware of the problem and of the advantages to be gained from crossing disciplinary boundaries. Addressing colleagues who were busy trying to identify groups within British colonial society that resisted the incursions of the market system, one historian of the "transition," Daniel Vickers, remarked, "Only on the far side of that frontier did there exist societies with real reservations about the legitimacy of political economy.... On the question of property right ... the English and the Indians were worlds apart.... If the strict English definition of private property right was a cultural weapon in the conquest of this continent, then the spirited Indian defense of their lands across the centuries can well be termed the only pure expression of moral economy in American history."[39] Several years later Steven Aron acknowledged the aptness of this comment and recommended that his fellow economic historians "be fitted with bifocals."[40] It cannot be said, though, that this recommendation has often been followed. Although the present study is not the work of an economic historian or ethnohistorian, I hope it contributes to the meaningful interrelation of the two fields.

THE FRENCH IN NORTH AMERICA

The encounter between modernity and its Other appears in its purest form in the British sphere of North American colonization, and this book focuses on the latter. But the French colonies constitute an interesting point of comparison. In the same period France also was moving toward modernity but following its own path and with some delay in relation to England, since it retained longer and more fully traces of the feudal past. In the first half of the seventeenth century it had participated in the creation of the new "Atlantic world" through the fur trade, drawing the indigenous peoples of Canada into a new system of economic relations.[41] In the sequel, though, France gave way increasingly to England and in its North American colonies never fully made the transition to capitalism, as the British did in theirs. In New France the stark opposition between the colonizing and colonized cultures that characterized British America was mitigated by several factors.

The first of these involves the difference in religion between the French and the English colonies. The Catholic missionaries were on the whole much more flexible than the English Protestants in their relations with the Indians. They lived among them and often allowed Indian beliefs to endure, coexisting with Catholic ones, as long as they were not patently in contradiction with Church doctrine. This attitude was facilitated by the affinities that certain aspects of Catholicism had with Amerindian paganism.[42] The Jesuits were particularly open from a cultural point of view, often living with Indians for a large part of their adult lives and adopting many of their ways.[43] A pan-American study of the encounters between native religions and Christianity—in its French and Spanish Catholic and English Protestant variants—has suggested that while New England Protestant ministers made little effort to bridge the gap and Spanish friars often employed or countenanced coercion, the French Jesuit priests reached out syncretically, to the point that they "seem to have actively sought to show themselves as superior shamans."[44]

Father Rasles, who lived with the Abenakis at the beginning of the eighteenth century, is a case in point. His letters show that he deployed all the pomp and pageantry of Catholic ceremony and display to attract the Indians. They in turn venerated him and admitted him to their councils. But this Jesuit missionary also participated in the daily activities and festivities of his hosts and came to identify with them to such an extent that he once wrote to his brother, "I assure you that I see, that I hear, that I speak, only as a savage."[45] In another letter he remarked that the strong adherence to Catholicism that he had been able to call forth in the Abenakis also predisposed them to prefer an alliance with the French rather than the English, in spite of the greater material advantages the latter could offer. The English indeed saw the sympathy between Father Rasles and his flock as a dangerous obstacle to the achievement of their aims and made repeated attempts to abduct and murder him.[46]

Another difference between the English and the French relates to economic activity. There was far less immigration to New France than to the British colonies in North America, and farming and plantation settlement were much less widespread. As a consequence the French experienced a considerably lower incidence of conflicts with Indians over possession of land.[47] Although they did engage in some settlement—particularly along the Saint Lawrence and Mississippi rivers—the French presence in North America overall cannot be characterized as "settler colonialism," as can the British.[48] As for the French fur trade, it was strongly regulated by the state and, according to Richard White, was "a hive of diverse interests which, while incorporating market concerns, tended to check their dominance."[49] In addition the so-called *coureurs des bois* were generally more adaptable to Indian lifeways and less inclined to cheating the Indians than were the English traders.[50]

Another group present in considerable numbers in New France was the French army. The officers were often aristocrats, and the ordinary foot soldiers peasants or rural poor.[51] These classes, present in the fur trade as well, were of precapitalist, feudal origin and tended to maintain attitudes (based on ideas of honor and independence) and practices (hunting, periods of idleness) that were close to those of the Indians. The French historian Marie-Noëlle Bourguet has argued that the aristocracy in New France, far removed from the overwhelming royal authority of the metropole, often was strongly attracted to "the indolent, undisciplined existence of the fur trade, precisely because this activity allowed it to conform to the code of the nobility, to live a life without work or subordination.... What was true of the aristocracy was also true of the people. A passion for hunting... is after all nothing other than the expression of an immemorial traditional penchant, which appears in the French countryside in the form of poaching and other minor offenses."[52] According to Bourguet, therefore, when the French colonists "went native" it corresponded to a deep social affinity.

In eighteenth-century New France, in fact, we find a mix of traditional and modernizing tendencies.[53] This complicates the pattern of sociocultural oppositions in the historical context, superimposing a triangular design onto the underlying binary polarity modernity/Other. The French in North America stand apart from the British in regard to their social configuration and their relations with Indians, constituting a distinct position and a mediating point between modernity and its Other. My study therefore includes consideration of a variety of French perspectives as counterpoints to the Anglo-American perspectives.[54]

My study explores this sociohistorical nexus not as historiography but through an approach that is "literary" in a broad sense, examining writings—fictional and nonfictional—that in their narrative and thematic developments engage with particular aspects of the conjuncture I am interested in. These texts are of two general sorts, dividing the work into two parts: accounts of discovery of the Anglo-American world—the world of modernity-in-the-making—and accounts of encounter with native peoples, the Other of modernity. They partially overlap, however, since dealing with one side of the dichotomy often leads into the other, commentary on colonial society inviting comparison with neighboring Amerindian groups and discovery of the latter recalling contrasting aspects of the former. The views of modernity in part 1 by St. John de Crèvecoeur, Philip Freneau, and Moreau de Saint-Méry, all of whom have some relation to French culture, though in highly divergent ways, take various literary forms: imaginary letters, sketches, tales, essays, poetry, travelogues. The texts of encounter with Indians in part 2 are also diverse, but the main focus is on one genre: the account of travel in "Indian territory." For that genre is, among the varieties of encounter literature, the one most propitious for "recognition" of the culture of the Other.

THE TRAVEL ACCOUNT

The travel account is a literary genre that was enormously popular in the eighteenth century, especially in the English-speaking world but also among the French. Its popularity was rivaled only by the novel, which came into being concurrently and in association with it.[55] Like the novel, the travel account reached a broad spectrum of readers. The Earl of Shaftsbury observed in 1710 that travel accounts "are the chief materials to furnish out a library.... These are in our present days what books of chivalry were in those of our forefathers."[56] This commentary applies well beyond the elite to which its author belonged. Though these accounts—both of maritime voyages and of terrestrial excursions—extended to all the known regions of the world, many had the "New World" as their setting.[57]

We can distinguish two general categories of North American travel account: those recounting trips made by colonists or foreign visitors within the settled parts of the colonies and those that concern travel beyond the "frontier," into territories still controlled by Indian nations. Some accounts incorporated expeditions in both kinds of areas. All of these narratives, but especially those involving Indian territory, were tailored to multiple expectations and publics. North American accounts were aimed first of all at certain circumscribed publics that were interested in gleaning useful information: colonial administrators and natural scientists, religious and royal authorities in the case of the French, land developers and potential settlers in the case of the English. However, they also addressed a much vaster public, one fascinated by the New World in general but more especially by the territories that remained "wilderness," still the realm of the "wild" Indian or *sauvage*. Publishers responded to this intense curiosity and taste for the exotic, and accounts of travel in Indian territory were among the early best sellers.

If one considers the literature of the period involving the Indian, the genre of travel in Indian territory clearly appears as the most favorable to a sympathetic awareness and understanding of the encountered culture.

It is at least partially based on firsthand experience,[58] and it narrates an encounter that often takes place in relatively favorable conditions. From these points of view the travel account can be differentiated from the other common forms of discourse on Indians: the captivity account (a narrative of *involuntary* travel), the military journal or report written by a soldier or militiaman in the "Indian wars" with which the period was studded, the histories of Indian nations or of colonies in their relations with them, and the novel or poem on an Indian theme. The first two picture a predominantly hostile contact with Indians, and the last two are often not based on personal contact.[59]

However, like the authors of works in other genres, writers of travel narratives were formed in the crucible of European civilization and of developing modernity. When confronted by the Other of their own *habitus*, and when this identity included an unquestioned sense of superiority, travelers were often predisposed to misunderstanding and to reactions of contempt and rejection. Recent studies of ethnographic travel accounts often foreground the "imperialist" position of the voyager and the ideological presuppositions ensuing from it. Mary-Louise Pratt's *Imperial Eyes: Travel Writing and Transculturation*, first published in 1992, is seminal for this trend.

While recognizing the significant contributions made from within that theoretical framework, I would argue that to understand the dynamics of travel encounter, analysis should take into account not only the overall society from which the traveler comes but also the specifics of the social, cultural, and ideological locations within it. As suggested by the opposition that I drew between modernity and its Other, the former is in a broad sense fragmented, individualistic, and inegalitarian, in contrast to the strongly unified, largely egalitarian aspect of the latter. A consequence of this difference is that travelers exhibit many differences that can have a significant bearing on their encounter experience. Taking into consideration specific sociocultural profiles of travelers allows us to identify different kinds of predispositions and in that way account for particular characteristics of travel texts.[60] In addition it seems necessary to acknowledge the possibility of a (partial) transcendence of initial prejudice or conditioning in the experience of encounter itself, thereby fulfilling to some degree the potential of the ethnographic travel account: "recognition" of the Other.

My approach, then, differs significantly from the trend of the "imperial gaze" in recent analysis of travel literature. But it also diverges from that of a prominent type of study relating to textual representations of Native Americans. This tendency, centered on the analysis of stereotyped images of American Indians (especially the "noble" vs. the "ignoble" savage), is an instance of the "history of ideas." Initiated by R. H. Pearce's study of "savagism," further developed notably by R. F. Berkhofer Jr. and later followers, it makes little or no attempt to explore the relations between ideas and socioeconomic contexts, restricting itself to tracing the anatomy of representations.[61] By contrast, I consider it crucial to take into consideration the rootedness of representations in concrete realities: the actual social forms and lifeways of Indians—their "praxis," to use a term instituted by a European tradition of social analysis[62]—the specific profiles and trajectories of the Europeans who encounter and textually represent them, and the particularized experience of encounter itself. Without underestimating the influence on Europeans of stereotypes, I treat them as elements in a concrete, often contradictory whole—the encounter experience. In view of the historical situation and thematic constellation I wish to explore, my discussion of authors of travel accounts focuses especially on their relation to modernity.

In the critical literature on the travel account, but also in the areas of anthropology and the history of non-Western civilizations, a broader epistemological controversy has been raging since the 1980s around the concept of alterity. To what extent is knowledge of the Other possible? Is the person who encounters an Other condemned to remain imprisoned in his or her own culture, systematically misinterpreting that of the Other? Do voyagers discover only themselves and their own society, the Other serving simply as a foil or an ideal contrasting with their familiar world?[63]

Anthony Pagden, author at a ten-year interval of two studies of the literature of encounter in the New World, stresses in the first that travelers applied to the Other an interpretative framework and system of classification stemming from ancient European intellectual traditions. Consequently their vision of the Other was thoroughly permeated with preconceptions.[64] In his second work, though, while recognizing that one can never escape the hermeneutic circle and that the Other ultimately remains a construction, Pagden insists that "we do not fabricate [the construction] out of nothing."[65] Those who ventured out to meet, on their own terrain, human beings strikingly different from themselves, found themselves necessarily in the cultural context of the Other. In this situation they often demonstrated flexibility of mind, adapting their "conceptual expectations" or "conceptual grid" to the newly perceived human phenomena.[66] The practice of ethnohistorians would tend to confirm this perspective since they often base their analyses on the observations and reflections of travelers, along with other sources, while "correcting" individual accounts by careful comparison with others.[67]

I adopt this intermediary position in the epistemological debate. Without assuming an innocent gaze of the voyager or an unproblematic transparency of the Other, I attempt to show that "recognition" can occur in spite of the predispositions of the traveler, sometimes even because of them. More precisely I explore the possibility that a critical vision of one's own society can lead to an understanding of the Other rooted in sympathy.

Such a perspective might be seen as raising the specter of one of the stereotypical polarities postulated by the historians of representations: the "noble savage." Reaching back at least as far as Michel de Montaigne's essay "On Cannibals" and classically articulated by many encyclopedists and romantic writers thereafter, this literary theme is nowadays often dismissed, implicitly or explicitly, as a sentimental myth or a deceptive, disingenuous ideology of colonialism.[68] There are undoubtedly many instances to which this debunking approach may be justly applied. Nonetheless it should be pointed out that often, particularly in earlier periods when "discovery" and exploration were ongoing, literary articulators of the theme had read widely in accounts of travel encounters and were thus drawing on firsthand testimony. More important, travelers themselves, among them some who had had long experience of contact, often portrayed the peoples they had visited and lived among in terms similar to the literary thematics. Washburn sees as "noble savages," for example, the Amerindians portrayed in the work by the veteran Indian trader James Adair.[69] This characterization is striking when one realizes that Adair spent the best part of his adult life—some forty years—living among several nations of southeastern Indians, principally the Chickasaws.[70]

For Washburn the term *noble savage* has no pejorative connotations, and he contends at the beginning of his article on Adair's representation of Indians that "the literature produced by those who knew the Indian best—whether missionary or soldier, French or English—provided legitimate evidence of a 'noble savage,' using that phrase, however, as a shorthand expression of a general though not uncritical admiration for Indian character and government in comparison with that of the white man."[71] This assertion, cited approvingly by another preeminent ethnohistorian, James Axtell,[72] suggests that sympathy and a certain degree of understanding deriving from it were relatively widespread in the literature of travel among Indians in North America. In my discussions of travel accounts I will test this hypothesis.

In *Manifest Manners*, his study of the Indian and "postindian" conditions, Native American writer Gerald Vizenor challenges the tradition of travel writing on "Indian territory," asserting that "the conventions of travel literature bear the causal contradictions of discoveries, translation, narrative representations of the other, and the simulations of dominance" and identifying "noble savagism" as one of its prime avatars.[73] More recently another native intellectual, Glen Coulthard, has written a critique of the politics of recognition—the concept I have posited as defining the potential of travel literature—as it applies to American Indian colonial and postcolonial situations.[74] As will be seen, many contradictions and severe limitations of Euro-American perspectives on Indians become apparent in my analysis of the texts in which they appear, notably in travel accounts. At the same time, though, a complex picture emerges in which stereotyping, misrepresentation, and imperial dominance, though frequent, also often give way to meaningful recognition in differing forms and degrees.

APPROACHES AND THEMES

In this two-faceted study I have attempted to capture different angles and components of a *lived* reality, a complex reality as it was experienced and as that experience was transposed into writing. I approach my subject through the lens of memory as opposed to history, in the sense of the distinction articulated by Paul Ricoeur, among others.[75] The written testimonies that I explore are situated and therefore multifarious, yet they often exhibit points in common, intersections of meaning. In the texts under consideration I take into account aspects of both comprehension and evaluation: observations and interpretations on the one hand, attitudes and value judgments on the other. In the analyses of travel accounts a third dimension comes into play: *interaction* between travelers and Amerindians, and thereby between two heterogeneous cultural formations.

The attitudes displayed in the texts examined here run the gamut from aggressive identification with modern European or Anglo-American civilization, along with horrified or contemptuous rejection of its Other, to celebration of indigenous cultures as the antithesis of the corrupted state of modernity. I have elsewhere, with Michael Löwy, elaborated a concept of romanticism as a cultural critique of capitalist modernity drawing on values and ideals taken from a premodern past.[76] In the present work I highlight a strong current of this kind of romantic vision in the confrontation between the two forms of civilization in eighteenth-century North America and show more generally that for many Europeans in this context Indian culture was a *temptation*. Even those who were not tempted were often struck—and this is a theme that recurs in different forms in the encounter narratives I analyze—by the recognition of a strange paradox: the beings labeled "savages" by Europeans regularly and effortlessly attained some of the key traditional European ideals. At the same time, though, my discussions often bring out the highly contradictory and ambivalent nature of the points of view expressed.

These points of view, and the representational forms that serve as vehicles for them, are essentially European or Anglo-American. Given the absence of writing in precontact Amerindian societies, we do not have the same access to their culture-specific perspectives that we do to European perspectives in the period. Textual representations of native discourse in the eighteenth century were in general filtered through and mediated by a European mental framework, through translation, selection, framing, interpretation, and so on, while those Amerindians who themselves wrote—most notably the Mohegan minister Samson Occom—had been formed and educated to a significant degree in white society. In spite of the difficulties of the enterprise, though, much fruitful work has been done to explore Indian perspectives in studies of early America, reversing the previous historiographic tendency by "facing east from Indian territory," as the title of one work expresses it.[77] A recent trend, coming particularly from Native American scholars, has been to use contemporary or recent oral testimony to understand tribal pasts. The hazards of such an approach have also been pointed out.[78] Aside from oral sources—whether contemporary or transcribed historical sources—many recent works have studied the long tradition of written productions by native peoples—their intellectual and literary history.[79]

Whatever may be the challenges of making Amerindian voices in nonliterate contexts heard, the reason for my focusing on European and Anglo-American perspectives is to be found elsewhere. I am concerned with the coming of modernity in the North American colonies and the confrontation with its Other, and *as lived experience* this double reality is that of the colonizers. My theme, in other words, is the experience of the advent of modernity and of the Amerindian *as Other*. Thus, since the authors I deal with have often reported, dramatized, or imagined Indian voices, framed by their own, Indian vantage points also will be part of the discussion, through refraction. In addition I bring in contextual, ethnohistorical material as a way of extending as far as possible the inclusion of the other side of the encounter in understanding it.

However, my subject is ultimately *memory* rather than *history*, and that involves the collective memory, from a multitude of vantage points,—of Europeans who experienced the encounter of two civilizational forms and explored it, most importantly, in the travel account. My study thus draws on European intellectual traditions that include cultural history, the study of collective memory, and textual analysis of travel literature.

There is clearly an area of overlap between historical or ethnohistorical study and these approaches that involve memory, but in spite of their interpenetration the fields are distinct.

It remains to give a brief overview of the general contours of this book. Part 1 examines three views of the development of modernity in the Anglo-American world of the late eighteenth century in the decades leading up to the Revolution, during the revolutionary crisis, and in the early Republic. The three authors discussed in this part—Saint-John de Crèvecoeur, Philip Freneau, and Moreau de Saint-Méry—have strong ties to France and French culture and extensive experience of Anglo-America, though in differing ways and degrees. Crèvecoeur was born and raised in France, served in the French army in Canada before moving to the British colonies and becoming a British subject, then returned to France during the American Revolution. After the conflict he spent another long period in the United States, before settling again in France. Freneau's relation to France is considerably more distant. He was born in British America to parents of French Huguenot ancestry. Culturally, though, the link was strong, as was the political link, since Freneau staunchly supported the Jacobin wing of the French Revolution. Moreau de Saint-Méry, the subject of the concluding chapter of the section, was only a visitor to the early United States. A Creole from Saint-Domingue who had lived also in the metropole, he fled the Terror in France to exile in Philadelphia. Although a foreigner, Saint-Méry remained for almost five years in the United States, a prolonged stay that allowed him to come to know America and Americans in considerable depth.

By virtue of their diverse links to French culture, in these three figures there is an interplay, different in each case, between an insider and an outsider status, and we can observe in them varying permutations of the tensions and contrasts between French and English mentalities. Two of the authors—Crèvecoeur and Freneau—also include views of the Indian in their writings, so in these cases the triangular dynamic referred to earlier comes into play. Although Saint-Méry does not bring Indians into his account, his friend La Rochefoucauld-Liancourt does so in his closely related travel narrative, and I will refer to his comments on them in conjunction with Saint-Méry.

Part 2 turns to views of modernity's Other. Four of the five chapters provide extended analysis of accounts of travel in Indian territory, exploring the genre to which I attach a heightened potentiality. The opening chapter, however, offers first a brief examination of other genres that textualize Indian encounter and a discussion of what I call the "zero degree" of contact. Here the encounter with Amerindians is at its most circumscribed, superficial, and negative, though it can at the same time be fascinating in the extreme: exposure to Indian violence in war, captivity, and torture and relations with Indians that are narrated as "adventure." This mode of confrontation forecloses fruitful cultural exchange, restricting interaction to a hostile exteriority but also giving rise to a rich popular literature. The zero degree thus understood is first discussed in relation to the principal genres in which it appears: the captivity account, the military journal, the colonial history, and the novel. Then, in the second part of the chapter, I analyze two nonfiction accounts of encounter with Indians to show how they produce adventure using literary techniques similar to those of fictional narratives. This form of representation tends to exclude cultural interaction and understanding, though in some cases they appear tangentially and sporadically.

Chapter 5 begins with a discussion of the ethnographic travel account in general, a genre that, although not excluding adventure, tends far more to the representation of cultural encounter. I follow Mary Campbell (*The Witness and the Other World*, 1988) in seeing the genre as a "literary instrument of consciousness" possessing a crucial potential for "cultural translation." This potential is achieved more or less fully in each individual case and is always manifested through a particular lens, conditioned by a specific sociocultural profile and itinerary. Following this discussion of genre, I examine the particular characteristics of the society of New France and of travelers within it, then turn to an extended analysis of two notable accounts of travel in Canada, in the area of the Great Lakes and down the Mississippi River—those of the baron de Lahontan and the Jesuit priest Charlevoix. The former was a soldier and aristocrat, the latter a Catholic priest engaged in the missionary effort. As such they are representative of the main types of traveler in New France.

Both being French, Lahontan and Charlevoix share the same broad sociocultural background, notably in terms of their relationship to modernity. However, within that shared matrix their affiliations and commitments are in large part divergent. They belong to the same class (the petty nobility) but stand starkly opposed in their relation to religion (freethinker vs. Jesuit) and the state (one was a renegade soldier who became stateless in the end, while the other undertook his travels "by order of the king"). These divergences help to explain the numerous differences in their relations with Indian tribes and people met on their voyages and in their ways of understanding and judging the natives.

In chapter 6 I analyze two of the most important accounts of travel by Anglo-Americans into Indian territories under English possession, that of John Lawson in Carolina at the beginning of the century, and that of Jonathan Carver during the 1760s in the region of the Great Lakes and upper reaches of the Mississippi, an area that had been only a short time before "annexed" by the English. These travelers have in common the overall Anglo-American sociocultural framework, yet they relate quite differently to it. As a land speculator and colonizer Lawson is closely identified with the main line of economic development, whereas Carver, as a militiaman and explorer serving the Crown, is linked to it in a more mediated way. These profiles allow us to understand some of the particularities of each of their accounts. Beyond the dissimilarities, however, convergences can be noticed among all the travel accounts considered in chapters 5 and 6, both the English and the French.

Chapter 7 is entirely devoted to a traveler who is exceptional in many respects: William Bartram, son of John Bartram, the celebrated Philadelphia botanist. William, who demonstrated artistic talent at a young age, accompanied his father on several of his botanizing expeditions, making sketches of plants. But he undertook alone the trip for which he is best known. Commissioned by a London collector of botanical specimens, William traveled, between 1774 and 1777, through a vast territory that included the Carolinas, Georgia, and Florida, west as far as the lower Mississippi, an area inhabited by Creeks, Seminoles, Cherokees, and Choctaws. The account of this trip, usually referred to simply as "Bartram's *Travels*," was acclaimed on its first publication, in 1791, and has become a classic in its genre.

The chapter highlights Bartram's difference in relation to his social and religious milieu, that of the Philadelphia Quaker elite, showing that he was entirely unadapted to their commercial pursuits and was closer to the radical, early Quaker vision than to their attenuated form of it. His sensibility also has strong affinities with romanticism. I argue that Bartram was particularly receptive to encounter with Indians, precisely insofar as they stood in opposition to his own society. His openness in this respect, which contributes to make his *Travels* an exemplary text within the genre, is inseparable from his felt alienation from the civilization of modernity. My analysis of Bartram includes discussion not only of the published travel account but also of the draft version and of several other manuscripts.

Chapter 8 takes up a specific category of traveler—the fur trader—at the very end of the century. Engaged in a commercial activity that employed Indians as providers of the raw material of the trade, fur traders were doubtless not among those most inclined to fulfill the travel genre's potential of recognition. Yet the fur trade had a complex dynamic and varied historical aspects and was practiced in significantly different ways by the French and the British. Consequently fur trader travelers were not all of the same cloth, as is illustrated by the accounts, one British and one French, analyzed in the chapter.

The first, by the fiercely competitive Scottish trader Alexander Mackenzie, chronicles his two attempts to find a water route to the Pacific—the "Northwest Passage"—starting from a trading post in the subarctic Northwest. Mackenzie's first trip (1789) took him, by mistake, to the Arctic Ocean. On the second (1793–94) he succeeded in reaching the Pacific but had to travel overland for part of it. Entirely bent on achieving his goal, which was meant ultimately to open up lucrative trade routes to the Orient, Mackenzie was interested in the Indians he met only insofar as they could serve to further that goal. My analysis of his travel narrative details how he manipulated them and how his mercantile mentality thoroughly permeates the text.

The second account, Jean-Baptiste Trudeau's record of a two-year journey on the upper Missouri River (1794–96), until recently unpublished, shows a far greater complexity of attitude and interaction. Sent by Spanish authorities in an effort to counter the English trading incursions in the area, Trudeau never got as far as the Mandan settlements on the Missouri that he had been instructed to reach but spent considerable time with both Mahas (Omahas) downriver, who had already had much trading contact, and the wilder Arikaras farther upriver. Although his mission was commercial and political in nature, Trudeau partially transcends this context in his account, coming to understand the destructive dynamic of European penetration and admire the wilder tribes, less affected by it. While Bartram and Mackenzie are polar opposites in terms of the potential of travel encounter, Trudeau exhibits internal conflicts similar to those of travelers treated earlier.

An epilogue looks beyond the eighteenth century into the nineteenth. Through treatment of one major artist-traveler, George Catlin, I illustrate how the encounter of modernity and its Other is transformed in the nineteenth century. Known principally as a painter of Western Indians, Catlin also published a number of accounts of travel among them. My discussion focuses on the most important of these, showing how the writing and the illustrations are closely linked. The text and images are also inseparable from the Indian exhibitions that Catlin produced, at home and abroad, following his years of western travel in the 1830s. I explore the sharp contradictions in Catlin's attitude toward and relation to Indians. While celebrating the "wild," uncorrupted western Indian, Catlin encouraged tourism and development in Indian country and made Indians the object of ethnographic displays and shows, reducing them ultimately to lifeless specimens and commodities.

The conclusion of the work draws together the preceding discussions in an overview, tracing the broad features of the encounter by bringing out some main thematic lines, discussing convergences and divergences, and emphasizing the ambivalent nature of many of the expressed viewpoints. It also raises the question of the relationship between those themes and attitudes and the Enlightenment and romantic perspectives. Finally it looks forward in time, to ask what becomes of the encounter subsequently.

PART ONE

Views of Modernity
Internal/External Discovery

CHAPTER ONE

Crèvecoeur

British America before and during the Revolutionary Upheaval

I will begin by looking at the onset of modernity in the English colonies through the eyes of Saint-John de Crèvecoeur, an author who has received considerable attention, but not in this perspective. The coming of a fully market-driven society to British America did not, of course, take place all at once; it occurred progressively and over the long term. Recent historiography has generally placed the beginnings of the transition period at the turn of the seventeenth and eighteenth centuries, particularly in the northern colonies. In the southern colonies the new trends really started to make themselves felt in the 1740s. By the time the revolutionary "troubles" broke out and the War of Independence got under way, the social metamorphosis was everywhere far advanced, and while the American Revolution was a key turning point it played this role by unleashing social forces that were already at work but still held back to a certain extent. Already present to some degree at the end of the seventeenth and beginning of the eighteenth centuries, the traits that defined the new socioeconomic order—individualism, competition, profit seeking and a form of religiosity that sanctified it—spread and developed considerably up to the revolutionary period.[1]

Firsthand testimony concerning the period preceding and including the Revolution is certainly not lacking. The literature is quite varied. There are in the first place many narratives of travel within the colonies, covering the countryside as well as cities and towns, on the coast and in the back country, from New England to Charlestown and Savannah. But other forms of writing were also commonly practiced that did not necessarily involve movement in space: the memoir, the diary, and the letter.[2] Two other types of writing, while not personal testimony per se, draw largely on individual experiences: the promotional tract, intended for potential immigrants, and the modern version of the ancient genre of chorography, which offers the "history and present state of" a particular province.[3]

The authors of these kinds of works were in the majority English, but one finds Scots, Germans, Swedes, and French among them as well. In the different national groups there were both colonial inhabitants and visitors. The social and professional situations of the writers were also diverse: they were European nobility, wealthy American landowners, merchants, doctors, scientists, churchmen, and military officers. Among the better known works are the travel accounts of the planter William Byrd II (1728), the doctor Alexander Hamilton (1744), the Swedish naturalist Pehr Kalm (1748–51), and the French aristocrat the Marquis de Chastellux (1780–82).[4] In a different genre we might cite the correspondence of Abigail Adams, wife of the second president of the United States.

In many such works the incursions of modernity in eighteenth-century British American society are apparent in various ways. One case in point is a travel account recently republished in several collections, Sarah Kemble Knight's journal of an expedition from Boston to New Haven and New York in 1705, which allows us to see to what extent the mercantile mentality was already pervasive in the Northeast at the beginning of the century. Daughter of a Boston merchant and wife of a maritime entrepreneur, Knight herself was a businesswoman. The purpose of her trip was to settle an inheritance, and her narrative is filled with observations and anecdotes that involve commercial transactions and practices, some exorbitant or questionable, all motivated by profit seeking, that she encounters on her way.[5]

But among these texts that bring particular perspectives to bear on the era, the writings of Saint-John de Crèvecoeur are of exceptional interest. In them we find a greater breadth and diversity of experience than are exhibited in most of the others.[6] Crèvecoeur's viewpoint is that of someone both on the inside and the outside, and his explorations of colonial realities are both intensive (based on long-time residence in one place) and extensive (based on much travel, covering virtually all of British America). What is more, his writings radically cut across generic lines. Situated at the intersection of autobiography and sociological documentary, his texts adopt just about all of the genres of nonfiction writing mentioned earlier while often giving them a new dimension by "fictionalizing" them. This literary aspect of the writing allows for a particularly rich and subtle exploration of the author's experience of the era. In what follows I will attempt to unfold Crèvecoeur's vision of British American modernity.

In 1988 Bernard Chevignard, the foremost French authority on the work of Crèvecoeur, pointed out the continuing deficiency in biographical knowledge of this author, who had been rediscovered at the beginning of the twentieth century after a long period of neglect.[7] It must be admitted that the progress since then has been slight. Although Dennis D. Moore's work on the manuscripts now held by the Library of Congress has clarified some issues, and Chevignard himself has encapsulated his own research in a short monograph,[8] we are still awaiting a more substantial biography. Many uncertainties remain concerning Crèvecoeur's life, but the broad outlines are nonetheless well established. I will sketch in those that are most relevant to my analysis.

Born in Caen, France, in 1735, into a family of the petty nobility, Michel-Guillaume-Jean de Crèvecoeur joined the French army at the age of twenty and embarked for New France.[9] Before this departure the young Crèvecoeur had visited England, and his stay there seems to have inspired him with considerable admiration for the country, particularly as regards the mechanical bent of its people. In New France he served as an engineer and cartographer but also as an artilleryman. He may have been wounded in the decisive battle in 1759 on the Plains of Abraham that was to spell defeat for the French in North America, but this is not certain.[10] Whatever the truth of the matter may have been, in the immediate aftermath of the battle Crèvecoeur resigned his military position and moved south into the English provinces. There he took on the name of J. Hector St. John, was naturalized as a British subject, and for a good part of the following ten years traveled throughout the colonies as a topographer, surveyor, and merchant. In 1769 he married Mehitable Tippet, a woman from a wealthy New York landowning family, and settled on a farm in the Hudson Valley. During the War of Independence Crèvecoeur seems to have leaned toward the Tory side,[11] as did his wife's family. At any rate he was harshly persecuted by local "patriots." In 1779 he crossed the patriot lines and entered New York City, then in the hands of the British. There also he encountered hostility; he was suspected of espionage for the rebels and was imprisoned for several months.

When he finally succeeded in reaching London in 1781, Crèvecoeur sold a large manuscript to a British publisher. A portion of it was published in 1782 under the title *Letters from an American Farmer*. Two-thirds of the whole remained in manuscript, however, until the twentieth century. A substantial part of that was published in 1925 as *Sketches of Eighteenth-Century America*, but the remainder appeared in book form only in 1995, in a definitive edition of the unpublished materials prepared by Moore from the original manuscripts.[12] After arranging for the first publication of *Letters*, Crèvecoeur crossed the Channel, settled in Paris, and began frequenting the salon of Mme d'Houtetot, the patroness of Rousseau. Under the influence of this intellectual milieu he produced a French version of the work that differed considerably from the original. A two-volume edition of *Lettres d'un cultivateur américain* was published in 1784, to be followed in 1787 by a further enlarged three-volume version.

Once he returned to France Crèvecoeur again redefined his national, cultural, and linguistic identity, thoroughly reaffirming his French self. Subsequently, after a period of residence in the fledgling United States as the French consul general in New York (1783–90), he came back for good to France (with a brief interlude in Germany during the Terror), and he died there in 1813. Throughout this later period of his life he wrote in French for a French public. His main publication, aside from the two editions of

Lettres d'un cultivateur américain, was *Voyage dans la haute Pensylvanie et dans l'état de New-York* (Voyage in Upper Pennsylvania and the State of New York), which appeared in three volumes in Paris in 1801.[13]

Crèvecoeur's writings can thus be divided into those written in English during his prolonged residency in British America and those written in French after his return to his homeland in 1781. Clearly that division also points to a deep split in his cultural identity. After reinventing himself as a British colonial he finally reentered his original French persona. The double national and cultural identification at the same time coincides with a social dichotomy. Born a French aristocrat, initiated into the traditions of a premodern class, Crèvecoeur found himself drawn, first in England and then in its colonies, to the technical prowess, industry, and mercantile enterprise that was part and parcel of British modernity.[14]

Contrary to what might be supposed, though, the two sensibilities that inhabited Crèvecoeur are not neatly divided between his English and French periods but rather remain in a state of internal contradiction in each corpus of writings. This contradiction sometimes appears baldly, with no attempt at conciliation, but the author often articulates a kind of unstable resolution. The form this takes is different, however, in the two periods of Crèvecoeur's literary production: in the English writings the adoption of the point of view of the big landowners of New York, whose mentality had feudal as well as capitalist aspects, and in the French writings the appropriation of the perspective of the intellectual circle he frequented in Paris, which combined a Rousseauist romanticism with the encyclopedists' fascination with certain aspects of modernity.

I will concentrate on the texts in English, while bringing in occasional commentaries on the French editions by way of comparison. My purpose is to explore Crèvecoeur's perceptions of the British colonies before and during the War of Independence, and the writings in English, before he underwent the influence of the Parisian salons, are much closer to the American realities he experienced.[15] I will draw on the original *Letters* and also on the *Sketches*, which, according to one commentator, are a kind of "shadow" to them,[16] and on some texts from the edition of 1995 that bring in new elements.

In the English corpus one finds very little on Indians, and there is no English-language account of the travel in Indian territory that Crèvecoeur himself had undertaken. It is in the French writings that the Indian is progressively introduced, finally taking up a significant portion—about one quarter—of his *Voyage dans la haute Pensylvanie*.[17] But in this book the passages dealing with Indians are largely borrowed from other sources, often from the accounts by Jonathan Carver and William Bartram that I analyze later.[18] Although the element of personal memoir concerning Indians is thus quite limited, at the end of the chapter I will briefly deal with Crèvecoeur's representations of them.

PORTRAIT OF THE BRITISH COLONIES

Before discussing how the colonies are depicted in Crèvecoeur's English texts, it is necessary to address the question of narrative point of view. The opening letters of the original 1782 edition of *Letters from an American Farmer* set out and develop a narrative persona—James, a farmer in Pennsylvania—and the entirety of the letters in this edition are purported to be his, addressed to a European correspondent. Recent American critical analysis of that work—in isolation from the other English writings and from the French works—has sometimes treated it as a kind of epistolary novel, in which the narrator's attitudes are satirized or critiqued by Crèvecoeur, the author.[19] The latter's point of view is thus posited as starkly different from that of James, the narrator. As scholars of Crèvecoeur's overall work have pointed out, however, Crèvecoeur himself made no such clear-cut distinction between his own voice and that of his narrator. In his personal copy of *Letters from an American Farmer* he at some point crossed out "James," writing "John" in its place, and in the subsequent French versions "James" became "St. John," clearly identified with the author.[20] To complicate matters further, there is no evidence that Crèvecoeur planned the original *Letters* to have a novelistic structure. It is not certain, for that matter, whether he or an editor, or both, were involved in making the choice of texts to be included in the original edition. It does seem plausible, though this also is unproven, that once they had been chosen Crèvecoeur retouched or revised at least some of the letters of the original edition so as to frame the work with a fictional narrative voice and render it what Katherine and Everett Emerson aptly term "moderately coherent."[21]

As I have already suggested, Crèvecoeur's was in fact a highly divided and conflicted sensibility, due in the first place to his social, cultural, and national displacements. His diversity of point of view is reflected in the heterogeneity of narrative voice in his writing. In the texts not included in the original edition of *Letters* he sometimes seems to articulate his own point of view directly,[22] but in many cases other fictional voices are introduced. Through these voices Crèvecoeur presents different angles of perception of the American scene he has observed and different aspects of his understanding and interpretation of it. Through them he displays his many ambivalences, hesitations, and inconsistencies, but at the same time provides an exceptionally revealing, multifaceted panorama of that scene. I will therefore treat the author's various narrative personae as representing partial aspects of himself.

In many passages of Crèvecoeur's English texts, but especially in those chosen for the first edition, there seems to be a clear intent to present the British colonies as a kind of ideal. The note is struck in the very first letters, in which Farmer James lavishes praise on them and states in summary, "We are the most perfect society now existing in the world."[23] Scattered throughout, but mainly concentrated at the beginning, one finds passages that construct an unambiguously positive conception of British America. It can be broken down into several propositions: (1) America is a melting pot ("Here individuals of all nations are melted into a new race of men": *Letters*, 64). (2) It is egalitarian, with little disparity between rich and poor. (3) The backbone of America is agriculture, and its characteristic social type is the farmer ("We are a race of cultivators," says James with pride: *Letters*, 37). (4) The typical American farm is more or less self-sufficient ("The philosopher's stone of an American farmer is to do everything within his own family.")[24] (5) The relentless labor of the new breed of people in America generally leads to growing wealth and a rise in social status—in short, "success." (6) American communities are characterized by solidarity, mutual aid, and hospitality.

Such is the vision that Crèvecoeur often seems to wish to project of colonial America, a vision that was doubtless nostalgic since it is likely that a considerable portion of the letters were revised, or even written, during the traumatic period of the war.[25] But he is too lucid an observer to remain a prisoner to this simplistic stereotype. A careful reading of *Letters*—and especially of *Sketches*, which is generally more critical and "realistic"—reveals that, while they are not entirely false, each of the elements of Crèvecoeur's ideal image hides another reality.[26] (1) The melting pot excludes at least two groups: blacks and Indians. (2) America in this period is in fact riven by sharp differences in wealth and status. (3) The dominant social type in America is not so much the farmer as the merchant, the land speculator, and the lawyer (as well as the *merchant* farmer in the North and the plantation owner in the South). (4) The typical farm is not truly self-sufficient but rather part of a market network. (5) The hard work of newly arrived colonists results at least as often in failure as in success. (6) Solidarity is rather marginal in the competitive society of British America.

In the letters that involve the period before the revolutionary troubles the author discusses in some detail five distinct social and geographical "conditions," or types of colonist: the new immigrant, the coastal fisherman, the "middle" farmer (the kind who, like Crèvecoeur himself after 1769, occupied land in the interior that had already been cleared and cultivated for a certain time), the pioneer or "back settler" who cleared forest land and introduced the first farms, and the southern planter. Of these, only the last is presented in an entirely negative light. Treatment of the others is contradictory. While some passages attempt to idealize them, others either subtly or bluntly undermine that image.

I shall first look at the case of the new immigrant, who is given a relatively limited treatment in the work as a whole but who is highlighted by appearing near the opening of *Letters*, in the now famous Letter 3 entitled "What Is an American?"[27] Here Crèvecoeur employs a technique that he often uses elsewhere as well, which consists of recounting the life story—considered to be exemplary and called an "epitome"—of either a real person or an imaginary construct based on a number of people. The epitome of the new immigrant is Andrew, who comes from the poverty-stricken

Hebrides Islands. The author describes the scene of his arrival in the port of Philadelphia, where he and his fellow passengers are lodged in the houses of the city's residents. The man who takes Andrew into his home immediately offers paid employment to him and his family, and later proposes apparently favorable conditions of land leasing.

The narrator mentions several concrete details, however, that undercut the impression the reader might have of an altruistic gift and act of solidarity on the part of the already established Philadelphians. He gives figures for both the employment offered to Andrew's family and the land lease. Andrew's salary—the usual one for new arrivals, he specifies—is to be four dollars a month rather than the five paid to more seasoned workers (at woodcutting). Andrew's wife's salary is to be two dollars a month (at spinning), while their son will earn one dollar a month driving a team. These figures clearly indicate that immigrants provided a relatively cheap source of labor, and that women and children were extremely underpaid in relation to men.

As for the land lease, while the landowner grants good terms of credit—Andrew will begin to pay only after several years, when he has gained a surplus from his crops—it is stipulated that during the first three years he must plant at least fifty trees and drain seven acres of marsh on his land. If one considers, as the author points out elsewhere, that draining marshland was one of the most difficult and costly tasks in the rural American economy, it is apparent that in this respect also local elites used immigrants to their own advantage.[28] Still, these conditions of work and land occupation might be considerably better than those the immigrant had left in Europe.

The author continues Andrew's story and brings it to a happy end. Andrew succeeds with the initial conditions offered him, becomes a wealthy landowner himself, and in the end aids other newcomers to America. Yet here also Crèvecoeur's commentary partially undermines the sanguine view of the immigration process that seems to be implied, placing in question the value of this epitome as a general rule. For in the view of the narrator some immigrants bring their "vices" and "indolence" with them from Europe, which often impedes their rise in society. According to him the rate of success depends on national origin. Of a total of twelve immigrants of each nationality, he claims, nine Germans, seven Scots, and only four Irish will "succeed." If one calculates the average from these hypothetical statistics, 6.6 of 12, or just over half, of the incoming immigrants will prosper. The national differences indicated are also interesting. Germans and Scots apparently have ethnic characteristics that are better adapted to American life than do the Irish. They presumably display traits of the "Protestant ethic" such as asceticism, devotion to work, and parsimony, whereas the Catholic Irish do not.[29]

The second of the "conditions" treated by Crèvecoeur—in Letters 4–8 of the first edition—is that of the fisherman in Nantucket (and Martha's Vineyard). Though half the inhabitants of Nantucket are Quakers and half are Presbyterians, they live in harmony, according to the narrator, because all are so absorbed with the things of this world that they are "less vehement about spiritual ones" (*Letters*, 144). These fisherfolk, who also engage in farming, turn out in fact to illustrate perfectly Weber's Protestant ethic and spirit of capitalism. They are frugal, sober, orderly, devoted to their occupation, and never cease to pursue useful activities, even in their spare time. (While chatting with friends they are in the habit of whittling practical objects out of pieces of wood.) Most important, they have made fishing into a large-scale business enterprise. After fishing for cod in nearby waters, they shift to whaling, seeking their prey farther and farther away, throughout the world. Since whale oil brings high prices, they will often stop at nothing to maximize their kill. "Sometimes men more intent on gain than on the preservation of their lives will run great risks" (*Letters*, 132), comments the narrator. When their expeditions sometimes end in failure, though, "they bear such misfortunes like true merchants, and as they never venture their all like gamesters, they try their fortunes again; the latter hope to win by chance alone, the former by industry, well-judged speculation, and some hazard" (*Letters*, 124). They are indeed merchants to the core, doing business everywhere they go, selling not only their own products but buying and reselling those of others, in particular in the Caribbean islands (*Letters*, 125).

Under these conditions Nantucket could hardly remain a community of equal members. At the beginning of his description Crèvecoeur explains how land on the island was uniformly distributed at the outset, but then shows that the number of shares held by families became more and more unequal, resulting in considerable differences in wealth. The imbalance is even greater on Nantucket than on the mainland, but on the island they do not arouse "those heart burnings which in other societies generate crimes" (*Letters*, 120). Although no reasons are given for this difference, one hypothesis might be that in the predominantly maritime economy of Nantucket landownership had relatively less importance.

Turning now to the continent, closest to the coast are the already well-established farms of the "middle" lands. If we look carefully at the passages involving this geographical zone, it appears that the image of the self-sufficient rural economy sometimes evoked by Crèvecoeur corresponds in fact more to a desire than a reality. For although the farmer makes some of his tools himself and often consumes the produce of his orchards and henhouses, he also buys much from merchants. He uses the sawmills in the neighborhood and in winter brings a large portion of the harvest to markets. There are marketplaces of two kinds: riverside storage depots for goods that will later be sent off to the international market, and mills that process produce—winnowing wheat, in particular—for local sale (*Sketches*, 73, 74, 145, 147, 150).[30]

In several places Crèvecoeur extols the hospitality and helping spirit of the farmers, but the customs that incarnate these traits are in fact part of a network of relationships of a different kind, one that obeys economic imperatives. Such, for example, is the moral obligation of farmers to open their doors to strangers during the winter. The text suggests that most of those who accept this hospitality are other farmers taking their produce to market, and although no allusion is made to them Indians clearly were not included in the open invitation. A similar economic underpinning can be discerned in the "bees" or "frolics" described; these are gatherings of neighboring farmers to carry out some piece of heavy work for one of them, followed by a banquet and dancing. This practice undoubtedly provided a kind of insurance for the farmers who provided the help, knowing that sooner or later they would need help themselves (*Sketches*, 49, 80, 96, 145).

But the conviviality of these frolics also engendered a kind of utopian space that set them apart from the normal daily lives and behavior of the farming families. When the narrator enumerates the general characteristics that define the mentality of the farmers, hospitality and helpfulness are not among them, whereas "selfishness" and litigiousness are. In one revealing passage the narrator admits that for him the essential function of the festivities seems to be to create "the union and the little society which subsists among us" (*Sketches*, 96). The frolics thus generate, at least for a time, the sense of community that is otherwise lacking.[31]

The farming society turns out to be markedly hierarchical as well. This is apparent in the first place as regards women, about whom the narrator seems to naïvely reflect the common male attitude in this context. The farm wife is a "useful acquisition" for the farmer (*Sketches*, 124), since within the family economy of which he is the head she manages a more limited domain, the house and farmyard. Her most important function is to make edible—and pleasant to eat—the perishables, like fruit and eggs, that cannot be transported to market (*Letters*, 39; *Sketches*, 41, 124). Although important, then, the woman's role is seen as both marginal to the main economic activity of the household and entirely subordinate.

In the society of the farm two categories occupy an inferior rank: day laborers and blacks. The blacks are most often slaves, both in the North and the South, but are freedmen in some cases, particularly in Quaker households. In one letter from the first edition Crèvecoeur relates a visit to John Bartram (the father of William) on his horticultural farm near Philadelphia.[32] In this Quaker ménage all eat at the same table but seated in a well-defined order: at the head of the table the family and guests, in the middle the day laborers, and at the far end the freedmen, clearly not on an equal footing with the white laborers (*Letters*, 182). While the living conditions of workers on the farms of the "middle" are shown to be relatively comfortable due to the chronic shortage of manpower, and those of blacks in the North to be better than in the South, both groups are nonetheless at the bottom of a sharply differentiated social scale (*Sketches*, 50, 82). The narrator gives an indication of the extent of wealth at the other end of the spectrum when he mentions that the "first man in our country" possesses 1,500 acres of prime land (*Sketches*, 83).

The fourth "condition" examined by Crèvecoeur is that of the "back settler." In several passages the narrator raises the question of the motivation of frontier settlers, the impulse "which drives people over the hills and far away" (*Sketches*, 151). Although the commentary is sometimes muddled, the predominant explanation offered is that they are most often poor debtors wishing to better their fortune or laborers preferring independence to salaried work. Another common case put forward is that of owners of small farms of the middle who want more land for their children. To colonize new land one ordinarily needed to borrow money to pay for the land, equipment, and often a slave. Many failed in the endeavor, having to give up their new property and begin again even farther west, or vegetating in a miserable state of inactivity and drunkenness, a half-civilized condition worse than the "savage" state, in the view of the narrator. Many remained in debt for the rest of their lives, sometimes bequeathing their indebtedness to later generations (*Sketches*, 90).

Some succeeded, however. As with whaling in Nantucket, new settlement constituted, in Crèvecoeur's phrase, "a very odd sort of speculation." Indeed, he adds, "the poor beginner toiling in the woods . . . greatly resembles the situation of the English manufacturer" (*Sketches*, 92). A striking passage in *Sketches* provides a portrait—in the form of a nonindividualized epitome—of the settler who succeeds. When this settler has managed to amass a surplus of wheat, and new arrivals in his area wish to purchase from him, in determining the price he does not deduct the cost of transport to a distant mill that he would have had to pay if he had not sold locally:

> This would appear just . . . [but] his neighbors absolutely want his supply. . . . He therefore concludes upon having the full price. He remembers his former difficulties; no one assisted him then. Why should he assist others? . . . How should he be merciful . . . ? He has never heard that it was a necessary qualification. . . . He, therefore, deals hardly with his neighbors. If they are not punctual in their payment, he prosecutes them at law. . . . He impeaches the cattle. . . . He secures himself. . . . His wealth and, therefore, his consequence increase with the progress of the settlement.

Later, at a crossroads that he has engineered, he builds a big house:

He becomes an innholder and a country-merchant. This introduces him into all the little mysteries of self-interest.... He sells for good that which perhaps he knows to be indifferent, because he also knows that ... the wheat he has taken in may not be so good or so clean as it was asserted. Fearful of fraud in all his dealings and transactions, he arms himself therefore with it. Strict integrity is not much wanted, as each is on his guard in his daily intercourse, and this mode of thinking and acting becomes habitual.... If it is not "bellum omnium contra omnes," 'tis a general mass of keenness and sagacious acting against another mass of equal sagacity; 'tis caution against caution. Happy, when it does not degenerate into fraud against fraud! (*Sketches*, 75–78)

This passage occurs in a letter from *Sketches* entitled "Reflections on the manners of the Americans," signaling the broad range of applicability the author intended to give the portrait.[33]

The last "condition," that of southern planters and plantations, calls forth strenuous condemnation by the narrator in some of the best known passages of *Letters*. Letter 9 contrasts the life of the idle and immensely rich Charleston plantation owners with that of their black slaves, sold "like horses at a fair" and perpetually toiling in appalling conditions (*Letters*, 162). The narrator also describes a horrifying scene that he happens upon while out walking: a black man, half-dead in a cage, is being eaten alive by birds and insects, in punishment for having killed an overseer. In dwelling on the all-pervading cruelty of southern slavery, the narrator of *Letters* points up by contrast the relative mildness of the treatment accorded to blacks in the North.[34] Yet Crèvecoeur suggests elsewhere that the difference is far from absolute. In a letter included in *Sketches*, one that concerns the North, the narrator tells of a punishment one landowner meted out to his slave that closely resembles the one witnessed in the South. The slave was tied to a pole in a salt marsh, and although in this case the intention was not to kill, the man eventually died from insect bites (*Sketches*, 110).

In the works in English by Crèvecoeur, the subject matter almost exclusively concerns British America. But in three exceptional texts the author brings in other colonies: French Canada, the Spanish possessions in America, and finally Jamaica and the Bermudas.[35] The first two of these, as treated by Crèvecoeur, are symmetrical but also opposite. France and Spain are the two other major colonial powers in the region, and each differs from British America in culture and religion. But one is looked upon positively, the other negatively. In "The English and the French before the Revolution," Canadian culture is presented as an ideal and implicitly opposed to certain traits in the British colonies criticized by Crèvecoeur. Compared with French Canada, the author comments, "no society of men could exhibit greater simplicity, more honesty, . . . less litigiousness" (*Sketches*, 172). In this piece from his Anglo-American period he fully identifies with a modified (colonial) version of his culture of origin against his adopted culture. In the essay comparing the Spanish and English colonies, on the other hand, it is the English that is given an ideal status—in terms similar to those already mentioned, with particular emphasis on the religious aspect—as against the notorious "Black Legend" of Spanish America.

The third comparative essay, "Sketches of Jamaica and Bermudas and Other Subjects," is the most interesting in terms of the themes I am exploring here, for two reasons. First of all, it makes a devastating appraisal, not of the islands named in the title but of British America itself. And second, the French version of the essay (in the 1784 edition of *Lettres*) revealingly illustrates the kind of transformation undergone by *Letters* in becoming *Lettres*.[36] This text, in its original form in English, does not appear to have been much reworked by its author—it was first published, as a transcription of the manuscript, in *More Letters* (1995)—and it is precisely its inconsistencies that make it interesting. The title suggests that Jamaica and the Bermudas will be central to it, but three-quarters of the letter in fact concerns the "other subjects." Moreover that plural is misleading since it refers to commentary on one colony alone: British America.

The letter opens with its author, the son of a wealthy farmer turned country merchant, bitterly resolving to cease being an honest man after he has made the painful discovery that honesty exists nowhere in "the country." It becomes clear in what follows that the country referred to is not Jamaica, of which the author is also highly critical, or the Bermudas but rather the British mainland colonies, where the author was born. He has indeed spent time in Jamaica, where he received bad treatment ("I was severely duped in several of my Transactions"), and subsequently in the Bermudas, where on the contrary he was delighted with the inhabitants (*More Letters*, 107, 109). But he has already been back home for some time. His traumatic experiences there, of deceitfulness stemming from egotistical calculation, form the main subject matter of the letter. His disillusionment is all the more severe since those he has had dealings with attend church regularly and display an elevated sense of morality. In closing out the affairs of his deceased father he encountered everywhere—with one exception, which of course proved the rule—behavior that was "Perverse, Insincere, often down right dishonest" (*More Letters*, 110). Among those who have mistreated him the author is particularly galled by an Irish immigrant whom his father aided when he arrived in America four years earlier. But the Irishman has now, without hesitation and without difficulty, taken advantage of the son, having learned how, through the school of experience in America (*More Letters*, 111) Here, then, is a dark counterpart to Andrew, the model immigrant from the Hebrides.

It is instructive to see what becomes of this caustic critique of British America in the French version of the text, inserted in the 1784 edition that purports to be a translation of *Letters* but is in fact a far-reaching revision. The French title, "Voyage à la Jamaïque et aux isles Bermudes" (Voyage to Jamaica and the Bermuda Islands), already announces the change of content, since the "other subjects" that were central to the English version disappear entirely. In this version, written after Crèvecoeur's return to France and under the influence of a Parisian intellectual milieu that was very supportive of the victorious American Revolution, criticism of British America would have been unwelcome, and so it has been deleted. The method is simple: the author announces at the outset that he has just returned from his trip to the islands, and the experiences that have grieved him are transferred (with a few modifications) from the mainland to Jamaica. Now it is on that island that he has become disillusioned and cynical: "I was exposed to such malice that I said to myself: let's be as nasty as they are; let's resist fraud by fraud."[37] At the same time, in this French version the description of Bermuda is further developed and projects the image of a quasi-paradisiacal society. The contrast between it and the hellishness of Jamaica becomes not only the principal but the sole subject of the essay. The coherence of the text is perhaps improved thereby, but only by eliminating what was the heart of the matter in the original.

THE REVOLUTION

Among the dozen or so English texts by Crèvecoeur that deal in one way or another with the revolutionary crisis, only one, "Distresses of a Frontier Man," appears in the first edition of *Letters*. This almost total absence of the Revolution in the original edition is consonant with its less critical stance regarding the prerevolutionary colonial society, compared with the group of texts excluded from it. In the first edition the editorial intention seems clear: to present the British colonies as a utopian society in the making.[38] "Distresses of a Frontier Man" shows only that this universe is threatened by the coming of the revolutionary "troubles," whereas many of the texts covering the revolutionary period that are not included in the first edition dramatize and analyze the rise of a new class that uses the Revolution to enrich itself.[39] A careful reading of these texts excluded from the 1782 edition reveals in the revolutionary process an exacerbation of the tendencies of development toward modernity that some texts and passages, most often also rejected from the first edition, had discerned in prerevolutionary society.[40] Crèvecoeur himself, however, never seems fully aware of the link between his latent critique of prerevolutionary society and his perception of the revolutionary crisis.

The narratives of the crisis are about equally divided between those situated on the frontier and those on the farmlands of the "middle." In the former the main emphasis is on physical violence, ferocity, and cruelty, all encouraged by distance from sources of authority. In the latter it is moral violence and cupidity that prevail, in situations where authority is changing hands and is being exercised for personal profit and social ascension. This last category of texts will interest us particularly here.[41]

Four texts have special relevance to the socioeconomic issues I have been discussing: "The American Belisarius" (*Sketches*), "Ingratitude Rewarded"

(*More Letters*), "The Commissioners" (*More Letters*), and *Landscapes* (*Sketches*). The first tells the story of a wealthy but generous farmer who is harassed by the rebels at the beginning of hostilities. His possessions are confiscated and he is put in prison, but later he is set free and allowed to live on a small portion of his original estate. The title points to a comparison of this landowner with the Byzantine general Belisarius, unjustly accused of conspiracy, imprisoned, and subsequently released. In this text as in several others, the author tells the reader he intends to bring attention to some disagreeable realities that will, he fears, end by being entirely effaced from official works consecrating the Revolution—the "journals, memoirs, elaborate essays [that] shall not fail hereafter to commemorate the heroes who have made their appearance on this new American stage" (*Sketches*, 228).

The opening passage introduces the narrator as a detached observer—"the inquisitive eye of an unnoticed individual mixing in crowds" (*Sketches*, 228)—but it soon becomes evident that he identifies passionately with the sufferings of the American Belisarius. This is not surprising if one remembers that Crèvecoeur himself underwent a similar ordeal. The account of the persecution of the landowner, accused by the patriots of being a Tory, is quasi-Orwellian. In a kind of self-fulfilling prophecy, the inquisitors themselves engender the guilt they are searching for. For the rebels' harassment is what drives the protagonist to flee to the Tory and Indian camp, with which he had had no previous contact.

One of the most original aspects of the narrative, though, is the revelation of the motive of greed at work on the side of the rebels. The revolutionary camp, which includes two brothers-in-law of the rural Belisarius who envy him his fortune, looks for any pretext to confiscate his wealth. Under the cloak of ideology lurks the desire for self-enrichment. These men, according to the narrator, "impiously affix to their new, fictitious zeal the sacred name of liberty on purpose to blind the unwary, whilst . . . they worship no deity but self-interest" (*Sketches*, 238).

In a remarkable passage that comes at the end of the text, one can see the germ of an interpretation of the revolutionary crisis as an attempt by a rising class—the puritan-minded lower middle class—to supplant the older elite: "His enemies, now become his masters, were, before these times, mostly poor, obscure, and unnoticed; great psalm-singers, zealous religionists.... They were meek,... prudent in their outward actions, ... men of plausible countenances, sleek-haired, but possessed at the same time of great duplicity of heart; sly in their common social intercourse, callous, pushing, with an affected charitable language, from their doors the poor, the orphan, the widow.... That affected meekness, that delusive softness of manners are now gone; they are discarded as useless" (*Sketches*, 247–48).[42] If he did not believe in a future punishment of evildoers, the narrator concludes, "I'd turn Manichaean like so many others. I'd worship the demon of the times.... I'd set myself calumniating my rich neighbours.... I'd build my new fortune on the depreciation of the money.... I'd become obdurate, merciless, and unjust. I'd grow rich.... I'd send others a-fighting, whilst I stayed at home to trade and to rule. I'd become a clamorous American, a modern Whig" (*Sketches*, 249).

In contrast to these grasping petty bourgeois who are using the Revolution for their own enrichment, the fallen landowner is presented as a quasi-aristocrat. Characterized as "princely," before the upheaval he was a patriarch who liberally gave to the poor. As we have seen, however, Crèvecoeur elsewhere portrays a colonial society in which mercenary mentalities and behaviors are to be found in nearly all of the diverse "conditions." In fact the big rural landowner of the middle possessed traits of both the entrepreneur and the nobleman, and, as I suggested at the beginning of the chapter, the glorification of this social type by the author may be seen as an ideological compromise that reconciles the aristocratic Frenchman and the plebeian American in himself. But in "The American Belisarius," as in other texts of the crisis, this personage appears as an unadulterated aristocrat and plays the key role in a nostalgic drama of paradise lost. This way of depicting the before and after of the Revolution, however, in effect precludes any realization that the revolutionary process and what preceded it are linked, any recognition that the worm was already in the apple, so to speak, and that the Revolution is part of a much broader social change.

Whereas "The American Belisarius," as the title indicates, focuses on one victim of the Revolution elevated to the status of paragon of a bygone era, "Ingratitude Rewarded" turns to a portrayal of the new rulers. As an antidote for "that vague artificial Splendor with which it is now fashionable to represent every thing," the author of this letter wishes to give his interlocutor precise delineations of facts, "some Real Sketches of our Times in the Picture of those Nefarious Agents who have occasioned all the Calamities they contain" (*More Letters*, 316). To do this the narrator chooses to recount one story among others, the story of one of the "insignificant" agents who have now taken the upper hand.

A benevolent patriarch is present in this narrative as well, but here the center of interest is the person who has been aided by him and who betrays him once the Revolution has raised him to a position of power. The beneficent landowner, and later his widow, pay for the education of this man of modest means and are crucially instrumental in his becoming a lawyer, but they thereby provide him with the very arms by which he can become an oppressor. In the course of the rebellion the young lawyer becomes a "Commissioner of Sequesteration; for Selling and Confiscating the Tories Estates" (*More Letters*, 321). In this capacity he declines to intervene, as he might have, to keep the estate of the man to whom he owes his success, which is now in the possession of the son, from being sold. Everything is finally put up for auction, including a painted portrait of the benefactor, which is bought at a low price for the value of its gold frame (*More Letters*, 322). As for the lawyer, "after he had been appointed to the Important Commission he Now holds, he was consulted about the Salary. He Modestly begged that None Should as Yet be Fixed, Untill his Country shou'd have had proper knowledge, and experiance of his Services, and Abilities. That is, he wanted the Settlement Shou'd be delay'd untill the Money Shou'd be better established" (*More Letters*, 323).

"Ingratitude Rewarded," then, takes up a single example from among the new rulers, as "The American Belasarius" shows a single victim. In the third text, "The Commissioners," Crèvecoeur sketches a group portrait and, while keeping the epistolary framing device, gives a prototheatrical form to the depiction. The author of the letter attempts to dramatize for the person to whom he is writing a meeting of the committee that interrogates those suspected of Tory sympathies. The first to appear before the committee is a well-intentioned landowner of the same type as the

"Belasarius." When he finally realizes, after a frustrating exchange, that it is impossible to reason with the commissioners, he openly alludes to the hidden agenda: "The Truth of ye Matter is that you want my Estate" (*More Letters*, 304). Following him, an English doctor, an Irish farmer, and a Quaker are interrogated. In each case the good faith of the person under suspicion is manifest, highlighting the irrationality of the commissioners. But at the same time the covert motive for this irrationality is insistently brought out, since those in the dock accuse their interrogators of wanting to profit personally from the spoils. The "Belasarius" of the text summarizes the situation more generally when he cries out at one point, "By you[r] new Policy there will be but one single standard of distinction left[,] that of Richesses[,] that of Monney I mean" (*More Letters*, 311).

The last text, *Landscapes*, maintains the plurality of voices introduced by "The Commissioners" and carries to its logical conclusion the evolution toward a new genre initiated in the latter. It is a short play, made up of six scenes—"scenes" being one possible meaning of the "landscapes" of the title. Although it has been largely ignored in the historiography of American theater—a situation that is perhaps understandable, given that it was never actually staged—*Landscapes* was one of the very first dramas to be written in America, a significant achievement in itself.[43] The play provides another and more elaborate representation of the situation delineated in the other texts under discussion: persecution by nouveau-riche revolutionaries, carried out for personal profit under the hypocritical guise of patriotism and religiosity.

In the introduction to the play, the author insists that he wishes to show not the "superb frame" of the Revolution but the "vulgar thread of the canvas," not the "august bird arrayed with majestic feathers [but] only the nest in which it was hatched, composed of sticks and twigs cemented with dirt" (*Sketches*, 250). The drama focuses on the persecution of a family of the gentry by the commander of a revolutionary militia unit who is also a deacon and a "Commissioner for Selling Tory Estates." Here the agent of harassment and expropriation is in fact a couple—the deacon and his wife—and the play illustrates how the corruption of values by money can thoroughly permeate the domestic sphere.[44] The action takes place on a

Sunday when, instead of attending church, as would be appropriate, the deacon lets his wife persuade him to visit the estate of a landowner who is to be dispossessed the next day, with the unacknowledged purpose of confiscating goods for themselves. While the couple are traveling to the estate, other characters are introduced: on the side of the exploiters of the Revolution, a certain Aaron Blue-skin,[45] "new-made squire" (*Sketches*, 278), and several other militia officers; on the side of the victims, the owner of a tavern who is having trouble making ends meet, a Quaker arrested for refusing military service, and two travelers suspected by the militiamen.

In the exercise of oppression that is dramatized in the middle section of the play, an atmosphere of dread develops that is even more Orwellian than in the previously discussed texts. The search for "counter-revolutionaries" becomes a witch hunt in which anything and its opposite can prove betrayal and in which, in particular, simply belonging to the gentry demonstrates ipso facto that one is a Tory enemy. History is rewritten as well. When the deacon learns, for example, that a former Whig has just been shot as a counterrevolutionary, he loudly proclaims that the man was never a Whig at all.

The main lesson taught by the play, however, is that the revolutionary crisis is systematically used as a vehicle for self-enrichment. When the deacon commissioner and his wife arrive, in the penultimate scene, at the estate to be dispossessed the next day, the wife succeeds in extorting many goods she wants, including a slave, from the wife of the landowner in a way that is both cruel and hypocritical. In doing so she has the approval of the deacon. In the last scene the couple give a final demonstration of turpitude. As they are returning home they encounter, wandering on the road, a woman who has already been dispossessed and who is in a state of near madness. The deacon's wife refuses her any aid at all, while the deacon finally grants her an absurdly small sum of money, clearly to assuage his conscience.

THE TEMPTATION OF INDIAN LIFEWAYS

Confronted with the materialistic civilization that was developing in British America, Crèvecoeur was aware that there existed a radically different alternative beyond the bounds of this civilization: the Amerindian communities. His attitude toward the diametrically opposed way of life practiced in these communities remained as ambiguous and contradictory, however, as that which he manifested toward the nascent capitalism of the British colonies and the early United States. He saw Indian lifeways as both a temptation and a danger, sometimes picturing their societies as enclaves of human happiness, sometimes as states of degradation.

As mentioned earlier, Crèvecoeur wrote little about Indians in his English-language works, while in the French texts much of the material involving them was borrowed from other sources. But the dearth of personal testimony in his publications does not mean that he entirely lacked experience of encounters with Indians. He refers to several trips into Indian territories made in the 1760s before settling on his farm—one in Vermont, probably in 1764,[46] during which by his account he was adopted by an Oneida tribe, and another beyond the Allegheny mountains as far as the Mississippi River in 1767. The latter gave rise to a handwritten report, in French, prepared much later (1785) in the framework of his mission as French consul in New York. In all probability Crèvecoeur also had contact with Indians at the end of the 1750s while he was still a French soldier in Canada, as well as on his excursions up the Susquehanna River during the revolutionary troubles of the mid-1770s.[47] With the exception of the 1785 manuscript report, however, he produced no narratives of these experiences. Moreover the subjective, experiential aspect of that text is quite limited, since it was intended for his consular superiors and meant only to provide useful, factual information (though it sometimes oversteps those bounds). The travel account per se takes up only a small portion of the report as a whole.

If one looks at the relatively few references to Indians in Crèvecoeur's English texts, one finds comments on both "civilized" Indians—those living on Nantucket, Martha's Vineyard, Cape Cod, and other coastal areas—and "wild" Indians living beyond the frontiers. For the most part, he observes, the first have adopted a mode of life similar to whites in the area (fishing, notably whaling, and agriculture) and abandoned many of their traditional ways. In general Crèvecoeur attempts to justify the treatment accorded these New England Indians, but he nonetheless brings out the ravages caused by contact with whites: epidemics, alcoholism, and the consequences of underhanded land transfers. He had visited Nantucket in 1764, immediately following a devastating epidemic, perhaps of yellow fever, which leads him to reflect, as many whites would later, on the probable demise of Native Americans through contact with Europeans.

It is interesting to note that Daniel Mandell's ethnohistorical study of Indian groups "behind the frontier" in eighteenth-century Eastern Massachusetts cites Crèvecoeur in several places and in general corroborates him, while pointing to the inevitable limitations of his perspective. According to Mandell, although "ethnocentric" in expression, the picture painted by Crèvecoeur is true as far as it goes. What remained invisible to Crèvecoeur, as it did to other white observers at the time, was how the native groups in the area succeeded, in the face of a daunting situation, in surviving and preserving a "core" of their traditions in new forms. While the old clans and tribes tended to disappear, a "new pan-indian ethnic identity" arose in the region in the later part of the eighteenth century.[48]

With regard to white dealings with Indians, Crèvecoeur is far more severe with the frontier settlers, finding that in their relations with natives beyond its limits they are regularly guilty of gross deception and thereby responsible for the massacres that periodically occur in the border areas. Yet his attitude toward the "savages" themselves is bizarrely inconsistent, reflecting the ambivalence of many whites in that period. On the one hand he is not insensitive to the "singular charm" of the Indian way of life (this is the phrase he uses several times: *Letters* 207; *Sketches* 194). Among its most attractive aspects for him are freedom from "care" and what he describes as "peace and harmony" (*Letters* 218). But the "singular charm" also constitutes a threat, since it can lead to the abandonment of civilization, indeed will necessarily have that effect if one tastes too much of the forbidden fruit. For while many instances are known, Crèvecoeur reports, of whites held prisoner by Indians choosing to remain once they were free to leave, no cases of the contrary have been reported (*Letters*, 208).[49]

Crèvecoeur offers an imaginary solution to this conundrum in terms that bring out all the complexity of his perspective, in a well-known passage from the twelfth and last letter of the 1782 edition, "Distresses of a Frontier Man." The narrator, finding himself in an unbearable situation at the beginning of the Revolutionary War, considers escaping his predicament by going to live in an Indian village where he is known and feels sure to be welcomed. But he is anxious about his family, especially the children. Without any doubt, he supposes, they will be lured by the primitive way of living and will not want to return to "civilization" after the war. He devises an extraordinary remedy for this foreseen evil, however. First, he will insist that his family engage in only agricultural activities and shun hunting. In his eyes, hunting constitutes the foundation of the primitive economy and, because of the great freedom it entails, one of the primary attractions of the Indian way of life. This measure will not be enough, though, since if it is put into practice in an Indian village it will necessarily take the form of subsistence farming, "[which] cannot have the same restrictive effects on our minds as when we tilled the earth on a more extensive scale. The surplus could be then realized into solid wealth ... [which] engrossed and fixed the attention of the labourer and cherished in his mind the hope of future riches.... [Therefore] I will keep an exact account of all that shall be gathered and give to each of them a regular credit for the amount of it, to be paid them in real property at the return of peace" (*Letters*, 217).

The narrator's plan, then, is to transfer English-style commercial farming into an Indian village. This is seen from the outset as a temporary expedient and is to be effected by the fiction of a "credit" account to be cashed in upon return to "civilization," presumably from wealth previously accumulated by the narrator, which he hopes will be restored to him. The scheme captures strikingly the deep ambivalence of Crèvecoeur, who was strongly influenced, if not totally transformed, by the mercantile ethos of the British colonies. While many passages in the English writings suggest that he retained a sharp critical distance and experienced a certain unease living in British colonial society—doubtless in part due to his aristocratic roots—and while he acknowledged the attractiveness of the Indian countermodel, he never crossed the threshold to full, sympathetic endorsement of it.

In the French writings, though there is a marked increase in expressions of pro-Indian sentiment that seems to have been stimulated by the

Parisian intellectual milieu that Crèvecoeur had joined, the ambiguous stance remains, taking on new forms. The 1784 edition of *Lettres* in French includes as an appendix an imaginary conversation between Metacomet (the Wampanoag leader in "King Philip's war" with the New England colonists in the late seventeenth century) and an old sachem, in which they discuss the possibility of resisting the white settlers.[50] Here for the first time Crèvecoeur seemingly allows Indians to speak for themselves, though he is of course himself constructing their discourse. In the dialogue the two speakers do not disagree about the harmfulness of the whites, but only about whether resistance has any chance of succeeding. This text thus adopts the point of view of Indians in conflict with colonists.[51] Although very different both in form and in content, it is in a certain way comparable to the travel account in the consular report, prepared a year later, in which Crèvecoeur describes his trip west of the Allegheny Mountains in 1767 almost entirely by water, via the Ohio, Mississippi, and Illinois rivers and Lake Erie. In that manuscript the author suggests that his trip, during which he spent more than five months in Indian territories, hunting and at least for part of it sharing the company of Indians (the only ones actually mentioned, however, are eight Ottawa guides who accompanied his party on one leg of the journey) was the happiest time of his life.[52]

In both of the larger, framing texts, however, the perspective is blurred. In each case the writer seems unaware of contradictions between different elements or aspects of them: in the *Lettres* of 1784, along with the Indian dialogue one finds a portrait of British America from which all traces of criticism have disappeared, and in the manuscript of 1785 the commercial purpose of the consular report clashes with the nostalgic memory of an idyll in "wild" Indian country.

In Crèvecoeur's last French work, *Voyage dans la haute Pensylvanie et dans l'état de New-York*, the same contradictions are displayed through a proliferation of voices and points of view. In this massive three-volume opus, which in spite of its title is quasi-encyclopedic in scope, one finds a play of mirrors in which whites converse about Indians, who discuss the invading colonizers.[53]

In one passage, in the course of a colloquy with his traveling companion, a certain Mr. Herman, the narrator denounces the brutality and coarseness of the Indians and mocks the declarations of some Europeans on the theme of the "noble savage," declarations that in his view "[are] only inspired by censoriousness and the desire to stand out; they take the side of the savage, whom they do not know, to satirize their contemporaries." Yet in another passage, a real-life person who has lived many years in close contact with Indians, Colonel George Croghan, makes the following reflection: "How can one call them barbarians after having observed the constant gentleness of their domestic habits, their serenity of mind, their disinterestedness, their continual inclination to help each other?" Moreover, in a reported debate that takes place during an Indian assembly, the two orators are portrayed as displaying dignity and intelligence, and one puts forward a compelling critique of the civilization of white men, dominated by money.[54]

Voyage juxtaposes discordant perspectives as regards the confrontation of European colonizers and Amerindians, but from among them a mediating point of view often reappears: the idea that the Indian, while maintaining his own specific qualities, must become a peaceful, sedentary farmer, similar to the ideal colonist in *Letters*. Here as elsewhere Crèvecoeur imagines a reconciliation of conflicting positions—ones that were inherent in the sociohistorical context in which he found himself but which could not find such easy resolution there.[55]

CHAPTER TWO

Philip Freneau
After the Revolution

The cessation of hostilities and independence initiated a decisive new point of departure in the socioeconomic development of the original thirteen colonies of British North America. J. Franklin Jameson, a pioneer historian in the sociological interpretation of the American Revolution, wrote in 1925 of the "transforming hand" of this event, which he saw as constituting a great leap toward "the America we know."[1] More recently historians of different schools of thought have insisted on the Revolution's role as a trigger in the unfolding of capitalist modernity by removing some of the traditional constraints that persisted in both economic structures and ideologies. In the ideological area the Revolution sanctified the principle of radical individualism in the pursuit of private interest.[2] According to one of the foremost cultural historians of early America, what occurred was in fact the coming to awareness of a social transformation already under way earlier in the eighteenth century: "[People's] mentality finally caught up with their experience."[3]

In the period following the Revolution there was a significant increase of writing about Anglo-America, stimulated by the creation of the new nation. Works continued to be produced in the genres mentioned at the beginning of chapter 1,[4] but there was especially a surge in travel accounts by visitors from abroad. The travelers came from different countries—in the first years of the Republic, for example, the Spaniard Francisco de Miranda and the Italian Francesco dal Verme visited[5]—but the most numerous were the French, who had been allies of the Americans in the conflict. Most notably the Marquis de Chastellux had traveled in the colonies during the war; he was followed by Brissot de Warville in 1788, who wrote his account as a rebuttal to that of Chastellux. Brissot, the future Girondin leader, came from a lower-middle-class family, and in his narration of a six-month stay in the United States, undertaken for commercial reasons, defended the widespread, vigorous pursuit of "economic advantage" in America against the nobleman Chastellux's criticism of mercantile practices, especially as carried out by Quakers. Brissot's polemic met with strong approval from many Americans at the time.[6] Several French accounts appeared later, though, that, like Chastellux's, projected more critical views from a Gallic perspective. One of these, from the end of the century, will be dealt with in chapter 3.

This chapter takes up a native-born American of French ancestry, Philip Freneau, who, like Crèvecoeur, was a literary author of some stature and knew the Anglo-American world in depth. The two writers stood at opposite ends of the political spectrum, but this divergence makes the similarities in their social themes—including some considerable ambiguities in their attitudes—all the more striking. Freneau began to produce a body of social commentary in the period following the Revolution, and his work provides a compelling view of and response to the intensification and maturation of modernity under its "transforming hand"—a literary representation of further developments in trends that Crèvecoeur had observed and analyzed in earlier periods.

Although Freneau began to publish exactly ten years before Crèvecoeur (his first publication dates from 1772), he belongs in fact to a later generation, since he was born in 1752, seventeen years after Crèvecoeur. Relatively little known today, Freneau is nonetheless recognized as having played a considerable role in both the general history and the literary history of the United States. As a journalist he counted politically in the first years of the nation, and as a poet he is often thought to be one of the founders of American literature. Like Crèvecoeur, he was of French extraction, but his relation to France is more distant. Descended from exiled Huguenots, both his father and he were born in America. His father was a wine merchant, and although he encountered financial difficulties near the end of his life he was able to send Philip to elite schools and to Princeton, one of the foremost universities of the British colonies.[7] There he met the future presidents Madison and Monroe and Hugh Henry Brackenridge, with whom he began his literary career. They composed together a poem of praise of the British colonies, "The Rising Glory of America," which they read at the Commencement ceremony of their class in 1771.[8]

After abortive attempts at teaching, and then theological studies, Freneau again turned to literature. Unlike Crèvecoeur, he sided with the "patriots" in the War of Independence and composed some polemical poems against the British after 1775. He spent more than two years in the Caribbean, however, far from the conflict, before joining the Revolutionary Army for a brief period in 1778. His most telling experience of the war occurred in 1780, when a ship on which he was sailing was captured by the English. His subsequent incarceration on a British prison ship in New York harbor, in extremely trying conditions, was the source of a violent hatred of the English.[9]

When the war ended Freneau divided his life between the sea (as ship's captain), the country (he owned a farm in New Jersey), and the city (New York, Charleston, and especially Philadelphia), and he divided his work life between poetry and journalism. His two careers were always closely intertwined in his writing, however. On the one hand, his poems often had political, social, and historical content, first appearing in newspapers—in many cases within articles—before being reissued in collections at a later date.[10] On the other hand, his journalistic prose usually called on his personal experience and imagination, giving it a poetic or literary dimension and taking the form of firsthand or fictive narration. In addition to the newspaper publications, a large number of his writings—both poetry and prose—initially came out as broadsides or pamphlets, aimed at a wide public. It should also be mentioned that during the 1780s and 1790s Freneau was editor, editor in chief, and owner of several newspapers, and in these capacities sought actively to advance a political agenda.[11]

Freneau was first and foremost, then, a "committed" writer.[12] As a journalist he published several hundred articles, essays, and editorials in about ten newspapers. In anti-British diatribes during the war and anti-Federalist polemics subsequently, he played a significant role in the political struggles that accompanied the birth of the United States. A personal friend of Jefferson (though politically more radical), Freneau was accused in 1791–92 of being, as a newspaper editor, Jefferson's hidden, paid mouthpiece.[13] He was a Jacobin sympathizer, on the far left wing of the Republican Party, and as such became the bête noire of the Federalist Hamilton, as well as of Washington. In referring to him as "that rascal Freneau," Washington provided the title for Freneau's principal biography.[14] More important from my point of view, though, this polemicist quickly became disillusioned as he observed the society being put in place after the coming of the independence he had so much wished for, and he came to articulate, in poetry and in prose, a body of strikingly lucid social criticism.

This aspect of Freneau's work—rather exceptional for the period—has generally been underemphasized. Most often the literary, intellectual, and general histories that mention him, as well as the monographs devoted to him by specialists, present him exclusively as either a political figure or a lyric poet. In his political conceptions, however, Freneau does not stand apart from Thomas Paine or from Benjamin Franklin Bache and William Duane, Jacobin editors of the *Aurora*, a newspaper of the radical Jeffersonian left that published a series of Freneau's essays at the end of the century.[15] Freneau's social perspective, on the other hand, is considerably more original. Literary anthologies generally include only a few of his poems—celebrations of nature and Indians or heroic narratives of the Revolutionary War—and leave out his literary prose, in which the social criticism figures prominently.[16] The image of Freneau that has come down to us, in short, has been largely amputated of its social radicalism.

In spite of their political differences, then, Freneau and Crèvecoeur have in common a clear-sighted, critical awareness of the nature of American society as it was developing in the late eighteenth century. But Freneau reached this awareness only slowly, undergoing a remarkable evolution from the time of his first youthful collaboration with Brackenridge in 1771. Only in the postwar period, and most fully in the 1790s, did he produce works of social criticism, when he could no longer ignore the gap between the ideals that he identified with the revolutionary struggle and the less noble realities that became apparent to him following it. Freneau's critical representations of the early United States, extending into the early decades of the nineteenth century (he died in 1832), thus offer a useful complement to Crèvecoeur's views of the colonial and revolutionary periods.

But Freneau also shares with Crèvecoeur a great ambivalence. Like Crèvecoeur, to the end of his life he vacillated between sharply contradictory ways of seeing. With Freneau, who is generally more sophisticated from a literary point of view, these contradictions take a quite different form, but fundamentally the two authors are similar in this respect. A final resemblance between Freneau and Crèvecoeur is their interest in and sympathy for the Indian, whom they saw as the antithesis of the society in which they were living.[17] But Freneau's representations of Indians differ from those of the author of *Letters from an American Farmer* in two divergent ways. First, Freneau had none of the firsthand knowledge of indigenous peoples that Crèvecoeur did, and the Indian who appears in his writings is a highly "literary" one.[18] Second, however, Freneau incorporates the (imagined) perspective of the Indian into his social criticism far more than Crèvecoeur does. What Crèvecoeur attempts only in a few of his French works, and with moderate success, Freneau carries out in many of his prose pieces, some of which are among his best.[19]

To frame Freneau's social critique in terms of intellectual currents I first look at the coexistence in his work of two largely opposed perspectives—the Enlightenment and romanticism—an instance of the often extreme ideological heterogeneity characteristic of the period.[20] Although I will show that only when he looks through the romantic lens does Freneau articulate a critical understanding of his society, the presence in some of his work of the mental framework of the Enlightenment, which leads him to a Whiggish view of history, is instructive as well in that it illustrates the diffuse penetration of the dominant ideology of the time. Then, to contextualize his approach to the postrevolutionary present, I will briefly discuss the evolution of his literary frescos of the colonial past. In this area Freneau is part of a general trend of reinterpretation of the prehistory of the new American nation.[21] Finally, I will turn at greater length to Freneau's vision of postrevolutionary society, notably focusing on some representations of it through the narrative point of view of the Indian.

ENLIGHTENMENT AND ROMANTICISM IN FRENEAU

Many commentators have noticed, and found disconcerting, the highly antinomic nature of Freneau's work. In my view his writing can best be understood as being ordered by two distinct, overall perspectives, or worldviews, opposed in most respects though not entirely incompatible: on the one hand romanticism, in the sense referred to in the introduction and that I have discussed elsewhere, as a protest against the conditions of life in modernity, in the name of values drawn from the premodern past, and on the other hand the so-called Enlightenment perspective.[22] Although these worldviews sometimes appear in mixture within a single text, they are more often separated.

In Freneau the Enlightenment viewpoint is always present and in its purest form in the revolutionary writings, that is, those texts that take as a subject the French or the American Revolution. Consequently, although the tension between the two kinds of vision persists throughout Freneau's career, the Enlightenment perspective is considerably more prominent during the revolutionary periods: from 1775 to the end of the War of Independence, and during the 1790s as the French Revolution unfolds across the Atlantic. During the interval between the two revolutions romanticism dominates, almost entirely eliminating the Enlightenment view. The latter is revived only when the events in France for a time restore Freneau's Enlightenment hopes. But in the 1790s the romantic perspective competes with it for pride of place in the author's works, since this period is also—and from Freneau's vantage point, more concretely—that of the *aftermath* of the American Revolution, which he experiences as disillusionment when he witnesses the growth and development of an inegalitarian society based on the power of money. In this context Freneau's romantic sensibility matures and deepens, side by side with moments of revolutionary Enlightenment fervor.

The contrast between the two visions manifests, on the most general level, sharply divergent conceptions of human history. When Freneau writes in the spirit of the Enlightenment, history takes the form of an upward movement of progress, and origins are devalued. Speaking of mankind, he declares, "At first a mere barbarian, he / Bore nothing good." Little by little humanity evolves—"Improvements gain'd, by slow advance"[23]—but only in the present does it truly come into its own, as the evils of past times give way before the thrusts of revolution. This historical movement is entirely reversed in Freneau's romantic vein of expression, in which mankind reaches plenitude in its beginnings. The earliest era of humanity is pictured as a paradise lost: "that age of innocence and ease / when men, yet social, knew no ills like these."[24] What follows is degradation, with social evils culminating in the present. Over the course of human history only isolated islands of humanity have managed to preserve traces of the golden age, notably American Indian cultures before the arrival of the white man. At present, however, these traces have all but disappeared, and Indian cultures will soon be "reckoned up among the lost things of the world."[25]

When expressing himself in the Enlightenment and romantic frames of mind Freneau conceives of evil in strongly contrasting terms. For the man of the Enlightenment it is the infernal trio of monarchy, aristocracy, and superstition that generates the worst human evils, and they are for the most part situated in the past. Some remain in the present, no doubt, but only as residues of a past not yet entirely overcome. Moreover they remain *elsewhere*—in Europe, not the United States. Evil for the romantic Freneau, on the other hand, is eminently present and fast spreading before his eyes. It is in his romantic persona that the author points to money as the source of all evils. Under its influence man comes to be motivated by egoism and greed alone, which distances him from his true being: he, "[a] stranger to himself[,] is found."[26] The rule of money, the author discovers, is particularly hostile to the intellectual and the artist. One of the characters Freneau creates to articulate his own views, "the Pilgrim," ironically advises a bookseller who can get only paltry sums for editions of Shakespeare and

Locke to "exchange his books for commodities in more demand, viz. a few casks of sugar, indigo, hides, tallow, soap, candles, etc., etc."[27]

In at least one passage Freneau seems to suggest that the principle of the modern world that is anathema to him is not only defined by the predominance of market relations but resides also in the perpetual expansion of capital. In the poem "The Hermit of Saba," three men shipwrecked on an island suspect—incorrectly—that a poor hermit living there is hiding a treasure. These men, who incarnate the logic of the system that the poem rejects, murder the hermit and justify their act in the following terms:

> Of useful wealth, he has not heart to use:—
> He builds no ships, employs no mariners;
> But like a miser, hides the ill-gotten store,
> And had he died before we wandered hither
> His gold had perished.[28]

According to these ideologically minded murderer-thieves, wealth must be kept in circulation to generate more wealth.

Freneau's contradictions are such, though, that the values he espouses when he shifts into the Enlightenment register can in some instances undermine his romantic critique of modernity. Thus, while most often he celebrates reason in a universalist, philosophical sense, in some passages he also glorifies utilitarian reason in the service of economic development. In one poem "the industrious mill" takes on positive value,[29] and the commercial enterprise condemned elsewhere is encouraged in certain texts on revolutionary themes. Before the victory of the patriots, Freneau anticipates with pleasure in one piece of verse an America liberated from the English, "When commerce shall extend her short'ned wing"; and long after it has come he jubilates in another that "Without a king, we trace the unbounded sea, / And traffic round the globe, through each degree."[30]

The two visions also refer to ideal modes of living in a certain relation to Nature. While they resemble each other to the extent that both value a way of living outside cities, the character of that kind of life is significantly different in each case. On the side of the Enlightenment we find the physiocratic ideal, shared by other republicans of the period (Jefferson and

Madison, in particular), which makes agriculture the foundation of the economy and glorifies the life of the farmer. The relation to Nature is active and in some places becomes aggressive, adopting the frontier mythology in which by dint of grueling labor the backwoodsman conquers the wilderness. Within this framework the rural life is not opposed to commerce but calls for it as a complement, as in one passage where the author speaks of agriculture "and its attendant, commerce."[31] In this state of mind the city and urban life sometimes also lose all their bad connotations, and the poet can come to dream of the happy future time "When one vast cultivated region teems, / From ocean's edge to Mississippi's streams."[32]

On the side of romanticism, on the contrary, the relation to Nature is passive; what Nature in its munificence provides is accepted with gratitude. Often echoing Horace, Freneau reminds the reader that mankind originally lived in this way and predicts that we will again in time to come. At present only the Indian preserves this mode of life. Rather than cultivating fields he subsists in wild forest lands.[33] There, rather than commerce, barter holds sway, which in one passage Freneau seems to wish to see extended to all Americans:

> At home a surer harvest springs
> From mutual interchange of things,
> Domestic duties to fulfill.[34]

Living thus man is united to man, who becomes a brother, and to the universe, which becomes a home.[35]

Similar to many European and American intellectuals at the end of the eighteenth century, Freneau held these two worldviews in some sort of equilibrium throughout his life. As a passionate partisan of the French and American revolutions, he was confronted with a serious dilemma. According to the logic of the Enlightenment, American postrevolutionary society should have been the culminating point of human history, the beginning of a millenarian process that would be extended and reinforced by the revolution in France. Yet this was a proposition that he saw contradicted in reality. Thus in his writings in the wake of the American Revolution

Freneau was impelled to express his bitterness and bring out the traits of the developing society that he reproved. When he did so it was in the romantic register. But as a political activist he did not give up hope. Up to the end of the century, while the French Revolution was under way and, under the administrations of Washington and Adams, the Republican Party had not yet triumphed in the United States, Freneau could continue to think that the problematic aspects of postrevolutionary society would finally be given a political solution. In some of his writing in that period he persevered in expressions of faith in the rise of humanity through "progress," and to the extent that this seemed inseparable from commerce and industry, he sometimes sang their praises.

At the beginning of the nineteenth century the situation changed. Between France and America the political configurations reversed. While the French Revolution gave way to the autocrat Napoleon, republicanism was bolstered in America with the election of Jefferson in 1801. Though nothing more was to be expected of France, the Jeffersonian victory should have in principle eventually corrected the early faults of the new nation, as Freneau saw them. This of course did not happen, since the faults were related to long-term socioeconomic developments that in fact the American Revolution stimulated rather than canceled. Thus Freneau found himself, perhaps more than ever before, in conflict with himself in the last decades of his life. In this period he wrote less, drawing back partially from both politics and literature. He continued to produce some critical texts of romantic inspiration but never entirely abandoned a Whiggish form of Enlightenment discourse as well, a kind of discourse that was destined more and more—though Freneau never seems cognizant of the problem—to turn into an apology for modern forms of domination.

INTERPRETATIONS OF THE COLONIAL PAST

In Freneau's poetry we find a number of works that deal with American history. While some concentrate on a particular period,[36] several attempt to present an overview. The first of the latter is "The Rising Glory of America," already mentioned, written by Freneau and Hugh Henry Brackenridge together. It was first published as a whole in pamphlet form in 1772, and then much later, in 1786, the parts written by Freneau were republished in modified form in a collection. Another poem of the same type, "The American Village," by Freneau alone, also appeared in 1772, and those early pieces were followed by "Sketches of American History," published in two parts in 1778 and 1784. A final historical survey, entitled "The Rising Empire," appeared in 1790. These works are interesting in that they reveal Freneau's changing perspectives on the history of the Americas, especially North America, at different moments over the course of two decades. In them a clear evolution is apparent, in the direction of a more disabused, critical understanding of the past of the British colonies. This new perception of the past goes hand in hand with the maturation of Freneau's apprehension of postrevolutionary society and serves as a framework for his social criticism of the world in which he is living. I will examine briefly how Freneau's appraisal of the nation's past is transformed through these historical frescos.[37]

"The Rising Glory of America" has the particularity of existing in two distinct versions, separated by the American Revolution—the original of 1772 and the rewritten excerpts in the 1786 collection. The latter retains only the passages written by Freneau, who revised and expanded them, which has the effect of attenuating the influence of Brackenridge's attitudes, in many ways different from Freneau's.[38] In particular Brackenridge unambiguously condemns the Indians as cruel and bestial and lauds the commercial prowess of Anglo-Americans. Although Freneau's stance on these issues does vacillate, as we have seen, his positions are never as extreme as Brackenridge's and they diverge progressively more and more from his. Though Freneau's ideas may have been relatively close to those of his friend while they were at the university, once Freneau began an independent literary career his thinking took a very different turn.

This divergence can be illustrated by comparing the two different versions of a passage of "The Rising Glory" involving Indians. The poem overall, in both its versions, contrasts the treatment accorded historically to Indians in North and in South America. The methods used by the Spaniards in the South are denounced as criminal.[39] In the first version of the passage in question, which concerns North American Indians, the author emphasizes their cruelty so as to highlight the clemency shown by the North American colonists:

> fierce Indian tribes
> With deadly malice arm'd and black design,
> Oft murder'd half the hapless colonies.[40]

The second version, however, as revised many years later by Freneau, subtly attenuates the responsibility of the Indians:

> fierce Indian tribes
> With vengeful malice arm'd, and black design,
> Oft murdered, or dispersed, these colonies. (1:63)

"Vengeful malice" implies that the Indians had in fact been provoked, and the added phrase acknowledges that the colonists were not always massacred but sometimes only "dispersed."

For the most part, though, the two versions of "The Rising Glory" are convergent and paint a highly idealized picture—one reflecting the two university students' early enthusiasms—of the Pilgrim fathers fleeing religious persecution, of the heroic pioneers who settled the back country, and of the millennium of peace and prosperity to come.

"The American Village," however, published the same year as "The Rising Glory" but without Brackenridge as coauthor, projects a startlingly split vision of this history, with no attempt at consistency. The poem begins in the same vein as "The Rising Glory," celebrating the rise of America to supremacy over the other nations of the world, as it takes over that role from England, now in decline (3:381). The Enlightenment perspective prevails: a dark wilderness is being pushed back to make of America a luminously and happily productive land.

Near the middle of the poem, however, the tone as well as the message abruptly change. When the poet looks into the future, the definitive triumph of America is no longer a prophetic certainty but only a possibility. Then the work makes a complete about-face, and the poet relocates true human fulfillment on American soil in the primitive, pre-Columbian past. The "discovery" of America by Europeans brings about a Fall:

> Renowned SACHEMS once their empires rais'd
> On wholesome laws; and sacrifices blaz'd.
> The gen'rous soul inspir'd the honest breast,
> And to be free, was doubly to be blest:
> 'Till the east winds did here COLUMBUS blow, ...
> And rav'nous nations with industrious toil,
> Conspir'd to rob them of their native soil. (3:387)

In this passage Freneau no longer justifies the North American treatment of Indians, for here its colonizers devastate indigenous peoples not through massacre, as in the South, but by illegitimately taking their land. Thus in this poem written soon after the collaboration with Brackenridge, Freneau already distances himself from his earlier position.

It was only after a considerable lapse of time that Freneau published his next historical piece, and by then his point of view had further evolved. Unlike "The American Village," "Sketches of American History" (1778, 1784) is not split into two contradictory halves but develops a single narrative thread that is harshly critical, albeit in a somewhat bantering style, of the role of whites in North America. The poem opens with a view of pre-Columbian Indians, defining their existence by contrast with that of whites; they did not suffer then from the civilizational evils introduced by the Europeans' merchant, minister, lawyer, and doctor. The arrival of Columbus—though the explorer himself is not condemned—is placed under the sign of cupidity. But it is the portrayal of the Pilgrim fathers and other, later North American colonists that undergoes the most striking evolution. Now the desire to escape religious or political persecution is only one motive among other, less honorable ones:

> They were, without doubt, a delightful collection;
> —Some came to be rid of a Stuart's direction,
> Some sailed with a view to dominion and riches,
> Some to pray without book, and a few to hang witches.
> Some, came on the Indians to shed a new light,
> Convinced long before that their own must be right. (2:270)

What follows is a long diatribe against puritanism in the colonial period, with its denial of the body, of pleasure, and of scientific truth.

As in the earlier historical poems, Freneau evokes the "discoveries" that followed Columbus's—those of Cabot, Drake, Hudson, and so on—but this time they are demystified. The author's irony is aimed at the "right" of property in American lands claimed by Europeans on the basis of having been the first to see them,[41] the sale of these lands, and the resolution of territorial conflicts by force. Thus the author comments on the colonial struggles between the Dutch and the British at the end of the poem:

> Force ended the contest—the right was a sham,
> And the Dutch were sent packing to hot Surinam....
> [But] Fate saw—though no wizzard could tell them as much—
> That the crown, in due time, was to fare like the Dutch. (2:276)

Here we are at a far remove from the heroic, eminently moral, upward movement of American colonization figured in "The Rising Glory."

In the last of the historical survey poems, "The Rising Empire" (1790), the critical tendency is even more accentuated and is carried into the present. The title itself is indicative of a significant shift when set against that of the first of the series. America is still rising, but now only to a position of power among nations ("empire") rather than of moral superiority ("glory," with its religious tonality). This poem deals far more with the present than did the earlier ones. After an introduction entitled "On American Antiquity" the following sections draw portraits, moral and physical, of particular states: Rhode Island, Connecticut, Massachusetts, Pennsylvania, Maryland, and Virginia. But their present characteristics are seen as the result of past developments, and the poet delineates some long-term historical processes that have been at work. Freneau recognizes some positive qualities in the states he describes, but the charges he levels against them in most cases weigh heavier in the balance: exploitation of man by man, religious hypocrisy, chicaneries in the North, slavery and decadence in the South, and throughout the thirst for money and luxury. This last attempt to give a poetic overview of the history of British America opens into a critical representation of what it has become in the postrevolutionary present.

AFTER THE REVOLUTION

In the 1780s, mainly the second half, when the revolutionary period was over, Freneau began to write social satire, and the trend was reinforced in the 1790s. During this period we find, as with Crèvecoeur, some rather idealized representations of the immigrant, the pioneer, and the farmer. One ode, to a "Crispin O'Connor, Esq. a backwoods Planter," appreciatively tells the story of O'Connor's immigration from Ireland forty years earlier, his settling on a piece of land in the West, swampy at first, but which by hard work he succeeds in making into a prosperous farm.[42] Another poem, entitled "The Bergen Planter" in one version, "The Pennsylvania Planter" in another, recalls some of Crèvecoeur's more idyllic evocations of the "American farmer."[43] But in many texts there is a depiction of a darker reality and critical reflection on it. Different elements of this reality, which is sometimes designated as "modern,"[44] appear in different texts. Overall they give a perception of the society that has both breadth and depth. In addition, in conjunction with its historical material, "The Rising Empire" provides a broad picture of the fledgling United States in its geographical diversity, though incomplete nonetheless since the author never finished the comprehensive series of sketches of states he intended to make.[45]

The penetration of modernity throughout this society—in North and South, in city and countryside—is revealed variously in the different texts. In cities, which were growing rapidly and taking on greater importance at the time, commercial activities and mentalities reign. Already in Freneau's first series of essays, "The Pilgrim" (1782), the narrator notices the omnipresence in towns of the storekeeper, that "idle scheming citizen, who sits perpetually behind his counter, like a spider in the web, watching his commodities."[46] But in a later prose piece we find a more fully developed portrait of "the man in business," presented in the manner of the "characters" of the French satirist La Bruyère:

> A man in business is at once known by his air and gait; and in my numerous and extensive walks through the streets of this large and populous city, I do not know that I was ever deceived in my judgment on the matter....
> A man in business always walks fast, not caring whose heels or toes

he treads upon; his shoes are constantly kept well blacked, his buckles cleaned.... His eye has an insolent glance, and is commonly fixed upon something at a distance before him, now and then upon the ground, but never upwards.... If your habit and person answers to his ideas of a man *in* business, he smiles upon you ..., if not, he bids you an everlasting adieu.... He rarely looks into the faces of those he meets ... and, in fine, is little better than a perambulating machine, till he comes to the scene of action, his counting house, or his law shop.[47]

This sketch is followed by one of "the man *out* of business," who by contrast shows sensitivity to others, humility—in short, "humanity."[48]

In the city are also to be found banks and the world of finance, and in a mock glossary entitled "Modern Explanation of a Few Terms, Commonly Misunderstood," Freneau defines the science of banking as the "real art of hocus pocus: or the sorceries of Simon Magus revived." In the same glossary "genius" is defined as "money-catching," and a "great genius" as "a great money-catcher."[49] But beside the rich in cities live the poor, and Freneau describes their miserable living conditions in a poem about a prison in a back street of Philadelphia, "Pewter Platter Alley."[50]

In several places the author laments more generally the state of unhealthiness, artificiality, and ugliness that he finds in the bigger cities of the East Coast, as in all modern metropolises. In one essay, "On Trees in Cities" (1791), he evokes "the tiresome uniform regularity" of streets, as well as the "smoke, foul air, and other squalid appendages of a large town," and expresses indignation at an attempt by the Corporation of Philadelphia some ten years earlier—successfully opposed by the citizens—to remove the only remaining traces of nature by cutting down all of the city's trees.[51] The following year Freneau returned to the same theme in a poem occasioned by a similar initiative made the year before by the Corporation of New York, and concludes:

> Men are not now what once they were,
> To hoard up gold is all their care:
> The busy tribe old Plutus calls
> To pebbled streets and painted walls;
> Trees now to grow, is held a crime.[52]

The mercantile turn of mind is, however, to be found in the country as well. Though village merchants are not always as clever and crafty as their urban counterparts—this is the theme of a humorous poem that appeared in 1792[53]—farmers are seen to be often in fact agricultural entrepreneurs. Those of Rhode Island, for example, are characterized thus in "The Rising Empire": "On grassy farms, their souls enslav'd to gain, / Reside the masters of the rural reign."[54] Moreover in the countryside early manifestations of industrialization are appearing in the guise of small factories. In the same Rhode Island sketch Freneau bitterly denounces the human suffering resulting from one such enterprise:

> One, bold in wrong, his paper fabric rears
> And steels his bosom to the orphan's tears
> To those he ruin'd grants no late relief!
> But leaves the wretched to subsist on grief![55]

Rural industrial production, like that of commercial farming and fishing (Freneau several times mentions the avid profit seeking of the whalers), is largely sent out to the international market, and the frenetic maritime trade that results is often condemned by the poet, notably in his sketch of Massachusetts in "The Rising Empire."[56]

The portrayals of several other northern states in the same poem reveal, each in specific terms, the diffusion of the commercial spirit in daily life. Here is Freneau's characterization of Connecticut, for instance, the proverbial home of the "yankee":

> All bow to lucre, all are bent on gain,
> In contact close their neat abodes are thrown,
> Its house, each acre; every mile, its town; ...
> Where fast-day sermons tell the hungry guest
> That a cameleon's dinner is the best ...
> Fond of discourse, with deep designing views
> They [the inhabitants of the state] pump the unwary traveller of his news
> Fond of that news, but fonder to be paid,
> Each house a tavern, claims a tavern's trade,

> While he that comes as surely hears them praise
> The hospitality of modern days.⁵⁷

As for the Dutch of Long Island (among whom Freneau lived for a time):

> All tends to something that must pelf produce,
> All for some end, and every thing its use ...
> The strong-ribbed lass no idle passions move,
> No frail ideas of romantic love;
> He to her heart the readiest path can find
> Who comes with gold ...
> She heeds not valour, learning, wit, or birth,
> Minds not the swain—but asks him what he's worth.⁵⁸

Even in Pennsylvania, the state that is treated most positively in "The Rising Empire," the author finds in the Quakers (whom he favors for the most part) an inclination toward "prudent foresight" in their own interest—a habit they developed long ago as "proof to the projects of the keenest knave." Consequently they "praise *other* worlds but keep their hold on *this*," seemingly ruled by the principle "Good will to all, themselves their first great care."⁵⁹ As for the southern states (Maryland and Virginia), while rural decay and a particularly cruel regime of slavery are the focus of opprobrium, the text points to signs of modernity as well. Baltimore has recently become the main port city of Maryland, surpassing Annapolis in its commercial dynamism. And in Virginia the Scots have set about creating a virtual trading monopoly:

> To these far climes the scheming Scotchman flies, ...
> Marks well the native—views his weaker side,
> And heaps up wealth from luxury and pride,
> Exports the produce of a thousand plains,
> Nor fears a rival, to divide his gains.⁶⁰

Elsewhere in Freneau's poetry one finds sketches of certain prevalent social types: the lawyer who puts his fees above all else ("A Modern Tale," 1797), the speculator who makes a fortune from one day to the next but loses all when the bubble bursts ("The Speculator," 1792), and finally the "projector," that is, the speculator on western land taken from the natives ("The Projectors," 1782).[61] This kind of speculation is the object of Freneau's most virulent scorn. In one passage he cries out directly to the "projectors":

> Base grasping souls, your pride repress;
> Beyond your wants must you possess?
> If ten poor acres will supply
> A rustic and his family,
> Why, grumblers, would you have ten score,
> Ten thousand and ten thousand more?[62]

Here the poet is pointedly incensed by the irrationality of the process of capital accumulation.

Beyond these types that play dominant roles in postindependence society, Freneau points in several texts to a diffuse frame of mind and an atmosphere that has become widespread: the reign of "rigid Reason" and of a "common sense" that thinks only in terms of material or commercial utility, the prosaic ennui of an era devoted to the pursuit of money—an "iron age" that is radically alien to the intellectual and the artist.[63] It is an era, finally, in which even activities that are in principle noble—science and politics, in particular—often come to be mere servants to the market economy.[64]

THE INDIAN AS SOCIAL CRITIC

In the same period Freneau published a series of texts that gave a new slant to his social criticism, adopting the point of view of the Indian to attack white society. The author had earlier written several poems that began to explore that approach. "The Prophecy of King Tammany," which appeared in the *Freeman's Journal* in 1782, depicts the famous Delaware Indian chief, known for his willing collaboration with Penn's colonists, watching in despair while ancestral lands are taken from his people and they are driven west; before killing himself, he predicts misfortune for whites. The ravages of the struggle with the "tyrant" (England) will be succeeded by the coming of an "odious train" of "little souls" who have not had the courage to take part in the struggle themselves.[65] In 1787 "The Indian Student" appeared, in which a gifted young Indian, sent to Harvard University by his family, eventually flees white society to return to the forest.[66] This story, which echoes several real occurrences that had appeared in the press, contains an implied criticism of the Anglo-American society the Indian fled, but its evils are only hinted at in passing.

A number of prose texts go considerably further. These constitute a kind of American equivalent of Montesquieu's *Lettres persanes* (Persian Letters): "The Voyage of Timberoo-Tabo-Eede, an Otaheite Indian" (1788); "Reflections on my journey from the Tallassee towns to the settlements on the river Hudson, By Opay Mico, one of the Indian Kings" (1790); and especially—probably Freneau's most successful attempt in the genre—a set of essays published in serial form in the *Jersey Chronicle* in 1795: "Tomo Cheeki, the Creek Indian in Philadelphia." This group of Indian texts, in which the "savage" visits and brings judgment on white civilization, represents a fictional reversal of the travel account in Indian territory that I examine in part 2.

The first, "The Voyage of Timberoo-Tabo-Eede," differs from the others in that its narrator is not an Amerindian but the inhabitant of a fictive Tahiti-like island,[67] and the satire comes in part from the fact that this imaginary people themselves wish to conquer and colonize. In addition to the barb thus directed against imperialism, slavery is attacked, along with the idolatry of "small circular plates of yellow metal," which the denizens of the country visited by Timberoo-Tabo-Eede seem to practice. The second text turns to the North American clash of cultures. Here an Indian from the South visits a city on the shores of the Hudson—presumably New York—sent with a delegation to negotiate a treaty. The text develops a lamentation on the fate of dispossessed Indians and a contrast between two ways of life—that of forest-dwelling Indians who "disturbed not the face of nature" and that of whites "satisfied with [their] stye amidst the heat, and dust, and the outcries of a large city."[68]

Freneau's largely literary conception of Indians is apparent in this second example, drawing as it does on certain current stereotypes. The Creek Indians of the Tallassee area, of whom Opay Mico is an imagined chief, would have engaged partly in agriculture and, like Indians in many other places, would have employed forms of land management, albeit nondestructive ones. The overall contrast between ways of life is not false per se but lacks grounding in concrete knowledge of native practices.

The implied protest against the specifically urban form of white civilization—which we have seen expressed elsewhere in Freneau's work—is further elaborated on in the "Tomo Cheeki" series. The eponymous protagonist is also a chief, named after a historical Creek leader. In the fictional framework of the series, he has come to a big city, Philadelphia, to engage in a diplomatic mission. What first strikes Tomo Cheeki on arrival in Philadelphia are "the anxious discontented countenances of all I meet; proving alas! too clearly that all are the slaves of care." This observation sets off a meditation on the vanity of the whites' values: "With all this sublimity of science are they not slaves to the earth?—do they not, notwithstanding their astonishing discoveries in the heavens, cast an eye of cruel anxiety upon the dust? Is not the hoarding up of *money* the object they have most at heart—that source of innumerable evils, the source of treachery, devastations, and murder?"[69]

Later in his stay in Philadelphia, Tomo Cheeki has a dream. He is in a "land of devils," a "hell" in which the inhabitants wear long beards because no one "has confidence enough in another to trust him a single moment with a razor at his throat." As he awakens he cries out, with heavy irony, "How happy am I to reside in a town, and among a species of beings who have barbers in every street!" The Indian chief later remarks that this "species of beings" is in fact quite miserable: "Perpetual jealousies of all around them, and a suspicious eye cast upon futurity, damp all their pleasures." The evils besetting them seem to come from their possessions, while, by contrast, the narrator insists, "In the forests, we acknowledge no distinction of property."[70]

Other problems involve the conditions under which city dwellers work and their relations of domination. Whites often pity us, Tomo Cheeki remarks, because of the primitive way of life allotted to us. But we pity *them*, imprisoned as they are "[in] dark cages and narrow boxes: in these deep alleys and narrow pathways reigns a perpetual gloom, the source of pining discontent and peevish melancholy. There sits the artist [the artisan, or worker] on his bench, pale as the grass beneath the thick spreading oak; actuated, like a machine, by the will of another." The sight of an elegant coach inspires in Tomo Cheeki the reflection that "the driver is driven," since he is propelled by the "idol" who is inside. The visiting Indian is also outraged at the kind of existence led by stable boys—representing to his way of thinking a profoundly degraded form of humanity—and rhetorically asks, "Why do the big-chiefs here hold long talks on the dignity of man, when such a wretch of their own species and colour is encouraged to live among them?"[71]

Thus in these texts that imagine Indian voices Freneau reformulates the themes of his social criticism from a different angle, combining them with an expression of sympathy for the premodern mode of life of the natives of the continent. In doing so he might have served as an example for the narrator of Crèvecoeur's *Voyage dans la haute Pensylvanie* when he ridicules those who are "only inspired by censoriousness and the desire to stand out; they take the side of the savage, whom they do not know, to satirize their contemporaries."[72] However, while it is true that Freneau did not know Indians firsthand, and that his Indian creations are largely literary constructs, there is—as we will see in part 2—much common ground between his thematics and that of many travelers who came into direct, sometimes lengthy contact with Amerindians.

As I suggested earlier, in the period following Jefferson's election in 1801, during the Republican administrations of Jefferson himself, and then of Madison and Monroe, Freneau was faced with the paradoxical situation that his political party had come to power while the kind of social change he wished for had not followed. Though in some of his later writings he continued nevertheless to cling to a Whiggish posture, in others he showed that he remained sharply aware of the persistence of the same social ills he had often chastised before. Some poems composed after the War of 1812, at the end of Freneau's life, bear witness to his continued critical acumen.

One in particular is worth mentioning in conclusion—a short satirical play in verse entitled "Elijah, the New England Emigrant," published in a newspaper in 1821. In this sketch of contemporary life it appears that colonization of western lands continues, now along the banks of the Alabama River and Lake Erie, as dishonestly as ever in relation to the Indians. Elijah Salem is planning to settle on Indian land that he has not bought, as his father-in-law Hezekiah, who displays great contempt for Indians, had earlier done.[73] However, Hezekiah has returned to New England, where he is a well-to-do merchant and deacon of his church. He has prospered by engaging in questionable business dealings, living, as his son-in-law avers, by "hook and crook" and "selling trash by inch of candle." Indeed it emerges from a conversation between members of the Salem family that to prosper in the land of the Yankee one "must cheat and juggle, / And life is one continual struggle." More than that, the motive of self-interest has so far permeated the lives of New Englanders that one can be "even by friends and cousins squeezed."[74] This late sketch by Freneau thus reveals a post-Jeffersonian social reality that in no way differs from that of the earlier, postrevolutionary period.

CHAPTER THREE

Moreau de Saint-Méry
Fin de Siècle

A third record of personal discovery of American modernity—the most external view of the three—is the little-known account of travel and sojourn in the early United States by Moreau de Saint-Méry, a French Creole from Martinique and Saint-Domingue who spent part of his adult life in the metropole. There had already been numerous accounts of the British colonies by French visitors during the War of Independence, but the volume of French travelers further increased in the late 1780s and early 1790s, first due to interest in the new national "experiment," then as a result of developments in France.[1] With the radicalization of the French Revolution and the advent of the Terror, one destination of émigrés was the United States. Some of these émigrés wrote accounts of their stay, including, most famously, Chateaubriand. The young Louis-Philippe, future king of France, also went to the United States and produced a travel account, as did the Duke de La Rochefoucauld-Liancourt, a prominent "enlightened" nobleman who published a far more substantial, eight-volume account in 1799.[2] But one such émigré who is now not well-known in that context, though at the time he played a crucial role in the émigré community in Philadelphia, is the good friend of La Rochefoucauld-Liancourt, Moreau de Saint-Méry.

Saint-Méry was born in Martinique in 1750, into a family of the colonial magistracy. He was sent to Paris at nineteen to study law, where he acquired at the same time a broad Enlightenment culture. Then he returned to the French West Indies, but this time to Saint-Domingue, where he practiced law, served on the upper council of the colony, and began a collection of documents on West Indian history and legal institutions. That collection was, in the words of one commentator, "a classic Enlightenment project, based on the idea that knowledge would promote better governance."[3] The vast documentation Saint-Méry accumulated became the basis for the later publications for which he is well-known to scholars of the Caribbean, some of them published while he resided in Philadelphia.[4] Because of his extensive knowledge of French West Indian society and institutions, he was invited in the early 1780s to return to Paris and join the central, colonial administration. A strong proponent of the French Revolution when it broke out, he quickly rose to a position of influence, serving as a member of the Assemblée constituante and being appointed president of the provisional government of Paris for a time after the taking of the Bastille. However, as a moderate (and, it should be noted, a strong advocate of the maintenance of slavery in the colonies),[5] he soon was attacked by the Jacobins and was targeted for arrest by Robespierre just before his flight to America in November 1793.

Saint-Méry's account of his voyage to the United States opens with his dramatic escape from Le Havre as agents of the Terror were on their way from Paris to arrest him. (A day's delay, he tells the reader, and he would surely have been guillotined.) After a grueling four-month Atlantic crossing, he and his family finally landed in Norfolk, Virginia. Their original intention was to proceed to Saint-Domingue once they had reached the United States, but it soon became clear that this would be impossible, since a revolutionary upheaval was under way in the French colony as well. So, after spending several months in Norfolk, they proceeded northward up the east coast by ship to Philadelphia, with a short stopover in Baltimore, then continued to New York by land. There followed a period of shuttling back and forth between New York and Philadelphia. The family finally stopped in Philadelphia, where they settled for the remainder of their stay in the country. They returned to France as soon as it became safe to do so, in August 1798. All in all Saint-Méry spent some four and a half years in the early United States, and during the bulk of that time—almost four years—he was in residence in Philadelphia. Because of the length of his sojourn, he can be considered, like Crèvecoeur and Freneau, an "insider" in Anglo-America. It will be apparent, though, that Saint-Méry remained extremely marginal and at odds with that society throughout his stay, and he is doubtless the most fully an outsider of the three.

The narrative of his American journey was never published during his lifetime. The manuscript was consigned to the shelves of the Archives coloniales in Paris and was discovered only in the early twentieth century by a professor of history at Yale, who published the first edition—in the original French—with Yale University Press in 1913.[6] Ironically, then, although originally published in French it has probably reached a largely Anglo-American audience. The first audience was limited and academic, but its readership extended considerably when Kenneth Roberts, the American historical novelist, came upon the edition in French, found it revealing and perceptive, and prepared an English translation with his wife, published in 1947.[7]

Saint-Méry is indeed an astute observer and commentator, and his sociocultural background is complex and multiple, resulting in an unusual viewpoint. Both metropolitan French and Creole in culture, he was also a cross between the aristocrat and the *grand bourgeois* in that he stemmed from the colonial *noblesse de robe*. A committed republican, he also became an émigré from the Revolution. But his writing exhibits a sensibility that was particularly swayed by the French, "enlightened" aristocratic milieu. He has much in common, in fact, with his friend La Rochefoucauld-Liancourt, and there are signs in Saint-Méry's work of an interaction between the travel accounts of the two men. Each seems to have drawn on ideas and experiences of the other.

The work takes the form of a dated diary alternating with general, descriptive sections dealing with the main cities Saint-Méry stayed in—most important and longest, Philadelphia. As with many travel accounts, although it was surely based on notes and a journal written on the spot, there are many indications of later reworking. The original material was evidently worked up at a later time, when Saint-Méry was living in France, with a view to publication. The text is written in French and there is no doubt that it is intended for a French, perhaps more largely European public, since it sometimes anticipates French or European reactions to the American phenomena being presented. The use of *we* clearly designates inhabitants of the Old World. (Remarkably Saint-Méry never seems to be addressing Creoles.) Throughout the text the author makes extended commentaries on American mores and character, generalizing from his overall experience but also using illustrative examples. He continually contrasts American traits, as he discovers them, with those of the French. What he discovers about Americans is not generally to his liking, in spite of a favorable prejudice he held at the outset due to his admiration for the goals of the American Revolution.

THE TRANSATLANTIC CROSSING AS PREMONITION

Saint-Méry's introduction to the American character begins on the trip over. What he observes once he reaches American shores only seems to corroborate and provide a broader framework for his shipboard experience, which he presents as a kind of premonitory epitome. The transatlantic crossing, which is recounted at considerable length, took an exceptionally long time to complete, even by the standards of the period. After an initial few weeks of normal weather, the ship was dogged by almost continual heavy storms, in which it was severely battered. These conditions created extreme discomfort for those on board, and at some moments real danger. But it was clearly not the length of the trip or its tribulations that caused the author to dwell on it in such detail. Relatively little space, in fact, is devoted to descriptions of storms or of shipboard life per se. The real focus of the opening section is on the sociocultural traits revealed. Heavy weather and the minutiae of life on board are evoked mostly insofar as they relate to cultural discovery and interaction.

The very first paragraph already hints at this focus. The author is informed by the captain that they will not be leaving that day because "it was Saturday, a day on which Americans did not like to start a voyage."[8]

The ship does finally leave that day, but by opening this way, the text has brought attention to the American identity of the ship and its crew and to the peculiarities of their ways. Further on we learn more details about the crew. They are ten, including a cabin boy and a cook, all Americans. The passengers, on the other hand, are all French or French Creole, sixteen in all. Most are members of Saint-Méry's extended family, including his wife, sister, brother-in-law, and children and their servants. Others are friends of the family. One man is a retired sea captain from Brittany whom they meet on board. The crew and passengers, then, are two sharply distinguished cultural groupings, and the main theme of the opening section, mirroring that of the later sections involving the American sojourn, is discovery of the American ethos in contrast with the French. In formal terms also the passage on the crossing mirrors the rest, since it is mostly in dated diary format, but contains a generalizing part as well that deals with regular aspects of life on the ship.

Very early on the author informs us that he was the only passenger to speak English (3). Consequently he is the one who must convey questions and requests from his group to the captain and negotiate courses of action with him, but also gather information from and interact with crew members. Thus he becomes the go-between for the French passengers, the pivot between the two microcommunities. As an English speaker he is a privileged observer of the American group and of the confrontation between the two cultural entities on board.

Also near the beginning the author identifies a principal characteristic of American seamen (4), which several pages further on he will broaden to be "the most conspicuous trait in the American character" as a whole (7). This he calls "lack of foresight" or "carelessness" in the English translation, *imprévoyance* or *insouciance* in the original French.[9] From then on Saint-Méry copiously instances this trait as it appears during the crossing and highlights harmful effects of different kinds, running from unpleasantness and discomfort to considerable suffering and sometimes serious danger. But it is only near the end of the section that this somewhat puzzling cultural trait is more fully contextualized in social terms.

As Saint-Méry and his compatriots soon discover, little has been provided for in the way of basic amenities such as the French understand them. The food produced by the American cook is primitive, and wine and spirits are not included in the price of passage. The passengers accordingly bring their own food and beverages, but careless treatment of them by the crew quickly decimates them. Chickens are left on deck to die, and poorly stacked bottles break and their contents leak away. To make matters worse, sanitary facilities are of a kind that totally ignore finer sensibilities. The toilet consists of a malodorous open hole in a cabin used also as living space. These instances of "carelessness" only involve the amenities of life, but the author also enumerates many that create serious hazards, in some cases mortal dangers. Lamps are used in a way that creates risk of fire. The ship's sails and rigging are in poor condition, while spares and repair materials are either inadequate or nonexistent. In one case the ship comes close to losing its masts because proper repairs have not been made on some of the gear. Moreover navigation is often done by what Saint-Méry considers to be guesswork rather than by use of the best nautical instruments. Finally, the author is at pains to show that these practices are not limited to his ship; he mentions several similar examples he was told of concerning other vessels. He has heard, for instance, that U.S. coasting boats without compasses are often blown out to sea.

Throughout most of the narrative of the crossing, the cases of lack of foresight or carelessness are detailed with little explanation. In one early passage reference is made to the desire to effect "savings," but without further elaboration (4). It is only near the end of the journey, when the crowning instance occurs—the most extreme and most revealing—that this American trait is framed in social terms. For as the *Sophie* approaches the U.S. coastline, food of any kind, good or bad, has almost run out because of accidents and the extreme length of the voyage. The passengers are exhausted and severely weakened by lack of food and by the prolonged buffeting of the ship by storms. Several are at risk of death, and one who is seriously ill is in immediate danger. The bad weather also shows no signs of abating. Yet in these dire circumstances the captain insists on pushing on in an attempt to land in New York, the port they were bound for, even though they have been blown much farther south. Saint-Méry, as spokesman for the passengers, begs the captain to put into the first port they can reach. But the captain is adamant: "He spoke a great deal about his shipowner's interests; also of the risks that an interrupted trip might cause to his own fortunes in a country where, according to him, the owners of vessels believe that non-success is a proof of incapacity (which they condemn) or of bad luck (which they avoid). He impressed upon me how important it was that any request to break the trip should come from the crew, since in that case their wages would not be paid during the stop, whereas the contrary would result if he stopped of his own accord" (22). Only almost two weeks later, because the continued heavy weather endangers the vessel itself, does the captain finally agree to come into Norfolk, Virginia.

The author seems to suggest, then, that the underlying and unifying motivational factor for the American trait exemplified earlier is the commercial mentality. At the heart of the society that he has not yet reached is the principle of economic gain. When he has actually stepped onto American soil, Saint-Méry will repeatedly find confirmed that behavior going against or simply indifferent to economic self-interest tends to be shunned or actively opposed.

The French passengers described on the ship stand in sharp contrast to this outlook, as will the French émigré community in Philadelphia as portrayed further on. "One would truly be able to say," comments the author regarding the passengers, "that the character attributed to the French had never been more evident than with us" (23). They prize the pleasures of good food and drink, investing time, money, and effort in enjoying them as much as is possible under adverse circumstances. They also savor lively conversation and the exercise of the intellect. Saint-Méry gives several of his fellow travelers lessons in English as they cross, more, it would seem, to stimulate their minds than to provide practical language skills. The French passengers also assiduously and enthusiastically practice various arts. Saint-Méry's son plays the violin, his daughter sketches, the retired sea captain plays the guitar, and they all sing a great deal on the way over. These qualitative and noncommercial interests and activities diverge sharply from the dominant ones of the Americans, as becomes increasingly apparent when the author encounters more Americans onshore.

FIRST IMPRESSIONS ONSHORE

In his entry for March 7, 1793, the day of landing, the author exclaims, "At last I am on this hospitable soil, on this land of freedom, this land which, if the inhabitants are wise, should one day astound the rest of the universe" (34). The clause "if the inhabitants are wise" introduces a caveat, perhaps added at the rewriting. But the following day's entry hints more strongly—through denial, paradoxically—at what is to come, when the author assures the reader, "My pen has not been guided by any wish to depreciate the great people who have given the world the magnificent spectacle of men successfully fighting for true liberty" (39). Depreciation, or at least strong criticism, is, however, what Saint-Méry's text goes on to produce in large measure. Drawn to the United States on the level of principle, its author is often put off, shocked, or revolted by the realities he encounters.

From the beginning of his travels there, Saint-Méry notices that economic utility and commercial self-interest most often take precedence over the pleasures of aesthetic enjoyment in public spaces. In Norfolk he first becomes aware of the chaotic ugliness of American ports, commenting, "New wharves completely fill the river front. These wharves, like all the others in America, are put up solely for the convenience of the owner, are built without any plan, and inconsiderately shut off the view of the river" (47). Farther up the coast he comments on how tedious and unattractive the view of the omnipresent American rail fence is, as opposed to European-style flowering hedges, of which he sees one exceptional stretch near Newcastle, Delaware (85–86).

Saint-Méry becomes equally aware of the manifold ways the primacy of the profit motive over considerations of comfort and safety is demonstrated, both in the private and the public sphere. He marvels, for example, that so many choose to remain in Baltimore when yellow fever is rampant there, because, as he sees it, they are loath to interrupt business activities: "An interest stronger than love of life ... holds those there who place the doubtful rewards of fortune above the danger of certain death" (80).[10] This example involves individual choice, but far more objectionable for Saint-Méry are those that affect public well-being, which sometimes can lead to disaster. In his travels along the eastern seaboard he employs both stagecoaches and packet boats. The latter, he finds, although admittedly very fast, are set up and operated with no regard for the convenience of the passenger (89–90); the former, also speedy, in addition to being extremely uncomfortable are usually driven by drunken coachmen, creating a high risk of accidents (96–97). The author is particularly outraged by dangerous negligence in public places when he visits a Brooklyn gunpowder depot, where the guards let in anyone who wishes to enter, where there is powder on the ground and children are free to make firecrackers with it. "What a country!" he exclaims (169).

PHILADELPHIA

As might be expected, given the length of Saint-Méry's stay there, the material on Philadelphia—the diary and descriptive sections together—takes up a large portion (almost half) of the book. In the end Philadelphia is a kind of microcosm of the whole. In treating this city the author brings in much material from elsewhere in America, and, even more than in the account of the Atlantic crossing, it becomes the locus for broader generalizations about Americans and American society.

During his stay in Philadelphia, Saint-Méry set up a bookstore and printing press, which became a center for the French émigrés who had flocked in large numbers to the city—their "Noah's arc," they called it. A good many of these were eminent personalities, often, like Saint-Méry, having participated in the first stages of the French Revolution. Among them was La Rochefoucauld-Liancourt and another of Saint-Méry's close friends, Talleyrand. Others were prominent members of the early revolutionary assemblies.[11] Saint-Méry's printing press published works, often in French, by émigré authors, including, as previously mentioned, some by Saint-Méry himself.[12] For a time also the press issued a gazette aimed at the Creole emigration.

During his residence in Philadelphia, then, Saint-Méry played a crucial social and cultural role for the milieu of French and French Creole émigrés living or visiting there. Much of his time was in fact spent with other émigrés, and the diary portion of his treatment is filled with comments on their comings and goings, as well as his personal, political, and business relations with them. I will focus here, though, on Saint-Méry's continuing discovery of American culture and society in Philadelphia.

Saint-Méry finds in and around Philadelphia manifestations of an overweening desire to amass and save, noticing for example that houses often are left with broken windows and locks out of reluctance to make costly repairs. And, as he adds, "leaks are common to every attic. These, the owners coldly insist, are impossible to prevent" (264). He also discovers there that all personal possessions are potentially for sale if the price is right: "Everywhere, even in Philadelphia, which is America's outstanding city, everything is for sale, provided the owner is offered a tempting price. He will part with his house, his carriage, his horse, his dog—anything at all" (279). More generally the author observes a calculating, utilitarian spirit. Everything is done for a practical purpose, and that purpose is the pursuit of wealth.

This pervasive mentality creates environments in which Saint-Méry is painfully aware of things lacking that he values and misses. As had already been the case in Norfolk, his aesthetic sense is affronted by the Philadelphia waterfront, disfigured by a hodgepodge of wharves put up by maritime entrepreneurs without concern for the overall view of the city. The author sees this situation as the triumph of selfish private interest over the public good and connects the absence of sensitivity to beauty with the "lack of foresight" that he finds more generally in Americans, since here anarchic commercialism negates the art of urban planning: "One feels real sadness when docking at Philadelphia.... The entire view is blocked by the construction of the wharves, which clearly show that their builders, moved solely by their own greed, had no consideration whatever for good taste, the appearance or well-being of the city.... All that Philadelphia has of beauty in its magnificent design preceded the influence of mercantile and narrow-minded speculations, which can never give birth to anything either beautiful or great" (89). He also wonders at the paucity of popular holidays or festivals, and the lack of gaiety or joyousness in those that are held (336).

Another lack that the author is made aware of as he meets and interacts with Americans are the bonds of social cohesiveness he is accustomed to, some of which, in his social background, take hierarchical forms. At one point he comments, "One singular American custom as compared with our own is that no traveler gives tips to servants in hotels" (298), and he cites an incident he observed in a Philadelphia lodging house where a servant was furiously beaten by the proprietor because she had accepted a small gift. Saint-Méry notices that philanthropy in general is often scant, although he does gratefully acknowledge the aid the Creole refugees have been offered by at least some Americans. Most galling for him, though, is what is lacking in more intimate relations. "Americans, indifferent in love and friendship, cling to nothing," he insists, "attach themselves to nothing. There is plenty of evidence of this among country dwellers. Four times running they will break land for a new home, abandoning without a thought the house in which they were born, . . . the tombs of their fathers, the friends of their childhood" (279). Most surprising perhaps is the coldness of lovers, who according to the author often fall asleep when alone together, while the women "always act as though everything they do is done for a purpose" (285). The general passionlessness in noncommercial matters that he observes even leads Saint-Méry to remark acidly when discussing the mental ward of a Philadelphia hospital, "There are generally from thirty to forty lunatics, most of them as a result of love, and it might be remarked in passing that the great majority of Americans are to be congratulated that this is something they don't need to worry about" (355).[13]

In the Philadelphia section the author again returns to the notion that there is a key to the American makeup, which he elaborates on in a series of passages. He first points out that the Americans in this overall definition much resemble the English, in spite of their claim to dislike them (267). Then, alluding to the rapidity of land settlement since independence, Saint-Méry finds the Americans' "mode of life . . . exactly adapted to their undertakings," the former being characterized as "trickiness and . . . commercialism" ("l'esprit mercantile et calculateur" in the French original).[14] As he had in the passage recounting his arrival on American shores, Saint-Méry holds out the hope that when these traits are "replaced by the virtues that citizens of a great nation ought to have, the country should enjoy perfect tranquillity" (269). But he does not elaborate on why and how "virtues" might take the place of such essential features of American mentality and behavior, and the expressed hope seems to have no basis in his observation and experience of American life.

In a subsequent passage he further refines his perception of the fundamental character of Americans when he argues that another nationality to which they have a particular affinity are the Dutch. As with the English, the distinctive nature of the Dutch is close to that of the Americans, and as a consequence "Americans descended from the Dutch combine to a pronounced degree the indolence of Americans with the avarice of the Dutch, thus emphasizing the eagerness for gain that is common to both" (272). Finally, in a later section of his generalizing comments the author goes on to specify that in thus speaking of the "general character" of Americans he is referring to white males in particular (276). Being the dominant race and gender, their mentality is recognized to be the crucial determinant factor.

Saint-Méry tells the reader in more than one passage that his own reaction to American sociocultural patterns—all ultimately stemming from the overriding trait of putting pecuniary gain before all else—was shared by many of his fellow exiles. Démeunier, another revolutionary leader who left France in 1793, chose to return home as soon as it was safely possible, in 1795, and explained to Saint-Méry on departure that America was a "country which I do not care for in any way" (205). Saint-Méry generalizes this cultural dissonance at one point: "I wouldn't be a faithful historian if I silently permitted it to be thought that a true feeling of affection exists between Americans and French colonials or Frenchmen in general" (275).[15] Just as many of his French and Creole friends seem to have harbored anti-American sentiments similar to his, Saint-Méry was also aware of coolness or worse on the part of Americans toward the French, even in the "pro-French" period that covered most of his stay in Philadelphia. He notes, for instance, "The adoption in this city of French styles in dress and manner does not ... indicate that it has any marked affection for the French nation, and its residents have no hesitation in charging the French higher prices and higher rents than anyone else" (284). He admits, however, that in some cases the French have betrayed the confidence of those Americans who did offer them welcome (276).

When the tide turned near the end, the general standoffishness of the Americans toward the French became open hostility. President Adams, who had earlier frequented Saint-Méry's shop and exchanged writings with him, now placed him on the list of aliens to be deported. When asked by an acquaintance why he had done so, Adams perhaps unwittingly puts the issue of sociocultural incompatibility in a nutshell: "He replied, 'Nothing in particular, but he's too French'" (253). Saint-Méry's travel account amply demonstrates that he had indeed been too well formed in a cultural matrix not as far advanced on the road to modernity to be adaptable to the American mold.

LA ROCHEFOUCAULD-LIANCOURT ON INDIANS

"We shall not speak of the Indians," Saint-Méry informs the reader in the same place where he identifies white males as the dominant group that determines the general ethos in the United States (276). Elsewhere he does make some comments on blacks and women, both dominated by white males, with whom he had contact over the course of his stay. He never seems to have encountered Native Americans, however. Consequently, unlike Crèvecoeur's and Freneau's works, his *Voyage* does not incorporate any kind of material involving them. His friend La Rochefoucauld-Liancourt, on the other hand, did have limited contact with Indians, and his travel account includes some significant commentary on them. Because of the closeness between Saint-Méry's point of view and La Rochefoucauld-Liancourt's, and of the intertwining of their texts, it seems relevant to conclude this chapter with a brief consideration of La Rochefoucauld-Liancourt's views on indigenous peoples in relation to Anglo-American modernity.

Although Saint-Méry's friend was not a Creole, the parallels between the two men are striking. Like Saint-Méry, Liancourt was an "enlightened" member of the upper classes who served on the Assemblée constituante at the beginning of the French Revolution, then fled and went into exile, in his case to England before the United States. The period he spent in the United States coincides almost exactly with that of Saint-Méry: 1794–98. He also spent much of that time in Philadelphia, and many of the commentaries on Americans in his voluminous travel account are based on that residence. Saint-Méry and Liancourt often exchanged views, experiences, and texts during their exile, and Liancourt's travelogue echoes many themes concerning Americans and modernity that I have been discussing in Saint-Méry's.

Liancourt also is at pains to counter the charge of severity in his treatment of the Americans, pays homage to their political ideal, and expresses hopes for their future welfare.[16] Like Saint-Méry, though, he is in fact strongly critical of American society as he encountered it, and his observations and diagnoses correspond closely to those of his friend. Some points of detail are the same—Liancourt, for example, complains that the "ever-present, rough wooden fences largely ruin . . . the landscape" with their "bleak uniformity" (59)—but more important, Liancourt's understanding of the crux of the American mentality is the same as Saint-Méry's. In one passage he characterizes it by a term similar to those employed by Saint-Méry, "nonchalance" (58), and in many other passages he makes it clear that this unconcern is for all else than making money: "As I have already stated many times, the desire to enrich themselves is their dominant passion, in fact their only one" (412). Like Saint-Méry he points to the difficulty most French have in adapting to American mores (e.g., 158–59), and his portrayal of Philadelphia is also consonant with Saint-Méry's; noting the extreme lack of hospitality in that city, he links it to the particularly intense pursuit of wealth there, which "necessarily produces egoism, isolating the person so engaged and leaving him no time for society" (340), that is, the cultivation of personal relations and friendships prized by the French.

Unlike Saint-Méry, however, Liancourt was interested in the Indian peoples who had been displaced by Anglo-American society, and he attempted to gain some firsthand knowledge of them. In May 1795 he left Philadelphia on a trip north and west, through upper New York state to Niagara and across the border to Canada. He hoped to continue his travel farther north and east. He was welcomed and entertained at the border by the lieutenant governor of Upper Canada, John Graves Simcoe, but was finally prohibited from proceeding farther by the governor general of British North America, Lord Dorchester, who feared that if the Frenchman entered Lower Canada (Quebec) he might cause trouble with the French Canadian population there.[17] Because of this foreshortening of his trip, Liancourt's actual contacts with Indians were relatively limited and included only communities living in close proximity to whites. While still in New York state he met several small groups of Iroquois and mentions having spoken with Joseph Brant, the Mohawk chief.[18] While on the Canadian border Liancourt was also a spectator to dances and games of a Tuscarora band. Although his account of these encounters includes a short generalizing section on the "habits and customs of the Indians" (*mœurs et usages des Indiens*),[19] due to the paucity of concrete interaction they are not particularly instructive. But going beyond the limitations of his direct experience, Liancourt reflected in some depth on the situation of Indians in North America, and his real contribution lies in his perceptive analysis.

Even before his first meeting with them, Liancourt notes, "Everything that I hear about the Indians interests me in their behalf" (71), and he recognizes them as victims of the colonizers, driven off their land. Here and in later passages he condemns the turpitude of frontier whites and soon generalizes the censure more broadly to whites in America, who have reduced the Indians under their influence to the "ultimate human degradation" such as he observes in the Indian groups he encounters (90). He also finds highly reprehensible the way the English and the Americans use the Indians in their conflicts with each other, calling their policies "low and barbarian" (120). He questions the state of civilization of the "civilized" invaders and concludes that, at least for the Indians not yet corrupted by contact with whites, becoming "civilized" would probably not be beneficial (124).

Liancourt's text, then, articulates a moral criticism in regard to the treatment of North American Indians. But the most interesting aspect of his commentary lies in his lucid and detailed understanding of the process of dispossession and its intimate connection with the nature of Anglo-American society. Early on he contends that the moral "stain" of Americans' conduct toward Indians—like the stain of slavery—is formidably difficult to eliminate because it is linked to that crucial American trait, "love of money" (90). Then, near the end of his work,[20] he returns to the issue and discusses at some length the linkage in its concrete historical manifestations.

After having discussed American commerce in general, the author informs the (implied European) reader that an essential part of it, land speculation, is peculiar to the United States and calls for further elucidation (395). He then describes the massive expansion of the practice following the American Revolution, starting with the wholesale marketing of land held by the states and stimulating a near-universal obsession on the part of Anglo-Americans of all walks of life with the buying and selling of uncultivated lands to the west. The speculative potential of these lands is based on the combination of the huge quantity of it available, the relatively small colonist population at present, and the probability of its great increase. Liancourt goes on to describe the process by which the commercialization of these lands spurred a continual cycle of settlement, in terms that sometimes recall Crèvecoeur (396, 399–400).

The "uncultivated" lands submitted to this speculative handling were, however, almost entirely occupied by indigenous peoples, whom it was therefore necessary to "remove" (*éloigner*). In the implementation of this displacement, the frontier settlers engaged in what amounted to systematic plunder and in self-justification relegated Indians to nonhuman status (407). This othering of the indigenous population and desire to "remove" them are rooted in the speculative logic of a thoroughly mercantile society and consequently, in Liancourt's view, manifest themselves much more widely than among frontier people alone. "There are few Americans," he contends, "who do not desire, or rather even plan, to push the Indians beyond the Mississippi, and beyond that, to the South Sea [the Pacific Ocean]" (408). Ultimately, he adds, given the felt need of Anglo-America for the vast stretches of wilderness land that allow Indians to practice their "savage way of life," only two possibilities present themselves: "either work to civilize [the Indians], or destroy them [*les détruire*]; but this last course of action cannot yet be openly acknowledged" (408). Since he finds the view very widespread, even among seemingly unprejudiced people, that Indians are entirely refractory to civilization, Liancourt seems to suggest that though it may not have been spoken out loud, an unacknowledged conviction was broadly shared by Americans that some form of "destruction" was the only feasible solution.

Here, then, is a deeply pessimistic assessment of the eighteenth-century confrontation between an inexorably expanding settler colonialism and the indigenous peoples in its path. The next section, which turns to accounts of encounter with Indians, opens with a portrayal of this zero degree of the relation between colonizers and Indians set forth by Liancourt. In subsequent chapters I examine a far more complex dynamics of contact in texts recounting travel into territories still largely the autonomous domain of Native Americans, still outside of the full control of the forces of modernity.

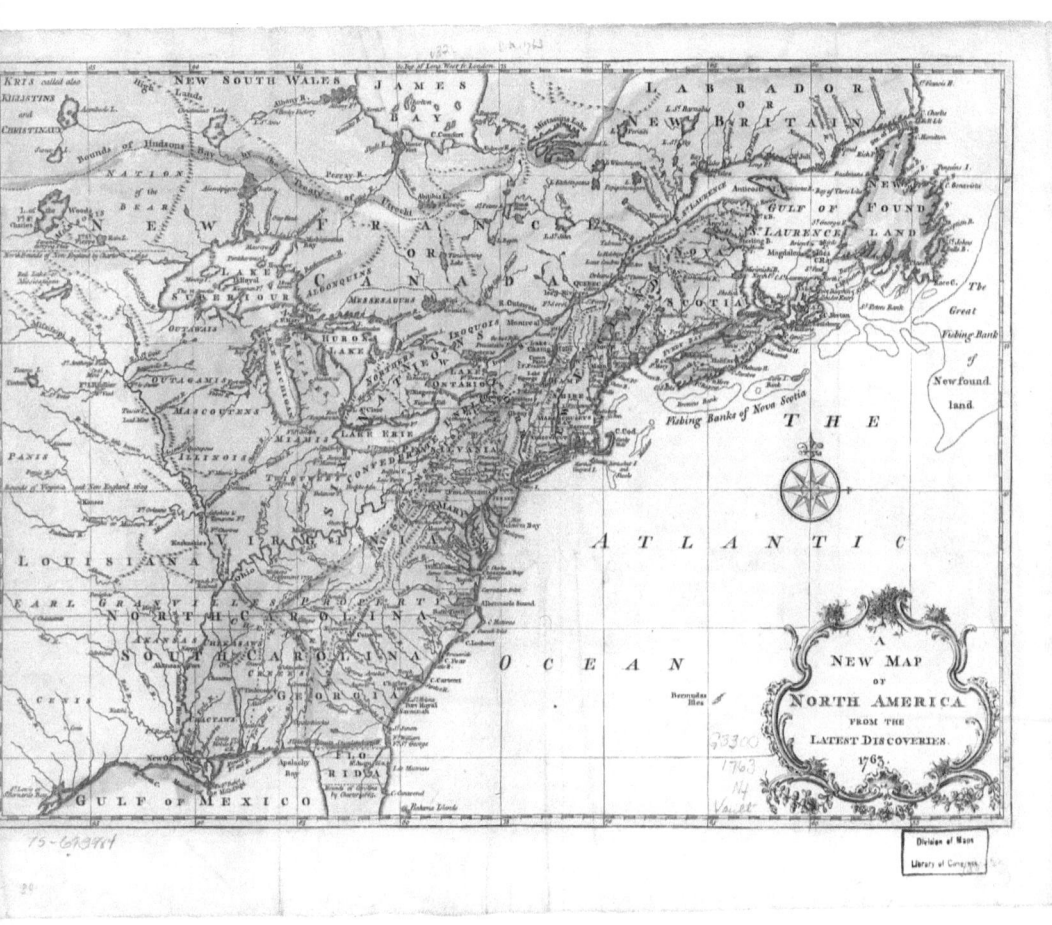

1. *A New Map of North America from the Latest Discoveries,*
1763. Map Collection, Library of Congress.

2. *Above*: *Tontine Coffee House, N.Y.C.*, by Francis Guy, ca. 1797. The neighborhood of the stock market in New York in the late eighteenth century. Oil on linen, lined to fiberglass. Unframed, 43 x 65 x 2 in. Object # 1907.32, New-York Historical Society. Photography © New-York Historical Society.

3. *Right*: *Elijah Boardman*, by Ralph Earl, 1789. A wealthy merchant in New Milford, Connecticut. Metropolitan Museum of Art. Bequest of Susan W. Tyler, 1979, www.metmuseum.org.

NARRATIVES

OF A LATE

EXPEDITION

AGAINST THE

INDIANS,

WITH

An ACCOUNT of the BARBAROUS
EXECUTION of Col. CRAWFORD;

AND

The WONDERFUL ESCAPE of Dr. *Knight* and
John Slover from CAPTIVITY, in 1782.

PHILADELPHIA:
Printed by FRANCIS BAILEY, in Market Street.
M,DCC,LXXXIII.

4. *Left: Marinus Willett*, by Ralph Earl, ca. 1791. A New York merchant and militiaman. Metropolitan Museum of Art. Bequest of George Willett Van Nest, 1916, www.metmuseum.org.

5. *Above:* Title page of Hugh Henry Brackenridge's *Narratives of a Late Expedition against the Indians*, 1783.

6. Portrait of Alexander Henry, frontispiece of his *Travels and Adventures in Canada and the Indian Territories*, 1809.

TRAVELS

AND ADVENTURES

IN

CANADA

AND

THE INDIAN TERRITORIES,

BETWEEN

THE YEARS 1760 AND 1776.

IN TWO PARTS.

BY ALEXANDER HENRY, ESQ.

NEW-YORK:
PRINTED AND PUBLISHED BY I. RILEY.
—
1809.

7. Title page of Alexander Henry's *Travels and Adventures in Canada and the Indian Territories.*

8. Frontispiece of Lahontan's travel account *Nouveaux voyages de M. le Baron de Lahontan dans l'Amérique septentrionale*, 1703.

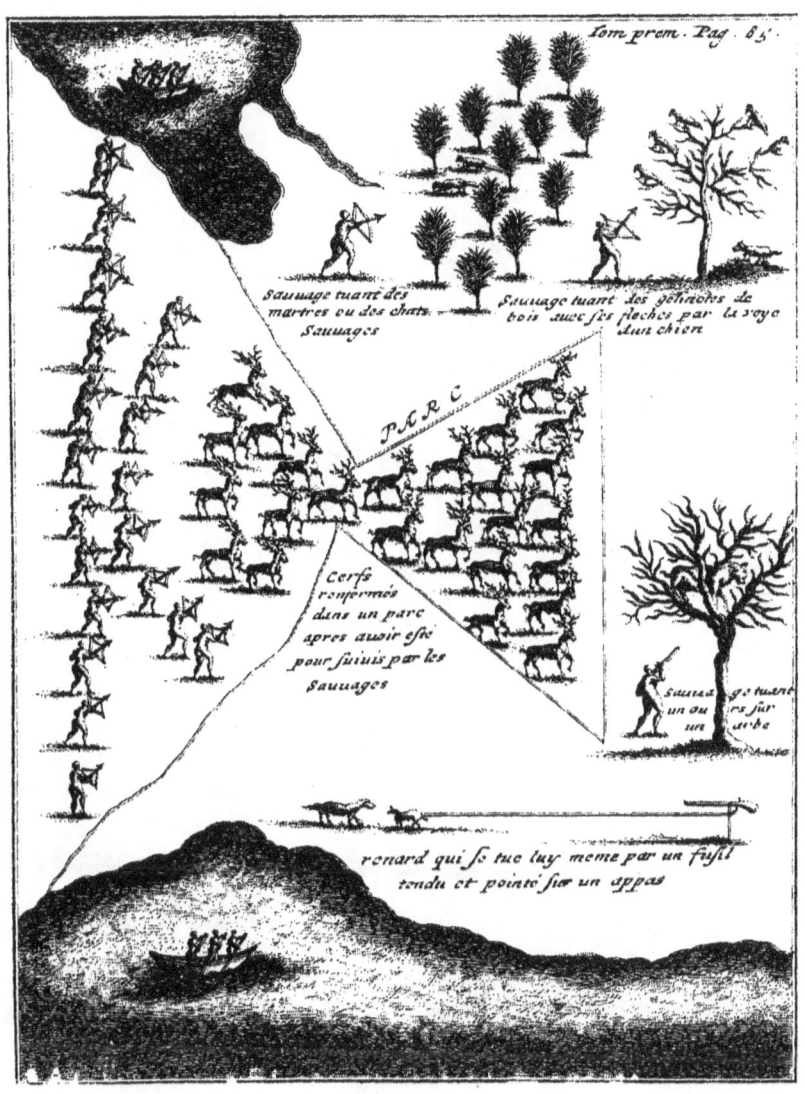

9. Illustration in Lahontan's *Nouveaux voyages* of Indian hunting practices.

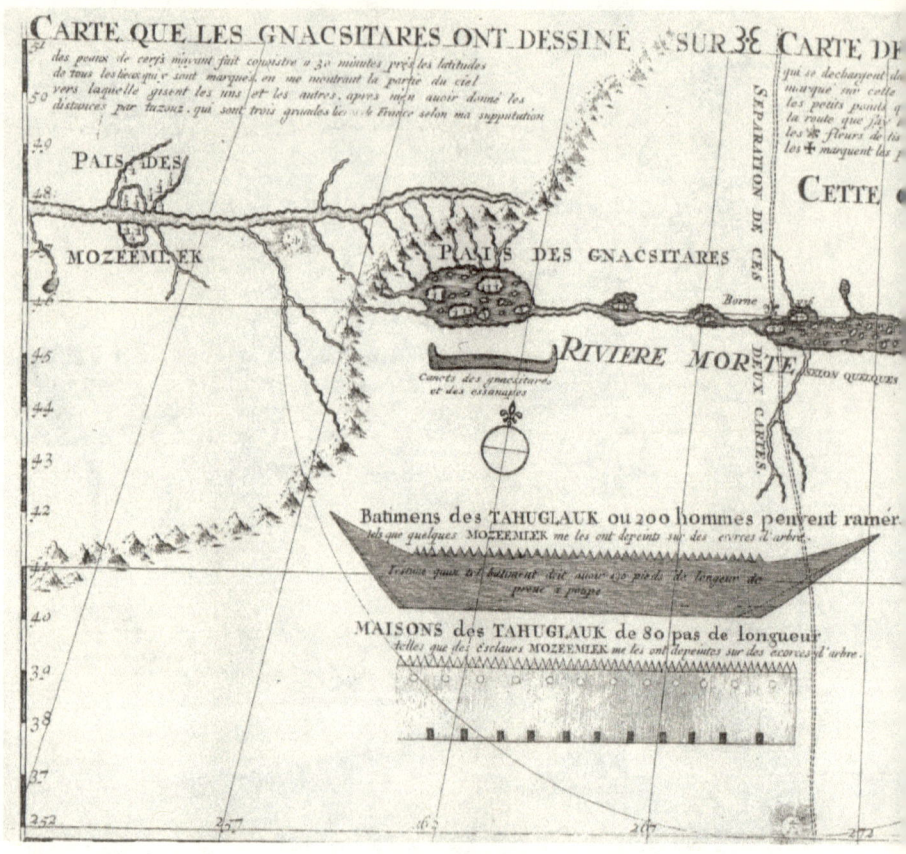

10. Map of the "Rivière longue," partly based on an Indian drawing, in Lahontan's *Nouveaux voyages*.

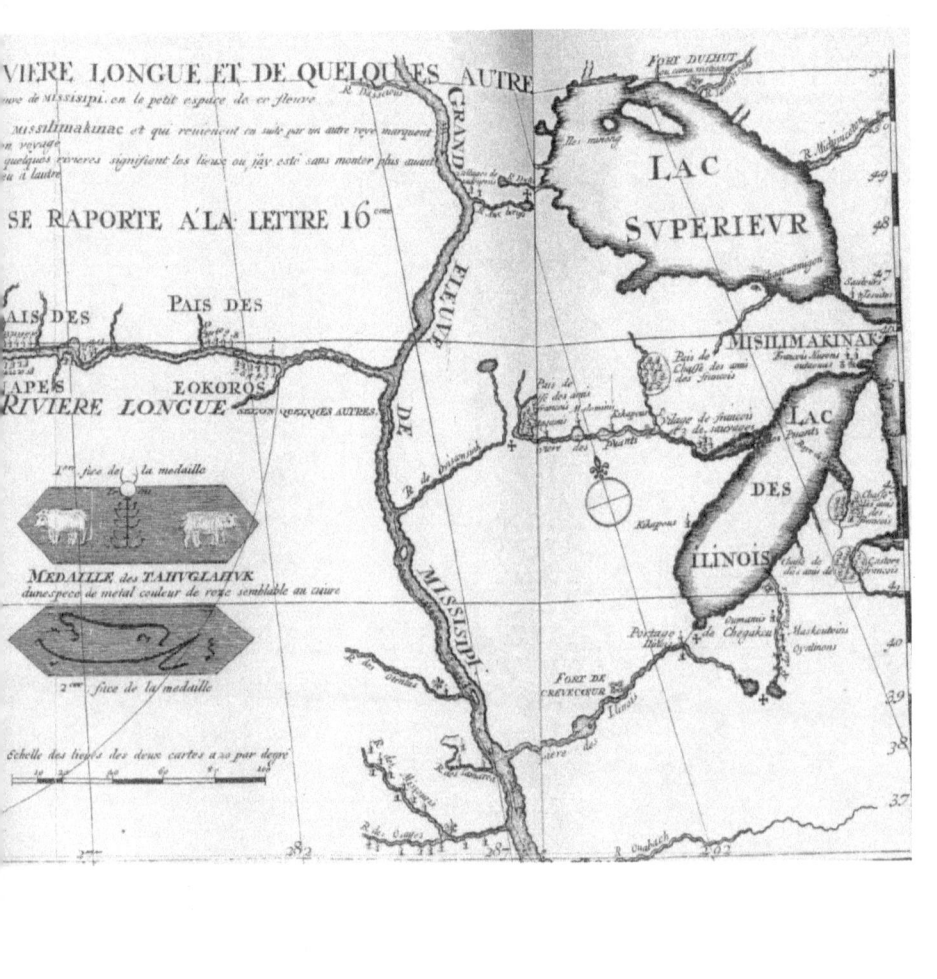

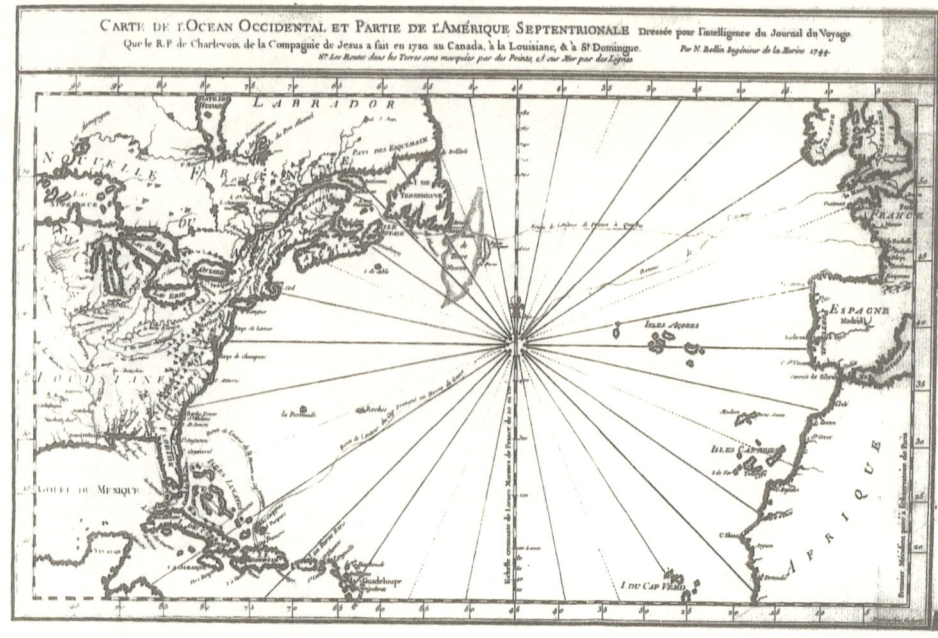

11. Map by the geographer and mapmaker Jacques-Nicolas Bellin to illustrate Charlevoix's *Journal d'un voyage fait par ordre du roi dans l'Amérique septentrionale*, 1744.

A NEW VOYAGE TO CAROLINA;

CONTAINING THE
Exact Description and *Natural History*
OF THAT
COUNTRY:

Together with the *Present State* thereof.

AND
A JOURNAL

Of a Thousand Miles, Travel'd thro' several Nations of *INDIANS*.

Giving a particular Account of their Customs, Manners, *&c.*

By JOHN LAWSON, Gent. Surveyor-General of *North Carolina*.

LONDON:
Printed in the Year 1709.

12. Title page of John Lawson's *A New Voyage to Carolina*, 1709.

13. Map of Carolina in Lawson's *A New Voyage to Carolina*.

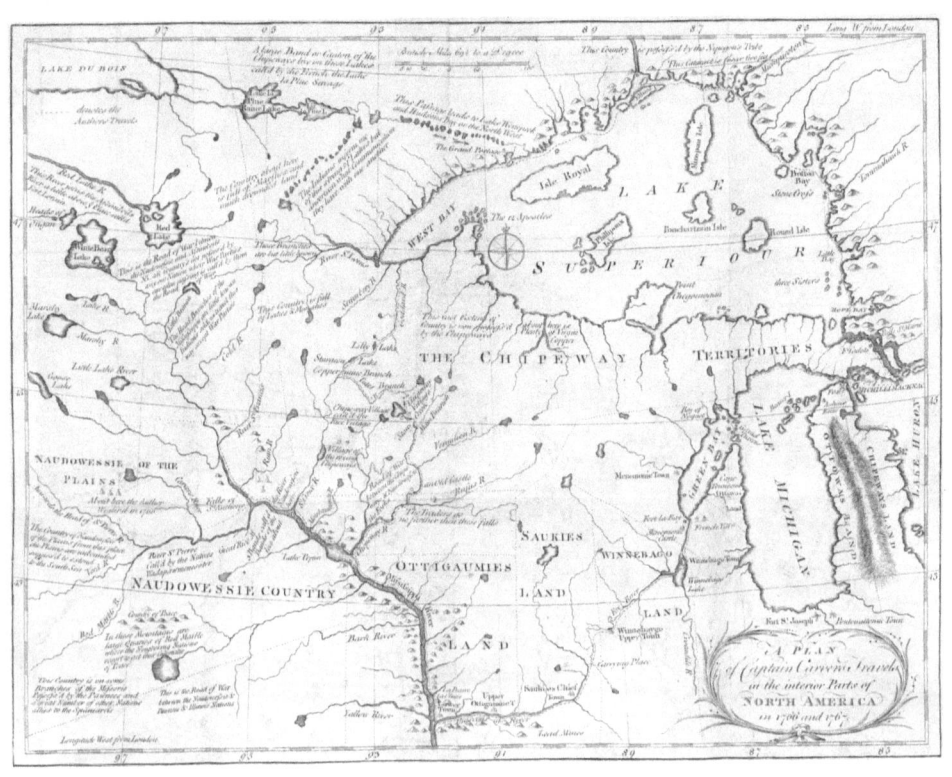

14. Map of the Great Lakes and upper Mississippi region in Jonathan Carver's *Travels through the Interior Parts of North America, in the Years 1766, 1767, and 1768*, 1778. AC7. C2566T.1778, Houghton Library, Harvard University.

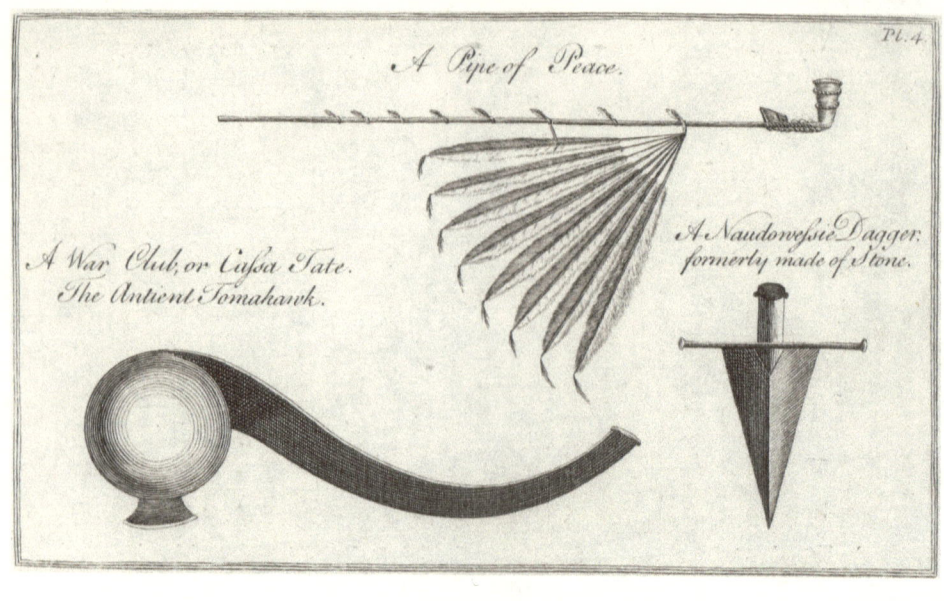

15. Illustration in Carver's *Travels: A Pipe of Peace*, etc. AC7.
C2566T.1778, Houghton Library, Harvard University.

16. Illustration in Carver's *Travels: A Man and Woman of the Ottigaumies.* AC7.C2566T.1778, Houghton Library, Harvard University

17. *Above*: Frontispiece (Mico Chlucco) and title page of William Bartram's *Travels*, 1791. AC7.B2861.791T, Houghton Library, Harvard University.

18. *Right*: Map of the Coast of East Florida from Bartram's *Travels* (London edition, 1792).

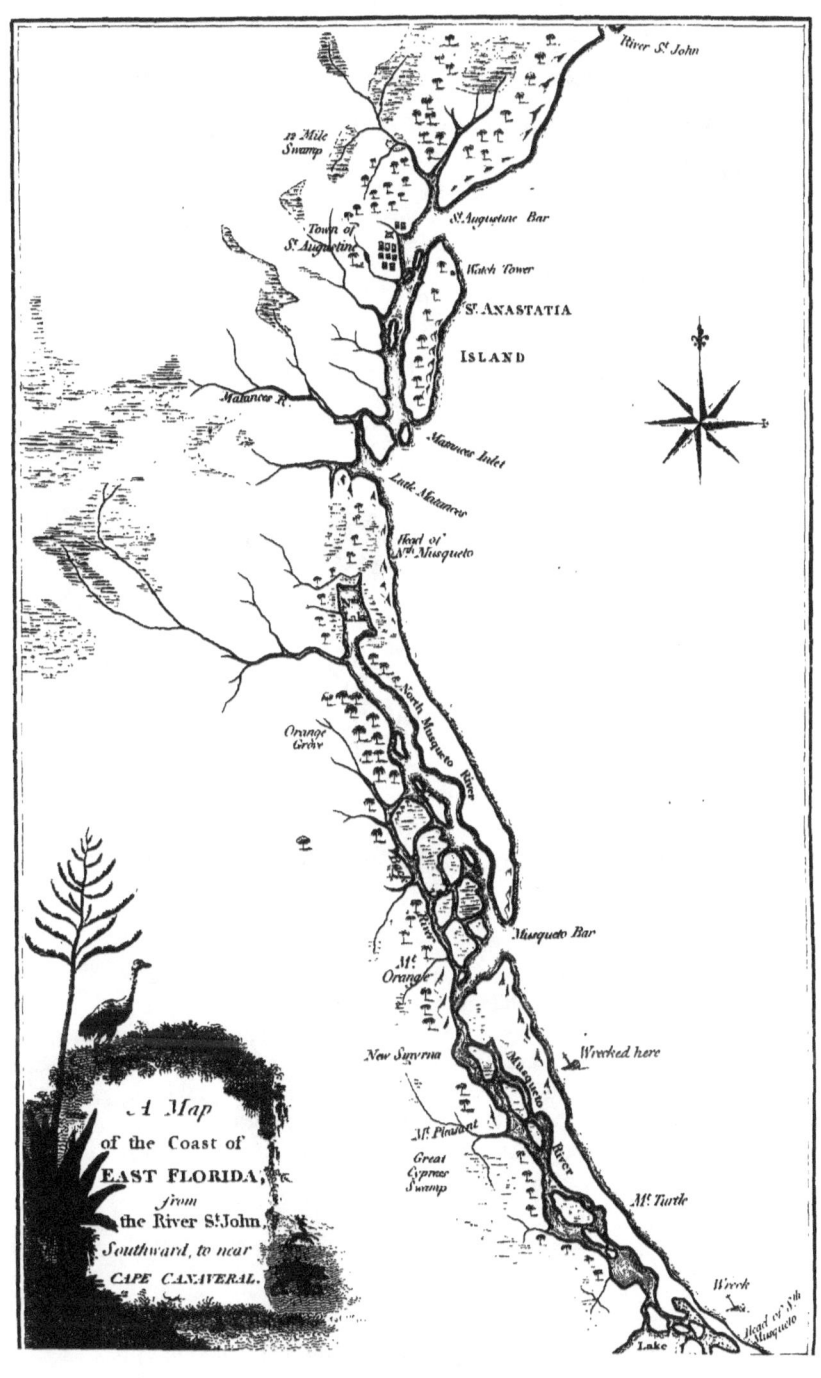

THE CREEK AND CHEROKEE INDIANS. 55

Indians themselves, is shown in the following engraved plan :—

A is the Rotunda ; *B*, the Public Square ; *C*, the grand area or Chunky-Yard. The habitations of the people are placed with considerable regularity in streets or ranges, as indicated in the plan.

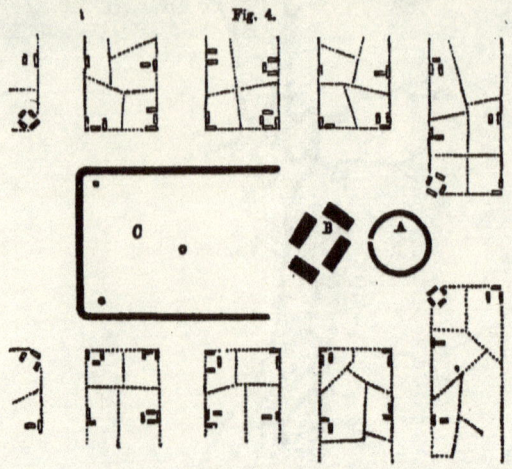

Fig. 4.

The dwellings of the Upper Creeks consist of little squares, or rather of four dwelling-houses inclosing a square area, exactly on the plan of the Public Square. (*See cut, fig.* 1, *p.* 38.) Every family, however, has not four of these houses ; some have but three, others not more than two, and some but one, according to the circumstances of the individual, or the number of his family. Those who have four buildings have a particular use for each building. One serves as a cook-room and winter lodging-house, another as a summer lodging-house and hall for receiving visitors, and a third for a granary or provision house, etc. The last is commonly two stories high, and divided into two apartments, transversely, the lower story

19. A page from E. G. Squier's edition of William Bartram's "Observations on the Creek and Cherokee Indians, 1789," 1853.

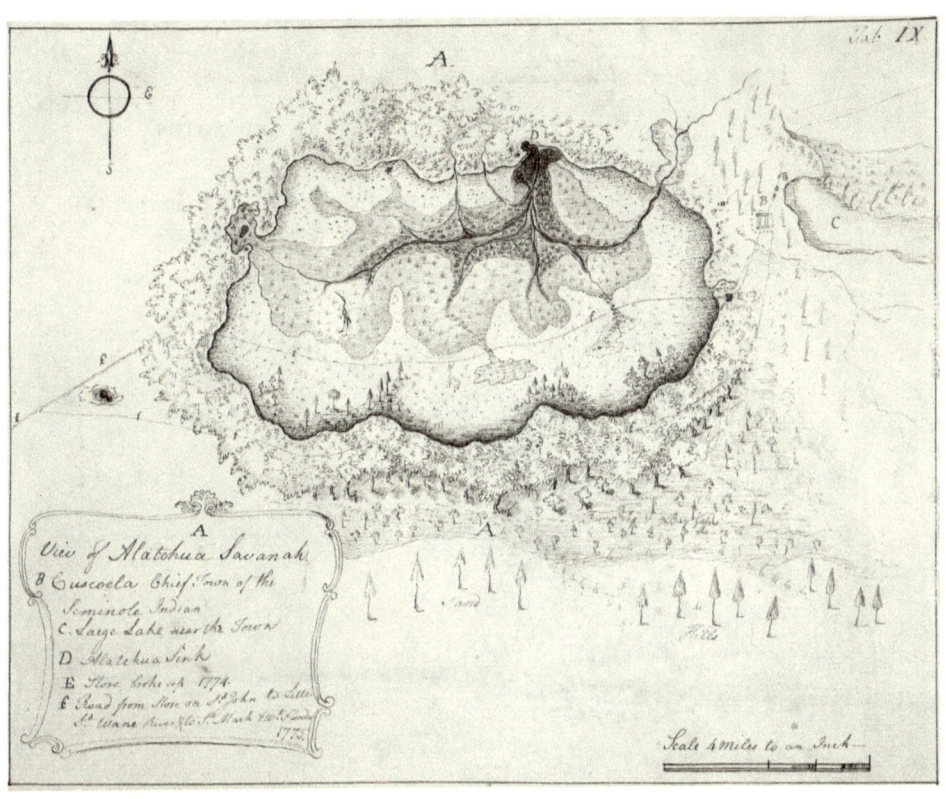

20. Map drawing by William Bartram, *The Great Alachua Savanah in the province of East Florida*. © The Natural History Museum / The Trustees of the Natural History Museum, London.

LETTERS AND NOTES
ON THE
MANNERS, CUSTOMS, AND CONDITION
OF THE
NORTH AMERICAN INDIANS.

BY GEO. CATLIN.

WRITTEN DURING EIGHT YEARS' TRAVEL AMONGST THE WILDEST TRIBES OF
INDIANS IN NORTH AMERICA.
IN 1832, 33, 34, 35, 36, 37, 38, AND 39.

IN TWO VOLUMES,
WITH FOUR HUNDRED ILLUSTRATIONS, CAREFULLY ENGRAVED FROM HIS ORIGINAL PAINTINGS.

VOL. I.

LONDON:
PUBLISHED BY THE AUTHOR, AT THE EGYPTIAN HALL, PICCADILLY.
PRINTED BY TOSSWILL AND MYERS, 24, BUDGE ROW.
1841.
[*Entered at Stationers' Hall.*]

21. Frontispiece of George Catlin's *Letters and Notes on the Manners, Customs, and Condition of the North American Indians,* 1841.

22. "Stu-mick-o-sucks, Buffalo's Back Fat, head chief" (Blackfoot). Line drawing in Catlin's *Letters and Notes*, 1841. Plate 11, vol. 1.

23. "One Horn, head chief of the Miniconjou." Line drawing in Catlin's *Letters and Notes*, 1841. Plate 86, vol. 1.

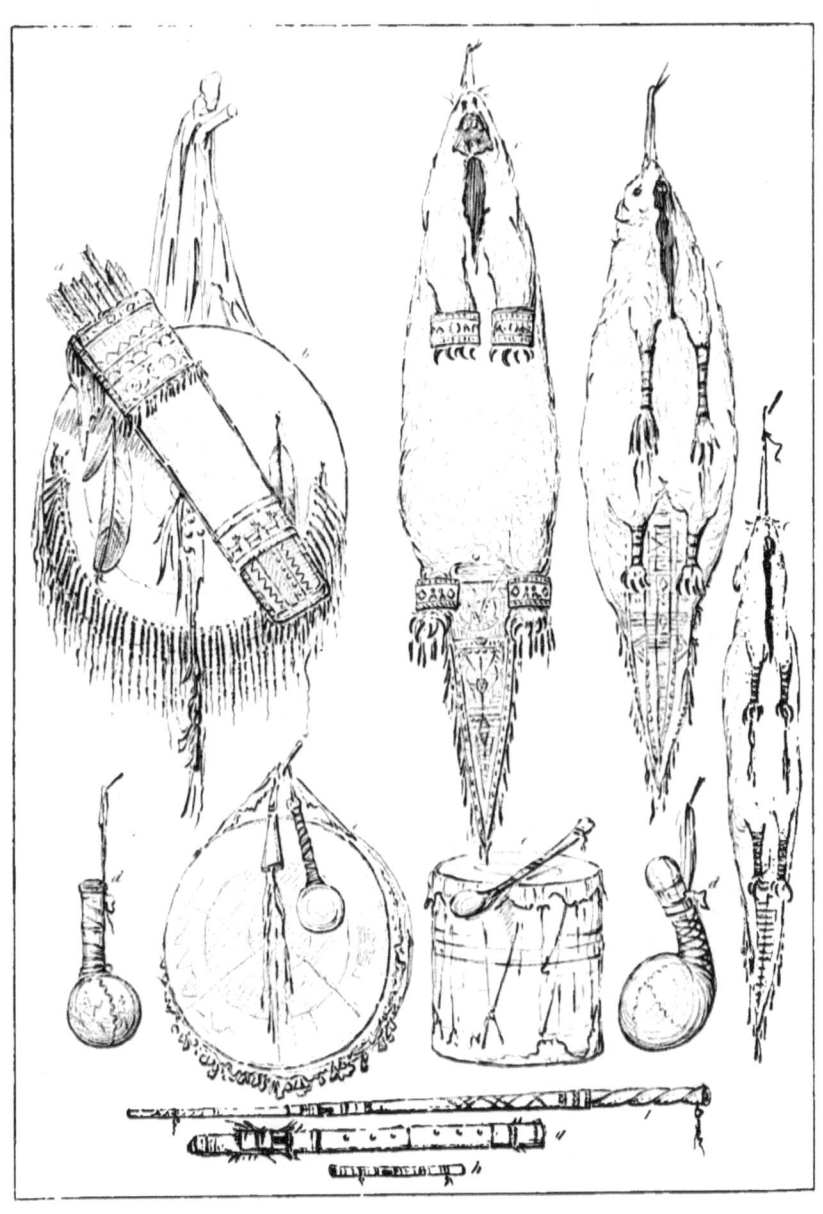

24. "Indian artifacts." Line drawing in Catlin's *Letters and Notes*, 1841. Plate 101½, vol. 1.

25. "Wi-jun-jon, Pigeon's Egg Head, going to and returning from Washington." Line drawing in Catlin's *Letters and Notes*, 1841. Plates 271 and 272, vol. 2.

PART TWO

Views of the Other

Travels in "Indian Territory"

CHAPTER FOUR

The Zero Degree of the Other
Indian Violence and "Adventure" with Indians

Since the early development of capitalism in Anglo-America was closely linked to the expropriation of land—land inhabited and used by Amerindians but also imbued with crucial cultural meanings for them—the relation between the natives and the settler colonists could only be highly conflictual.[1] A merciless struggle for control and possession of land was engaged, and the Indians responded to the continual incursions of whites by a ferocious resistance that often took violent forms.[2] By its very nature the situation discouraged fruitful cultural exchange, naturally tending toward the "zero degree" of contact—confrontation, misunderstanding, rejection, and hatred. In these circumstances the violence exercised by the Indian enemy came to haunt the Anglo-American settlers' imagination, and encounter with this adversary was often experienced and figured in writing solely as dangerous "adventure."

In this first chapter of part 2, which shifts the focus from experiences of modernity to those of its Other, I begin by looking at this lowest common denominator of the encounter. I will first briefly examine representations of Indian violence in the eighteenth century in the principal genres that stage it, and then illustrate, through two examples, the textual creation of adventure in "true" narratives of Indian encounter through the use of literary techniques similar to those of the adventure novel. As should be apparent, such adventure—generated out of violence and the risk of violence—is a representational mode that excites the reader's fascination but generally stifles the kind of cultural encounter that will come into play in subsequent chapters.

REPRESENTATIONS OF INDIAN VIOLENCE

The "Indian wars"—armed conflicts in North America between European colonizers and indigenous peoples—extend from the very first European implantations to the last Indian resistance at the end of the nineteenth century. Much has been written about the violence of this history. Richard Slotkin's now classic study, *Regeneration through Violence*, analyzes the whole sweep of it, up to the Civil War, in terms of the creation of a national mythology. More recently Bernard Bailyn, one of the foremost historians of British America, has focused on the brutality of its early years.[3] But within that history the eighteenth century—at the turning point in the development of modernity—constitutes a particularly intense moment; it was punctuated by a succession of British, French, and Indian wars up to the Treaty of Paris in 1763, followed by the War of Independence and its sequels—which were in part also Indian wars—and permeated throughout by the advance of armed Anglo-American colonization.[4] By the end of the century, however, or at least after the defeat of the movement led by Tecumseh in the War of 1812, the Indians of the eastern United States were almost entirely subjugated, and the Indian wars moved to the West.[5]

Apart from this continuum of violent Indian-colonizer relations during the period, raids and local wars between tribes constituted an essential aspect of the lives of Amerindians east of the Mississippi. Although specialists are divided on the exact role and importance to be attributed to war in Indian societies, and although the arrival of whites without a doubt considerably aggravated conflicts between Indians, it is clear that warlike violence was endemic to the way of life of many eastern Indians.[6]

Throughout the eighteenth century hostile confrontation between the colonists and these often warring peoples produced a voluminous literature, one that pictured Indian violence directed both toward whites and toward other Indians. Although generally negative, the reactions of whites to these phenomena were often to some extent ambivalent. While even authors favorable to Indians usually saw the practices of war and torture as constituting their dark side, Europeans not uncommonly found aspects of this behavior worthy of admiration. The counterpoint to the image of the bloody and inhuman butcher was that of the heroic warrior of almost superhuman courage, endurance, and skill.

The literature of Indian violence evoked many different moments of warfare in the indigenous style: dances, body painting, and other war preparations, stratagems, ambushes, and surprise attacks, scalping, running the gauntlet, and the putting to death of prisoners.[7] But some scenes occupied a privileged position, especially depictions of the torture of prisoners, a practice specific to the eastern tribes that was likely to create the most dreadful of impressions in the European observer (or reader).[8]

There were as many things at stake in these representations as there were publics to which they were directed. In certain cases they served ideological purposes, justifying or calling for repressive measures against the Indians.[9] They sometimes were useful pedagogically, when they analyzed Indian war practices to better combat them. The choice not to represent violence could also have a utilitarian goal, since the presence of such depictions might discourage potential colonizers. But often commercial considerations were involved, since publishers of periodicals as well as books were keen to meet the expectations of their readers. In England and North America alike writings about Indians were exceedingly popular.

In what genres did representations of Indian violence mainly appear? Putting aside the account of travel in Indian territory, in which they played a lesser role, four genres stand out (though they often appear in mixture): military accounts, captivity narratives, historical writings, and works of fiction. I will look briefly at each in turn.

MILITARY ACCOUNTS

Unlike those of the seventeenth century, often penned by colonial dignitaries to demonstrate "the observable Dispensations of God," as Cotton Mather expressed it,[10] eighteenth-century accounts were generally written by the participants themselves, and their purpose was in part the utilitarian one of teaching readers how to counter enemy tactics. Thus Robert Rogers, the most famous of the colonial militia leaders, who had developed his own methods during the Seven Years' War based on the Indian model, opens his *Journals* by observing, "Should the troubles in America be renewed, and the savages repeat those scenes of barbarity they so often have acted on the British subjects, which there is great reason to believe will happen, I flatter myself, that such as are immediately concerned may reap some advantage from these pages."[11] The narrative of a 1764 expedition led by the Swiss officer Henri Bouquet against the Indians in the region of the Ohio declares the same goal. The author is not Bouquet himself, but the account is based on the eyewitness testimony of officers who accompanied him, and it includes an appendix entitled "Reflections on the War with the Savages of North America"—a kind of manual of Indian warfare written by one of the officers.[12]

In these military writings one finds a tendency to minimize or play down and sometimes to shift the responsibility for Indian acts of violence. The laconic, emotionless style in which they are often written doubtless comes largely from the fact that the narrator shares the warrior mentality and does not let himself be overly affected by scenes of carnage. But another factor may come into play as well, that leads the author to put the blame on other shoulders, as we find, for example, in Rogers's journals.

The series of wars involving Indians that ended with the Treaty of Paris were fought principally between the English and the French, using Indian intermediaries, just as subsequently multiple frontier conflicts occurred between Loyalists and Patriots, instrumentalizing Indian fighters. A militiaman like Rogers, fighting in what the British termed the French and Indian War (1754–60), thus felt impelled to show that the French were responsible for Indian atrocities on the other side and to designate the perpetrators as "French Indians." It was important to insist on the French origin of the acts because the British also used Indian combatants who acted in similar ways. Thus Rogers informs his readers that the French paid their Indian allies sixty pounds for each English scalp and quotes a letter from his superior officer lamenting "the unheard-of-cruelties committed by the French, and the Indians, by their instigation."[13]

He does not hesitate to report elsewhere, however, that an Indian of his own camp has returned with "two French scalps, agreeable to their barbarous custom."[14] Here responsibility for the acts, mentioned only in passing, is attributed not to the English but to an unfortunate Indian custom. The same kind of nonrecognition of their own agency and accusations of responsibility on the other side took place between the Americans and the English during the revolutionary warfare in frontier areas, in which Indians participated.

CAPTIVITY NARRATIVES

This form of writing became an important American genre at the end of the seventeenth century, when Mary Rowlandson's famous account appeared, and continued to have great popularity into the mid-nineteenth century.[15] These texts dealt with the very common experience of colonists—in the eighteenth century there were thousands of them—being captured by Indians during raids of frontier towns or war skirmishes. Taken by force, sometimes in horrific circumstances, they often endured tremendous suffering during the first phases of captivity. In some cases they were tortured and killed; in others they were adopted by a tribe, sold to the French, or finally "redeemed" by the English. Among those who survived and returned home, some recounted the vicissitudes of their captivity, either by becoming authors themselves or by means of an amanuensis.

Eighteenth-century captivity accounts were not framed as demonstrations of the workings of divine providence, as seventeenth-century accounts often were, but rather reported purely secular realities that were often frightful, incomprehensible, and chaotic. Contrary to the military narrative, the narrator's relation to Indian violence is mainly passive, that of the victim undergoing it or observing it as a helpless witness. Like the narrator, the reader becomes a mesmerized voyeur watching scenes of horror unfold—bodies mutilated, scalps torn off, refined torture carried out, and so on—since, by contrast with the phlegmatic, restrained military account, the tale of captivity often lingers on the atrocious details of those scenes.

This sensationalistic aspect surely contributed to the success of the genre with a wide public, and it also explains the ideological uses it could be put to. For the violence that was so vividly displayed in the captivity narrative was generally not contextualized and therefore encouraged the demonization of the Indian.[16] One example can serve as an illustration. In the course of a punitive expedition against British-affiliated Indians of the Ohio region at the Wyandot town of Upper Sandusky in 1782, undertaken by a militia under the orders of Col. William Crawford—a friend of George Washington and a fellow land speculator[17]—Crawford was captured with some of his men and put to death after prolonged torture. Two of the prisoners managed to escape, and their accounts of the events were taken down by Hugh Henry Brackenridge, Philip Freneau's friend and poetic collaborator.

From the beginning Brackenridge had been and continued to be bitterly hostile to Indians, and for propaganda purposes he published the two versions of the incident in Philadelphia in 1783, first in a newspaper and then as a pamphlet.[18] These texts, which are full of shocking details on the treatment of the prisoners by their captors, make no allusion to massacres that Crawford had directed in Ohio Indian villages in earlier years.[19] In his remarks introducing the narratives, Brackenridge praises Crawford as an Indian fighter and treats as a commendable exploit his having "taken" a number of Indian towns. Further on he mentions the notorious massacre at Gnadenhütten earlier in the same year of peaceful, unarmed Delaware (Lenape) Indians who had been converted by the Moravians. But while condemning the murder of women and children, Brackenridge minimizes and relativizes the incident as a whole and most significantly denies any relation between it and Crawford's death.[20] Several members of Crawford's expedition had been members of the Pennsylvania militia that carried out the Gnadenhütten massacre (although Crawford himself had not been), and the putting to death of those captured near Upper Sandusky was in retaliation for that massacre.[21]

Although captives occasionally managed to escape, in some cases by exercising violence themselves, most often they remained powerless. This predicament generally increased their anxiety, fed by received stereotypes of Indians. Charles Johnston, taken during a journey on the Ohio River in 1790 in the service of John May, a speculator in Kentucky lands, speaks in his account of the terror that he felt at the moment of capture by a party he later learned was made up of Shawnees, Wyandots, Delawares, and Cherokees. Johnston had been raised in the fear and hatred of Indians, and he immediately imagined himself burned at the stake. This did not occur, but his fears were again stirred up when two scalps, freshly cut from the heads of his traveling companions, were placed next to him to dry by the fire.[22]

A captive's lack of familiarity with the customs and language of his captors could lead to serious misunderstanding in this kind of situation. James Smith, a workman captured during Braddock's campaign in 1755, tells how at a certain point the Kahnawake Mohawks who were holding him began to pull out his hair and attach rings to his ears and nose. He assumed they were getting him ready to be put to death, but he soon discovered that they were preparing to adopt him.[23] Conversely, previous knowledge of Indian ways might provide reassurance. O. M. Spencer was captured by Shawnees in 1792 at the age of eleven, near his family's frontier home in the Ohio country. After seeing another captive attacked and scalped, he was approached by an Indian holding out his hand. "I took it," he writes, "and from what I had heard of the character and customs of the Indians, feeling assured of present safety, became at once calm."[24] Knowledge could in other cases, of course, increase anxiety rather than reduce it, as happened with John Slover, one of those whose accounts Brackenridge recorded. When his captors painted one of the other prisoners black, Slover knew that their action amounted to a sentence of death; the captive who had been painted was at first unsure of its meaning but began to weep as he came to suspect the truth.[25] The man did in fact meet this fate, while Slover, who was also blackened, but much later, did not only because he was eventually able to escape.

Many accounts of Indian captivity emphasize the fortuitous—or apparently fortuitous—nature of the experience in its early stages. Sudden, incomprehensible changes in one's status and prospects were common, and the combination of horror and total uncertainty could produce tremendous emotional strain. Charles Johnston was struck by the reactions to her tribulations of one of his fellow captives, Peggy Fleming. After having been brutalized at the moment of capture and seeing her sister killed before her eyes, she seemed strangely happy and vivacious during the first days of captivity. But when Johnston crossed paths with her later—they had been separated into different Indian bands—she appeared deeply dejected and miserable.[26] She apparently was manifesting a delayed reaction to the trauma of capture, perhaps combined with response to further trauma in the interim, after an initial compensatory reflex.

The nightmare, however, sometimes ended. If one survived the initial period of trials, one might be adopted into a tribe and treated as one of its members. From then on captivity could open onto an encounter of a very different kind. The narrative would be transformed as well, becoming a sketch of daily life in an Indian community.

HISTORICAL AND DESCRIPTIVE WRITINGS

Although their authors may draw on some experiences of their own, these are not the only resources used, and they are integrated into a larger, collective story of past and present. Historiographic and descriptive writing on Indians thus stands at a greater distance from its object and often attempts to explain the manifestations of violence it describes by contextualizing them. One finds this kind of treatment in chorographies of the colonial provinces, notably in Robert Beverley's portrait of Virginia.[27] One of the several chapters on Indian customs, entitled "War and Peace," provides a short description of warrior practices, along with explanations of motivation. The tone is moderate and the evident intention is to understand.

The same purpose is manifest in George Henry Loskiel's history of a different kind of collective entity—the Moravian Indian mission in the Ohio region. But here the author also alludes to the extreme nature of Indian violence so as to demonstrate the power of the Christian message and the mission's work. Thus Loskiel writes in his preface, "The heathen nations, with whom the Missionaries are here engaged, are more remarkable for their ferocity, obstinacy, and hardness of heart, than all other nations of the earth, and yet the power of the word of atonement conquers their unbroken and inflexible dispositions."[28]

Several secular Anglo-American works focus on larger communities of Indians: Cadwallader Colden's *History of the Five Indian Nations* in two parts (1727, 1747) and James Adair's *History of the American Indians* (1775), mainly on the Indians of the Southeast, of which the author had firsthand knowledge. These works differ considerably in the weight of personal experience. Colden, an officer in the provincial government of New York, drew mainly on archives for his history of the Iroquois confederacy, whereas Adair, a trader for some forty years with the Cherokees, Chickasaws, and to a lesser extent the Choctaws, shared their life fully over long stretches of time, even participating on occasion in war expeditions. At one point he gives the reader a general description of these from personal experience. Once the battle is engaged, he writes,

> now the hot work begins—The guns are firing; the chewed bullets flying; the strong hiccory bows a twanging; the dangerous barbed arrows whizzing . . . the well-aimed tomohawk killing, or disabling. . . . Nothing scarcely can be heard for the shrill echoing noise of the war and death-whoop, every one furiously pursues his adversary from tree to tree, striving to incircle him for his prey. . . . One dying foe is intangled in the hateful and faltering arms of another. . . . On returning to the place of battle, the victors begin, with mad rapture, to cut and slash those unfortunate persons, who fell by their arms and power.[29]

Both Adair and Colden offer descriptions of torture—perhaps largely or entirely from secondhand accounts in both cases—and the way these are handled is indicative of the extreme ambivalence of European reactions to the practice. Particularly revealing are the ways the two authors introduce the subject and prepare the reader before exhibiting scenes that may be perceived to be both fascinating and repugnant, ignoble and admirable. Colden, a political official, brings to bear an anti-French strategy in his opening remarks, pointedly choosing to describe only an instance of torture that the Comte de Frontenac ordered some of his Indian allies to carry out. "Such a Piece of monstrous Cruelty," Colden writes, "though I have frequently mentioned to have been done by the Indians, yet I forbore giving the Particulars . . . , suspecting it might be too offensive to Christian

Ears." In this particular case, however, he intends to give a circumstantial account, "to shew on the one hand, what Courage and Resolution, Virtue, the Love of Glory, and the Love of one's Country can instill into Mens Minds [those of the Indians undergoing torture] . . . and on the other Hand, how far a false Policy, under a corrupt Religion, can debase even great Minds [those of the French, who are responsible for it]."[30]

In the case of Adair, who is almost as hostile toward inept British Indian policy as he is toward the French, and who seems to be aiming for a large public, the sensationalist impulse appears to be uppermost. "No representation can possibly be given," he tells the reader, "so shocking to humanity, as [the Indians'] unmerciful method of tormenting their devoted prisoner; and as it is so contrary to the standard of the rest of the known world, I shall relate the circumstances, so far as to convey proper information thereof to the reader."[31] "Information" is a weak word for the wrenching depiction that follows. Moreover, after adding that this was the most favorable outcome that could be hoped for when a warrior was captured, Adair admits that he cannot resist the temptation to present "one or two" more exemplary instances of the practice. He finally recounts four such stories. Though the author insists that he does not do this to wallow in blood but because he sees in the tortured warriors illustrations of a greatness of soul unequaled since the first Christian martyrs, it is hard not to believe that he is also playing to the morbid curiosity of the reader.[32]

LITERARY WORKS

Almost nonexistent in the seventeenth century, works of fiction and imagination that portray Indians are rare in the first half of the eighteenth, both in America and England. Only in the last half, and especially in the last quarter of the century, does the Indian begin to appear often in poems, tales, and novels. (Works of fiction in general are rare in the colonies before independence.) In poetry a minor genre develops near the end of the eighteenth century and continues into the early nineteenth, the "Indian death song," which pictures a warrior dying under torture. Several of the best in the genre are by Philip Freneau. In his as in others' poems on this theme, the emphasis is on the nobility of the tortured Indian.[33] As for

Crèvecoeur's fictions, Indian violence plays an important role in the letters that concern the revolutionary struggles in the frontier areas. But in these texts what is highlighted is not so much the acts of violence of the Indians themselves as the brutality and cruelty exercised by the Loyalist officers who direct attacks on settlers and the equal ruthlessness of the backcountry Patriots.[34]

In his study of the Indian in eighteenth-century English literature, Benjamin Bissell enumerates some fifteen novels in which Amerindians play a significant role.[35] In these prose narratives, mainly concentrated in the second half of the century and largely forgotten today, the torture scene recurs often (it is the subject of the frontispiece of one of the first novels in the genre, published in 1720),[36] sometimes emphasizing the cruelty of the torturers, sometimes the heroism of the tortured. Many of these novels present a generally positive image of the Indian, even though scenes of war and captivity are included. Military prowess itself is in certain cases glorified, but elsewhere nonmilitary attributes of Indians are the ones valued in spite of "that pernicious principle of glory, which delights in war and slaughter."[37]

Whether Indian violence is represented as noble or ignoble in these literary works, it is always treated in a serious vein, as the nature of the subject might seem to dictate. There is, however, an exception—perhaps unique—in the major English novel *The Expedition of Humphry Clinker* (1771) by Tobias Smollett. For in a secondary plot development Smollett manages the tour de force of treating torture with humor.

Near the middle of the novel, during the course of their peregrinations in Great Britain, the entourage of the protagonist Matthew Bramble encounters the Scottish lieutenant Lismahago. He is a quixotic character who, as he tells his story, had been sent to America to fight in the French and Indian War, had lost his scalp at Ticonderoga, and subsequently had been captured, along with a fellow soldier named Murphy, by Miami Indians. The sequel, as recounted by Lismahago, shows that Smollett had some acquaintance with the available literature on North American Indians, which he manipulates for comic effect. Murphy, the younger of the two prisoners, should have been adopted to replace a dead warrior and marry his intended wife: "But in passing through the different whigwhams or villages of the Miamis, poor Murphy was so mangled by the women and children, who have the privilege of torturing all prisoners in their passage, that, by the time they arrived ... he was rendered unfit for the purposes of marriage." For this reason he must finally be burned at the stake: "The Indians themselves allowed that Murphy died with great heroism, singing, as his death song, the *Drimmendoo*, in concert with Mr Lismahago, who was present at the solemnity."[38]

The comic punch line, though, comes with the reaction to Lismahago's tale of Tabitha, Matthew Bramble's sister, who is looking for a husband: "The description of poor Murphy's sufferings ... extracted some sighs from the breast of Mrs Tabby: when she understood he had been rendered unfit for marriage, she began to spit, and ejaculated, 'Jesus, what cruel barbarians!'"[39] Seen through the lens of Smollett's comic vision, then, the horror usually provoked by Indian violence is conjured away by irony.

Looking at these representations of the Indian in a context of intense conflict and hostility, one is struck by the diversity, and often the ambiguity, of the attitudes expressed by the Anglo-American colonizers. While the zero degree of encounter is strongly encouraged by the structural basis of the historical situation, it is only the far limit toward which discourse on Indians tends. Often the feelings that surface are mixed or mitigated, notably in those who have had firsthand experience of violent contact: soldiers and captives. Even Robert Rogers, who was a professional Indian fighter, after the Seven Years' War published a verse play in which the rebel chief Pontiac is the tragic hero, portrayed as noble although blind, and as motivated in part by legitimate griefs against the English.[40]

As for captives, John Slover is typical of the kind of vacillation or hesitation between the two cultures experienced by many of them. He had been captured before, as a boy of eight, and had lived twelve years in all with native tribes, six years with the Miamis who had captured him, then six more with Shawnees. In 1773, on the occasion of a prisoner exchange, he was prevailed upon by white relatives to leave the "life of a savage," but, as he comments in his account, he did so "with some reluctance, this manner of life having become natural to me, inasmuch as I had scarcely known any other." About ten years later, though, after having served in the Continental Army early in the War of Independence, Slover agreed to act as a guide for Crawford's expedition. At the moment of his capture, he was recognized by one of his captors, who belonged to one of the tribes he had earlier lived with. (Slover does not say which.) In a gesture that reveals the uncomfortable in-between status of the newly captured man, the Indian then, as Slover recounts it, "came up and spoke to me calling me by my Indian name, Mannucheothee, and upbraiding me for coming to war against them." From the Indian's point of view, Slover was a compatriot who had betrayed them. In spite of this betrayal, Slover was subsequently accorded special treatment—left unbound and invited to war dances and councils—that suggests he was still considered a member of his tribe by adoption. Only when a general council of all the allied Ohio Indians came to an overall decision was Slover condemned to death, which he succeeded in evading, along with the remaining prisoners.[41]

In a certain number of cases, several of which became famous, even after severe mistreatment at the hands of Indians the captive finally chose to remain with them when it became possible to return to "civilization." In doing so he or she became a "white Indian."[42] Such was the case of John Tanner, captured in 1790 at the age of nine by a band of Ojibwe near his father's homestead in Kentucky on the Ohio River. Taken north by the Ojibwes, Tanner lived in the Great Lakes area with Ottawa and Ojibwe bands for almost thirty years. He finally decided to return to Kentucky and later became an interpreter for the Indian agent and ethnologist Henry Schoolcraft, but was never able to readapt to life in white society.[43]

Even better known than Tanner was Mary Jemison. In her old age she, like Tanner, told her story to a white man, James Everett Seaver, who took it down and published it in 1824. *A Narrative of the Life of Mrs. Mary Jemison* was an immediate success and was often republished (with considerable editorial transformations) throughout the nineteenth and into the early twentieth century.[44] Although at the moment of her capture in 1758 she had seen her parents, two brothers, and a sister killed, she continued until the end of her long life to live voluntarily in the Seneca community that had adopted her. Though in her memoir she confides that some warrior practices distress her,[45] her pride in being an Indian and sense of well-being living with the Senecas are evident throughout. In one passage she exclaims, "No people can live more happy than the Indians did in times of peace."[46]

Neither the overall context nor the particular harshness of personal experience, then, leads necessarily to the zero degree of encounter. But the logic of the face-to-face of modernity with its Other often brought those who fully identified with commercial civilization, or those who profited most from it, close to that polar extreme. There was certainly a pragmatic point of view that recommended compromise and cohabitation. James Adair, a trader, but one whose long relationship with Indians had partially drawn him into their way of life, strongly advised his British compatriots to follow this course. In his magnum opus on the Indians he insists, "It is certainly our interest, as a trading people, to use proper measures to conciliate [the] affections [of the Indians]; for whether we are conquerors, or conquered, we are always great losers in an Indian war."[47]

Thus Adair attempts to encourage a conciliatory approach by appealing to precisely what makes the Indian the Other of Anglo-American society: commercial calculation. This advice, however, was not always heeded; increasingly as the century progressed, the opposite inclination came to the fore: to see the Indian as irremediably an enemy, who must be totally removed or destroyed. Signs of this developing attitude are to be found at midcentury, during the French and Indian War. In 1757 the General Court of Massachusetts published an edict that promised three hundred pounds in bounty for each scalp of an "enemy Indian." Since no specific military target was indicated, the term could apply to any Indian and the edict amounted to declaring open hunting season on Indians.[48]

Reduced to an absolute negative otherness, the Indian as irreducible enemy was dehumanized, identified with the bestial or the diabolic. In this perspective his elimination, pure and simple, could come to seem desirable. In the preceding century one also finds statements of radical dehumanization, as in Cotton Mather's accounts of "King Philip's War" in which he calls Indians "wolves," "serpents," "monsters," and "Fierce Things in the Shape of Men."[49] But it is in the eighteenth century, especially near its end, with the victory of the Patriots in the War of Independence that the threshold is sometimes crossed and an actual desire to exterminate expressed.

In 1764, after having suppressed the Indian revolt in the Ohio region, Henri Bouquet presented an ultimatum to those he had defeated—Delawares, Shawnees, and Mingos—accompanied by the threat that it was in the power of the English "totally to extirpate you from being a people."[50] But in that case the statement was aimed at a particular Indian population and used as a means of pressuring them to accept the terms of capitulation the English wanted to impose. During and after the Revolutionary War, however, it became increasingly acceptable to envisage and call for the general extinction of the indigenous peoples of the continent, who were henceforth an obstacle to the advance of the new nation, which became a standard-bearer of the values of modernity.[51] In his study of American settler colonialism Walter Hixson sees the Gnadenhütten massacre of 1782 as emblematic and a sign that a turning point had been reached. The Moravian mission had embodied the possibility of accommodation between Indians and colonial settlers, but the massacre there pointed to the fact that henceforth for many "*the very existence* of Indians [was] an impediment to individual and national aspirations."[52]

We find a brutally explicit statement of this perspective in Brackenridge's remarks in a letter to the editor appended to *Narratives of a Late Expedition against the Indians*. "I subjoin," he begins, "some observations with regard to the animals, vulgarly called Indians." A series of identifications of the Indian with different animals follows—pigs, cattle, and finally the buffalo. "Would you ask a buffalo to grant you land?"[53] Brackenridge asks, before concluding that the Indians have no right to the lands they occupy since they do not use them.

But beyond this dehumanization Brackenridge does not hesitate to assert that the North American natives *deserve to be annihilated*. It is precisely their violence that founds this proposition. "The tortures which they exercise on the bodies of their prisoners, justify extermination," he claims in one passage, and he returns to the idea a page later, using the same vocabulary; the fact that they are murderers constitutes "a sufficient order to exterminate the whole brood." He develops a further train of thought

The Zero Degree of the Other · 115

that makes clear the racist underpinning of his point of view. Musing, at first, that he would be rather disposed to let the "savages" live if they demonstrated their willingness to renounce war and torture, he retracts the point immediately: "Even reforming from these practices, they ought not to live: These nations are so degenerate from the life of man … and so incapable of all civilization, that it is dangerous to the good order of the world that they should exist in it." The proof of their incorrigibility, according to Brackenridge, is that even if they are raised in "civilization" the Indians "retain the temper of their race."[54]

Here, then, is an unambiguous expression of the true zero degree of the encounter between modernity and its Other. As we see, the violence exercised by Indians is cited by Brackenridge as the primary indicator of their absolute otherness, their inferiority to "civilized" men, and the threat they represent. In fact, however, the relationship of Indian violence to Anglo-American modernity is complex, since it is linked at the same time to the premodern specificity of Indian societies, to their resistance to the imperial incursion of modernity, and also to a certain extent to their involvement in some of its networks. As an expression of the cult of personal honor associated with uncompromising commitment of self to a tribal community, it stands sharply opposed to the ethos of modernity as it developed in the attitudes and behaviors of Anglo-Americans, notably in their relation to war and violence.[55] But Indian violence was exacerbated—as well as transformed—on the one hand by the struggle against the carriers of modernity and on the other by the involvement of the Indians in one of its manifestations, albeit a complex, multifarious, ambiguous one: the fur trade, which put Indian groups in competition with one other.[56] In the perspective of the zero degree, however, Indian violence is experienced simply as a "bad" alterity, an absolute negative difference with respect to modern civilization (which of course ignores "civilized" violence altogether).

In the case of Brackenridge this rejection of the Indian, carried to its most extreme, genocidal conclusions, is asserted in the name of Enlightenment values.[57] Yet such an ideological linkage is by no means a necessary one. As we saw, Freneau's work is split between a romantic and an Enlightenment perspective, but nowhere in his articulations of the latter does he express hatred and the desire to annihilate the Indian. It should be added, though, as several historians of ideas have argued, that the contradictory conceptions and initiatives of Enlightenment "liberals" on the Indian question—notably those of Jefferson and the Jeffersonians—contributed more finally to the subsequent destruction of Indians and Indian culture than did the radical will to do the same expressed by others.[58]

"ADVENTURE" IN INDIAN COUNTRY

The zero degree of the encounter with the Amerindian cannot be limited, however, to the rhetoric of rejection, hatred, and ultimately extermination. In terms of writing, and of the kinds of experience that it conveys, the notion should also be extended to depictions of the confrontation in the form of "adventure." For adventure is one mode of relation to the Other that tends to limit contact to an externalized minimum and to focus on aggression or the possibility of aggression in the contact. While in the preceding century encounters with Indians were generally figured quite differently (though in ways that also often tended to the zero degree), starting in the eighteenth century the narrative of adventure came to be a major form of representation.

Adventure, as I use it here, is a form of narrative that focuses on external events, ones that happen to individuals or small groups and that involve chance, or at least the unexpected, and danger or risk. While seventeenth-century texts tend to frame relations with Indians by the unified Puritan community and to see them as ultimately determined by God's will,[59] with the eighteenth-century tendency toward secularization and individualism the literature of encounter with Indians often takes the form of adventure. Such narratives depict experiences of contact with Indians of an individual (or individuals), treated as such, and those experiences notably feature contingency and danger.

This is not the case—except episodically—in the historical-descriptive genre, in which the subject is a collective, but all of the genres that involve a narrator or individual protagonist are potential generators of adventure. It is not enough, though, for the elements of danger and contingency to be present. The account must also be written *as* adventure, creating, through literary means, an adventure "effect." This sort of effect is typically established through the dramatization of a persona, however rudimentary, who is the subjective center of the adventure; often this is the first-person narrator. The state of mind of this subject is explored or at least evoked, and the reader is brought to identify with it. The personality of the subject may be more or less active, sometimes heroic (the "adventurer" type), sometimes passive and suffering (the victim). Certain narrative techniques recur frequently to elicit vicarious emotions of adventure in the reader: the build-up of excitement, fear, or horror; the intimation of possibilities (suspense, foreboding); the continual introduction of sudden, unexpected new developments; and the narrow escape from danger. In a repeated cycle we are given a build-up of tension, a release from it, and then more of the same.

In eighteenth-century encounter literature the dimension of adventure is often present in texts that are addressed to a broad reading public. Clearly this kind of public, both in North America and in England, was strongly drawn to the particular mix of ingredients in Indian adventure: the combination of extreme forms of uncertainty, danger, and violence, potential or real, with the exoticism of mysterious, "primitive" peoples, these two aspects often being linked. This literature, at least in its purest forms, constitutes another manifestation of the zero degree of contact, for the version of encounter that it presents is one in which the Indian is reduced to the status of pure object. He functions solely as the source of danger, or fear of it, for the protagonist-subject of the adventure. The Indian's difference—potentially rich in what it can reveal—thus becomes depleted to the extreme, as it is objectified and limited to producing the sense of danger necessary for the subject of the adventure.

As already mentioned, a current of eighteenth-century English and American novels depict encounter with North American Indians. Many of these would qualify as adventures in the sense that I have been discussing, and in some cases their titles use the word itself.[60] Here, though, I will not be dealing with fictional representations but with several texts that report "true" incidents. They illustrate how nonfiction accounts can construct adventure through the use of techniques similar to those used in fiction, and how this form of narrative produces a truncated image of the Indian that largely excludes authentic cultural encounter. I will take one example from each of the two nonfiction genres discussed earlier that feature individual protagonists: the military and the captivity account.

THOMAS MORRIS'S MILITARY JOURNAL

In terms of mere quantity of dangerous encounter, and especially in view of the peculiar nature of colonial American warfare, one might expect the military journal to be a prize terrain for the discourse of adventure. William Smith, the author of the report on Bouquet's expedition in the Ohio region in 1764, shows that he is aware of the adventure potential of his narrative. In the introduction he muses on the particularity of his subject:

> Those who have only experienced the severities and dangers of a campaign in Europe, can scarcely form an idea of what is to be done and endured in an American war.... In an American campaign every thing is terrible; the face of the country, the climate, the enemy ...; simple death is the least misfortune, which can happen to [American soldiers].... If the actions of these rude campaigns are of less dignity, the adventures in them are more interesting to the heart, and more amusing to the imagination, than the events of a regular war.[61]

However, for the adventures that transpired during these "rude campaigns" to be "interesting to the heart" and "amusing to the imagination" they had to be written in a way that made them so, and this sine qua non is often not fulfilled in the genre of the military journal. The *Historical Account of the Expedition against the Ohio Indians* does not do so generally, even though it was authored by a cultivated noncombatant.[62] The explanation doubtless lies in the purpose of the writing and the public addressed, the former being to provide practical instruction on the conditions of Indian warfare to the latter, consisting of those involved or who might become involved in this type of conflict. If we add to this the fact that in the most common case the author was a person whose principal activity was soldiering and whose concern was with the pragmatics of combat, it is understandable that in the writing of such accounts events bloody and fraught with peril seldom become adventures. In the introduction to his *Journals*, for instance, Robert Rogers informs the reader that they were written under difficult conditions in the field and that they are limited to the recounting of "matters of fact."[63] Not surprisingly these matters of fact rarely come to life in the text, and the characteristics of adventure are almost entirely absent.

One case in which an account by a military man is written as adventure is the *Journal of Captain Thomas Morris*, published in exceptional circumstances for that kind of material. Although written immediately after the events it recounts—a mission in 1764 into the Illinois territories, in the immediate aftermath of Pontiac's rebellion—it was published only much later, in 1791, as part of a collection of literary pieces by the same author entitled *Miscellanies in Prose and Verse*. The journal was thus presented as a literary production, and although no explicit mention is made of it, the manuscript probably underwent a later rewriting to make it more suitable to the intended public.[64] However that may be, Morris's journal presents his trials and tribulations with Indians in the guise of an adventure story. He seems in fact to have conceived of it as such, since in the "preamble" he uses the term *adventure* several times in alluding to the experience he is setting before the reader.[65]

The journal begins by establishing a sense of foreboding in the suggestion that the author has been chosen for a doomed mission. The aide-de-camp of his commander, General Bradstreet, approaches Morris and asks him to recommend officers who would have the necessary caliber to take possession of the Illinois lands for the British, but immediately rejects each of Morris's suggestions. When Morris begins to volunteer himself, the officer accepts before he has finished his sentence, and when Morris asks why this was not proposed in the first place, "he said, with an oath: 'It is not a thing to be asked of any man'" (2). Morris is then treated to dinner with the general himself, who offers to send with him, as a translator, a French prisoner who has been sentenced to hang but will be pardoned to go on the mission. As a final sign of ill augur, the aide-de-camp tells Morris that unless certain Indian "deputies" arrive beforehand, an Ottawa village where he is to spend the first night will be attacked in the middle of the night. But, he adds cavalierly, "that . . . will make no difference in your affairs" (3). Only as Morris is stepping into his canoe to depart do the deputies finally appear.

One day out on their voyage, Morris reports, "passing by the encampment of the Miamis, while I was admiring the regularity and contrivance of it, I heard a yell, and found myself surrounded by Pondiac's army, consisting of six hundred savages, with tommahawks in their hands, who beat my horse, and endeavoured to separate me from my Indians." "By their malicious smiles," he adds, "it was easy for me to guess their intention of putting me to death" (5–6). But Morris is then brought before Pontiac himself, who protects him from those who wish to kill him by insisting on the importance of allowing safe conduct to ambassadors.

What follows is a vertiginous tale in which Morris is repeatedly buffeted between two kinds of treatment: extreme hostility, often with murderous intent, and respect, even occasional friendliness (though this is not the case with Pontiac). It becomes clear that Morris has stepped into a highly charged and confused situation, in which many different tribal groups are intermingled, only very partially under the control of Pontiac, and in which Indians and groups of Indians act out upon Morris their differing, volatile, mostly antagonistic attitudes toward the British.[66] As Morris persists in penetrating deeper and deeper into rebellious territory in a desperate attempt to fulfill his mission, he is often saved from torture and death only in extremis.

For example, immediately after being saved by Pontiac's intervention, Morris is almost killed in an unruly attack that ironically originates from an action by a supposedly friendly Indian of his own party. This man, a Mohawk, has robbed him of "almost every thing" and sold rum to the young Ottawa warriors present. They get drunk, and one of them swipes at Morris with his knife. Godefroi, the French translator, grabs his arm just in time. "He certainly saved my life," comments Morris, "for I was sitting, and could not have avoided the blow though I saw it coming" (10). Morris senses that others also wish to kill him, and he first hides under a mattress, then disguises himself in Indian clothing and retreats to a neighboring field outside the encampment. Here he is visited by several chiefs, Kickapoos and Miamis, who speak kindly to him and tell him he is welcome. These encouraging signs are, however, immediately contradicted when a Huron woman, whose son has been killed by the English, berates him. Later, when Morris has returned to the Indian camp, he is insulted by a Delaware, who, "passing by the cabin where I lay, called out in broken English: 'D—d son of a b—ch'" (11).

Much of the later narrative continues in this vein: ominous signs, close calls, moments of good fortune only to be followed by another dire predicament. The story is sometimes awkwardly or confusedly rendered, but there is a clear attempt to interest readers and engage their emotions. Two passages are particularly striking in different ways—one for its whimsical linkage of chance and the mix of cultures, the other for its evocation of the most fearful of adventures imaginable. In the first we are shown how Morris was saved on one occasion by none other than Shakespeare. Several pages before the incident itself the author mentions, apparently in passing, that one of the chiefs favorable to him "made me a present of a volume of Shakespear's plays; a singular gift from a savage" (12). The Shakespeare volume then disappears from the narrative and seems to have been brought in solely for its incongruity. A week further into the trip, though, the expedition stops at a village. In reporting this the author immediately informs the reader of what he was to discover only later: that here again the natives have designs on his life. But "I had the good fortune," Morris explains, "to stay in the canoe, reading the tragedy of Anthony and Cleopatra.... Though perfectly ignorant of their intention, I pushed the canoe over to the other side of the river" (17).

The presentation of this episode is rather poorly handled. Morris flatly apprises the reader of the villagers' malevolent aims at the outset, precluding any effect of dawning awareness or sudden revelation on the part of the reader. Moreover there is no real follow-up. The story trails off, and the reader never knows how Morris subsequently left the village without being caught. The story remains an isolated anecdote, yet its point is not lost. In a highly fortuitous sense Morris was saved by one Indian from other Indians through the mediation of the ultimate icon of English culture.

The second passage is far more somber in tone and involves the dreaded fate of torture. The scene is part of an extended series of developments that follow a seesaw pattern of repeated tension and release but interrupts it at a moment of heightened intensity. Godefroi, the French interpreter, has again intervened with a saving gesture, reminding an angry Miami chief that if Morris were killed the chief's children, who are in Detroit with the British, would be in danger. The chief has relented but inexplicably does not impede another, who has been pursuing Morris, from tying him by the neck to a post. Suddenly all present are preparing for torture. At this point the author pauses in the account to insert a description of usual Indian practices of torture, explaining, "These modes of torture I should not have mentioned, if the gentleman who advised me to publish my journal, had not thought it necessary" (21). Once having made sure the reader understands what the prospect of torture by Indians means, Morris adds, "It may easily be conceived what I must have felt at the thought of such horrors which I was to endure," and he describes feeling "myself as it were going to plunge into a gulf, vast, immeasurable," and then falling into "torpor and insensibility" (22). Morris is unexpectedly extricated from this fearful situation by the intervention of a Miami chief who suddenly appears on horseback, and the author's vicissitudes continue to unfold.

Morris's text clearly presents his experience in the contested Illinois territory as an adventure in the sense that I have given the term, manifesting many of its typical stylistic and structural characteristics. In this textual format the Indian plays a severely reduced role, one that is negative and external, appearing only in the guise of the frightening, unpredictable adversary who at any moment can become deadly. The English protagonist who undergoes the adventure (he is portrayed mainly as a victim) makes no attempt to analyze the Indians' motivations but only parries their attacks. The area of contact with Indians is almost entirely physical. When an element of culture is momentarily introduced, it is an English one (Shakespeare). Near the end of his narrative Morris does make a few general comments in which he shows some sympathy for Indians who are exploited by English traders (and praises the contrasting French policy toward them). On the whole, though, Morris's journal remains firmly positioned within the limiting perspective of adventure.

THE CAPTIVITY OF ALEXANDER HENRY

Unlike the military journal, the captivity account, starting in the eighteenth century, is frequently cast in the adventure mold. The events that made up its raw material were, from the point of view of the captive, marked to the highest degree by peril, contingency, and the unforeseen, and the adventure mode could readily be made to serve the purposes of authors seeking wide readership. The nature of the captive's experiences, on which the narrative was based, usually dictated a tripartite structure: first, the capture, often after a struggle in which there was the immanent prospect of sudden death; then the compelled voyage to the Indian homeland, during which many accidents could occur that might cause suffering and death; finally, arrival and determination of the prisoner's fate—adoption, slavery, "redemption," or torture and death. Built into the very situation was sustained suspense, an intense, life-or-death uncertainty. If the emotions of the victim were at all effectively delved into, a powerful adventure "effect" could be produced. In many of these accounts there is indeed a quality of descent into the "heart of darkness."

The captivity narrative that I will look at here is an example of the overlap and interpenetration of genres often found in the literature of encounter with Indians. The work from which it is taken, *Travels and Adventures in Canada and the Indian Territories between 1760 and 1776*, by Alexander Henry the Elder,[67] was written by a combatant in the French and Indian War (though no longer a soldier when captured), and, as the title indicates, involves free travels as well as captivity. The presence of the word *adventure* suggests a conscious intent on the part of its author, as was the case with Morris. Like that author's journal, Henry's work was published only long after the period involved, in 1809. Henry's captivity also took place during the period of Pontiac's rebellion, though in quite different circumstances from those that gave rise to Morris's experiences. After his demobilization in 1760, Henry became a fur trader and was one of the first British American traders to move into the western lands newly won from the French. It was at Michilimackinac, a key fort and trading post in the Great Lakes region, that Henry was captured during the massacre that occurred there in early June 1763. He was one of the

British who survived the massacre, and his eyewitness account is not only a valuable source for historians but also a striking illustration of captivity written in the mode of adventure.

The Michilimackinac massacre, which became notorious in the annals of frontier history, was the result of a stratagem on the part of the Ojibwes of Mackinac Island and nearby, who were answering the call of Pontiac, from Detroit, to attack the British at forts all over the area in an attempt to drive them out, allowing the French to reestablish control as a bastion against the advance of British settlement. As such, the assault was in fact the opening salvo of what came to be known as Pontiac's War. Although the attack itself succeeded, the situation was very quickly reversed due to the fact that other Indians in the area—especially the Ottawas of a village in the vicinity and the Ojibwes of further distant Sault Sainte Marie—had not been included in the plan and did not agree with it. This political context for the massacre, however, is not laid out by Henry in his narrative. Instead he recounts it largely as a personal adventure.[68]

The account opens with Henry's return to Fort Michilimackinac after an absence, in late May 1763, when he is warned by several traders of the hostile mood of the Indians encamped in the area, Indians who far outnumber the soldiers and merchants in the fort. Henry attempts to alert the fort's commander, Major Etherington, to the danger, only to be laughed at. Yet by his own admission, "if this officer neglected admonition, on his part, so did I, on mine."[69] The author then explains that a year earlier, soon after his first arrival at Michilimackinac, he had been adopted by Wawatam, an Ojibwe (Henry uses the term Chippewa) trading at the fort who was directed in a dream to adopt an Englishman. Now, in the first days of June, Wawatam visits Henry several times, speaking ominously of the "noise of evil birds" and attempting to persuade Henry leave the fort. But Henry disregards the warning, explaining, "Nothing induced me to believe that serious mischief was at hand" (74, 76). However, when another Chippewa tells Henry that on the king's birthday the Chippewas are to play the Sauks at "baggatiway" (lacrosse) just outside the fort, and that the match is to be attended by the commander, Henry tries again to convince Etherington that trouble is afoot. Enigmatically, then, this textual prelude to the massacre attempts to convince the reader that Henry was both suspicious and unconcerned as disaster approached.

Henry's text goes on to relate the horrific event once the atmosphere of suspense has been created. Seemingly by mistake the lacrosse ball is hurled over the wall of the fort during the match, and Indians run in as if to retrieve it. Then mayhem breaks loose. Henry has chosen not to watch the game and is writing letters. Brought to the window by war cries, he sees his fellow Englishmen being slaughtered and scalped. He takes refuge in the house of one of the "Canadian inhabitants of the fort," who are "neither opposing the Indians nor suffering injury" (79). Hiding in the garret, he looks outside again, to behold butchered bodies and the "barbarian conquerors" drinking their blood. "I was shaken," Henry tells the reader, "not only with horror, but with fear. The sufferings which I witnessed, I seemed on the point of experiencing" (81).

Indeed Indians soon are at the door of Monsieur Langlade, the neighbor to whom he has fled,[70] and then they are at the garret door. The text goes on:

> The state of my mind will be imagined. Arrived at the door, some delay was occasioned by the absence of the key, and a few moments were thus allowed me, in which to look around for a hiding-place. In one corner of the garret was a heap of those vessels of birch-bark, used in maple-sugar making.... The door was unlocked, and opening, and the Indians ascending the stairs, before I had completely crept into a small opening, which presented itself, at one end of the heap. An instant after, four Indians entered the room, all armed with tomahawks, and all besmeared with blood, upon every part of their bodies. The die appeared to be cast. I could scarcely breathe; but I thought that the throbbing of my heart occasioned a noise loud enough to betray me. (82)

The Indians do not discover Henry's hiding place. They leave, and Henry falls asleep, "exhausted as I was, by the agitation of my mind" (83).

The saga goes on. Monsieur Langlade, fearing for his family's safety, informs the Indians of Henry's presence, and the dread induced by their mounting the garret steps and bursting in is again evoked. This time they are drunk, and one of them, whom Henry knows personally, "seized me, with one hand, by the collar of the coat, while in the other he held a large carving-knife, as if to plunge it into my breast; his eyes, meanwhile, were fixed stedfastly on mine. At length, after some seconds, of the most anxious suspense, he dropped his arm, saying, 'I won't kill you!' To this he added ... that, on a certain occasion, he had lost a brother, whose name was Musinigon, and I should be called after him" (87–88). A moment of choice is depicted here which in many captivities occurred later, when the captive arrived at the village of the captors.[71] This adoption of Henry does not, however, put an end to his immanent danger, for in the anarchic situation reigning at the fort he is several times within an inch of being killed by an Indian who holds a grudge against him, even before the prisoners are embarked on their voyage to the captors' home.

During that trip by canoe there are more accidents, reversals, rising and falling fortunes. The Ojibwe captors have no sooner departed than they are waylaid and robbed of their prisoners by the nearby Ottawas, who resent not having been consulted before the taking of the fort. At this point Henry interjects an authorial aside: "The reader's imagination is here distracted by the variety of our fortunes ... who were the sport, or the victims, of a series of events, more like dreams than realities, more like fiction than truth!" (96). All parties return to Michilimackinac, and a council meeting follows between Ojibwes and Ottawas, in which the former attempt to convince the latter to join them against the British. The fate of the prisoners hangs in the balance overnight, since, as Henry informs the reader, "the Indians rarely make their answers till the day after they have heard the arguments offered" (97). The prisoners are finally returned to the Ojibwes.

Before departure from Michilimackinac to resume the voyage, Wawatam, who had earlier warned Henry of the impending massacre, reappears and is allowed to keep Henry as a brother, so Henry here changes adoptive families.[72] Although thenceforth protected by Wawatam, he, like all the prisoners, is in continual danger of violence from other members of the returning war party or from those who join it. On occasion he is hidden or dressed as an Indian to hide his identity. One day he sees seven corpses of white men and is "informed, that a certain chief, called, by the Canadians, Le

Grand Sable, ... having been absent when the war begun, [was] now desirous of manifesting to the Indians at large, his hearty concurrence in what they had done" (104). By a stroke of luck Henry has been spared their fate.

After arriving at the Ojibwe village that is their destination, Henry continues to be insulted by other Indians. Only when he accompanies his adoptive brother Wawatam's family to their wintering ground, where they are relatively isolated, does full integration into Indian life ensue, and the narrative changes. No longer a captive but rather a family member, Henry becomes for a time a "white Indian." The text then ceases to be an adventure and becomes a proto-ethnographic portrait of Ojibwe life patterns.

Like the period of adventure, though, Henry's life on the other side also comes to an end. He returns finally to fur trading, and in the second part of the book the narrative reverts to the form of the travel account with which it began. While some adopted captives chose to remain permanently with their Indian captors, Henry, after some hesitation, did not. He notes that after a time living with his Ojibwe band he felt his needs diminishing, to the point where barter for simple "necessaries" seemed able to satisfy them (116), and he speaks of the increasing pleasure he took in hunting and other Indian activities that gave him a sense of "personal freedom" (127). He continued to be reluctant, however, to fully accept this way of life. There remained "the idea of which I could not divest my mind, that I was living among savages," and he continued to hear "the whispers of a lingering hope, that I should one day be released from it" (132).

So when he and his Indian family at one point visit the British fort of Niagara he decides to return to his previous life. He first agrees to accompany General Bradstreet on his expedition to lift the siege of Detroit, but only on condition that once the military operation is concluded he will be aided in retrieving his equipment and merchandise at Michilimackinac. Knowing that his goods remained there, Henry comments, "The reader will ... be far from attributing to me any idle or unaccountable motive, when he finds me returning to the scene of my misfortunes" (181).

Throughout the noncaptivity portions of his work Henry appears to be ruled largely by mercantile interests and motivations. Having originally gone to Michilimackinac because the region around it was reputed to be richer in furs than anywhere else (10), once there he obstinately ignores the warnings of danger so as "to remain with my property" (39). The travel that he recounts in the second part of the book is undertaken with the general purpose of developing and extending his network of Indian trade, and at one moment he is also sidetracked into pursuing the mirage of an easy fortune, becoming a partner in a gold and silver mining venture. The enterprise fails miserably, but only after having prospected several times, fruitlessly, on islands in northeastern Lake Superior held to be sacred and legendary by Ojibwe Indians in the area (part 2, chaps. 4–7).

Following his captivity Henry seems to have fully readopted his former role and mentality. In recounting his later trading sojourns with Indians—in areas extending into the far North and West—he sometimes offers descriptions of native customs, but always does so in a purely neutral manner, unemotionally and without value judgments, as he had declared in the work's preface to be his general intention (vi). Clearly the Indians have again become for him what they were before: "customers," as he calls them explicitly in one passage (324).[73]

At the end of this chapter on the zero degree of encounter, I have chosen to focus on Alexander Henry the Elder's captivity narrative, embedded within a larger travel account, as an instance of the adventure mode. His overall work, though, is part of the generic tradition that I will now take up. The accounts of travel in Indian territories that will be dealt with in subsequent chapters are highly diversified in terms of the national and social backgrounds of their authors and also of the degree and quality of their engagement with Indian cultures. As an English trader, and one with a thoroughgoing commercial mentality, Alexander Henry stands at a far remove from the travelers I will begin with in the next chapter: two Frenchmen, one an aristocrat and the other a Jesuit priest.

CHAPTER FIVE

Accounts of Travel in New France
Lahontan and Charlevoix

In my view the travel account holds the preeminent place in the literature of encounter with Amerindians, moving decisively away from the zero degree of violence and adventure, though not excluding it entirely. I begin with two French voyagers and their narratives, which will serve as cultural counterpoints for the Anglo-American accounts that follow. Before taking up the French texts, though, I will make some preliminary remarks on the travel account as a genre and on New France and its travelers.

THE TRAVEL ACCOUNT

The type of text that I am concerned with here is strictly speaking a subgenre of the travel account per se, though undoubtedly a large proportion of travel accounts fall within it: it is an ethnographic account, which deals with encounters during the course of travel with peoples who are different from the social community to which the traveler belongs. There exist, of course, accounts of travel on the open seas and in areas devoid of human habitation and accounts of travel in which the traveler does not leave his or her own cultural environment. But sea voyages often end by arrival in unfamiliar lands, much "wilderness" is at least sparsely inhabited, and cultural differences can appear even near the point of departure. Consequently encounter with some Other is characteristic of and often one of the main focuses of a large portion of travel literature as a whole.[1]

The travel account, and more specifically the ethnographic version, is not easy to define since, as has often been noted,[2] its contours are fuzzy and permeable, and it mixes often with other genres. I adopt here the minimal definition proposed by Friedrich Wolfzettel, cited in the introduction: "a personal discourse (most often in the first person) recounting an experience of encounter with the Other, that is, of a real voyage."[3] Using different formulations, and with some variations, other authors who have studied the genre have articulated similar notions.[4] For Mary Campbell—who has traced its prehistory from late antiquity to the Renaissance, when she contends that it first appeared in its true form—the travel account is above all a "witness." The genre as such aims for "truth" in its representation of the Other and founds its authority on the narration of a personal experience.[5] However, this narration is in general a reconstruction or rewriting of the raw material of experience based on notes, a journal, or a log made during the trip itself. In its final form the travel account is thus a literary creation and conforms, or at least makes reference to, a tradition and a set of implicit rules of the genre.[6]

Campbell sees in this new genre that arises on the threshold of the modern era a "literary instrument of consciousness." As a "genre of cultural translation," it possesses a crucial potential that in her view verges on the "ethical." In regard to a text by Sir Walter Raleigh that she considers to be one of the first travel accounts in the full sense, Campbell claims that the author is already "self-conscious about the problem of presenting difference in terms that neither inadvertently domesticate nor entirely alienate." Campbell recognizes, however, that the birth of the travel account is only a "new opportunity for [European] consciousness," a possibility of "cultural translation" that is not always achieved, and she acknowledges that many aspects of the texts are "reductive, false, and inadequate."[7] The highest degree of the potentiality of the genre is, according to Campbell, an actual reversal of perspective on the part of the traveler, who comes to identify entirely with the encountered Other. She cites the "Relacion" of Cabeza de Vaca as a rare—and precocious—example of such a fulfillment of the genre.[8]

For Campbell the potentiality of the genre is linked to its individual, subjective narrative voice—one of the genre's principal defining traits, as I have suggested. (Without the presence of such a voice, a text cannot be considered a travel account.) Other elements are often added to this core, however. In many cases the account of the trip per se is combined with a second type of discourse, which is related to another genre. A synchronic and synthetic form of presentation that makes generalizations is juxtaposed with the diachronic relation of particular events that occurred during the journey. First and foremost these generalizations involve the customs and character of the indigenous peoples encountered, but sometimes the fauna and flora of the areas traversed are also treated. Although the two textual elements are most often separated into distinct sections, in some instances the line of narration is interspersed with generalizing commentary.

The static, synchronic passages that are thus grafted onto many travel accounts are to be associated with chorography, the descriptive genre I have already referred to in several places. In regard to description (often combined with analysis) of Amerindians, some such texts are not joined to a travel account but rather make up the entirety of the work, most notably the Jesuit Joseph-François Lafitau's *Mœurs des sauvages américains comparées aux mœurs des premiers temps* (1724; Customs of the American Natives Compared with the Customs of Ancient Times).[9] More impersonal than the recounting of an individual itinerary, the synthetic presentation lends itself particularly well to wholesale borrowing from other authors—the kind of plagiarism that was commonly accepted practice until the nineteenth century. It also testifies to what Pierre Berthiaume calls the "encyclopedic aim haunting the mind of all travelers."[10] The universality of this assertion seems excessive since the generalizing dimension is not found in all travel accounts. As a heterogeneous element, though, it is present often enough to be called typical, if not constitutive, of the genre.[11]

In spite of the habitual presence of these seemingly impersonal descriptive sections or passages in the travel account, in the final analysis it must be said that the authorial point of view controls the text as a whole. The author in principle composes, constructs the presentation of, or at least chooses all the materials used in the text. Consequently a travel account that includes both diachronic and synchronic parts must be considered a single textual entity projecting an authorial perspective. While it is true that in many cases in the eighteenth century editors and ghostwriters—usually anonymous—inflected published work in significant ways, we often have little or no indication of how much and in what respects they modified the text and are obliged to assume the responsibility of the author who signed the work for its entirety.[12]

It was precisely to overcome the limitations of singular authorial points of view that, under the impetus of the encyclopedic spirit of the Enlightenment, large anthologies of travel accounts were published in the eighteenth century (as they were in the Renaissance).[13] Among French publications the most famous was that of l'abbé Prévost, which appeared between 1746 and 1761. In this Enlightenment perspective, as Wolfzettel notes, the individual account "is seen as useful only as one particular document to be inserted in a general collection.... The value of voyages is measured against the critical, encyclopedic ideal."[14] Indeed in her now-classic study, *Anthropologie et histoire au siècle des Lumières* (1971; Anthropology and History in the Century of the Enlightenment), Michèle Duchet conceives of individual travel accounts—of the eighteenth century and earlier—as pieces of empirical documentation, "sources" that provide "observations," data, in short, that must be gathered as evidence but that are only preliminaries for the philosophers' reflection. Only this reflection, in her view, produces knowledge and creates the conditions of possibility of anthropological science.[15] In the perspective of the present work, however, travel accounts in their unique individuality offer more than that and something of a different nature. I am concerned with travel accounts as particular texts rather than as fragments of general documentation, and this focus raises the question of the method of approach I adopt in studying them.

I argued in the introduction to this work that, among the different genres that represent the encounter with Amerindians, the travel account is the one in which the fulfillment of the potential inherent in that situation is most likely to appear. This potential corresponds to the notion of "cultural translation" postulated by Campbell. Such translation as may occur in a travel account is at least partially a form of knowledge, though the knowledge gained is not necessarily encyclopedic in scope. Since the knowledge that a traveler comes to have of the Other is in large part the result of an experience, what is involved is a living form of it that cannot be entirely assimilated with that which is attained by reading or thought. Each way of experiencing and textualizing the encounter is different, and analysis of the travel text should attempt to understand it as a whole, in its complexity and in terms of the multiplicity of its determinations.

Thus, rather than examining the literature of travel in Indian territory by themes, drawing on examples from many texts, I present a limited number of selected works in their entirety—as meaningful totalities, that is, as literary texts—and this includes their synchronic as well as diachronic dimension, when the former is present, the "voyage-as-description" along with the "voyage-as-itinerary," to use Berthiaume's terms.[16]

I will analyze these textual totalities in terms of three distinct aspects: *interaction* (the lived experience of contact), which paradoxically is sometimes present in the generalizing, descriptive sections as well as in the narrative sequences; *understanding* (reading or interpreting the Other), which is at least partly founded on interaction and firsthand observation but also, in some cases, on information furnished by others or gleaned by reading; and *evaluation* (value judgments made about the culture of the Other), either about the whole of the society or culture encountered, or particular elements thereof. Although it is useful to distinguish these categories for the sake of analysis, very often they are linked and intermingled in the texts to be considered.

The encounter with the Other, in all of these aspects, is conditioned by the different contexts of the meeting, on the one hand, and the various sociocultural traits of the traveler, on the other. A multiplicity of factors can come into play in honing the particular lens through which the experience is perceived by the traveler: ethnic or national culture (thus the pertinence of a comparative study) but also social class and more particularized experiences, affiliations, and ideologies (professional, philosophical, religious, political, etc.). I will attempt to identify and examine the parameters that are most relevant in each case. First and foremost in discussing these encounters with the Other of modernity I am concerned with defining the position of the traveler within the matrix of that modernity.

NEW FRANCE

The geopolitical area designated by this name, used in its most inclusive sense—encompassing Louisiana and the "Illinois country" as well as Canada—was immense in 1763, at the moment when France lost it almost entirely. Its contours were, however, far from clearly defined. The region claimed by France covered the greater part of the eastern half of the North American continent below the Hudson's Bay watershed, extending across the North from Cape Breton to west of Lake Superior and running southward to the Gulf of Mexico over a vast territory from the Appalachians at its eastern extremity to an undetermined boundary beyond the Mississippi River in the West.[17] Considered exclusively from the point of view of their surface area, the French colonies were considerably greater than those of the English, which—with the exception of "Rupert's Land" around Hudson's Bay, entirely devoted to the fur trade—were restricted to the Atlantic coastal strip. But their density of population was far less than those of the British coastal colonies, and the mode of occupation of the land extremely different. New France exhibited these differences in relation to the English model of colonization, and some others as well, throughout its history—both in the seventeenth century, when it covered only the Canadian Northeast, and in the eighteenth, when Louisiana and the Illinois country were added. In spite of some points of similarity,[18] a specific set of traits define French colonial society largely by contrast with that of the Anglo-Americans. These traits are highly relevant with respect to the relations of the French with the Amerindians.

At the most general level—and most important, as regards the framework of this study—the degree of advancement of France and its North American colonies toward capitalist modernity was considerably less than in the English case. While they were definitely situated within the zone of the "economy-world" (Wallerstein) that was moving toward the transition to capitalism, they remained clearly behind the Netherlands and England (with their colonies), which dominated this movement—the former in the seventeenth and the latter in the eighteenth century.[19] Centered on the fur trade, the economy of New France was largely commercial, but that sector of colonial commerce was not nearly as productive or as profitable as that of sugar in the Caribbean islands. Its agriculture, much less widespread than in the British colonies, was governed in the Saint Lawrence River valley by a seigneurial system dominated by the aristocracy, which produced little surplus. There landowners in general sought prestige (sometimes through ennoblement) more than profit, and proceeds from the fur trade were more often converted into rents and appointments than into capital investment.[20] Although historians differ to some extent on the relative weight of tradition and modernity in New France, their work suggests overall that while it was engaged in a process similar to that of the English colonies in North America, it stayed behind at an earlier stage of development of that trend.[21] On the basis of their findings it seems safe to say that unlike the English colonies and the early United States, New France never fully effected the transition to a capitalist economy.[22]

New France also differs from the British colonies in the strongly pervasive influence of the Catholic Church and the controlling power of the state. The banning of Huguenot immigration in 1627 ensured that the Catholics—priests, monks, and missionaries—would have a quasi-monopoly on the religious life of the colony. With regard to predominant religious tendencies, I referred in the introduction to this work to Weber's theory that closely associates Protestantism with the inception of capitalism, particularly in the English colonies in America. Similarly to the Protestant ethos (especially in Calvinism), capitalism is characterized by what Weber terms the "disenchantment of the world": the propensity to elimination of magic and the marvelous. On the other hand, although he does not study it in detail, Weber suggests in *The Protestant Ethic and the Spirit of Capitalism* that Catholicism is by nature more open to magic and hostile to capitalism.[23] The case of the French colonies in North America would seem to support this hypothesis. A recent cultural history of New France has demonstrated the importance of magic and "superstition" in the religious universe of its inhabitants,[24] and its socioeconomic evolution never culminated in capitalism.

As for the state, its sovereignty was far more potent in New France than under the British colonial regime, especially after 1663, when Louis XIV personally took charge of the administration of the colony. Throughout the territories claimed by the French, even though it sometimes became diluted in far-flung outposts, the presence of the absolutist state made itself felt. And by its initiatives and regulations the state vigorously counterbalanced the free development of market forces.[25] At the level of ideology, in the context of the extreme authoritarianism cultivated by the Sun King—and as a study of administrative reports from the period shows—the "ideal figure" of a Frenchman was that of a subject owing obedience to a hierarchy.[26]

A final particularity of New France is the one I alluded to at the beginning of this section: geographical distribution of population and land use. Lands used for farming were limited, concentrated for the most part in the Saint Lawrence River valley and along the Mississippi River. Regarding the small areas of French farms in the Illinois country, especially along the Mississippi, a historian of the region in the eighteenth century has recently shown that its nonexpansive system of land use followed a pattern closely resembling that of rural northern France starting in the Middle Ages.[27] The vast majority of the French "colony" was in fact situated in Indian territory, "controlled" by a sparse network of forts, missions, and trading posts. W. J. Eccles, author of *The Canadian Frontier*, recognizes that the meaning of the term *frontier* applied to New France is radically different from the commonly accepted definition based on the Anglo-American model. In a real sense the frontier was everywhere in New France.[28]

The relevance of this aspect of the French colony for relations with Indians is clear. Conflicts around land occupation were minimal compared with those provoked by the Anglo-American advance westward, and this made for a more harmonious coexistence between colonists and natives. There were some exceptions—in particular, exacerbated relations with the Natchez Indians on the southern Mississippi River when the French introduced tobacco plantations nearby in the 1720s—but in general the French intruded far less on Indian lands, and this considerably reduced hostilities between the French and the Indians.[29]

The other traits I have mentioned are equally germane to relations between natives and French colonists. The Catholic version of the Christian faith is closer to Indian religions than is the Protestant, in that Catholics do not carry the "disenchantment of the world" so far and leave room for the marvelous. Moreover Catholic priests, unlike Protestant ministers, in their zeal to convert the native peoples were willing to live in their communities and often showed considerable tolerance—to the extent that Church doctrine authorized it—for Indian beliefs and practices.[30] More than that, in their strenuous effort to bring Catholic doctrine to the Indians Jesuit missionaries often found themselves obliged to translate it into the cultural universe of the natives they were engaging, so that a two-way process occurred, "through which Indians were christianized and Christianity was Indianized."[31]

In regard to the state, because of its power and the ubiquity of its agents imperial policy almost always prevailed over particular interests in dealings with Indians. This policy underwent some variation, but essentially it aimed to impose royal authority and progressively reinforce French governance over the Indians, most often without attempting either to dispossess or to destroy them.[32] In terms of attitudes, the central place occupied by the French ideology of the all-powerful state brought the Indians and the French alike to perceive the stance toward authority and subordination as constituting the main difference between the two peoples.[33] (The principal point of differentiation between Indians and English people, on the other hand, was often seen to be the approach to property and money.) At the same time, though, the *insubordinate* frame of mind of many Frenchmen in New France—aristocrats and peasants and landless poor were all susceptible to this kind of resistance to the imposition of centralized authority from above—provided a terrain on which affinities might be felt with Amerindian ways of living.[34]

WRITERS AND TRAVELERS IN NEW FRANCE

In this context, what writing developed around the encounter with the Indian? What kinds of texts were involved, and from what social groups did their authors come? It should first be said that the literature of New France was for the most part the work of *visitors*, of French people sojourning in the North American colonies for different lengths of time. These residencies were usually followed by a return to France, and in any case the writings were always published in the metropole for a largely French public.[35] Two groups that were more firmly settled in New France did not express themselves in writing, or only rarely: the *habitants*, or farmer colonists, who were considerably less numerous than their English counterparts and often did not have sustained relations with Indians; and, of greater note in relation to the subject at hand, the *coureurs de bois* (literally, "forest runners"), who played a crucial role in colonial life. Contrary to the *habitants*, they were in intimate contact with the natives as agents in the fur trade.

To remedy the textual silence of the *coureurs de bois*, whom he calls "men of the wind," Philippe Jacquin published a study of them several decades ago.[36] In this work Jacquin analyzes the partial acculturation of *coureurs de bois* in the Indian societies with which they were in contact and shows how they practiced a form of cultural *métissage* (amalgamation), seemingly often experiencing a marked sympathy for native peoples. Being especially attracted by the sexual freedom of the indigenous peoples and by other traits of Indian culture that corresponded to those of the French or French Canadian peasantry, from which they often came (marvelous tales, magic, a cyclical vision of life, premonitory dreams, etc.), they integrated themselves to a large extent into Indian communities, without entirely assimilating in most cases. Jacquin emphasizes the ambiguity of the position of the *coureurs de bois*. As agents of a colonial power and at the same time commercial traders, they were capable of acting like "Caesars" (according to Pierre-Esprit Radisson's expression) and engaging in trickery and "base actions" to amass furs.[37] However, it seems clear that these Frenchmen were on the whole less intensely motivated by monetary gain than their English counterparts, less inclined to cheating, and closer to Indian culture.[38]

The writers of New France can be divided into three groups: members of religious orders (principally Récollets and Jesuits), soldiers and officers of the French Army, and administrators who represented the state and the king in the colonies. The social origins of those who fell within these groups were diverse, but the aristocracy was well represented and influential throughout. Aside from the "relations" of the Jesuits, which constitute a genre in themselves, writing that stages the Amerindian takes several forms: descriptive works (depicting the customs of Indians, but also often fauna and flora, geography and landscape), historical works (on New France, the Indian wars, the origins of Amerindians, etc.), and travel accounts. But most often the works are hybrid, exhibiting diverse generic traits, sometimes combining characteristics of all the relevant genres. The travel account in particular is almost always mixed with other forms of discourse, especially the "customs of the savages" genre mentioned earlier. To further complicate the picture, the titles of the works are often misleading, for example designating only one of the generic elements of the content, and sometimes a secondary one at that. In other cases the title suggests subject matter more broad than that which is actually to be found in the work. This literature, in all its variety, was extremely abundant from the early seventeenth century on.[39]

If one compares this production with the equivalent literature in the Anglo-American sphere, one is struck by the absence—doubtless due to the differences between the two colonies—of the discourse of the zero degree of encounter and of the will to destroy the Indian that is expressed in its most extreme form by Brackenridge. Moreover, as Annie Jacob points out in her comparison of the "Indian of the English" with the "Indian of the French," for the French "Indians became part of the ideological debate. They provided arguments in philosophical discussions and in social criticism."[40] As we shall see, this proposition is well illustrated in the works that I now take up.

LAHONTAN

Ever since Gilbert Chinard brought him to light in the early twentieth century, and until recently, Louis-Armand de Lom d'Arce, baron de Lahontan (1666–1716) has been known and studied mainly for his *Dialogues de M. le Baron de Lahontan et d'un sauvage* (Dialogues of the Baron de Lahontan with a Savage). This philosophical conversation, however, is only a part of the third and last tome—published as a supplement a year after the others—of a multivolume set of which the first two volumes are entitled *Nouveaux Voyages de M. le Baron de Lahontan dans l'Amérique septentrionale* (New Voyages of the Baron de Lahontan in North America) and *Mémoires de l'Amérique septentrionale* (Memoirs of North America; vols. 1–2: 1703; vol. 3: 1704). This focus on the *Dialogues* is understandable, coming from historians of ideas who saw Lahontan as one of the creators of the "myth of the noble savage," a precursor of the Enlightenment and of the values of the French Revolution and, in the framework of Paul Hazard, a major exponent of the "crisis of the European consciousness" at the turn of the seventeenth and eighteenth centuries.[41] In the *Dialogues*, which are clearly fictional (though perhaps in part based on real conversations between the author and the Huron chief Kondiaronk), the philosophical issues are explicitly articulated and a sustained intellectual debate is staged. Yet Lahontan's critical vision is equally manifest in the first two volumes, and more recently, as interest in the study of travel literature has grown, an edition of the complete work has appeared.[42] Critical analyses of Lahontan's triptych as a whole have also appeared, both in the context of the travel genre and of the crisis that prefigured or introduced the Enlightenment.[43]

Lahontan came from a family of the lower nobility in the Pyrenees-Atlantic region, near Bayonne. According to his own account, in 1683, at age seventeen, he shipped out for Canada with a troop of the marines and participated in two campaigns carried out by the French and their Indian allies against the Iroquois (in 1684 and 1687).[44] Once in New France Lahontan quickly rose in rank, and in 1687 he took command of a fort (Saint-Joseph). From September 1688 to May 1689 he undertook on his own initiative a long exploratory trip into the interior of the continent, during which he claimed to have traveled up a western tributary of the Mississippi River that he called the "Long River."[45] After returning to the Mississippi, he descended it as far as its juncture with the Ohio, then returned to the point of departure of his unofficial journey, Michilimackinac, the fort situated between Lakes Michigan and Huron at which Alexander Henry was to be captured three-quarters of a century later. Several months later, in October 1689, when back in the town of Quebec, he learned that a judicial decision in France had resulted in the loss of the ancestral château of Lahontan. Before his departure for North America, Lahontan already knew that his father had endangered the family fortune by running up a massive debt, and financial insecurity may have influenced his decision to leave home. But only in Quebec, six years after his departure, did he receive news of his family's ruin.

Lahontan remained four more years in New France. After becoming a favorite of Frontenac, he was promoted to captain, then named "king's lieutenant" at Plaisance (Placentia, Newfoundland) in 1693. There he immediately became involved in a bitter dispute with the governor of Newfoundland, who accused him of insubordination. In return Lahontan attacked the governor for engaging in illicit activities for personal gain. In December 1693 he fled to Europe. Treated as a deserter in France, Lahontan wandered thereafter from country to country and published his works in exile, at La Haye, almost ten years later. In the course of his last years in Europe, he was suspected of working for foreign countries, most notably by providing the English with the manuscript of his *Mémoires* to help them in their conflict with the French in America. (After an initial infatuation for England, Lahontan seems to have become quickly disillusioned during his stay in that country.)[46] Considered a traitor, he continued to be banned from returning to France and died in Hanover, a man without a country.[47]

Several elements of this brief sketch of his life are particularly relevant for an understanding of Lahontan's sociocultural profile. First, as a provincial nobleman in the period when the absolute monarchy was being imposed in France, Lahontan exhibited a strong spirit of resistance characteristic of the Fronde, a proud refusal to submit to centralized authority. Moreover, as a ruined aristocrat who left home to seek his fortune in the colonial army, he was an uprooted person and a *déclassé* freed from traditional attachments, a "citizen of the world" who thereby was better able to think outside established boundaries. Though he participated in the military and administrative apparatus of New France, he came to criticize it from the inside, and finally he broke from it. Lahontan ultimately became a renegade, but he maintained an ambiguous relationship with the colonial project throughout his career.[48]

This context sheds light on some of the major themes of Lahontan's work, particularly insofar as they involve representation of the Indian. The main thrust of his criticism is clearly directed against authoritarian power—that of the state but also of the Catholic Church. This focus is already strikingly demonstrated by the frontispiece illustrations of one of the first editions of *Nouveaux voyages*.⁴⁹ On one page an Indian brandishes a bow and arrow, his feet triumphantly planted on a crown and a book. The caption, in Latin, is *et leges et sceptra terit*, "he tramples underfoot the law and the scepter." On the other, a bird rises toward a globe surmounted by the inscription *orbis patria*. The citizen of the world in free flight seems thus to be an ally of the Indian annihilating royal and ecclesiastical rule.⁵⁰

Although absolutist authority is consistently the prime target for Lahontan, there is another that also holds great importance: private property and the power of money—the rule of "mine" and "thine" that the author finds to be absent from Amerindian societies. The relative predominance of the first critical theme can be explained, it seems clear, by the characteristics of New France mentioned previously: the domination exercised by the state and the Church and the weaker development of commercial society there than in the English colonies. This hierarchy of targets that are both nonetheless important for Lahontan may help to explain his turnabout following his flight from Newfoundland, when, after first turning to England against France, he soon reconsidered. He was perhaps initially tempted by the English model as a "lesser evil" but then came to see it simply as another evil that he could not support.⁵¹

Nouveaux voyages and *Mémoires*, published together, make up a whole that takes the typical composite form of the travel account, placing the narrative part in volume 1 and the synchronic and synthetic part in volume 2. Though the two textual dimensions are thus clearly separated, occasionally the author introduces into one volume elements that should logically be in the other. A system of cross-referencing from *Mémoires* to *Nouveaux Voyages* reinforces the unity of the two texts. Still another unifying aspect is that while the first volume is presented as a series of letters sent to an elderly relative, the second is identified as a synthesis sent later to the same person.⁵² *Dialogues*, on the other hand, is both a distinct publication and a literary creation of a very different sort. Consequently it constitutes a work apart, one that steps out of the framework of the travel account and stands at a further remove from the experience of encounter.[53]

Though Lahontan did not make any prolonged stays in Indian communities, he had many contacts with different indigenous peoples in the course of his peregrinations in New France: Algonquins in the Saint Lawrence Valley, Hurons, Ottawas, Fox, Potawatomis, Ojibwes, and Miamis in the Great Lakes region, and others as well.[54] In reporting these encounters he often shows a sensitivity, quite unusual in travel accounts of the time, to the *linguistic* problems involved in such interactions—the pitfalls of communication in indigenous languages that Europeans often imperfectly mastered. While he expresses pride in knowing several Indian languages (it seems likely, however, that his knowledge was more rudimentary than he claims),[55] he alludes to the active participation of interpreters providing their services when he was unable to communicate directly. In several places Lahontan brings the reader's attention to a linguistic hesitation or confusion, when he was not sure he understood correctly, for example, or he feared that the interpreters were translating badly. This lucidity in regard to the role of languages and translation is exceptional among travelers of that period and place. However, in recounting some other episodes the author presents the exchange as if it were linguistically transparent, while an editorial footnote points out a problem of interpretation of meaning based on extratextual evidence.[56]

The influence on Lahontan of these contacts during the approximately ten years of his North American travels seems considerable. He discovered deep affinities with Indians he encountered, and in his account expresses a growing admiration for their way of life. But the progression is not entirely linear. The most intense and decisive moment occurred at the beginning of his American sojourn. During the first winters in New France, while he was garrisoned in Quebec and then in Montreal, Lahontan reports that he took off on expeditions in the surrounding forests with several bands of Algonquin hunters, for periods that are not clearly defined (perhaps several weeks or several months). During these excursions he began to learn their language and took immense pleasure in the hunt (330). He compares this experience of happiness with the ennui of his life in town, and this fuels his anger at the deadening censorship imposed by the priests.

According to Lahontan, the priests exercised a despotic power over the lives of the inhabitants of the towns. He himself was once subjected to an uninvited intrusion into his quarters by a priest who wanted to see what books he had in his possession. When the cleric found Petronius's *Satiricon* on a table, he tore it up. Lahontan comments that the priests "aren't content just to keep a watch on people's actions, but also want to pry into their thoughts" (314). The great freedom he experiences hunting with Indians stands in stark contrast to this repressive ecclesiastical regime. It is surely no accident that the hunt is Lahontan's point of entry into Indian life, the point at which an intense rapport is established and a breach opens up onto what remains to be discovered about that way of life. Hunting is precisely a prime activity shared by the European aristocrat and the Amerindians of the forested Northeast.[57] It is hardly accidental also that, later in his stay in New France, his most vivid relationship with an individual Indian, the "Petun" Huron chief Kondiaronk, called the "Rat," develops while they are hunting together (660).[58]

On later excursions, in his roles as soldier, officer, and explorer, Lahontan often maintains more conventional relations with natives, when for example he is received and feasted by chiefs. In general these contacts do not appear to touch him to the same extent, and his responses seem more stereotyped.[59] He sometimes intervenes actively, as when he attempts to stop the execution of what he considers an unjust punishment meted out by Indians of his party to some Christianized Iroquois near Fort Frontenac (345–46), or, contrariwise, when he accedes to the burning of a village of Missouri Indians at the request of the Fox who are accompanying him on the lower Missouri River (427–28). But throughout his accounts the author *de-dramatizes* scenes of action and danger, systematically refusing to emphasize his peril or to give himself heroic airs. Lahontan's narrative never seeks to create "adventure." Indeed most of the interactions that are staged in his text are not acts but words.[60]

Aside from hunting, and sometimes as an accompaniment to it, his preferred mode of relation with Indians is conversation—or rather discussion, since often an exchange of ideas is involved. Lahontan generally portrays his relationship with Indians as *rational*. They, unlike priests, who refuse debate and want only to preach their own truth, are amenable to this form of dialogue, and Lahontan, breaking with common preconceptions, proclaims that he has "reasoned with these peoples" (630). Recounting his journey up the "Long River," which took him away from territories frequented by whites, he writes, "The further up the river I went, the more the Savages seemed reasonable to me" (410).[61] Depending on which hypothesis is favored regarding the identity of the river, Minnesota or Missouri, those upriver Indians may have been either Dakota Sioux or Mandans, quite different tribes but ones that shared the characteristic of having experienced little contact with Europeans at that time.

Particularly in the *Mémoires*, Lahontan recalls long philosophical and religious discussions with natives, which he reports generally in an ironic tone: "I found myself fifty times with them, very puzzled as to how to counter their absurd objections.... I always got out of the difficulty by bidding them to lend an ear to the words of the Jesuits" (655). Here, as elsewhere, the "empirical subjectivity" of the traveler and real conversation tend to be superseded by invented dialogue.[62] Knowing Lahontan's attitude toward Jesuits, it is hard to imagine him actually answering the Indians in that way.[63] At any rate his interactions with Indians typically take place on a verbal, intellectual plane.

One situation that unavoidably arises many times, however, is totally foreign to reason: the torture of prisoners by Indians allied with the French—Lahontan claims that only some nations engage in the practice (718–19)—often with the tacit approval of the French authorities or even, on occasion, at their instigation. The Indians are offended if their French allies do not attend these events, but Lahontan is horrified by them. In one instance, when visiting a Miami encampment, he finds them preparing to "burn" several Iroquois and invents an excuse allowing him to leave before the torture begins (432). In another, in which this form of execution has (exceptionally, by Lahontan's account) been ordered by Monsieur de Frontenac himself in Quebec, Lahontan painfully endures the spectacle until he can take no more, and then flees (482–84).

The polemical aspect of Lahontan's writing has often been used to discredit him as an observer of Amerindian societies. The editors of the *Œuvres complètes*, however, have checked his reports against other sources and have generally found them confirmed.[64] Some modern historians are also convinced of the value of his testimony and quote his observations on the Hurons and Algonquins, as well as on the colonists of New France.[65] As for his interpretations of what he saw, the issue is doubtless more complex.

Lahontan often portrays himself as a teller of unpalatable truths, especially with regard to the Church and the state. He fiercely criticizes, among other things, the missionaries' "relations," which in his view "are grossly inaccurate in their account of the customs and manners of the Savages" (630).[66] They have deceived themselves and others, in particular on the question of whether the Indians are amenable to Christianization. Lahontan also ridicules the stupidity of the priests, who, through a faulty translation of the word *Matchi Manitou*, persuade themselves that the Indians worship the "devil" and speak to him (665). Compared with the missionaries and with others who have spent many years with Indians, Lahontan credits himself with having understood them more astutely: "I know the character [*le génie*] of the Savages better than a great many Frenchmen who have spent their entire lives with them, because I have studied their customs very precisely" (669).

The general descriptions and commentaries of Lahontan on Indian cultures with which he has come into contact, developed mainly in the *Mémoires*, do not cover all the areas usually treated by other travelers. Noting the absence of any significant material on the education of children or culinary practices, for example, some have suggested that Lahontan chose his themes solely according to whether or not they were relevant for colonial policy.[67] This criterion may have played some role, but it seems nonetheless that many themes were chosen because they interested Lahontan himself and nourished his reflections on Indians rather than because of their usefulness for colonization. This appears to be true of passages relating to love and marriage. The author couples his depiction of sexual and matrimonial customs with a theory. In his view Indians shun feelings of passionate love because of the importance they attribute to *freedom*:

"[They] always take care to guard their hearts' independence [*la liberté du cœur*], which they regard as the most precious treasure in the world" (669).

Religious beliefs are another interest of Lahontan. What seems to motivate this concern most strongly is his desire to mount a campaign against Catholicism, as is suggested by the title of one section, "Beliefs of the Savages and Obstacles to Their Conversion" (653). But beyond this polemical intention, and going deeper, is the affinity he perceives between the religious sensibility of Indians he encountered and his own form of deism. According to him, Indians believe that mankind "is the work of a principle that is superior in wisdom and knowledge, that they call the GREAT SPIRIT or Master of life, and that they worship in the most abstract way. . . . The existence of God being inseparably joined with its essence, it contains everything, appears in everything, acts on everything and imparts movement to all things. In a word, all that we see and all that we conceive of is this God. . . . This leads [the Indians] to worship it in everything that appears in the world" (654).[68]

Lahontan devotes several sections of the *Mémoires* to other aspects of the "Customs and Manners of the Savages" (637), such as "sicknesses and remedies," war and hunting. Though all of these have some utilitarian value, he also clearly takes a personal interest in them. On the subject of war, he claims that in the course of their conversations Kondiaronk confided to him on several occasions "that the thing that most vexed his mind was to see men making war against men" (711), a point of view that Lahontan surely shared. But, like many other travelers, Lahontan also offers an explanation for why the Indians war among themselves: "The Savages war with each other over questions of hunting, or passage on their lands, since there are fixed boundaries. Each nation knows the borders of its own country" (712). While other travelers often cite revenge as a common motive for war (712n645), Lahontan mentions only the protection of customary limits to land use. Both of these reasons for Indian warfare aim for the preservation of a certain equilibrium and in this way contrast with the expansionist purposes—extension of power and wealth—that are regularly at the source of "civilized" wars. But Lahontan's choice to highlight defense of territorial hunting prerogatives important for survival, ignoring the impulse for revenge, may well have stemmed from his perception of the first as a clearly rational motive while the second appeared to be born of unreasoning passion.[69]

Beyond these particular aspects of Amerindian society, and sometimes through them, Lahontan attempts to characterize it as a whole, with reference to its underlying principles. In *Mémoires* two essential qualities are put forward. First, and this idea introduces the section of the work devoted to customs and manners, Indian society evinces a seamless cohesion that is expressed especially through sharing and mutual aid.[70] This trait is moreover integrally linked to the absence of private property and money. Thus "the Savages know no mine or thine, for it can be said that what belongs to one belongs to the others as well. When a Savage has not been successful in a beaver hunt, his companions help him without being asked. If his gun bursts or breaks, the others all hasten to offer him another.... The only ones who use money are those who are Christians and live near the gates of our towns. The others do not want to touch it, or even to see it" (637–38).

At the same time, Lahontan sets out a second broad characteristic of Indian culture, expressing it negatively: one finds among Indians no "subordination" (639) and, more specifically, "no laws, judges or priests" (643). The positive counterpart to this absence—freedom, independence of individuals, a kind of libertarian equality—manifests itself in many ways in different areas of the culture, for example in "love and marriage," as already mentioned. Although the word is not used in *Mémoires*, in the preface to the second volume the author goes so far as to define Amerindian society as "Anarchy" (2:797).

What is to be said of the interpretations that Lahontan makes on the basis of these observations? First, they agree on many points with those made by other travelers, as is attested by the editorial notes in the *Œuvres complètes*. However, a particular inflection is often given to Lahontan's explanations, coming from his peculiar angle of vision as a *déclassé* aristocrat and "citizen of the world." While this perspective allows him to perceive lucidly, through both his attractions and his antagonisms, important dimensions of Amerindian society and point out some of the blind spots of other observers—notably the missionaries—it also imposes some limitations or distortions. In particular Lahontan's thoroughgoing rationalism and "Pyrrhonian" skepticism make him insensitive to the whole area of nonrational beliefs in premodern cultures: the interpretation of dreams, magic, rituals, and so on. He either ignores them or does not take them seriously. Yet in this respect his weaknesses are also strengths, for by portraying "reasoning" Indians, Lahontan foregrounds a basic, universally shared human quality and undermines the negative stereotype of the Indian as a wild beast.[71]

As for the author's evaluation of Indian culture, a clear but complex progression is evident from the first to the second volume, and beyond that, to the *Dialogues*. In *Nouveaux voyages*, which recounts the concrete experiences of the voyager, the depiction of and attitude toward North American natives are situated on a relatively prosaic plane, and value judgments, although generally positive, are mixed. Lahontan sometimes shows himself to be as ironic or even contemptuous toward Indians as he is toward priests and missionaries, mocking, for example, the infatuation of a chief (perhaps Dakota) for what he calls "trifles" (*bagatelles*, 407) or calling the members of a certain band "rascals" (*canailles*, 414). On the other hand, in *Mémoires* and even more so in *Dialogues*, Amerindians tend increasingly to take on symbolic value and to serve as foils for the defects of European civilization. Yet this evolution is by no means absolute. In *Mémoires* one still finds, though less often, pejorative remarks about Indians, and in the *Dialogues* distancing devices block any total identification with them.

What are the specific traits of North American natives—such as he knows them—that Lahontan praises? First and foremost, those that contrast with authoritarianism and the constraints of private property. Most important, the Indians are *free*, but they are at the same time *egalitarian* and *fraternal*, since they know no hierarchy, no "mine" and "thine," and systematically practice gift-giving and mutual aid. All of the components of what will later become the motto of the French Revolution are valued by the author, but he places special emphasis on the notion of freedom. His descriptions of particular aspects of Indian communities suggest that this spirit permeates the whole and includes not only men but also women (who can freely choose, and leave, their partners) and children (who do not undergo the severe discipline and punishments imposed on European children). Finally, linked to these characteristics and central to his system of values, Lahontan applauds the exercise of reason that he has found so prevalent in Indian culture. According to the author, for Indians reason constitutes "the noblest faculty" (657), and because they cultivate it, one "never regrets the time one has spent with these rustic philosophers" (644). A corollary to their powers of reason is the astuteness with which Indians carry on their public affairs, making decisions involving the community through discussions in council, exhibiting the "shrewd political sense [*la fine politique*] of this kind of beings whom [Europeans] consider beasts" (364).

Contrariwise, Lahontan deprecates those practices he considers "unreasonable" or irrational, that is, those that seem impossible to fit into a rational framework. In some cases he simply omits to discuss them (as with magical usages), and in others mentions them only to disparage or dismiss them. He makes no more attempt, for example, to understand the kind of music made by Indians than he does the "trifles" they seem to prize so highly. On being regaled once by Sauks, Menominees, and Potawatomis on the Fox (Wisconsin) River, Lahontan comments, "These songs and dances lasted two hours. They were accompanied by the cries of joy and buffooneries that they mix into their ridiculous music" (385). Moreover, for the protoscientific man that he is, Indian medicine seems insane. Their remedies, he says, are "as wild [*sauvages*] as they themselves are."[72] It is a matter of pure luck if they survive their treatments, since "they do everything necessary to kill themselves [*tout ce qu'il faut faire pour se crever*]" (696). Finally, in a period when concern for historical truth is beginning to threaten myth and legend, Lahontan declares himself convinced from his experience with Indians in Canada "that tradition is too unreliable, unstable, murky, uncertain, misleading and vague to be trusted" (629).[73]

These reservations are minor, though, compared with the overall appreciation of native culture that the author expresses. However, that appreciation often comes across only indirectly, through the use of irony and paradox. Thus when Lahontan elaborates at length on Indians' opinions of Europeans—especially their criticism of money and subordination in European societies—he suggests, without saying so explicitly, that he shares their point of view, only to ironically conclude, "I wish I had the time to tell you all the foolish things they say about our customs—it would take me ten or twelve days" (640). The central paradox articulated by the author is the reversal of the civilized/savage opposition imposed by European colonizers. At the end of the passage on love, for example, he remarks that if the Indians insist on keeping themselves free even in this area, "they are not quite as savage as we are" (669). Thus it is most often obliquely—and shrinking from any definitive pronouncements—that Lahontan transmits his admiration for Amerindian in contrast to European culture.

Clearly what Lahontan admires most are all the aspects of their way of life that correspond to the values of the nascent Enlightenment, of which he was a prime exponent. In chapter 4 I showed how, a century later, Hugh Henry Brackenridge came to situate himself, based also on an Enlightenment perspective, at the opposite end of the spectrum of attitudes toward Indians: rejection carried to its ultimate extreme, the urge to exterminate. Aside from the Enlightenment framework of vision, everything separates the two men: period and place, nation, class, and profession. These differences doubtless partially account for their diametrically opposed views of the Indian. But this astonishing contrast should also remind us that philosophical standpoints in general, and that of the Enlightenment in particular, include great ideological diversity and constitute only one determining factor in the encounter with the Other.

CHARLEVOIX

Charlevoix, whose work also stands out among accounts of travel in New France, is in many respects the antithesis of Lahontan. Several decades later he followed an itinerary similar to that of Lahontan, but he was Lahontan's declared enemy and actively attempted to discredit him. Despite the extreme ideological opposition between them, however, their perceptions and many of their opinions concerning Amerindians show striking resemblances. François-Xavier de Charlevoix (1682–1761) was a Jesuit. He took his vows at the age of eighteen and spent most of his long life as a priest in France. For ten years he was a teacher at the illustrious Parisian school Louis-le-Grand (1709–19). Later he served for many years as the editor of the Jesuit journal *Mémoires de Trévoux* (1723–41). His first stay in Canada was between 1705 and 1709, when he taught at the Company of Jesus's school in the town of Quebec.

In 1720 Charlevoix was again sent to New France, this time by order of the king, on an expedition of exploration in the region of the Great Lakes and along the Mississippi River. Catholic clergy were often sent on exploratory missions mandated by the state for the purpose of exercising control over the behavior of members of the party, censuring both "immorality" and unauthorized trading. The expedition in question was intended to be a preliminary probe to determine what the prospects might be for a larger-scale French voyage of discovery, seeking a route to the "Western sea," that is, the famous Northwest Passage. Midway through the trip, on Lake Michigan, Charlevoix was given information suggesting that a route west of Lake Superior was the most promising, but because of the lateness of the season he decided to postpone that northern exploration and proceed south, down the Mississippi River. In the course of his trip, which lasted just over a year (from March 1721 to April 1722), Charlevoix descended the Saint Lawrence River from Quebec, navigated through Lakes Ontario, Erie, Huron, and Michigan; then, once the southern route was decided on, he went down the Illinois River to the Mississippi and all the way to its mouth. This trajectory, with the exception of the last leg on the lower Mississippi, overlaps considerably Lahontan's journey.[74] Unlike Lahontan, though, Charlevoix was not able to return to his Canadian point of departure. (He fell sick, and also learned that some tribes on the route back were engaged in hostilities.) Instead he returned to France from the Gulf of Mexico at the end of 1722, having learned little of interest from the point of view of the mission's purpose.[75]

Although he announced his intention to publish it immediately upon return to France in 1723, the account of his trip, entitled *Journal d'un voyage fait par ordre du Roi dans l'Amérique Septentrionale* (Journal of a Voyage in North America, Made by Order of the King) appeared only much later, in 1744, appended to his *Histoire et description générale de la Nouvelle France* (History and General Description of New France).[76] The latter work was itself only one part of a vast series of projected historical publications. After first bringing out a history of Saint-Domingue, in 1735 Charlevoix published "Project for a Set of Histories of the New World" in the *Journal de Trévoux*. In Charlevoix's usage, the "New World" covered all the countries discovered by Europe since the Renaissance, in the Orient as well as in the West. He planned to write a historical monograph for each country, making a critical survey of works that had appeared on the subject, so that "one will know what to think of those [authors] who have written about the country up to now." By reading the synthesis, he promised, "one will be able to gain a complete understanding of each region of the New World."[77] The aim of the overall project was thus encyclopedic, synthetic, and evaluative, and those qualities are reflected in the *Journal d'un voyage*, Charlevoix's only published work that is part of the project but pertains to another genre than the historical study.[78]

Like that of Lahontan, Charlevoix's account uses the epistolary format. It is presented as a series of thirty-three letters sent during the course of the voyage to a noblewoman, the Duchess of Lesdiguières. As in the case of Lahontan, though, there can be no doubt that the correspondence is imaginary. When the work first appeared the public seems not to have understood that it had in fact been written in France. The author surely used notes he had taken during the trip, but the text as a whole gives relatively little attention to personal experience. Charlevoix was a scholar, like many Jesuits, and in preparing his manuscript followed the directions he had laid out for his overall project of New World histories. He surveyed the existing literature on the different territories, the fauna and the flora, and the indigenous peoples that lay in the path of his excursion, and made extensive use of the sources he judged to be most trustworthy. He drew much from the Jesuit relations, and even more from Lafitau's *Mœurs des sauvages américains comparées aux mœurs des premiers temps* (1724; Customs of the American Savages Compared to the Customs of Antiquity). Though the borrowings from this work are considerable, Charlevoix makes them his own and reworks them, selecting, pruning, reformulating, and, most important, integrating into them his own point of view, which is much more normative than Lafitau's.

The synchronic and synthetic material included in *Journal d'un voyage* is much more voluminous than the narrative of travel. Since Charlevoix's trip was quite real, and the account of it not in any way plagiarized, the borrowings from other sources are to be found in that synchronic material. Unlike Lahontan's work, Charlevoix's does not separate the diachronic and the synchronic elements into distinct sections. The synchronic materials are simply divided into blocks of text and artificially interpolated into the narration of events, itself reconstituted after the fact, though it feigns to be written as the trip is taking place.[79]

Thus Charlevoix's work is a literary creation as well as a personal testimony, and a compendium of knowledge as well as the projection of a particular perspective. While he drew heavily on the works of others, Charlevoix's own publications on New France—both the travel account and the larger history—were often later "reutilized," among others by Jonathan Carver, whom I discuss in chapter 6.[80] Beyond these borrowings his writings on the subject exercised a very powerful influence. According to one historian, Charlevoix "for almost a century . . . remained the chief source for the writing of early Canadian history."[81]

In Charlevoix's text, then, the relative importance of personal experience is small when compared with the long interpolations on general subjects. In *Journal d'un voyage* depictions of situations in which the author confronts and interacts with actual Indians are rare. When he does pause to describe an encounter of this kind, it is often with Indians who are either Christianized already or in the process of becoming so. In particular Charlevoix reports visits he made to two Christian communities at the beginning of his trip, at the Huron village of La Lorette near Québec and then, midway through his account, at another near the fort of Detroit. Even when he is speaking of Christian Indians he is circumspect in referring to his own experience with them and quickly turns to broad descriptions or other generalities. Most often the actual encounter is only glimpsed.

During his stay at La Lorette, Charlevoix attended some ceremonies that included dancing and singing. Like Lahontan, he does not find the latter to his liking: "The music is in fact quite boring and unpleasant, at least judging from what I saw of it. [Sung with] pinched throats, continuously monotonous, airs that always have something ferocious or lugubrious about them. But their voices are entirely different when they sing in the church."[82] Several pages earlier the author had told the addressee of the letter how affected he was when he heard this other kind of music: "Nothing is more touching than to hear sung, by two choirs—the men on one side and the women on the other—church prayers and canticles in their language" (1:239). Among the ceremonies practiced by the natives Charlevoix most appreciates the "harangue." In expressing his admiration for one such oration he heard at La Lorette, he is brought to raise the issue—though he is generally less alert to it than Lahontan—of translation: "The orator of the Hurons said that day so many witty things [*des choses si spirituelles*], that we suspected the interpreter, who was the missionary himself, of having lent him his wit [*esprit*] and polish [*politesse*] along with his voice. But he protested that he had added nothing of his own, and we believed him since he is known to be one of the most frank and honest of men" (1:241–42).

Later in the trip, when Charlevoix arrived at the fort of Detroit, a council was announced with the purpose of communicating to the Indians of the region—non-Christian Ottawas and Potawatomis as well as Christianized "Petun" Hurons, who had moved there from farther north—some orders recently received from the governor of Louisiana himself, the Marquis de Vaudreuil. The commander of the fort, Monsieur de Tonti, desired Charlevoix's presence. Charlevoix reports that he was once again impressed by the eloquence of an Indian orator, a Huron here also, and in this case was convinced just from listening that the effect created could not have come from the interpreter: "His air, the sound of his voice, and the way he acted, though he made no gestures, seemed to me noble and imposing, and what he said must have been very eloquent, since even though shorn of all the ornaments of language by the interpreter, who was a simple man, we were all charmed by it. I will even have to admit that if he had spoken for two hours I wouldn't have been bored for a minute" (1:541).[83]

The following day Charlevoix visited the Huron village. He listened to the complaints of "matrons" who had for a long time been awaiting the arrival of a missionary, and then went to inquire about the situation with the authorities at the fort. Charlevoix was concerned mainly with the religious affairs of these Indians, who are presented as good Christians. Nonetheless he candidly acknowledges that he was more favorably impressed by the neighboring Potawatomis whom he visited afterward: "I was even better received by the infidel Potawatomis than by the Christian Hurons.... Onanguicé, their chief, treated me very politely, which gave me as good an opinion of his turn of mind [*esprit*] as had the speech he had made to us in the council" (1:543). Onanguicé had followed the Huron orator in speaking the night before, and Charlevoix was impressed with the ingenious succinctness of his delivery.

Over the course of his journal Charlevoix only occasionally, and fleetingly, puts himself on stage, either externally or internally. He recounts his discovery, for example, of two Indian cadavers while he was walking in the Illinois country: "The rain, and even more than that a sight that horrified me, kept me from going around those rocks, from whence I hoped to have a view of a large sweep of country. I saw at the edge, and just above the village, the bodies of two Savages that had been abandoned, according to custom, to the birds of prey" (2:739).[84] But instead of further elaborating on his feelings at this sight, or of speculating on the specific circumstances that might have led to it, Charlevoix immediately shifts to a general description of the way prisoners of the Illinois are brought into their towns and in many cases put to death. The personal experience seems here little more than a pretext allowing the author to introduce discussion of an aspect of Indian warfare.

Elsewhere one finds the opposite procedure: the author's experience is briefly alluded to as an illustration within a general presentation. Under the heading "Concerning the Miamis" in Letter 23, the passage opens as follows: "The Savages in this area are habitual thieves, and consider well taken whatever they can lay their hands on."[85] After giving further details on the ways in which Miamis put this habit into practice, the author adds, without further embellishment, "I was submitted to the same the day after my arrival, and was spared no quarter" (2:642).

In one case Charlevoix does dwell at greater length on a difficult situation in which he found himself, soon after having seen the two hanging enemy cadavers, and near the spot. But while recounting the event he drops the main line of narrative and shifts his focus to religious themes. In a neighboring Illinois village with his men, he was informed that they were surrounded by four bands of Fox warriors. The circumstances that led to the mishap are explained at some length. According to his telling of the story, Charlevoix was impatient to continue on his way, but the village chief tried to dissuade him. Charlevoix at first wondered whether the chief had some reason of his own for doing this, but finally decided that the chief's behavior was disinterested and generous. Up to this point the incident is told as a story with a developing plot.

Then, however, the main thread of the plot is broken off by another, extraneous narrative. Reported at secondhand, as told to him by several French Canadian *voyageurs* he met in the village, this narrative involves the origin of an image of the Virgin that the chief wore around his neck. Charlevoix had been told by the chief that he was not a Christian, and the *voyageurs* provide an explanation for his wearing the image. Having asked the meaning of the image when it first came into his hands, the chief was told that Christians ask the Virgin for protection in times of danger and that She rarely fails them; he therefore called on Her once when he encountered a Fox warrior while hunting alone. The Fox's gun failed to fire five times in a row. Following this incident the Illinois chief never left the village without his talisman. This story—and Charlevoix's response to it—is an illuminating illustration of the complex interaction of the Amerindian and Catholic religious perspectives. While the Indian has clearly made the Virgin into a powerful spirit, without embracing the overall Christian worldview, Charlevoix interprets what has happened as an instance of the Virgin's efficacy and supposes "that only the lack of a missionary has up to now kept him from becoming a Christian, and that the Mother of God, after having saved him from a temporal death, will obtain for him the grace of a sincere conversion" (2:747).

This diversion from Charlevoix's own predicament of entrapment in the village is followed by still another religious sidelight, in which he tells of baptizing in extremis a dying girl as he was about to leave the village. The center of interest is thus deflected onto these religious vignettes, and the main thrust of the story—the author's need to continue his journey and the threat of a possible attack—is lost. At the beginning of the following letter he mentions his anxiety at the moment of leaving the village, but he never returns to the question of what danger, if any, he encountered in escaping (2:743–52). Here, as elsewhere in his work, Charlevoix refuses to generate any sense of *adventure*. In this respect his writing resembles Lahontan's, though his eschewing of adventure stems from a very different perspective.

While Charlevoix's narrative does occasionally allow limited views of his experience of encounter, his work is first and foremost characterized by its "didactic fervor" and is presented to the reader as a compilation of information.[86] Having systematically studied the existing literature, Charlevoix transmits what he has found most interesting and reliable. The understanding of the Indian proposed by the text is in this sense a collective production. Yet he also draws on his own observations and filters the other materials through his own lens.

The author of *Journal d'un voyage* is particularly interested in the motivations behind the collective actions taken by Indians—their political decisions and their reasons for going to war. In his view, "as a general rule the fame and reputation [*gloire*] of the Nation, and reasons of honor, are the principal motives impelling all their endeavors" (1:559). As for war, Charlevoix is convinced, like Lahontan, that Indians never have recourse to it out of "interest" or for the purpose of expanding their territories (1:528). Unlike Lahontan, however, he sees revenge—which he takes to be a corollary of the principle of honor—as the predominant motive (1:475), perhaps since he more readily recognizes the role of the nonrational in the behavior of the natives. For this reason too, it would seem, he is more willing to confront and try to understand the practice of torture. Reflecting on what he calls the "principle of barbarism" at work in those who torture, he supposes that "they came to it by degrees, habitual practice [*l'usage*] slowly accustoming them to it" (1:525). He accounts for the behavior of those who undergo the torture most importantly by a simple psychological mechanism: their songs, and the insults they hurl at their torturers, distract them from the pain and raise them above suffering (1:524).

In defining the general nature of social relations and the deepest impulses at work in Indian societies, however, Charlevoix agrees remarkably with his freethinking adversary, while giving his own Christian inflection to their common themes. For him too freedom constitutes the overriding imperative for indigenous peoples: "These American natives [*ces Amériquains*] are absolutely convinced that Man is born free, that no power on earth has the right to violate his freedom, and that nothing can compensate him for its loss." As an indication of how profoundly true this is, he adds, we have "even had much difficulty in convincing the Christian [Indians] of the contrary" (1:563).[87]

In addition to this fundamental trait Charlevoix is equally struck by the fraternal egalitarianism of those societies. In regard to their practices of gift-giving and sharing, which he sees as exhibiting a generosity of spirit that resembles Christian charity (1:295), he points out a paradox: "What is absolutely amazing is to see these men, whose exterior promises nothing but barbarity, treat each other with a tenderness and consideration that one never finds among the people in the most civilized nations."[88] Charlevoix finds a source of this harmonious community in the same phenomenon postulated by Lahontan, but he gives a Catholic twist to his formulation: "This doubtless comes partly from the fact that mine and thine, those cold words, as SAINT CHRYSOSTOME calls them, which while extinguishing in our hearts the flame of charity ignite that of greed, are not yet known among these Savages" (2:627).[89]

Further on Charlevoix brings to light another paradox: the "virtues" that Christians try to put into practice in their relations with others follow naturally from the Indians' communitarian principles, even though the Indians do not see them as virtues. Thus he comments:

> As for what is known as ... qualities of heart, the Savages do not take pride in them, or more precisely, they are not virtues for them. It even seems that they are incapable of looking at them from that point of view. Friendship, compassion, gratitude, attachment—[the natives] possess something of

all that, but not in their hearts, and [these qualities] are not so much the result of good character as of reflection, or instinct.... [These qualities] are for them nothing more than a consequence of the conviction, which they hold, that everything should be in common between Men. (2:629)[90]

In this passage Charlevoix explicitly rejects any explanation based on the natural goodness of man and prefers that of a collective ideology ("reflexion," "conviction") that, in practice, becomes an "instinct."

At some points, admittedly, Charlevoix seems incapable of transcending the European cultural grid, and his interpretations of Indian ways of living suffer in consequence. Such is surely the case when he observes that the members of Indian families "often live like people brought together by chance, and that no bond links them to each other" (1:564). This statement, which is clearly in contradiction with other passages in his work, does not recognize the possibility of networks of human relationship following a logic other than that of the European family. Indigenous networks of kin and clan were probably invisible to this Frenchman. But the limitations of Charlevoix's viewpoint are most evident when he is dealing with questions of religious belief and worship. The Jesuit is first of all convinced that the Indians are rather "easy to convert" (1:551), the main obstacle to this conversion being a lack of missionaries. As for Indian beliefs, he rarely attempts to understand them. In one passage, for example, he simply remarks that the feast he is partaking in is "dedicated to I don't know what Spirit [*Génie*]" (1:298). Charlevoix is manifestly disturbed by Indian magical practices, however, and his explanations of them are confused and contradictory. He sometimes asserts that the shamans are simply charlatans, which he calls "jugglers" (*jongleurs*), using a term that was current at the time, and that the Indians do not really believe in them. But elsewhere he considers that both the "good" and the "bad" spirits raised by these sorcerers are devils or demonic powers (1:482, 2:705–12).

However, Charlevoix's intellectual honesty asserts itself in many of his analyses. I have already cited the instance in which he recognizes that he was better received by "infidels" than by Christianized Indians, and in several other places he admits to the reader how astonished he was to discover that his first ideas had been proven wrong. Thus, for example, he reports that he initially had assumed the "poorly disciplined" childhood of Indian children would lead to a "turbulent" and "corrupt" (*corrompue*) youth, but finally realizes that this does not occur (2:656). Although he falters in his understanding of phenomena that are too foreign to his own mental universe, Charlevoix nonetheless acknowledges, at least in some passages, the complexity of the Other with whom he is faced.

Beyond these attempts to depict and transmit knowledge of the Amerindian, Charlevoix's "didactic fervor" extends also to value judgments. The author consistently views Indians from the standpoint of a moralist imbued with Catholic doctrine. Unlike Father Lafitau, from whom he drew abundantly as a source, his analyses are almost always accompanied by moral criticism. An important aspect of his didacticism consists of conveying evaluations, and his writing is strewn with words like *quality* and *virtue*, *defect* and *vice*. Like the Jesuits in general, Charlevoix nonetheless shows some flexibility in this area while trying to remain within the bounds of Church teachings. Before all else Charlevoix measures Indian culture against a fervently held Catholic ethic. This sometimes turns out to be a risky endeavor, leaving him with insoluble contradictions.

Some aspects of Indian life meet with his disapproval. As a man of the Church he castigates the "lasciviousness" that, according to him, is to be found especially to the south, in the Illinois tribes, but that has recently also reached farther north. He is particularly scandalized by transsexuals, or what recently have come to be called "two-spirit" identities and practices. While acknowledging that the phenomenon—men taking on women's roles and dressing like them—is seen by the Indians of this area as having spiritual meaning, Charlevoix nonetheless forces it into his traditional Catholic framework, reducing it finally to a sin of the flesh: "It has been claimed that this custom comes from I don't know what kind of religious principle; but this religion ... was born out of the depravity of the heart, or, if the practice I am speaking of began with the spirit, it ended with the flesh." He laments that the males who follow this path give themselves up to "loathsome passions," by which he doubtless means homosexuality (2:620).

Accounts of Travel in New France · 163

Here his condemnation is absolute. On the subject of war, on the other hand, Charlevoix makes a distinction between the general motivation that is at its source—honor, which he finds praiseworthy—and the application of this principle to the carrying out of revenge, which he does not. In his view a noble quality is here misapplied to an activity he terms "frivolous" (1:475). Worse still, revenge can lead to great excesses: "What cannot be excused in them is that most often they stake their honor on revenge, and then set no limits to that revenge. This is a fault that only Christianity can correct, but our polite manners and our religion do not always succeed in doing it" (2:559).

Among the fundamental traits of Indian society identified by the author, one is strongly rejected: the lack of a spirit of subordination to authority, which he finds visible in many areas—in too great a tolerance toward children, in the absence of a "criminal justice" system, and in the many expressions of "pride," which he pinpoints as one of the most highly developed characteristics of the Indians (1:562–63, 2:628). Stated positively, this set of traits corresponds to the spirited assertion of individual freedom and independence. These qualities, which are the most highly valued by Lahontan, are the antithesis of the obedience and humility advocated by the Church. Nonetheless Charlevoix considerably softens his criticism of lack of discipline and pride by admitting that these traits do not produce the same baneful effects in Amerindians as they do elsewhere. On the contrary, he recognizes that affection, mutual understanding, and cooperation characterize normal relations in tribes, and even concedes that the great freedom Indians enjoy is what contributes most essentially to their happiness (2:647).

In fact the positive attributes that Charlevoix assigns to Indians far outweigh the objects of criticism. "It must be admitted, Madame," he writes in Letter 18, "that the more one sees our Savages at close range, the more estimable qualities one discovers in them" (1:551). Surprisingly, though, many of the qualities Charlevoix admires most are not Christian qualities. More than that, they are often linked to the very principles of freedom and independence that he reproves in his priestly role—among them, self-mastery, courage, the ability to overcome physical suffering, and more generally a "nobility of feeling" (*noblesse de sentimens*, 1:528) or "greatness of soul" (*grandeur d'âme*, 2:624), which are clearly linked to the sense of honor. All of these features of Indian character are more closely related to the aristocratic code than to Christian dogma and reveal a hidden affinity between Charlevoix and Lahontan. This subterranean—and paradoxical—kinship of perspective can perhaps be at least partially accounted for by their common social origin, both coming from the petty nobility.[91]

Another area of Charlevoix's valuation of the Indian is on the contrary directly related to his religious faith. Here also he shares with Lahontan the same value judgments, but in this case from a different angle of approach. Charlevoix also esteems in indigenous peoples all that stems from the absence of "mine" and "thine" in their societies: disinterestedness, generosity, the systematic refusal (except in war) to "do wrong" (*faire tort*) to others (2:628), the "tenderness" and "consideration" they show each other. Since he is aware of the resemblance of these practices with the ethical teachings of the Church concerning how one should relate to one's neighbor and fellow man, he cannot but suppose that the "Savages" already possess these Christian virtues to a superior degree and that their virtuous practices need only be complemented by instruction in Catholic doctrine and conversion by missionaries.

This awareness, however, produces a painful dilemma. Charlevoix is conscious of the fact that the Indians often lose their "virtues" through contact with "civilization." "It must be admitted," he writes, "that those with whom we have the most intercourse have already lost some of their generosity of earlier times, and of their admirable disinterestedness. Nothing is more contagious than the spirit of self-interest [*l'esprit d'intérêt*], and nothing is more able to debase morals" (1:295). In spite of this recognition, Charlevoix presents the Hurons of La Lorette as an example of the complete success of Christianization, which brings together the best of both worlds: they "retain of their birth and origin only what is estimable in them, that is, the simplicity and moral stature [*droiture*] of the First Age of the World, along with what has been added to it by Grace" (1:239). On the other hand, Charlevoix notices that while the inhabitants of the Christianized Huron village near Detroit are "industrious" and provide subsistence to other tribes through their work, they do not do so "for free, it must be said, since one cannot count disinterestedness among their good qualities" (1:543).[92]

The fundamental problem is that *francisation*—the introduction of French cultural patterns into indigenous societies—comes with Christianization, and while the former encourages (in its norms, at least) the spirit of subordination that Charlevoix approves of, it also often cultivates the spirit of self-interest, and even "greed."[93] Though he hesitates on the question of whether it is wiser to begin by *francisation* or Christianization,[94] in principle Charlevoix wishes that both objectives were carried out. However, he would like the Indians to adopt the hierarchical sense of European society, but not its egoism. Although he seems to be aware that this is ultimately impossible, he remains a prisoner to the contradiction throughout the *Journal d'un voyage*.

In the conclusion of Letter 3 Charlevoix devotes a paragraph to a comparison of the English and French colonies:

> There reigns in New England and the other provinces of the American continent subject to the British Empire, an opulence that it would seem they do not know how to enjoy, and in New France a poverty that is hidden by an air of affluence. . . . The English colonist amasses wealth, and makes no superfluous expenditure. The Frenchman enjoys what he has, and often shows off what he doesn't have. . . . The Anglo-Americans do not want war, because they have much to lose. They don't spare the Savages, because they don't think they need them. French youth, for the opposite reasons, hate peace and get along well with the natives of the country. (1:235)

Here we find succinctly and perceptively expressed the contrast between the two colonies, in terms of their socioeconomic mores and their stance with regard to the Indian. In the following chapter I will cross that border, taking up two accounts of travel that originated in the Anglo-American sphere of influence.

CHAPTER SIX

Anglo-American Travelers
John Lawson and Jonathan Carver

Until the end of the Seven Years' War, which opened to the British the vast regions to which the French had earlier laid claim, the genre of the travel account in Indian territory was dominated by French authors.[1] Accounts of trips made by travelers from the English provinces are not lacking, especially from the beginning of the eighteenth century on, but most of the travel they chronicle took place near the coast, not beyond the "frontier," and involved the kind of discovery of British colonial society discussed in part 1. Before the middle of the century accounts of journeys beyond the "civilized" zone are rare, particularly published ones. Those that were written were for the most part reports that remained buried in archives. After 1750, though, the number of accounts, especially published ones, increased, and during the 1760s several important trips that eventually gave rise to publications were made by Anglo-Americans into areas inhabited mainly by Amerindians.[2]

Among the Anglo-Americans—or more generally those who lived, temporarily or permanently, in the English colonies—there were several kinds of persons who were most likely to cross the frontier, to encounter Indians on their own terrain, and in some cases to put their experience into writing. First there were soldiers and militiamen, who on occasion wrote accounts that were more than just diaries of military campaigns. Sometimes traveling with them were geographers, cartographers, and engineers specialized in fortifications. Finally, related to these categories by their official role, and themselves sometimes members of the military, there were envoys sent by the provincial governments as Indian "agents." These agents generally knew the tribes they visited intimately and served as interpreters and diplomats in negotiations with them.[3]

A second group was made up of merchants of several kinds: fur traders—the approximate Anglo-American equivalent of the French *coureurs de bois*—and a type of person rarely to be found among the French, the land speculator or agent of a land company, who often traveled into Indian territories on reconnaissance missions. A surveyor often accompanied the private speculator and the government official to measure land and set out boundaries.

In addition to these types of travelers, who were sometimes in conflict among themselves but whose purposes coincided more generally—extension of the territory under colonial control, and exploitation of it—two other, less numerous categories of individuals made forays into Indian territory: the naturalist and the missionary. The latter, sent by Protestant denominations into the peripheries of the English colonies, were far fewer in number than the priests of New France. In the eighteenth century this missionary effort was undertaken mainly by Moravians, who, like the French Catholics but unlike most other Protestant sects, showed considerable sympathy for Amerindian cultures.[4] In many instances the travelers and authors of accounts belonged to several of the groups mentioned. Their social origins were diverse but rarely included the aristocracy.[5]

In the first half of the eighteenth century, then, the accounts that have come down to us of encounter with Indians by travelers coming from the British colonies are limited. Aside from John Lawson's narrative, there were several reports by officers on diplomatic missions to the Cherokees and Creeks in 1725 and that of a militiaman who accompanied General Oglethorpe, founder of the colony of Georgia, on another mission to the Creeks in 1739.[6] But toward the middle of the century the volume of accounts—some of note—began to increase. In 1743 an expedition left Philadelphia for Onondaga, the seat of the Iroquois in the western part of the province of New York. Its leader was Conrad Weiser. Sent as an envoy to engage in negotiations aimed at resolving a situation of conflict, Weiser was one of the most prominent Indian agents of the colonial period. Two other men were of the party: Lewis Evans, a cartographer and surveyor, and John Bartram, a botanist who would later become famous, the father of the William Bartram I discuss in chapter 7. Each of the men kept a journal during the trip, but only Bartram's was published—in London in 1751—because of its scientific interest.[7]

Weiser kept several other journals on diplomatic missions, most notably on an excursion beyond the Allegheny Mountains in 1748. His assistant on this trip was George Crogan, who became as important an intermediary as Weiser over the course of the next fifteen years, and who himself authored numerous accounts in epistolary or journal formats. In addition to his activities on behalf of provincial governments, Crogan took up fur trading, successfully for a time. Still another envoy sent officially by colonial authorities was the Moravian missionary Christian Frederick Post, who penned accounts of his expeditions starting in 1758.[8]

But it was after 1760, with the end of the French and Indian War, that travels in Indian territories, and accounts of such trips, took on real importance in Anglo-America. In this period the fur merchant Alexander Henry engaged in the multiple peregrinations that were recounted in *Travels and Adventures in Canada and the Indian Territories, between the Years 1760 and 1776*, discussed in chapter 4.[9] In 1762 a young soldier by the name of Henry Timberlake volunteered for a diplomatic mission to the Cherokees. This mission led him much farther than was usually the case. After having been taken hostage by the Cherokees and living among them for some time as such, Timberlake gained their confidence and finally accompanied several of their chiefs to England to meet the king. In 1765 he published, in London, *The Memoirs of Lieutenant Henry Timberlake (Who Accompanied the Three Cherokee Indians to England in the Year 1762)*, partly to justify to the British authorities his request for reimbursement of expenses. But he also addresses himself to a larger public in his narrative.[10] In the year following that publication Jonathan Carver undertook his long voyage in the region of the Great Lakes. Subsequently, up to the end of the eighteenth century and beyond, Anglo-American accounts of this kind abound.

The two works that I will now examine in detail are, along with that of William Bartram, arguably the most significant and best of this literature. They were certainly the most popular, both calling forth multiple reissues and translations in the years following their first publication. Both are based on substantial experience of contact with Amerindians over a period of years rather than days or months. The work by John Lawson, dating from very early in the eighteenth century, is exceptional for its time,[11] and Jonathan Carver's stands well above others in terms of its interest in the period when the genre was beginning to come into its own in the Anglo-American sphere. As will be seen, in spite of significant differences (dates, regions traveled, tribes encountered, sociocultural profiles and attitudes of the authors), these works converge in some important ways.

JOHN LAWSON

Next to nothing is known for sure about the author of *A New Voyage to Carolina* (1709) before his arrival in Carolina.[12] His birth date has not been established with certainty, though there is some indication it may have been 1674.[13] He probably came from a well-to-do family (though nothing suggests it was a noble one), and he seems to have received a university education. Concerning his reasons for going to America, Lawson explains in the introduction to his book that, desiring to travel, he spoke with a man "who was very well acquainted with the Ways of Living in both Indies; of whom, having made Enquiry concerning them, he assur'd me, that *Carolina* was the best country I could go to" (7). Before his departure Lawson may also have met James Petiver, a London apothecary and collector of botanical specimens, with whom he later corresponded, sending him plant samples and observations on their environment. A significant portion of *A New Voyage to Carolina* is devoted to descriptions of fauna and flora, especially the latter, in this recently colonized province that remained largely "wild."

Lawson shipped out from London in May 1700 and arrived in Charles

Town (Charleston SC) in September of that year, after a stopover in New York. He spent several months there, and then set out on an expedition to explore the interior of the country, in regions little known to the English at the time. He may have been commissioned to undertake the trip by the governors of the province, by James Petiver, or by both, but these are only suppositions.[14] Whatever the case may be, this first foray lasted about two months (December 1700 to February 1701) and covered some five hundred miles (although the author claims a thousand miles in the subtitle of his book).[15] He was accompanied at the outset by five other Englishmen, along with three Indian men and the Indian wife of one of them—all of unidentified tribal origin—to serve as guides. Later on the trip the party took on local native guides. Their course of travel took them in a wide curve to the west, into the piedmont area, and north. Then, with one of his fellow travelers, while the others continued on their inland path, Lawson returned to the coast, but far north of Charles Town, near the then contested Virginia border, in what had recently been differentiated as North Carolina. (Lawson sometimes refers to Carolina as a whole, and sometimes distinguishes between North and South.)

He settled in this area, around the Neuse and Pamlico rivers, which was inhabited by a small but growing number of settlers, with Indian tribes (particularly Tuscaroras) still located nearby. Lawson remained there for most of the eight years preceding publication of his book, periodically making further trips, some into the interior, and frequenting the Indians of the region. He engaged in various activities in this period: botanizing for Petiver, surveying (he seems to have practiced the trade in a private capacity before being named "deputy surveyor" [1705] and then "surveyor general" [1708] of the province), fur trading, and above all real estate speculation. He bought large tracts of land near his residence and was instrumental, along with several other entrepreneurs, in founding Bath, the first town of North Carolina, incorporated in 1706. He did the surveying of the town's layout as well.

Lawson left North Carolina, however, to spend more than a year (February 1709 to April 1710) in London preparing for the publication of his book. There he met Baron von Graffenried and several others who were planning to found a colony in North Carolina. Lawson joined their company, and upon his return to America helped them settle the colonists—Swiss and German refugees—in a freshly created town near Bath, named New Bern.

Lawson was very centrally involved, then, in the British colonization effort in the area. As such he was clearly perceived to be a threat by his Indian neighbors. He was captured in the company of von Graffenried, tortured, and put to death by Tuscaroras in the late summer of 1711 when on an exploratory trip. Its exact purpose is not known, but it almost certainly was made with a view to new settlement. New Bern, on the Neuse River, was created on the site of an earlier Indian village, and this displacement—following on other settler incursions and repeated mistreatment of Indians in the area by traders—triggered the outbreak of violent conflict. Lawson's death was the first skirmish in the "Tuscarora War," which culminated two years later in the defeat of that tribe and the immigration farther north of its survivors.[16]

Lawson's sole work was published two years before his death, and it enjoyed considerable posthumous success in the decade following. In that period it was reissued several times in English and appeared in two German editions.[17] The work's colonizing perspective is immediately manifest. *A New Voyage to Carolina* is dedicated to the Lords Proprietors, the governing body of the province. "I here present Your Lordships," Lawson tells them in the dedication, "with a Description of your own Country" (3). He proposes, then, to reveal to the possessors their possession, hitherto largely terra incognita to them, inhabited by alien Others.[18] But a public larger than the English governors is of course intended as well, and one group specifically targeted is potential immigrants. In his introduction the author claims, "This Place is more plentiful in Money, than most, or indeed any of the Plantations on the Continent" (10), and one of the work's five parts, entitled "The Present State of Carolina," is a kind of advertisement for the province.[19]

A rhetorical figure recurs regularly in the travel account, which imagines future, concrete appropriation of the land by the English. It might be called "prospective vision." As the traveler gazes on land now occupied by Indians, he sees in his mind's eye what that land could become in the hands of the English. Lawson describes, for example, a prairie near a village of Saponi Indians—one of the small tribes soon to meld into the Catawba Nation—that is perfectly adapted to cultivation and well irrigated by rivers that are "very convenient for the Transportation of what Commodities this Place may produce" (51–52), and then a "Neck of Land" of "many thousand Acres [that] may be fenced in, without much Cost or Labour" (55). In another passage the author says of the site of the Congaree Indians' town, to which his party has been welcomed, that it "would prove an exceeding thriving range for Cattle, and Hogs, provided the English were seated thereon" (34). Also, as if to buttress these prefigurations of English possession, Lawson often emphasizes the fidelity and submission to the British settlers of the Indian tribes that, like the Congarees, are already in close contact with them. Early on he insists that "they [the settlers] have an entire Friendship with the neighbouring *Indians* of several Nations, which are a very warlike People, ever faithful to the *English* . . . and are a great Help and Strength to this Colony' (10). So, although Lawson points out that "the Savages do, indeed, still possess the Flower of Carolina, the English enjoying only the Fag-end of that fine Country" (61), his text asserts present control and strongly projects a future possession by the English that has not yet been fully accomplished.

The map that Lawson drew up to serve as the frontispiece to his account provides an iconographic figuration of this thoroughly colonizing viewpoint. Its cartouche has two parts: below, a dedication of the map to the Lords Proprietors; above, the great seal of the dominion of Carolina: *Magnum Sigilium Carolinae Dominorum*. Within the latter two Indians stand on each side. In the center, cornucopias below and a deer above symbolize the natural produce over which the Indians preside and to which they seem to promise access. On the map itself the eastern coastal strip shows the land already divided into counties. Beyond the coast the few indications given mostly involve the quality of the land: *stony land, rich land, no poor land here*. Other notations point to mineral deposits: *iron mines, marble rocks. A pleasant vally with a lake* is also noted, perhaps as a potential site for settlement.

Such a perspective would hardly seem to lend itself to sympathy in the encounter with Amerindians. Yet from the very outset Lawson's text asserts a desire to write truly and justly about them. He opens his preface by expressing his determination to rectify erroneous notions purveyed by earlier English travelers: "Tis a great Misfortune, that most of our Travellers . . . are Persons of the meaner Sort, and generally of a very slender Education; who being hir'd by the Merchants, to trade amongst the Indians, in which Voyages they often spend several Years, are yet, at their Return, uncapable of giving any reasonable Account of what they met withal in those remote Parts. . . . In this Point, I think, the *French* outstrip us" (5). The main reason for this French superiority, in his view, is that their monarch "does not often let Money or Interest make Men of Parts [their missionaries and noblemen, both devoted to the service of their superiors] give Place to others of less Worth." From the start, then, Lawson displays a wish to remedy the shortcomings of the English accounts and in his status as a gentleman to vie with the finer French practitioners of the genre.

A sizable gap becomes apparent, however, between this initial distancing of himself from his compatriot travelers and his unconscious turn of mind expressed later in the text. For in his representation of his interactions with the natives Lawson reveals his own entanglement in the English colonialist mentality. His relation to the Indians who serve as guides and hunters for his expedition is formulated in the possessive mode—they are "our Indians"—though in one passage he recognizes that he owes his life to the canoeing skill of one of them (21). Lawson also seems naïvely to reflect the comfortable assumption that the Indians who have the best character are those who are most favorable to the English (62). In several places he contemplates the idea of exploiting Indian lands he has come upon in the interior. He muses in one passage, for example, "If it be my Chance, once more to visit these Hilly Parts, I shall make a longer Stay amongst them: For were a good Vein of Lead found out, and work'd by an ingenious Hand, it might be of no small Advantage to the Undertaker" (56–57). Here the author shows no concern for the fact, highlighted in the synthetic part of his work, that the Indians avoid showing the English the location of mineral deposits because doing so would "bereave [them] of the best Hunting-Quarters [they] have" (214).

In many passages Lawson seems to take for granted a hierarchical relation between Europeans and Indians, and his comments sometimes show condescendence toward the Indians, as when he notes that he and his traveling companions, going upstream on the Wateree River, received a Waxhaw Indian messenger "with a great many Ceremonies, acceptable to those sort of Creatures" (39). But perhaps Lawson's most characteristic approach to the Indians he encounters could be defined as domestication, or a "de-othering" of their otherness. This tendency surfaces notably in a linguistic practice, apparently adopted by the group of travelers as a whole and echoed in Lawson's text. The individual Indians with whom he and his fellow travelers develop particular relations (most often the chiefs that host them) are designated by familiar English nicknames, such as "Santee Jack," "Keyauwees Jack," and "Enoe Will" (31, 57, 61). Thus Indians' own names are replaced by attributed Anglo-Saxon names. The kind of Anglo-Saxon name given, well illustrated by the example of "Jack," which is used several times, not only conjures away cultural difference and distance but also imposes an impoverishment of identity. Whereas, as Gerald Vizenor comments, in native usage "personal names and tribal nicknames are stories" that concretely and intimately link individuals to their communities, here they are replaced by particularly commonplace, quasi-anonymous English monikers.[20] In the case of chiefs, the renaming also would have the effect of removing the aura of moral authority that was inherent in their position and integral to their identity.

But this refusal of alterity goes beyond naming and often permeates the style of the narrative. For Lawson often translates what he observes of Indian life into an English frame of reference, forcing what he sees into familiar molds that eliminate the specificity of difference. This can be seen in his choice of vocabulary in portraying scenes involving Indians and interactions with them. In describing a ceremony, for instance, Lawson speaks of a "ditty" being sung; the best hunters are termed the "chief Sportsmen"; and he calls the woman with whose family he was lodged on one occasion his "landlady" (45).[21] Beyond isolated vocabulary, this tendency can infect an entire narrative sequence. Lawson recounts one incident in which another of the Englishmen in his party becomes interested in having sex with an Indian woman,[22] gives her gifts to gain her assent, then goes off with her. When he returns she has taken some of his things and disappeared. But the story is told in a jovial, burlesque style, in the tones of an English picaresque novel, with the two protagonists called "Mr Bridegroom" and "Mrs Bride" and their coupling a "Winchester-Wedding."[23] The story ends in mock pathos, with the author waking early to see a melancholy figure "who in less than 12 Hours, was Batchelor, Husband, and Widdower, his dear Spouse having pick'd his Pocket of the Beads, Cadis, and what else should have gratified the Indians for the Victuals we receiv'd of them. However, that did not serve her turn, but she had also got his Shooes away.... Thus dearly did our Spark already repent his new Bargain, walking bare-foot, in his Penitentials, like some poor Pilgrim to *Loretto*" (47).

The interactions on which Lawson dwells are often sexual, although he never admits to himself engaging in such relations.[24] In several instances, though, an interaction of a very different order is staged, a "spiritual" one in which he is the main actor. What is involved is an attempt at proselytism, which imposes its own limitations on the encounter. During a stay in a Keyauwee village, Lawson shows the "king" an image of King David, since he is convinced that the only effective way to bring the truths of Christianity to the Indians is to show them, as do the French Jesuits, "some lively carnal Representation" (58). The king and his entourage seem to acquiesce in the Christian teachings that Lawson draws from the devotional image (although Indians notoriously often hid their real responses to attempts to change their ideas or beliefs). Several weeks later Lawson again uses the image, with the same goal in mind, this time addressing himself to his guide at the end of the trip—"Enoe Will," already mentioned—and the result is more mitigated: "[Will] asked me several Questions concerning the Book, and Picture, which I resolv'd him, and invited him to become a Christian. He made me a very sharp Reply, assuring me, That he lov'd the English extraordinary well, and did believe their Ways to be very good for those that had already practis'd them, and had been brought up therein; But as for himself, he was too much in Years to think of a

Change" (64–65). The guide nevertheless proposes to entrust his son, rebaptised Jack by the English, to the spiritual care of Lawson. The son is never mentioned again, though, and it would seem that the author did not take up the father's offer.[25]

The tendency to translate the experience of the Other into familiar frameworks of the Self often seems to stymie Lawson's attempts to understand what he witnesses. For he is confronted with an overall culture that is entirely alien, in which particular elements that superficially resemble elements of his own culture in fact take on entirely different meanings. In the scene in which the Englishman loses his shoes, Lawson seems to interpret the Indian woman's act as a way of taking payment for the food offered by the Indians to the English, though such a motive would presumably be inimical to the Indian ethic of hospitality. Rather than remuneration for goods, the woman's "thievery" more probably stemmed from a perception that the English had not provided adequately generous gifts.

Similarly in another passage the sexual freedom of girls before marriage is called "Whorish" ("the more Whorish, the more Honourable," Lawson exclaims [40]), and the women who play a diplomatic role in giving their favors to visitors are described in language suggesting actual prostitution: "They are mercenary, and whoever makes Use of them, first hires them, the greatest Share of the Gain going to the King's Purse, who is the chief Bawd" (41). Here the emphasis is also on the monetary. Coming himself from a thoroughly commercial culture and society, Lawson often depicts Indian society in mercantile terms. According to his account, Indian brides are "sold," and Indians can "buy off" a murder with wampum, "their Mammon" as he calls it (204).

While in this way he changes many observed aspects of Indian social relations into the currency, often in a literal sense, of his own social background, in the realm of religion Lawson is confronted with practices entirely alien to English Protestantism, and these call forth other domesticating strategies. In fact he hesitates between two alternative means of bringing the Indians' religious rites and beliefs into synch with his own worldview. In a few passages he suggests that Indians may be devil worshippers, thus bringing their practices into the Christian universe of discourse but as blasphemous negation (223). He seems to have trouble believing this explanation, though, and more often opts for a debunking approach, based on another element of his own culture—a kind of empiricist rationalism. Often myths and legends become simply "lies." He treats in this way, for example, the tale of how the Tuscaroras came to possess lightning in the form of a partridge (221). Ceremonies are simply "foolish" (219), and shamans are "quacks" or "cunning knaves" who are purposely deceiving a credulous people (27, 222).

In spite of his scornful debunking of Indian beliefs and magical practices in many instances, his responses in this area are in fact contradictory and hesitant, for he informs the reader that he has been witness to and has been told of efficacious Indian cures, and he concedes that they compare well with European medicine (18, 26, 225–26). Even more puzzling and disturbing—since the cures could be explained, without abandoning European medical principles, by the use of effective herbs—are instances in which he sees a prophecy fulfilled or seemingly supernatural control exercised by a shaman over a natural phenomenon (in one case, a thunder storm [30, 55]). Lawson appears to be at a loss to account for these occurrences within the terms of his system of belief and understanding and is reduced to reporting them without commentary.

At the same time Lawson shows signs of frustration in his desire to understand more fully. For Indians refuse to answer certain questions that he asks, especially those that involve their religious beliefs and practices. In one instance he observes several Indians who have joined his party for a time—probably Enos or Shakoris—approaching a concave stone, placing tobacco in it, and spitting; they remain silent when he asks them why (63). Lawson also becomes curious regarding the custom of circumcision practiced by some Machapunga Indians he encounters, but he is not able to get an explanation, which leads him to a general comment on the reticence of Indians: "Perhaps, if you ask them, what is the Reason they do so, they will make you no Manner of Answer; which is as much as to say, I will not tell you. Many other Customs they have, for which they will render no Reason or Account . . . for there are a great many of their Absurdities, which, for some Reason, they reserve as a Secret amongst themselves"

(219). Lawson's irritation is palpable in this passage. He cannot fathom why his interlocutors will not simply explain everything straightaway. This inability to understand the Indians' reluctance to accede to a demand that they reveal secrets to a stranger—and one who dismisses them as "absurdities"—in itself exemplifies the kind of barriers that Lawson's perspective puts in the way of penetration of the Amerindian Other.[26]

In spite of the many times his cultural "blinders" get in the way, Lawson does at points seem to show a lucid awareness of a number of areas of Indian culture, broadly conceived on the basis of the groups he has been in contact with and perceived as significantly different from English (and European) modes of thought and behavior.[27] Like Lahontan, he points out the absence of passionate love among the Indians, and more generally their control of their emotions (195, 209–10). But more surprisingly, in contradiction with his commercialization of Indian culture elsewhere, in certain places in his text Lawson develops the idea that Indian money, means of measurement, and sense of time and work are all fundamentally different from those of Europeans, and that these are interrelated.

The Indians never push themselves to work so as to accumulate goods or wealth, he claims, but only do as much as is necessary to provide subsistence. When traveling or hunting, though, they often exert themselves enthusiastically and tirelessly because these activities bring both pleasure to them and practical advantage to their group (176). Lawson points out in another place that the production of wampum is extraordinarily painstaking and time-consuming, but since the Indians "never value their time ... they can afford to make them" (204). He also makes the related observation that the Indian method of measuring the length of a wampum belt is to extend it from the elbow to the little finger, but "they never stand to question, whether it is a tall Man, or a short one, that measures it" (203). Clearly the standardized quantification of commercial transactions does not hold sway with Indians Lawson has known.

At many points—in the continuation of his remarks on wampum, for example—Lawson's attempts to analyze Indian culture are confused, contradictory, or fragmentary. For the most part he does not manage to formulate his observations and interpretations in terms (concepts and language) other than those that are thoroughly familiar to him.[28] Yet in one passage he also shows that he is aware of the nature of the problem, admitting that the Indians'"way of living is so contrary to ours, that neither we nor they can fathom one anothers Designs and Methods" (240).

In spite of this opacity of the Other, Lawson's text, like those of the French travelers, does on occasion point to an underlying principle of Indian societies that is at loggerheads with English and European principles: the tight-knit, integrated nature of their communities. Although often belied by the textual practices I have illustrated, Lawson does in some places emphasize the Indians' egalitarian sharing of material goods, deep attachments, generosity and mutual aid, the predominance of the common good over that of the individual, and so on (34, 38, 184–85, 220). The Indians value human qualities such as prowess in hunting and war rather than possessions, and greed for wealth is foreign to their mentality: "For a great Dealer, amongst the *Indians*, is no otherwise respected and esteemed, than as a Man that strains his Wits, and fatigues himself, to furnish others with the Necessaries of Life, that live much easier and enjoy more of the World, than he himself does with all his Pelf" (206).

Indeed, as Lawson observes elsewhere, the Indians "never walk backward and forward as we do, nor contemplate on the Affairs of Loss and Gain; the things which daily perplex us" (175). According to him this characteristic results in a striking lack of dissension: "They never fight with one another, unless drunk.... They say, the Europeans are always rangling and uneasy, and wonder they do not go out of this World, since they are so uneasy and discontented in it" (184). Although ostensibly just reporting what Indians say, Lawson seems to be speaking with them as well.

As regards evaluation of Indian societies, *A New Voyage to Carolina* is shot through with contradiction and ambivalence, swinging from expressions of contempt, summary negative judgments typical of Lawson's social milieu,[29] and an admiration that he seems unable to resist. But with value judgment, as with understanding, an appreciable difference is apparent between the travel account and the customs-of-the-Indians sections of the work. On the whole it is in the latter part that one finds the more subtle analyses and more favorable attitudes toward Indians. One possible explanation might be that in the travel narrative the writer remains too close to his experience to be able readily to transcend conditioned reflexes, whereas the distance implied by the form of the treatise favors the taking of that step.[30]

In the final section of his work, which gives a general portrait of the Indian peoples he has known, Lawson expresses admiration for specific aspects of Indian society that seem to correspond to his own predilections (the lenient treatment of children and funeral customs that do not include burial of the body, for example). On other themes his attitude seems conflicted or confused. Strangely, for example, he speaks of torture within a single sentence as "what they are seemingly guilty of an Error in (I mean as to a natural Failing)," and as diabolic and an "inhumane butchery" (207). Similarly with Indian languages: after transcribing a small dictionary of three languages spoken in North Carolina (Tuskeruro, Pampticough, and Woccon), which he has spent time learning,[31] he excuses himself for boring the reader with a "Jargon" that he deems "deficient" and incapable of the "Flight of Stile, as Authors would have you believe" (239). These incongruities may at least partially be due to a strategy—conscious or not—of appeal to different intended publics of the work.

Whatever the case may be, the difference between the travel account and the study of customs remains partial and relative, and the ambiguities of point of view subsist up to the end of the synchronic section. Only in the final summation, in drawing lessons from the scattered threads of his experiences and reflections, does the author seem to become fully conscious of a conclusion toward which he had been tending. In a passage that is astonishing because what has preceded it has little prepared the reader for it, Lawson makes an eloquent plea in favor of the Indians, combined with severe criticism of the colonists:

> They are really better to us, than we are to them.... We look upon them with Scorn and Distain, and think them little better than Beasts in Humane Shape, though if well examined, we shall find that, for all our Religion and Education, we possess more Moral Deformities, and Evils than these Savages do.... These Indians are the freest People in the World,

and so far from being Intruders upon us . . . we have abandon'd our own Native Soil, to drive them out, and possess theirs; neither have we any true Balance, in Judging of these poor Heathens, because we neither give Allowance for their Natural Disposition, nor the Sylvian Education, and strange Customs, (uncouth to us) they lie under. (243–44)

He continues, "[We] daily cheat them in every thing we sell, and esteem it a Gift of Christianity, not to sell to them so cheap as we do to the Christians, as we call our selves" (244). Here an underlying tension between the economic and the religious dimensions of Lawson's sensibility becomes apparent, and the latter strongly presses its claims. To be fair with the Indians, Lawson concludes, would consist in putting an end to this behavior that is unworthy of true Christians, recognizing and encouraging the good qualities of the natives and attempting, by gentle means, to correct the bad ones. No indication is given as to what the latter consist of, but it seems likely he is referring above all to the Indians' violent practices, since several pages before he declared himself convinced that if they were not continually warring the Indians "would enjoy the happiest State (in this World) of all Mankind" (239).

It is true that this passage occurs in the context of final recommendations to the settlers (and Lords Proprietors) as to how to "make these People serviceable to us, and better themselves thereby" (243), that is, to civilize and convert them and extend British rule. Lawson recommends doing so by persuasion and intermarriage rather than by force and trickery, but this does not change the nature of the goal. In spite of the imperial context, though, this statement as well as some other passages preceding it stand in strange contrast to the discourse of domination and de-othering that I have discussed, and to a certain extent undermine it. In the confrontation between the two cultures, the moral hierarchy is reversed. The Indians turn out to be superior to the colonists from an ethical point of view, according to the colonists' own religious framework. At the same time, since they are "very happy" and the most free people in the world, they perhaps—though the author never explicitly asserts this—hold the key to a better way of life.[32]

JONATHAN CARVER

Unlike Lawson, Jonathan Carver (1710–80) was an American by birth. He was born in Wehmouth, on the coast of Massachusetts, not far from Boston. When he was about eight years old his parents moved to Canterbury, a Connecticut village in the interior but still far from the frontier. Carver's ancestors had arrived in New England in the early seventeenth century. His family was well-off but not rich, his father a small property owner and minor official in the different towns in which they lived. After marrying in Canterbury in 1746, Carver moved several years later with his wife and two children to another town, this one closer to the frontier, in northwestern Massachusetts. His occupations there are not known with any certainty, though he may have been a shoemaker, a trade that had considerable status in that time and place. When the Seven Years' War broke out Carver joined a local militia and served periodically as a militiaman until the end of the conflict. When he left the colonial army in 1763 he had reached the rank of captain.

Three years later, after the defeat of Pontiac's rebellion, when British control of the lands west of the Appalachians became better established, Carver was taken on as a cartographer and surveyor for an exploratory expedition by the famous ranger Robert Rogers. The two had probably met during the war. As with Charlevoix's journey under the auspices of the French Crown many years earlier, the ultimate goal of this expedition was the discovery of the Northwest Passage.[33] Carver may not have been fully aware of Rogers's long-range plans at the outset; at any rate they were very quickly stymied. But in the course of the preliminary probe Carver covered a vast territory (according to his own calculations he traveled 4,800 miles overall) in the region of the Great Lakes and upper Mississippi, an area still little known to the English at the time.

Leaving from Boston in May 1766, Carver first traveled to Michilimackinac. From there he set out in September on the exploratory part of the trip. Two other members of the expedition—the commander, James Tute, an ex-ranger, and the secretary, J. S. Goddard, a fur merchant—were to meet Carver near the Falls of Saint Anthony on the upper Mississippi River (the site of present-day Minneapolis). Winter set in before they were able to meet, however, and Carver was obliged to stop during the coldest months with a band of "Naudowessies" of the Plains (Dakota Sioux).[34] On the map that he published with his travel account, Carver locates this tribe at a considerable distance to the west of the Falls, on the north side of the St. Pierre River (now the Minnesota River).[35] He prolonged his stay with them until the end of April 1767, when he finally linked up with the two other men and headed farther north. By the time they had reached the northwest of Lake Superior in mid-July, their supplies had run out. Moreover Rogers's direction of the venture had been challenged by the British authorities, and he was finally arrested on accusations of treason. The voyagers were consequently obliged to return to Michilimackinac before the real search for a water passage to the west had begun. Carver spent the winter of 1767–68 at the fort, where he probably worked on the first version of a travel journal based on notes taken previously. He returned to the East Coast in the course of the following summer and arrived in Boston on September 1, 1768. During his two-year journey he made contact with many Indian communities—including Ottawas, Winnebagos, Sauks, Fox, Ojibwes, and Crees—and stayed with a number of them in addition to the Naudowessies, though for shorter periods.[36]

It was only ten years later, in 1778, that *Travels through the Interior Parts of North America in the Years 1766, 1767, and 1768* was published, in London. The work is the fruit of a series of textual revisions effected during that period, starting from the original journal. Soon after the trip had come to an end, in February 1769, Carver traveled to London to petition the royal authorities. He sought remuneration for the expedition, which had been withheld due to Rogers's difficulties, and hoped also to be granted a new mission as administrator of an Indian territory. In 1770 he was granted a simple reimbursement of expenses. In 1773, still in London and having exhausted his resources, he petitioned Lord Dartmouth for a post. After this request was refused, he made repeated attempts in the two years that followed to interest officials in several projects for exploitation of the western territories he had traveled over: a mining monopoly and—even more detrimental in its possible consequences for Indians in the region—a distillery of spirits that, since they would be produced on the spot, could be advantageously sold to the natives for furs. In addition Carver claimed, in all probability fraudulently, that the Naudowessies had made him a land concession.[37]

None of these propositions was accepted, partly due to English policy, which since 1763 had discouraged further colonization west of the Appalachians, and partly because the British were already confronted with colonial revolt. As Carver saw his chances of obtaining sources of revenue and appointments dwindle, he apparently began to reorient his hopes toward the financial rewards of a publishing venture that addressed a wide public. In this he clearly succeeded, for by the second decade of the nineteenth century his *Travels* had gone through more than twenty editions in the United States, Great Britain, and Europe.[38] Yet its author never tasted this success. Carver died in London, impoverished, little more than a year after the first edition appeared.

The publishing success of Carver's work went far beyond that of Lawson. Norman Gelb, the editor of a 1993 paperback edition of the text that is an attempt to revive interest in Carver, calls his account the "first genuinely popular American travel book."[39] After 1778 the book went through one edition (or reissue) per year in London for the next three years, while in the same period a Dublin edition and a German translation appeared. In the following three decades—through to the close of the War of 1812—the book went through some fifteen more editions, both in the British Isles (among other places, in Edinburgh and Glasgow) and the United States (in Philadelphia, New York, Boston, and several towns in New Hampshire), as well as being translated into French and Dutch.

After the war, however, Carver's literary fortunes began to change. During the rest of the nineteenth century only one more complete edition came out (1838, in New York), though abridged versions in German and French intended for young people continued to appear up to 1870. Over the course of the century, and especially after midcentury, Carver increasingly fell out of favor and was largely forgotten. In part this situation was due to the disrepute in which the text came to be held, for growing doubts were expressed as to the genuineness of Carver's account. It was noticed that significant segments of the text closely resembled passages from earlier

French travelers (notably, Lahontan and Charlevoix), and James Adair's *History of the American Indians* as well.[40] Some questioned whether Carver was its author at all, or whether the trip had ever taken place.

In 1909, however, the historian John Thomas Lee contributed to proving its authenticity by publishing two items he had found in the *Boston Chronicle* of 1768: the text of a letter from Carver to his wife while still on the trip, and a call for subscriptions for publication of an account of the trip.[41] Much more important, soon thereafter manuscripts of several versions of an original journal of Carver's voyage, in his own hand, were found in the British Museum. They had earlier been in the personal library of Joseph Banks of the Royal Society, to whom Carver had dedicated his *Travels*.[42] These manuscripts clearly establish that Carver was indeed the author of the nucleus of the published book, even though additional material was added and the original journal was considerably modified. But because such documentation is often lacking their discovery is also important in that it provides a relatively rare opportunity to study the genesis of a travel account—the developmental process that leads up to the final product in its published and generic form.[43]

The manuscript journals, now in the British Library,[44] exist in four versions, but versions 3 and 4 are in the main simply clear copies of 1 and 2 respectively. Version 2 makes significant changes in version 1, and expands it considerably. At the end of version 2, moreover, there are a series of fourteen inserts. Numbered pointers in the text indicate where these inserts were to be placed. Since these additions were afterthoughts to version 2, we can speak of three main stages in the development of the journals: version 1, version 2, and version 2 inserts. Although none of the manuscript stages is dated, it seems likely that version 1 was drafted in Michilimackinac during the winter of 1767–68, whereas version 2 and the inserts were written once Carver was in London (from early 1769).

The stage following the version 2 inserts is the published work—the first edition of 1778—and it introduces further changes involving reorganization, rewriting, and addition (including material taken from the French travelers). At least some of these are due to the intervention of another hand than Carver's. For along with the inserts at the end of version 2 is to be found a note "to the reviser," who is encouraged to make additions that will "embellish or give better sence [sic] to the journal."[45] Thus Carver was clearly aided in the final transformation of the original journal into a published travel account by an editor or by one of the literary hacks that abounded in eighteenth-century London.[46] We have no way of determining, however, exactly how they collaborated and the extent of the responsibility of each for the changes made. Since Carver published the work under his own name, it is legitimate—and necessary—to consider him ultimately the sole author of the work.

If we compare the two ends of the process of revision, it appears that the most significant and generalized changes are related to a shift in intended public. The early stages of the journal still show the marks of Carver's intention of providing a report—first, probably, to Rogers, and later, once he was in London, to the Crown's Board of Trade. But then the work was progressively revised to better appeal to a broad public. It should be emphasized, though, that the shift is not an absolute one, since, as already mentioned, Carver attempted to raise subscriptions for a publication immediately upon return to Boston. It is plausible that the first subscription campaign failed precisely because the manuscript was not yet deemed to be a travel account that could succeed on the literary market. When reaching that goal became Carver's more single-minded purpose some years later in London, he agreed to undertake the major revisions that would make it attainable.

Looking at the changes themselves, it seems possible to identify at least four principal tendencies. First, Carver eliminated many concrete specifics of the trip that would be of little interest to the general public. Second, he bolstered the importance of his own role. Not only is Rogers erased as leader of the expedition, but the two other members (who were with Carver, it is true, for only part of the trip) disappear entirely from the text as well. In this way Carver becomes the initiator and sole protagonist of the journey as narrated in *Travels*. Closely linked to this modification, a third development is increased attention to stimulating reader interest through anecdotes, particularly "adventures," of which the author himself is usually the hero. The fourth and final transformation is the restructuring of the text according to a pattern commonly found in the travel account genre: the division of the work into separate parts, including the narrative of the trip, a "customs of the natives" section, and a descriptive enumeration of fauna and flora.[47]

The evolution of the different versions of Carver's work are thus consequential. Yet it would be a mistake to conclude that *Travels* is a radically different work from the original journal. For beyond the textual variation, the fundamental perspective of the voyager remains unchanged. In the following analysis I will refer exclusively, with one exception, to the published text, since that is the final form in which Carver wished his work to be received by the public. But one element of the textual transformation is of special interest: the construction of adventure. This mode of representing experience, as I suggested in chapter 4, tends to constrict the range and impoverish the image of encounter with the Amerindian Other, ultimately becoming its zero degree. Though generally less present in travel accounts than in some of the other genres of encounter, the adventure mode is not entirely absent from them. In Carver's *Travels* adventure plays a considerably more important role than in the travel accounts I have already discussed. For this reason, in examining the dimension of interaction in Carver's work I will take a heightened example of adventure as it appears in the published text and trace its genesis through comparison with the first version of the account.

In its final form Carver's work is addressed above all to the greater British public, curious to discover the far-off western territories recently acquired by the Crown, and their native populations. Specialized publics such as administrative patrons, potential immigrants, and investors are less centrally addressed than in Lawson's account. Yet we do find an explicit appeal in the introduction to a double audience. On the one hand, for those interested in the area because of "the contiguity of their possessions or commercial engagements," the work "will be extremely useful"; on the other, for those who "from a laudable curiosity" wish to gain information, the book "will furnish an ample fund of amusement."[48] In laying out the reasons for the expedition he is going to recount Carver presents himself as a disinterested public servant (though his motives were doubtless more mixed than he acknowledges),[49] claiming that after his military campaigns he sought "to be still serviceable and contribute... to make that vast acquisition of territory gained by Great Britain in North America advantageous to it" (57). But in several passages he holds up the promise of immense riches for those who may follow in his footsteps. Early on, for example, he claims that those who penetrate farther into the continent "will reap, exclusive of the national advantages that must ensue, Emoluments beyond their most sanguine expectations" (59).[50]

On the whole, though, the emphasis is on riveting the interest of the general reader through the vivacity of the narrative and the appeal of exoticism. The book is filled with colorful incidents and tales concerning the Indians Carver was in contact with, culled from his own experience, from that of persons encountered on the way (both Indians and traders), and from previously published books (that he does not identify). Carver demonstrates that he is quite aware of what he is doing, and in justifying the brevity of his generalizations on Indian character near the end of his work he comments that "anecdotes and relations of particular events, however trifling they might appear, enable us to form a truer judgment of the manners and customs of a people" (212). Also in keeping with a concern to win over the reader, Carver's style—after its reworking by the "reviser," that is—is substantially more polished and literary than that of Lawson. At one point Carver asks the reader's pardon for his book's failings in this regard (62), but this apology both reveals a literary intention and is itself a literary device.

Among the anecdotes brought into the narrative, many involve Carver's own interactions with the natives, and these are often recounted with brio. The author tells, for instance, of his surprise and anxiety upon approaching an Indian encampment, when its inhabitants inexplicably and without warning began firing at him (though over his head) and he saw them "[running] from one tree or stump to another shouting and behaving as if they were in the heat of battle." Carver prepared to give the order to fire back, but happily another, more knowledgeable member of his party informed him in time "that this was their usual method of receiving the chiefs of other nations" (66).

This incident involved the very first meeting with Indians on his trip: his expedition's arrival at an Ottawa village on Green Bay.[51] In subsequent accounts of initial contacts, Carver usually portrays himself as peaceable and friendly even when the situation seemed threatening. The dramatization of the scenes generally pictures the author in a favorable light compared with his companions, guides, and servants. In several instances the text emphasizes that he courageously and level-headedly stood fast when others were tempted to flee (77, 93–94). Carver even claims that by interposing himself between them and negotiating, he was once able to reestablish peace between two warring tribes only a few days after having arrived in the camp of one of them (80). This was a band of Naudowessies "of the river," visited while Carver was still on the Mississippi, before he met—farther to the west—those "of the plains," with whom he was to spend five months. The author attributes to his peacemaking mission for the former his friendly treatment at the hands of the latter and, in a later encounter, also at the hands of the Ojibwe tribe that was the opposing party in his negotiation (81).

Among the first-contact incidents recounted, one is developed at greater length, clearly manifesting the author's intention of manipulating reader response to create adventure. There is, however, a striking contrast in this regard between the published version and the original manuscript version, in that the adventure elements are almost entirely missing from the latter. I will first discuss the published text as a fully realized adventure sequence, and then compare the earlier version with it.

The scene occurs after Carver's winter and spring with the plains Naudowessies, when he is heading north through Ojibwe country toward Lake Superior. Smoke appears on the horizon, and then a dozen tents. In spite of his apprehension—he fears they are a roving, tribeless band of Indians, and therefore dangerous—and in spite of an attempt by his companions to convince him to skirt them on the other side of the river, Carver resolves to "meet them boldly," since he knows from experience that this approach is "the best way to ensure a friendly reception" (93–94). His party disembarks from their canoes and goes to meet the Indians now standing on the shore. The first in line receive the voyagers cordially, but behind these stands

> a chief remarkably tall and well made, but of so stern an aspect that the most undaunted person could not behold him without feeling some degree of terror.... However, I approached him in a courteous manner, and expected to have met with the same reception I had done from the others. But to my great surprize he with-held his hand and, looking fiercely at me, said in the Chipeway [Ojibwe] tongue, "Cawin nishishin saganosh," that is, "The English are no good." As he had his tomahawk in his hand, I expected that this laconick sentence would have been followed by a blow, to prevent which I drew a pistol from my belt and, holding it in a careless position, passed close by him to let him see I was not afraid of him. (94)

Carver soon is told that this man is an important chief, called the "Grand Sautor" by the French,[52] of whom he is a faithful ally. Carver decides to stay on his guard but to remain overnight near the Indian camp to show that he is not intimidated. The narrative goes on: "I pitched my tent at some distance from the Indians and had no sooner laid myself down to rest than I was awakened by my French servant. Having been alarmed by the sound of Indian music, he had run to the outside of the tent where he beheld a party of the young savages dancing towards us in an extraordinary manner, each carrying in his hand a torch fixed on the top of a long pole" (94–95). Following on the menacing reception by the "Grand Sautor," it appears as if these dancing men mean Carver no good. The reader continues with aroused interest, only to be stopped short by the following sentence: "But I shall defer any further account of this uncommon entertainment, which at once surprized and alarmed me, till I treat of the Indian dances" (95). This sentence ends the paragraph, and the paragraph following it begins: "The next morning I continued my voyage and before night reached La Prairie le Chien." Thus the tense scene that has just been described is frozen, like a tableau vivant, setting up a prolonged "suspense," in the etymological sense of the word.

In this monumental deferment Carver transfers the adventure out of the narrative section and into the ethnographic—synchronic, in principle—which follows it. There are surely good reasons why he (or perhaps his editor) might have done so. In this way a bridge is thrown up between the two parts of the work; the reader of the travel narrative is encouraged to continue into the ethnographic description, while the spice of adventure breaks up the tedium of the latter.[53]

The story is taken up again, in the "customs" section, following descriptions of fearsome war dances and mention of the "Black Dance," thought by some Europeans to raise the devil. "I know not under what class of dances to rank that performed by the Indians who came to my tent when I landed near Lake Pepin ... as related in my Journals," he goes on. "When I looked out, I saw about twenty naked young Indians ... coming towards me and dancing as they approached" (141). They are painted red and black, as when Indians "go against the enemy," and some war dance gestures are part of their dancing. Carver resolves "to sell my life as dear as possible" and sits down, rifle on one side and pistols on the other. The Indians continue to dance, singing their war song while violently striking the tent poles with war clubs. The author exclaims, "I never found my apprehensions more tumultuous on any occasion" (141). He offers a peace pipe, which is refused, and then, as a last resort, several gifts. After consultation the Indians ultimately accept the gifts, along with the peace pipe, and depart in a friendly manner.

A final surprise is in store for the reader, however. After having created and sustained a sense of immanent danger in this incident, Carver admits that he was never able to find out what the intentions of the young dancers were: "I was afterwards informed that [their visit] might be intended as a compliment which they usually pay to the chiefs of every other nation who happen to fall in with them" (143). Thus the author seems to discover after the fact that what he had experienced as an adventure was perhaps not one at all. This dénouement closely resembles that of the story of arrival in the Ottawa village, except that in that case the author was given cultural information about these Ojibwes on the spot rather than later and unambiguously rather than as a mere supposition. Since the Ottawa and Ojibwe nations are closely related culturally, geographically, and historically, the similarity of the stories involving customs of reception of visitors is hardly surprising.

Comparison of this treatment of the Ojibwe encounter with the corresponding material in the original journal manuscript is revealing. Two differences between them are particularly important. First, in the journal there is no division of the text into diachronic and synchronic parts; the entire text is a narrative of travel, within which ethnological commentary is inserted. Consequently there is no hiatus of suspense. Second, in the journal the incident of confrontation with the Grand Sautor is absent. What remains in the earlier version is a single passage, far shorter than the two separated passages of the final version. I quote it in full:

> May 3, 1767. Passd Lake of Tears or Lake St. Anthony, came to the enterance of the Chipeway River. Here I found two chiefs of this [Ojibwe] nation, a trader from Louisiania, and one from Michillimackinac. At the evening a number of their young men came to give me a dance. Their ceremony began with a sort of a drum and rattle shell at some distance, advancing slowly and stoping now and then to dance, each being dressd with short leather breeches like a highland kelt with the edges very beautifully figured with quills and long feathers on their heads. When they came to the door of my tent I was informd that the dance was intended for me. I stepd to the door and bid them welcom.
>
> They entered and soon began their dance, each one of them having a tomehawk in his hand or a club calld breakhead which every now and then they would strike upon the tent poles over head and make a short speech on something extraordinary that they have done before, either in war or hunting, after which they gave a loud coohoop with their hands on their mouths interupting the sound with a sort of tremour attended with such postures and motions of body as appeared both hostile and terrible, which I was informd by the French with me was their constant custom when they gave a dance to any strange chief that came among them. I was informed by people with me that they expected some presents, which I was very willing to bestow in order to get shot of my guests.[54]

Clearly in this version all the details contribute to give a different aspect to the incident than that of the adventure in *Travels*. Aside from the absence of a threat from the Grand Sautor, the action of the dancers is from the outset presented as a "ceremony" that is "given" to the author, and it is described in ethnographic detail. In the first sentence of the second paragraph the modulation of verb tense from past to present perfect—"something extraordinary that they have done before"—suggests a surreptitious shift to description of usual practices. The emphasis on the beauty of the Indians' dress—the breeches with their "edges very beautifully figured"—is also not conducive to the arousal of fear in the reader, and when the author bids the dancers "welcom" it appears that the person undergoing the experience felt none.

The "hostile and terrible" appearance of the dancers is evoked only near the end of the passage, and when it is, the threat is unambiguously dissipated in the same sentence (the author was informed that this was the Indians' "common custom"). In the published version, as I have already pointed out, this interpretation of the Indians' behavior is only a possible hypothesis that the author became aware of after the fact. A final difference of a similar kind between the two versions occurs in the conclusion of the incident. In the manuscript journal the author is simply told by his informers—specifically identified as French, who, because of their intimate experience with the Ojibwes, would be likely to know—that the Indians expect gifts; he obliges, he seems to be telling the reader, only so as to be rid of unwanted "guests." In the published version, on the other hand, he tries gifts (after a peace pipe, which is not mentioned in the early version) as a strategy to pacify potential assailants.

The incident as recounted in the journal is thus quite different from the final version, in which the earlier text has been thoroughly reworked to become an adventure intended for a large public. It is doubtless impossible to determine exactly what corresponds, in the two versions, to the author's "real" experience,[55] but it is noteworthy that the first version—the one that is closest (at least temporally) to the experience of encounter—is more ethnological and less adventurous. And the adventure, even in the published version, is partially deflated, or placed in question, at the end of the account. This episode, then, in its two versions, illustrates the point that while the travel account may use the rhetoric of adventure, it cannot be reduced to that dimension.

The incident I have just discussed involves a first encounter, but Carver's relations with Indians went far beyond such initial contacts, giving rise to the development of deeper ties, particularly during his stay with the Naudowessies. It would seem that Carver participated to a much greater extent than Lawson in Indian life. Carver claims, for example, that he learned the Naudowessie language (though his knowledge was seemingly rudimentary), that he was admitted to council meetings and was adopted as a "chief" (90). Doubtless more important than the honorific function and title, however, was the fact that Carver often hunted with his hosts and exchanged war stories over a pipe, drawing on his memories of the war against the French (88–89). Later on his trip he spent shorter periods with other Indian nations, notably the Ojibwes, and in the "customs" section of his work he mentions that in his willingness to become involved he often went so far as to join in war dances, in spite of his fear of being wounded by the sharpened knives with which they mimicked combat (141).

Two details from their narratives are indicative of the gap between Carver and Lawson in terms of their degree of projection into the culture of the Other. Carver, like Lawson, mentions the importance for the Indians of speeches and ceremonies in encounters with other groups. But instead of speaking of what is "acceptable to those sort of Creatures," Carver transcribes a speech that he made on one occasion "to give my Readers a specimen of the language and manner in which it is necessary to address the Indians so as to engage their attention and to render the speaker's expressions consonant to their ideas" (90). The idea is the same, but the tone has shifted.[56] Second, instead of giving English nicknames to the natives, as Lawson and his companions do, Carver allows himself to be named by them (and reports the naming to the reader). The Naudowessies call Carver "Shebaygo," which signifies, he tells us, "a writer, or a person that is curious in making hieropglyphicks, as they saw me often writing" (189).

Though the difference of empathy between the two travelers is appreciable, it should not be overestimated. Of his friendly discussions with the Naudowessies, Carver tells the reader, "I held these conversations with them in a great measure to procure from them some information relative to the chief point I had constantly in view, that of gaining a knowledge of the situation and produce, both of their own country and those that lay to the westward" (89). If we are to believe the author, then behind the seemingly pleasurable interaction was a pragmatic goal in the service of the interests of the colonizers. Yet this statement itself may be at least partly disingenuous. It seems to be largely directed to Carver's more restricted public of governmental patrons in an attempt to convince them of his seriousness. Even if we take the statement at face value, though, such a hidden agenda in his dealings with the Naudowessies would not necessarily have kept him from appreciating the relationships and activities that he took part in while he was among them.

Like Lawson before him, Carver wishes to reassure the reader as to the veracity of his testimony, especially regarding the native peoples he met. At the beginning of *Travels* he thus distinguishes himself from many earlier writers: "I shall in no instance exceed the bounds of truth, or have recourse to those useless and extravagent exaggerations too often made use of by travellers to excite the curiosity of the public or to increase their own importance. Nor shall I insert any observations but such as I have made myself or, from the credibility of those by whom they were related, am enabled to vouch for their authenticity" (63). In several places in his narrative also Carver reiterates his claim that what he has reported is entirely true. Whatever the case may be as to their authenticity, he generally seems to penetrate further than Lawson in the analysis of the phenomena he observes. Less dominated by prejudice, Carver comes closer to achieving something like an ethnological perspective.

Unlike the Carolina traveler and settler at the opening of the century, Carver expresses no irritation when he comes up against the opacity of Indianness—the difficulty of interpretation and the refusal of natives to reveal themselves, particularly on the subject of their beliefs. The synthetic chapter on religion opens as follows: "It is very difficult to attain a perfect knowledge of the religious principles of the Indians. Their ceremonies and doctrines have been so often ridiculed by the Europeans that they endeavour to conceal them; and if, after the greatest intimacy, you desire any of them to explain to you their system of religion, to prevent your ridicule they intermix with it many of the tenets they have received from the French missionaries, so that it is at last rendered an unintelligible jargon, and not to be depended upon" (191). For this reason Carver prefers to limit himself to what he has been able to understand of the religion of the Naudowessies, who have not undergone any French influence. As for myths and legends, rejected by Lawson as pure lies, the author of *Travels* calls them "fabulous" (104) but does not disdain them; indeed he transcribes several of them in the course of his narrative.

Like Lawson, Carver is troubled by the apparent efficacy in some cases of Indian magic. He is unable to explain what he has been witness to and simply takes note of the mystery, assuring the reader of the truth of the events related. Soon before his return to Michilimackinac, at the Grand Portage, he converses one day with a group of Killistinoe (Cree) Indians. Their "chief priest" announces that he is going to attempt to obtain a prediction from the Great Spirit of the time of arrival of a party of traders. The shaman conducts a consultation, during which he seems to be possessed, and the divination is communicated: a canoe will arrive the next day, and those in the canoe will know when the traders will come. As they wait, Carver senses that the Killistinoes are surreptitiously watching for his reaction, aware of his skepticism. Everything takes place as the shaman has foretold. The Killistinoes seem triumphant before the doubting European, and Carver concludes by offering the story for the reflection of his readers, without "wishing to . . . make superstititous impressions on their minds, but leaving them to draw from it what conclusions they please" (103).[57]

The author of these lines is doubtless playing on the exotic appeal for a portion of his public of the "primitive" supernatural. Yet it appears in Carver's account of this incident and others of a similar kind that he was personally shaken by what he saw and came close to giving credence to some Indian beliefs. Consequently, in some passages he is at pains to convince the skeptical reader who might accuse him of gullibility. Quite clearly some were incredulous, as is indicated by an introductory note, titled "An Address to the Public," added to the third edition of *Travels*. In it the author responds to doubts having been expressed by some readers of the earlier editions concerning the veracity of this story of a prophecy that came true and another involving prediction by a Menominee Indian of the return of a tamed rattlesnake at a precise time and place (73–74). In the note Carver attempts to explain the story of the snake—which he says he was told by a trustworthy Frenchman—in terms of natural phenomena. In the case of the Killistinoe shaman, however, the only proof offered is the fact that he was himself a witness to the events.[58]

In a passage that immediately follows that story Carver makes a remark about the Killistinoes that exemplifies the contrast between his epistemological approach and that of Lawson. I have pointed out that in Lawson's text Indian women offered to strangers are considered prostitutes. Here is Carver's comment on the same or a similar phenomenon: "I observed that this people still continued a custom, that appeared to have been universal before any of them became acquinted with the manners of the Europeans, that of complimenting strangers with the company of their wives. This is not only practised by the lower ranks, but by the chiefs themselves, who esteem it the greatest proof of courtesy they can give a stranger" (103).[59] Carver thus refers to the meaning the Indians themselves appear to attribute to the act and suggests the role that the practice would have in the framework of Indian culture.

The explanation is perhaps rudimentary, but it is significantly different from the way Lawson deals with the issue. Instead of reading the Other through his own cultural grid, Carver attempts to imagine that of the Other and to use it in interpreting observed phenomena. Nonetheless Carver does not always follow this procedure. For example he reproduces without question the commonplace notion held by many European travelers of the period, that Indian men were "remarkably indolent, leav[ing] to [the women] every kind of drudgery" (121). This statement simply carries over a European idea that defines certain tasks as "drudgery" without asking if the status and social role of the tasks are not different in Amerindian cultures.

In identifying the most fundamental aspects of Indian societies he has knowledge of, Carver is often in agreement with Lawson, and with the French voyagers of chapter 5 as well. In his view Indians show great self-control and prudence while also demonstrating the most ardent and tender family feelings. They are hospitable, generous, and free-spirited, and in normal circumstances enjoy an exceptional peace of mind. He attaches particular importance to the attitude and behavior of Indians with regard to property: "strangers to all distinctions of property, except in the articles of domestic use" (127), they practice a continual sharing that produces "nearly ... the same effect" as if they held all in common (137). As for money, those who live far from the colonies, like the Naudowessies, have no notion of it, and "they consider it, when they are made acquainted with the uses to which it is applied by other nations, as the sources of innumerable evils" (127).[60] Rather than money or property, it is "the honour of their tribe and the welfare of their nation [that] is the first and most predominant emotion of their hearts." When they go to war it is "as if they were actuated only by one soul" (211).

These broad tendencies of Indian culture are clearly viewed by Carver in a thoroughly positive light. The ambiguities that characterized Lawson's attitude are almost entirely absent. The opinions expressed, both in the narrative and in the generalizing treatise, are enthusiastic, almost without reservation. Rather than coming to such a perspective only at the end, and in partial contradiction with what preceded it, in the opening pages Carver shows his cards to the reader: "I must here observe that, notwithstanding the inhabitants of Europe are apt to entertain horrid ideas of the ferocity of these savages, as they are termed, I received from every tribe of them in the interior parts the most hospitable and courteous treatment and am convinced that till they are contaminated by the example and spirituous liquors of their more refined neighbours, they retain this friendly and inoffensive conduct towards strangers" (66).[61]

Nothing that comes after contradicts this overall assessment.[62] Though Carver recognizes that he at first shared certain prejudices "in common with every other traveller" (206), his experiences lead him to question them and to alter his views. We find in Carver's work few of the reactions of boredom, disgust, or irritation that travelers sometimes report when brought into prolonged contact with the daily life of Indians. When he exclaims on one occasion that the inhabitants of a particular Ojibwe village "seemed to be the nastiest people I had ever been among" because of their habit of picking and eating fleas from each other's scalps, he immediately contextualizes his censure by adding that the practice is "common in some degree throughout every Indian nation" and that it is held to be repulsive only "according to our ideas" (96).

The only substantial criticism leveled by Carver against Indian lifeways involves their ferocity in war and relentless practice of torture. He never stresses this point, however, and nowhere expresses the kind of dread felt by other travelers, perhaps because he was never obliged to witness such an event. The following commentary, which comes after the overall evaluation of Indians cited above, reveals a dispassionate, understanding point of view: "Their inveteracy and cruelty to their enemies I acknowledge to be a great abatement of the favourable opinion I would wish to entertain. But this failing is hereditary of them, and having received the sanction of immemorial custom, has taken too deep root in their minds to be ever extirpated" (66).

Aside from this dark spot on the picture, which concerns only relations with the outside world, the disposition of Indian societies internally seems to Carver conducive to bringing out the best in human beings and forwarding the "general good," since it is founded on the "plain and equitable laws of nature" (127). He does not cite Rousseau or any other Enlightenment thinker, and nothing indicates that he was familiar with them, but the portrait he sketches of North American Indians constitutes, as with Lahontan, an incarnation of their ideals, and more specifically of the motto of the French Revolution. Unlike Lahontan, however, Carver does not give more weight to the idea of freedom. Equality and fraternity, as they appear in Indian communities, are from Carver's perspective at least as important.

The author often compares Amerindians with modern Europeans on the one hand, and ancient Greeks and Romans on the other, the Indians being judged superior to the former and equal to the latter. Even in war, in which their negative qualities come to the fore, the Indians are placed above Europeans since their motives for engaging in it are "in general more rational and just" (153). Moreover in pursuing war they display heroic virtues—such as courage and stoicism in the face of suffering, misfortune, and death—that are worthy of Greco-Roman antiquity. These commentaries are sometimes accompanied by illustrations. Carver tells of a Winnebago "prince," for example, whom he saw throw all his possessions into the Falls of Saint Anthony as an homage to the Great Spirit,[63] and who, while they were together, gave Carver "innumerable proofs of the most generous and disinterested friendship." While with him, Carver avers, he "could not help drawing a comparison between him and some of the more refined inhabitants of civilized countries" (84). Similarly the author relates that he saw a Naudowessie woman demonstrate tremendous self-control and familial tenderness when confronted with the death of a husband and a child. This Indian woman displayed, he concludes, "sentiments that would have done honour to a Roman matron" (206).

In several places Carver seems to wish to provide a balanced appraisal of the Indians. He tells the reader that they are "the worst enemies, and the best friends of any people in the whole world" (126), and that they exhibit "passions and appetites, which they hold in common with the fiercest beasts . . . and are possessed of virtues which do honour to human nature" (209). He hopes, in making his judgments, to avoid two pitfalls: "I shall endeavour to forget on the one hand the prejudices of Europeans . . . whilst with equal care I avoid any partiality towards [the Indians], as some must naturally arise from the favourable reception I met with during my stay among them" (209). In this passage, situated near the end of the synthetic section of his work in a chapter entitled "A Concise Character of the Indians," the author acknowledges the diversity of Amerindians throughout the continent and specifies that his comments are limited to the western tribes, "such as the Naudowessies, the Ottagaumies [Fox], the Chipaways [Ojibwe], the Winnebagoes, and the Saukies," that he knows best. In the final analysis, though, in spite of Carver's desire to equilibrate the pros and cons, the scale clearly tips toward admiration for Amerindian culture and society.

Although this stance applies to Amerindians in general, Carver clearly singles out the Naudowessies as the focus of his conception of Indians as incarnations of an ideal. This quasi-utopian designation appears strikingly in the manuscript map he drew up in 1769, an early version of the map published with *Travels*. The handwritten notations on it mostly concern the Indian nations in the area, showing the ways they use the land, divide it among themselves, and so on. There is virtually no reference to European presence, and the large divisions are all zones of sovereignty exercised by the different Indian nations. Yet there is a suggestive variation in the terminology used to construe this sovereignty. In the case of the *Chipeways* (Ojibwes) south of Lake Superior, the neutral term *territories* is used. Farther south the domains of the *Monomonies* (Menominees) *Winebaygoes* (Winnebagos) *Saugies* (Sauks), and *Ottigaumies* (Fox) are called *kingdoms*, also an essentially neutral term since the assimilation of Indian chiefs with the notion of kingship was current.

The one exception is the designation of the land lying west of the Mississippi as the *Naudowessie Republic*. This people is presented as incarnating the egalitarian ideals of antiquity or of the English Revolution. Clear proof of how subversive this naming of the Naudowessie nation as a republic was in the context, is provided by comparison of the manuscript map with that which finally was included in the first edition of the published work. Appearing in London in 1778, as the American War of Independence was under way, the edition simply erased the utopian political overtones from the map by substituting *land* where *kingdom* had been, and *country* for *republic*.

In the discussion I have been developing of two major Anglo-American travel accounts, one is struck by the disparity, in terms of openness toward the Other, between their two authors. This difference is due in large part, in my view, to their sociocultural specificities. Lawson, as a colonist, surveyor, trader, and speculator, was more directly implicated in the process of expropriation against which the Indians were struggling. Carver, a militiaman, adventurer, and cartographer, did not have as immediate a personal interest in the process, although he was tempted by several projects involving colonizing and exploiting Indian lands and remained committed to the state-sponsored enterprise of exploration that was creating the groundwork for private appropriation.

Beyond the differences, however, I have pointed to some convergences between the two accounts, convergences that link them also with the

French texts treated in chapter 5. These common features seem to stem from the intercultural encounter itself and to be rooted in the character of the Amerindian Other. There seems to be a general recognition, expressed with greater or lesser coherency in each case, of a crucial paradox: a culture considered by modern Europe to be savage, primitive, or even bestial fulfills the ideals that are the traditional patrimony of the Europeans. In the following chapter I will show how this recognition is carried to a higher level of awareness in the work of William Bartram.

CHAPTER SEVEN

Travels of William Bartram, Quaker Botanist

Following Jonathan Carver's expedition in the 1760s, Anglo-American travel—and accounts of it—increased in "Indian territories" as well as in areas of colonial settlement. Those who crossed the frontier in the last third of the century and sometimes recorded their experiences included explorers and fur traders such as Alexander Henry (discussed in chapter 4), John Long and Alexander Mackenzie (treated in chapter 8), speculators such as John Filson, settlers moving west, naturalists, and British visitors whose itineraries took them into "wild" parts.[1] But none of the Anglo-American narratives of encounters with North American Indians in this period has the stature of William Bartram's *Travels*.

This work was first published in Philadelphia in 1791 and the following year in London, long after the travel itself, which took place between 1773 and 1777.[2] It then went through a rapid series of European republications and translations: in Dublin, Berlin, and Vienna in 1793; in Holland and again in London in 1794; in Paris in 1799 and 1801.[3] After being largely forgotten during the nineteenth century, *Travels* was rediscovered in the twentieth century and met with remarkable success, both scholarly/critical and popular (featuring Bartram societies and websites, Bartram trails and trail guides, etc.). Bartram's entry into the Library of America in 1996 is probably the clearest indication of his recent "canonization." The author of *Travels* has been studied and admired as a nature writer, and he arguably was an important forerunner of environmentalism.[4] I will be concerned here, though, with his travel account as the textual representation of a particularly fruitful encounter with Amerindians. While sharing many aspects of the Anglo-American accounts already analyzed, it surpasses them and approaches, in my view, fulfillment of the potential of the travel account as an "instrument of consciousness" and a vehicle of "cultural translation," in the terms proposed by Mary Campbell.[5] I will attempt to show that the quality of Bartram's encounter with Indians is rooted in a sympathy and affinity that is linked to a radical alienation from his own society.

LIFE AND TRAVELS

William Bartram (1739–1823) was the son of John Bartram, the renowned Quaker botanist of Philadelphia. Bartram Senior was a well-to-do farmer whose rural properties near Philadelphia included a botanical garden—one of the first in the colonies—at Kingsessing on the banks of the Schuylkill River. He corresponded with and provided specimens for some of the leading lights of European horticulture and natural history and was named botanist of the king for the North American colonies by George III in 1765. When his son William's artistic talent became apparent at a young age, John took him on botanizing trips to make sketches of plants—several times in New York and Connecticut (1753–55) and then, most decisively for his later trip, in the area around the St. John's River in East Florida in 1765–66.

In spite of William's artistic disposition and manifest taste for "wild" natural settings, his father wished him to go into business and set him up first as an apprentice to a Philadelphia merchant (1756–61), then as the proprietor of a trading store in rural North Carolina for the four following years. After the trip to Florida in 1765–66, during which he became deeply attached to the region, William seems to have wanted to reconcile his love of beautiful natural sites with the commercial vocation his father hoped for him, by becoming a rice and indigo planter on the St. John's River. But this agricultural experiment—carried out with the manual labor of several slaves bought by his father—ended miserably, as had the earlier attempts at mercantile activity. The farm remained unproductive, and William became sick. He returned to Philadelphia after less than a year and persisted there for another three years in trying to fulfill his father's expectations. In 1770, heavily in debt, he returned to North Carolina, not to reopen the trading store of earlier years, however, but to take refuge with the beloved uncle he had lived with then. William remained in North Carolina until soon before he left on the trip for which he is famous.[6]

During his years of commercial endeavor Bartram had continued to draw. He had obtained several modest orders for sketches of fauna and flora from English patrons of the natural sciences. But in 1773 he managed to procure a more substantial subsidy for an extended expedition from John Fothergill, a wealthy London Quaker who was the owner of the largest English botanical garden of the period. This trip, which Bartram undertook alone, was to last four years and take him through the Carolinas, Georgia, and the Floridas as far west as the lower Mississippi River. Bartram was commissioned to report regularly to Fothergill and to send him samples and sketches. While Fothergill sometimes expressed dissatisfaction with Bartram's diligence in collecting samples, and in certain cases with the scientific precision of the sketches,[7] the travel account that came out of the trip—based on a written report that Bartram drew up for Fothergill—constitutes the more enduring success of the expedition.

In North Carolina and Florida Bartram had already had contacts with Indians, but this long period of travel—in a vast area still effectively controlled by native groups[8]—greatly expanded them. Bartram crossed the lands of a variety of Indian tribes and nations, notably Cherokees (North and South Carolina), Muscogulges or Creeks (South Carolina, Georgia), Seminoles (East Florida), and Choctaws (West Florida, present-day Alabama and Mississippi). In regular contact with these Indians, he often lived in their communities for weeks or months at a time. The Indian people Bartram knew best, the "confederation" of the Creeks (broadly divided into "Upper" and "Lower" Creeks), was the dominant power in the southeast region.⁹ But his wanderings in the area came at a turning point for them. His long excursion coincided with the first stage of the American Revolution, and in the aftermath of the revolutionary period the autonomy of the Creeks and the integrity of their culture came to be seriously compromised.¹⁰ By the end of the eighteenth century, as Robbie Ethridge asserts in her study of the Creeks at the turn of the century, they had become fully a part of the "modern world system."¹¹ During the time when Bartram was traveling in the Southeast, tensions and conflicts between patriots and loyalists erupted in some of the places he visited, particularly near the coast. But he chose to exclude them entirely from his narrative and to focus on the natural world and the Indians living in close relation to it.¹²

At his return to Philadelphia in January 1777, Bartram moved into the family house in Kingsessing, with its botanical garden. He remained there until his death almost a half-century later, continuing his botanical drawings and devoting himself to the cultivation of the garden along with one of his brothers, who became the owner of the property after their father's death in September 1777. In the course of the 1780s William also prepared the manuscript of his *Travels*. After his trip, then, he had definitively abandoned the idea of making a career in commerce. Though the Bartrams carried on a business of selling plants and seeds, its purpose was not principally profit, and William's brother was the owner of it. From an economic point of view, William lived to the end of his life under the protection of and dependent upon his brother John. Extremely modest and retiring by temperament, William also shied away from the honors and offers of positions that his growing notoriety inevitably brought. He let pass a chair in botany at the University of Pennsylvania and later declined to take part in the Lewis and Clark expedition. Though elected to membership in the Academy of Natural Sciences, he never attended their meetings.

QUAKER MILIEU AND WORLDVIEW

In his classic study of Philadelphia Quakers in the eighteenth century, Frederick Tolles distinguishes between two types: the radical Quakers, who witnessed deeply to the original ideals of Quaker faith, in particular the values of egalitarianism and affirmation of the oneness of the human and natural community, and those who practiced a moderate, mitigated form of their religion, one that was compatible with commercial activity, the pursuit of individual profit, and the accumulation of wealth. This second type of Quakerism grew in importance in eighteenth-century Philadelphia and had become predominant by the middle of the century. The ideological perspective of the second kind of Quakerism was close to that of other Protestant groups studied by Weber in *Protestantism and the Spirit of Capitalism*, which created a favorable terrain for the development of a market society. The Philadelphia Quakers indeed came to constitute a wealthy and powerful commercial elite in the middle of the eighteenth century, an elite made up of merchants and manufacturers who were often patrons of scientific activity as well.[13] This was the milieu within which William Bartram was raised, one that was in tune with the larger currents of British America at the time. It was a paradoxical milieu, though, since it contained a tension between the dominant worldly Quakerism and a minority strain that retained traces of the purer, primitive inspiration of early Quakerism.

Although not a merchant per se, William's father was clearly on the side of commercial Quakerism, vigorously attempting to steer his son's career in that direction, as I have indicated. John's desire for such an outcome was such that he persisted in spite of the repeated failures, while William's complete lack of aptitude for commercial activities appeared evident to a number of family friends. John received several letters on the subject. One friend, for example, expressed surprise that "you Should not have encouraged this Genius of his as a Naturalist sooner; for, tho' you endeavour'd to curb it by putting him to be a Merch[an]t, &c, yet Nature prevailed So far as to disqualify him from Pursuits of this Sort."[14] Fothergill himself commented in a letter to John, written while William was on his trip, that even though brought up to it his son clearly had no inclination or aptitude for commerce.[15] William had in fact come to the same awareness before setting off on the trip and had written his father telling him of his resolution to henceforth devote himself to drawing and studying the natural world.

John's lack of understanding of his son stems in large part, it would seem, from a marked difference between their worldviews, William's having been strongly inflected by the radicalism of early Quakerism, in particular that of its founder, George Fox.[16] In this respect William's vision is close to that of John Woolman, author of the famous *Journal*. Unlike Bartram, however, Woolman was successful in a small business venture that he found congenial at the moment when, as the result of an intense moral crisis, he resolved to retire completely from commercial life and devote himself to his inner, spiritual being.[17] Bartram's vision is also less narrowly expressive of Quaker theology than that of Woolman, and his perception of Nature has a quasi-pantheistic quality.[18] For Bartram, all the creatures of the world—plants, animals, and humans—are manifestations of the divine, and as such possess equal value. Profoundly linked, they are part of an overarching unity of life forms, which human beings should be in touch with and embrace. Yet while all created beings are part of a nonhierarchical whole, this does not mean a leveling down to the lowest common denominator. On the contrary, as Pamela Regis has noted, "the general movement is toward elevation—the plants Bartram mentions are animal-like; the animals are humanlike; the savages are not savage at all."[19] Only those who are called "civilized" are devalued, because their mode of life constitutes a negation of vital principles.

Among Bartram's unpublished manuscripts there are two fragments that develop the implications of these convictions in sociocultural terms. They present in condensed form some of the main themes that ran through the first manuscript version of *Travels*, some of which were edited out of the final published version. As such they provide an important philosophical and social background for the travel narrative.[20] Interestingly Bartram also drew several pictures over one of these texts, and these can be seen to project supplemental meaning visually and in palimpsest. On the lower part of the page there are two images: one of a small house that seems to be beside a river, the other of a man walking alone among trees, leaning on a stick. Above these is a third drawing, of a horse that seems to be galloping, or possibly jumping, since it is oriented upward. The images all involve the natural world, showing fauna and flora, and human beings in a natural setting, both living and moving (traveling) within it. The drawing of the man walking in woods might be a self-portrait of Bartram the "Philosophic Pilgrim," as he repeatedly called himself in the manuscript version of *Travels*.[21]

In the texts themselves Bartram levels a scathing critique at so-called civilized society. In this society "the more Any Man or Woman, approaches to Honesty and simplicity, the more he is accounted a Fool and he is in the broad Road, and hastening on to Poverty, contempt and Misery." It is a society in which "the Passion of covetousness is One of the most formidable . . . Enimies. This passion if we give way to it becomes insatiable It is the parant of contention . . . and contention begets violence and Warr" (304). The pursuit of wealth, and the work ethic (or "industry," the term Bartram uses) that accompanies it, turn civilized human beings away from the true source of life in nature, leading ultimately to "even a species of suicide. How common is it for Men Whose Aim is for excessive affluance, Riches and fashion able Luxery to ruin their constitution and shorten their Lives, through excessive and constant Labour, fatigue and Watching" (305). For Bartram, then, mercantile civilization constitutes a system of interrelated parts that is unnatural, and as such deeply damaging from a moral as well as a physical point of view.

The author of these fragments goes on to draw the following conclusions: "Thus it appears I think that we act most rationally and virtuously when our Actions *seem to* operate from simple instinct [or] aparoach nearest to the maners of the Animal creation" (italics mine). Those nations "who yet remain in the simple state of primitive Nature as our Indians, who had had but little intercourse with White People," are closest to this apparently instinctive life, and therefore to true morality (306). The "seem to" is important, since in a number of passages in *Travels* Bartram strongly rejects the notion, held by other whites, that Indians have no developed social institutions but are instinctive "children of nature." For Bartram they have structured societies, but ones that are in consonance with and integrated into the rest of living creation.

As for animals, with which he associates the Indians in the passage, it is clear elsewhere that Bartram means to raise their status rather than to lower that of human beings to a debased animality. In other portions of the fragments the author ironizes about the self-styled "Dignity of Human Nature," an unmerited distinction since mankind behaves as an "Absolute tyrant" (310) toward other animals and "probably would long ere this have destroyd the whold animal creation if his Arms were not withheld, by the Supreme Creatory & preserver" (319). Bartram, on the other hand, affirms the "Dignity of Animal Nature" (317) and is convinced that animals express themselves by means of actual languages and demonstrate rational intelligence (308, 319).[22]

This sketch of William Bartram's life and worldview points clearly to a particularly favorable predisposition to encounter with Amerindians—what could be called an "elective affinity" with their culture, directly related to his marginality to and estrangement from the civilization of modernity.[23] The Bartramian vision of the intimate, nonhierarchical unity of living things—plants, animals, and humans—as equal incarnations of divinity has a strong resemblance to Amerindian systems of belief. Moreover Bartram's fervent adherence to primitive Quakerism leads him to yearn for the union of human beings in friendship and cooperation, a state of being that he found in Indian societies. In his writings he portrays the lifeways of the Indians as an affirmation of life, and those of his compatriots as something like the negation of it. The fecundity of the encounter in *Travels*, then, is indissociable from its author's alienation from his own society.

Bartram's vision, with its harsh critique of modern society and aspiration to human community as part of an "enchanted" Nature, is entirely congruent with romanticism. This shared outlook doubtless explains the strong interest and admiration for *Travels* shown by many romantic literary authors, such as Wordsworth, Coleridge, Carlyle, and Chateaubriand.[24] Coleridge copied long excerpts from *Travels* into his notebooks, and several of his best-known poems, notably "Kubla Khan," are strikingly marked by it in different ways.[25] Echoes of Bartram's book can also be heard in passages from works by Wordsworth and Chateaubriand, in terms of imagery, description of place, phraseology, and even closely parallel passages.[26] In a letter to Emerson in 1851, Carlyle expressed a sense of nostalgic wonder at Bartram's text that must have been felt by other romantics as well: "Do you know Bartram's 'Travels'? Treats of Florida chiefly, has a wonderful kind of floundering eloquence in it; and has grown immeasurably old. All American libraries ought to provide themselves with that kind of book; and keep them as a future *biblical* article."[27]

VERSIONS OF THE TRAVEL ACCOUNT

Bartram's writings on his trip, like those of Jonathan Carver, went through several stages and versions. He first wrote a two-part report, already in the form of a travel narrative and based on notes that have not survived, to Fothergill in England, sent from the South before the expedition had been completed. This report, which has been published, puts the greatest emphasis on descriptions and enumerations of fauna, flora, and habitats of the kind that its addressee had instructed the traveler to provide.[28] Even in this document aimed at providing "objective" information, Bartram gives voice to subjective impressions and effusions, but that dimension is much expanded in the draft version of an account of his trip that Bartram probably began soon after his return to Philadelphia in 1777. Three sizable fragments of this first manuscript version of *Travels* have survived, in which many social and philosophical reflections and literary embellishments appear.[29] This early version then underwent an editing process (clearly with the aid of persons other than Bartram himself) before the work was finally published, fourteen years after the conclusion of the trip.[30]

In terms of my analysis of Bartram and his work, the most relevant changes made in the manuscript for the published book were the editing out—doubtless by editors thinking of the intended readership of the publication—of many passages in which the narrator, presenting himself as a "Philosophic Pilgrim," develops reflections on Indian as opposed to "civilized" societies. More precisely, many passages were eliminated that castigated the colonists, pinpointing avarice as the major evil and calling on the civilized—though without much hope of being heard—to reform themselves by imitating the virtues embodied in Indian culture.[31] As

Hoffmann, the editor of the manuscript, points out, "Bartram's draft is a candid statement, rendered seemingly without concern about how it would strike an audience who didn't share his vision of a philosophic pilgrimage." In summarizing major differences between it and the publication, Hoffmann also maintains that "in contrast to the published book there is a nostalgic quality about the prose of the draft manuscript that suggests its author's longing to a return to a simpler era in more natural surroundings."[32] This is a theme with a strong romantic resonance, but that might not appeal to many in postrevolutionary British America.

In spite of these differences I will concentrate my discussion on the published version of the work, that is to say, the first edition of 1791.[33] First of all, most of the passages involving Indians have been retained there, with few changes in content. What mainly has been erased is the critique of civilized society and the links between that and the commentary on Indians. But since the essay fragments I have presented provide an encapsulation of the views that appear more diffusely in the manuscript draft of the travel account,[34] they should allow for a reading of *Travels* that restores the dimension that was attenuated in the published version. Moreover it is important to emphasize that the published version did not completely adulterate the manuscript. *Travels* is not a different work, keeping, after all, enough of the qualities of Bartram's original inspiration to appeal to (among others) the romantic readership I have referred to.

TRAVELS

From a structural point of view, *Travels* adopts the classic form of separation into a diachronic narration of the trip and a synchronic treatise on the customs of Indian peoples encountered.[35] It is divided into four parts. The first three constitute the travel account, and the fourth is demarcated by a separate title page indicating that it contains general remarks on Indians known to the author, especially Creeks, Seminoles, Cherokees, and Choctaws.

The itinerary of the expedition, as it appears in the first three parts, begins with a voyage by ship from Philadelphia to Charleston and finally Savannah. From there the author travels inland, attends negotiations with the Creeks, and accompanies a surveying expedition that comes out of them, then returns to Savannah (first part). From there he descends the coast into Florida, travels up the St. John River that he explored with his father in 1765–66, and returns north to Charleston (second part). In the final stage of his circuitous wanderings Bartram goes west—northwest first, into Cherokee territories, then southwest through Creek lands and on to those of the Choctaws near the lower Mississippi. He visits Pensacola and Mobile on the Gulf of Mexico and ascends the Mississippi a short distance beyond Lake Pontchartrain. The return trip takes Bartram again through the domain of the Creeks, to Charleston, and from there back to Philadelphia by land (third part). These are the broad outlines of a peregrination spread over more than three years that includes detours, backtracking, and prolonged stays in some places. Although this textual itinerary corresponds overall to the reality of Bartram's trip—he did indeed visit all the places he writes of—recent research has established that the author of *Travels* rearranged some locations and events, in certain cases probably by mistake but in others for dramatic effect.[36]

In 1773, when Bartram begins his trip, a major transfer of Indian land, referred to as the "New Purchase," is in the offing in Georgia. It is the subject of the negotiations that the author observes on his first trek inland. Called for by merchants as reimbursement for debts, and by the governor as an opening for new colonization and speculation, this cession of land is far from unanimously approved by the Indians in the region. There are disagreements between Creeks and Cherokees over who is entitled to decide, as well as over the policy to adopt in relation to the English, whose recent incursions have led to some violent skirmishes. Within the Creek Nation there are also differences of opinion between young and old warriors.[37]

This situation, and other problems farther south, create a climate of tension and hostility in the larger region that makes parts of the projected path of travel dangerous.[38] There are rumors of massacre, but in spite of the risks Bartram continues the trip, changing his plans at some points. His decision to leave for East Florida in part 1 is largely determined by the fact that it is too risky to visit the Cherokees at the time (69). He is able to do that only much later (in part 3), and then cannot go as far as originally intended (296). The author sometimes, however, carries out his initial plan in spite of warnings, even when traveling alone, as is often the case. If the danger of proceeding alone seems too great, he joins a caravan of travelers (348). Despite these difficulties engendered by friction between Indians and colonists, during the entire trip, as he recounts it, Bartram maintains an extremely positive attitude toward the Indians, often taking their side in disputes with whites (58, 86).

Beyond that, Bartram is often sharply critical of the behavior of whites with whom he comes into contact in the wilderness areas. Those whom he encounters are settlers, surveyors, and traders, but most often traders. Although he does befriend some, particularly among the older and more experienced, whose sagacity he occasionally praises, they are exceptional cases, as he points out himself. When traveling with traders, Bartram most often chooses to stay apart from them on the trail, preferring the society of plants and animals. Recounting one such expedition with a company of traders crossing some of his most beloved terrain in Florida, Bartram notes, "Having a good spirited horse under me, I generally kept a-head of my companions, which I often chose to do, as circumstances offered and invited, for the sake of retirement and observation" (187).

The mode of travel of these white men is entirely different from that of Indians, and Bartram roundly censures their practices. They break camp late in the morning and stop their trek already in midafternoon. But what outrages Bartram most, as he comments in relation to a later excursion in Choctaw country farther west, is that they press their horses mercilessly with loud cries and curses, accompanied by continual whipping, filling the air with "an incessant uproar and confusion, inexpressibly disagreeble" (351). Such a manner of traveling exhibits the traders' insensitivity to the suffering of animals and at the same time their indifference to the natural scenes they pass through. (Bartram is particularly distressed on the trip in Choctaw territory by the suffering of his own horse, which becomes exhausted by the caravan's "infernal" pace.)

The cruelty of the white travelers extends to wild animals. Bartram tells of one incident in which he and his traveling companions are approached by an alligator at night. The person who has discovered it is quickly joined by all the others in the party, "for it was a rare piece of sport." They attack the alligator with firebrands and ram javelins down its throat. While a few are in favor of "putting an end to his life and sufferings with a rifle ball ... the majority thought this would too soon deprive them of the diversion and pleasure of exercising their various inventions of torture" (210). Only when they grow tired of the game do they put the animal out of its misery. Bartram reports a similar occurrence at a much later date, when another company of traders spies a litter of wolf cubs, chase them, and capture one of them: "One of our people caught it by the hind legs, and another beat out its brains with the but [sic] of his gun,—barbarous sport!" (319).

This seemingly widespread indifference to the suffering of animals is often accompanied by a lack of concern with wasting natural resources. Bartram becomes indignant at one point when his fellow travelers kill and cook a tortoise of which they know they will not be able to eat more than half: "My companions, however, seemed regardless, being in the midst of plenty and variety, at any time within our reach, and to be obtained with little or no trouble or fatigue on our part" (159). Even one of the older traders, with whom Bartram is on friendly terms, seems to share this attitude. When a party that the two of them are traveling with sight a herd of deer, "I endeavoured to plead for their lives; but my old friend, though he was a sensible rational and good sort of man, would not yield to my philosophy" (174). These examples highlight the exceptional nature of Bartram's awareness of ecological issues in the eighteenth-century North American context of seemingly infinite natural abundance.

As for the traders' behavior toward Indians, Bartram is aware that their frequent practice of marriage with Indian women is, aside from sexual attraction, dictated by pragmatic motives: "the white traders are fully sensible how greatly it is to their advantage to gain their affections and friendship in matters of trade and commerce," since "there are but few instances of their neglecting or betraying the interests and views of their temporary husbands; they labour and watch constantly to promote their private interests" (170).[39] Moreover, though Bartram acknowledges that some traders act honorably in their relations with tribes they are living with and are sometimes loved and respected by their hosts, that "is somewhat of a prodigy; as it is a fact, I am afraid too true, that the white traders in their commerce with the Indians, give great and frequent occasions of complaint of their dishonesty and violence" (286).

INDIANS AND THE NATURAL WORLD

In contrast to his disapproval of these behaviors on the part of whites, throughout *Travels* its author expresses a passionate interest in and respect for Amerindians in their natural environment. At the outset Bartram reveals his vision of nature through metaphor. The travel narrative per se is preceded by an introduction. After a preamble stating his hope to provide useful knowledge, particularly for the botanist and zoologist, the author announces his philosophical and religious credo: "This world, as a glorious apartment of the boundless palace of the sovereign Creator, is furnished with an infinite variety of animated scenes, inexpressibly beautiful and pleasing" (15). Several pages further on we read, "In every order of nature we perceive a variety of qualities distributed amongst individuals, designed for different purposes and uses; yet it appears evident, that the great Author has impartially distributed his favours to his creatures, so that the attributes of each one seem to be of sufficient importance to manifest the divine and inimitable workmanship" (17).

Subsequently recurrent passages (though less numerous and less accentuated than in the first manuscript) reinforce and develop this vision, proclaiming the nonhierarchical unity of living things (20, 22), the wonder of "scenes of primitive nature, as yet unmodified by the hand of man" (65), the majesty of Creation (82), the happiness of a free life in Nature (107–10), the peaceful character of animals (222), and a feeling of communication with them (282). Bartram avows a preference for wild Nature as opposed to sites "improved" by the work of settlers, when he travels from one to the other, for example (42), or when he revisits a spot that has been transformed since an earlier visit (101–2). Nature, finally, which "is not to be imitated by the united ingenuity and labour of man" (169), is in Bartram's mind intimately linked to the Indian (205).

Bartram perceives Indians to be *at home* in their natural habitats, which they treat in ways that seem to maintain rather than destroy them—habitats that constitute a kind of utopian home for Bartram himself. Here, for example, is his comment on a scene he came upon in East Florida:

> I penetrated the grove, and afterwards entered some almost unlimited savannas and plains, which were absolutely enchanting; they had been lately burnt by the Indian hunters, and had just now recovered their vernal verdure and gaiety. How happily situated is this retired spot of earth! What an elysium it is! where the wandering Siminole, the naked red warrior, roams at large, and after the vigorous chase retires from the scorching heat of the meridian sun.... Seduced by these ... visions of terrestrial happiness ... I had roved far away.... I turned about, and in the evening regained our camp. (107)

In this passage Bartram displays both an understanding of Indians' active role in modifying (without destroying) the natural environment and a lyrical sense of their being the inhabitants of Nature's utopia.

The author's perspective is not, however, without its contradictions. At the end of the introduction Bartram states what he claims to have learned in his relations with Indians: "They were desirous of becoming united with us, in civil and religious society." He encourages governmental authorities to send well-disposed agents among them, as a preliminary to the elaboration of a plan "for their civilization and union with us" (26).[40] He also expresses admiration in several instances for the "improvements" made by the commercial planters near the coast who host him (37, 77, 85) and praises the characters of the planters themselves. Moreover there are a few occurrences in Bartram's narrative of the rhetorical figure of "prospective vision" that I pointed to in Lawson's and Carver's texts, in which the voyager looks at a landscape presently occupied by Indians and imagines what it could become under English ownership. When describing a site discovered in Creek territory, for example, the author exclaims that it promises to be "a delightful and fruitful region in some future day" because of the richness of its soil and the convenience of means of transportation for commerce (309).

Yet these passages are limited in number. One of them is revealing because in it Bartram seems to betray his true viewpoint in spite of himself: "This vast plain, together with the forests contiguous to it, if permitted (by the

Siminoles who are sovereigns of these realms) to be in possession and under the culture of industrious planters and mechanics, would in a little time exhibit other scenes than it does at present, delightful as it is; for by the arts of agriculture and commerce, almost every desirable thing in life might be produced and made plentiful here" (199). Two things distinguish this passage from usual formulations in other travel accounts. First, the Seminoles are designated "sovereigns," who would have to freely cede their lands if the change were to take place. Second, the phrase "delightful as it is" reveals the underlying regret felt by the author at the thought that the natural beauty of the spot, maintained by the Indians, could disappear. In other passages, in fact, Bartram severely criticizes settlers for the destruction of natural beauty (e.g., 213).

It would seem, then, that the dissonant passages, limited as they are, can be attributed either to editorial intervention or to the pressure exercised by strong prevailing norms on a sensibility that was atypical and marginal to the extreme. The difference in this respect between the early manuscript version and the published work would tend to corroborate the contention that these passages do not correspond to Bartram's deepest sensibilities. As Thomas Hallock has noted, "the genetic text shows little interest in expansion . . . and portrays nature as a source of inspiration rather than as a commodity."[41] The same can be said of Bartram's being generally well disposed in *Travels* toward the planters near the coast. Christopher Iannini, a commentator who has recently laid emphasis on Bartram's implication in British colonialism, acknowledges that the figure of the "benevolent planter" does not appear in any known manuscript versions.[42] As for the project to civilize the Indians announced in the introduction, the main thrust of what follows flagrantly contradicts the idea by suggesting—sometimes explicitly—the superiority of Indian culture over that of the Europeans. Here too the author seems to be making a concession to the dominant ideological position, perhaps out of an overriding desire to see some form of peaceful coexistence with Indians implemented by the United States.[43]

RELATIONS WITH INDIANS

In the turbulent situation that obtained in much of the area of his travels, it was inevitable that not all of Bartram's interactions with Indians would be free of tension. He recounts in detail one particular incident in which he not only reacted calmly and courageously—as Carver prides himself on doing in similar situations—but according to a philosophy of human relations rather than simple pragmatism. This is the only case wherein Bartram recounts an "adventure," and it differs from others I have discussed in that he transmutes it into a "spiritual" adventure.[44]

The incident occurs in part 1 when Bartram is traveling entirely alone over savannas near the border between Georgia and East Florida, "beyond the utmost frontier of the white settlements" (44). When an armed Seminole horseback rider appears far off, Bartram first tries to hide from the Indian's view. But the Indian sees him and gallops up. Bartram's first response is fear: "I never before this was afraid at the sight of an Indian, but at this time, I must own that my spirits were very much agitated: I saw at once, that, being unarmed, I was in his power." However, he continues, "having now but a few moments to prepare, I resigned myself entirely to the will of the Almighty . . . : my mind then became tranquil" (44). When the Indian comes close, clearly angry, "I advanced towards him, and with an air of confidence offered him my hand, hailing him, brother" (45).

The Indian at first jerks back his hand "with a look of malice, rage, and disdain," but "when again looking at me more attentively, he instantly spurred up to me, and with dignity in his look and action, gave me his hand." The author then attempts to project himself into this Seminole's mind: "Possibly the silent language of his soul, during the moment of suspense (for I believe his design was to kill me when he first came up) was after this manner: 'White man, thou art my enemy, and thou and thy brethren may have killed mine; yet it may not be so, and even were that the case, thou art now alone, and in my power. Live, the Great Spirit forbids me to touch thy life; go to thy brethren, tell them thou sawest an Indian in the forests, who knew how to be humane and compassionate'" (45).

Bartram later learns that this Indian is a murderer, exiled from his tribe, who has just been beaten by traders and has vowed to take revenge by killing the first white he meets. Reflecting on the incident afterward, Bartram comes to see it as a clear sign of the "ray of divine light" (46), or innate moral sense, that exists in all human beings according to the Quaker faith. The story is indeed recounted as an exemplar, intended seemingly to demonstrate at least two other things to the reader: the efficacy of friendliness (in the Quaker sense) as a moral force and the amenability of Indians (even the "worst," the most hostile and violently inclined) to peaceful association with whites if they are treated with the openness and cordiality due to all fellow human beings.

Bartram carried this approach to interaction with Indians into all his more extended dealings with them. In a context in which Indian antagonism toward whites was rampant, he was often treated as an exception, as a white man whose intentions were manifestly innocuous. (He had no interest in taking their land and only wanted to observe—not take—wildlife.) For example, when Bartram met the Seminole chief Ahaye, named "Cowkeeper" by the British, in East Florida, the chief gave him "unlimited permission to travel over the country for the purpose of collecting flowers, medicinal plants, etc. saluting me by the name of Puc Puggy, or the Flower hunter, recommending me to the friendship and protection of his people" (163).[45] Here Bartram takes pride in being given an Indian name. In this he resembles Carver, but Bartram's relations with Indians, unlike Carver's, were not tinged with motives potentially inimical to Indian interests. Bartram was given similarly exceptional treatment in other instances as well. Another Seminole chief, the "White King" of Talahosochte, calls him "one of his own children or people" (201), and a Cherokee leader gives orders that his horse be given corn, an honor, he is told, that "is conferred on those only to whom they manifest the highest esteem" (285).[46]

Bartram never seems to have betrayed the trust the Indians placed in him. His conduct, as he reports it, always appears to be respectful of their customs and their persons. One indication is that even when whites he is traveling with prefer other kinds of entertainment, he chooses to take part in the Indians' ceremonies and celebrations (170). Another illustration of this attitude comes when his Indian guide on the St. John's River complains of having to paddle under a hot sun. Bartram freely lets him go, "knowing the impossibility of compelling an Indian against his own inclinations . . . when labour is in the question" (113). He imagines that his guide will perhaps return the next morning after having refreshed himself by hunting, but when he does not Bartram continues on alone, without recrimination.

Two more lengthily recounted incidents reflect different facets of Bartram's interaction with Indians. The first occurs when he is staying for a time with a Seminole party preparing to go to war with the Choctaws. The occurrence illustrates, according to the author, these Indians' "extraordinary veneration or dread of the rattle snake" (218). While sketching flowers one day, Bartram hears a racket. He is told by another white in the camp that a rattlesnake has appeared and that the Indians want Puc Puggy to kill it. He asks the other white man to tell the Indians that he is busy and would not like to get involved. But three warriors are already approaching. Bartram tries to leave his hut, but too late. They arrive, "richly dressed and ornamented . . . with a countenance and action of noble simplicity, amity and complaisance" (218), and explain that they are not allowed to expel the snake themselves. Knowing that Bartram collects plants and animals, they beg him to rid them of the snake.

Seeing the terror that reigns in the camp, Bartram finally agrees, kills the snake, and takes off its rattles for his collection. The Indians keenly thank him for giving them this "heroic" token of friendship. But soon thereafter a delegation returns, saying that they want to "scratch" him. Among the three Indians who have come Bartram recognizes a warrior who until then "had declared himself my friend and protector" (219). The two others, though, display their "scratching instruments," saying Bartram is "too heroic and violent, that it would be good for me to lose some of my blood to make me more mild and tame" (219). They threaten to do the same, but Bartram's protector objects, and the hostile behavior of the others immediately turns into boisterous demonstrations of friendship. This incident—which has something in common with the one discussed in Carver's text—could have been treated as an adventure but is not. At no point is a sense of danger generated. The anecdote is presented as an illustration of the power of certain beliefs over Indians, and the momentary expression of hostility, manifestly contradicting the warriors' first reactions, is shown to be a ritual enactment (which Bartram refers to, it is true, as a "farce") meant to "satisfy their people and appease the manes of the dead rattle snake" (220). In it the author demonstrates that he is ready to intervene—albeit unwillingly at first—in response to the imperatives of an Indian belief system.

The tone of the second incident is quite different. While staying at the village of Cowe in Cherokee territory, the author takes a walk in the hills in the company of a trader. On returning, an "enchanting" vista suddenly opens up before them: vast prairies, fields of strawberries, green groves, beds of flowers, a winding river on the banks of which can be seen wild turkey, deer, and "companies of young, innocent Cherokee virgins" (289). Some of them are picking berries, others are resting in the shade of trees and sweet-smelling, flowering shrubs, "disclosing their beauties to the fluttering breeze, and bathing their limbs in the cool fleeting streams." Still others, "more gay and libertine, were ... wantonly chasing their companions, tantalising them, staining their lips and cheeks with the rich fruit." This "sylvan scene of primitive innocence" was "perhaps too enticing for hearty young men long to continue idle spectators" (289).

The two men stealthily approach the "gay assembly of hamadryades," animated only by the desire to join in the frolicking, the author claims, though adding that he will leave it to the reader to decide "to what lengths our passions might have hurried us" if several "matrons" had not then appeared. The two then turn toward another group of young women, farther off, who on seeing them come forward and "[present] their little baskets, merrily telling us their fruit [is] ripe and sound" (289). The episode closes with the two men seated on the grass eating fruit, surrounded by both the younger and the older women. Bartram's companion politely apologizes for the intrusion, arranges for more fruit to be brought to their cabin later, and then, concludes the author, "we parted friendly" (290). The incident as recounted by Bartram thus takes place without sexual compulsion or pressure being exerted, though the encounter is clearly experienced by the men—and presented by the author—as sensual and erotic. In the scene as depicted, the Indians are assimilated to Nature in an Edenic setting. Bartram doubtless betrays a good deal of naïveté, or ignorance of Indian sexual mores, in characterizing the women as "virgins."[47] But though they are largely mythologized in the text—and portrayed in a somewhat questionable literary style—the Indian women are in no way demeaned by the textual treatment of them.

THE NATURE OF INDIAN CULTURE

The long title of the first chapter of part 4, the synthetic presentation of the knowledge of Indians gathered by Bartram on his trip,[48] enumerates the sources of his information: "Description of the character, customs and persons of the American aborigines, from my own observations, as well as from the general and impartial report of ancient respectable men, either of their own people, or white traders, who have spent many days of their lives amongst them" (380). Bartram is here concerned—as writers of travel accounts often are—to establish the reliability of his assertions through the credibility of his sources. Concerning information reported to him, this credibility is based on age (implicitly experience) and trustworthiness. As for his firsthand testimony, he insists elsewhere that it comes out of considerable immersion in indigenous cultures, involving stays of weeks or months in some Indian villages (385).

Bartram's attraction to Indian culture from the outset sharpens his curiosity, exciting interest in all he comes across that is related to them. Unlike Lawson and Carver, he seems almost as fascinated by the aboriginal past as by the present condition of Indian societies. As he travels he often stops when he comes across apparent vestiges of precontact times, known now to archaeologists as ruins of the hierarchical Mississippian cultures[49]: mounds and man-made waterways, terraces, "obelisks," ruins of buildings, traces of ancient roadways. In the course of his narrative the author often describes these phenomena and then reflects on their meanings and functions (56–57, 265–66, 300). Though they appear to Bartram to be remnants of earlier civilizations that were more grandiose from a material point of view, he can only hypothesize since the Creeks and Cherokees living nearby know nothing of them (297, 361–62). However, though the ruins are mute for the contemporary Indians as well as for Bartram, the Indians do have a collective memory, and Bartram reports stories he has heard from them or from older traders that tell of their past and origins (68–69, 307, 314–15).[50]

Just as the author attempts, as best he can, to "read" the monuments of American Indian antiquity, he "reads" the landscapes he travels through for what they can tell about the more recent past. When he sees battlefields, burial grounds, and dwellings or entire villages abandoned or partially destroyed, he attempts to reconstruct the events and historical developments that can account for them. He observes and comments, for example, on signs of Indian defeat at the hands of colonial militia, and of violent expropriation by settlers (270–71, 283). One day, while walking in a wild area, his pleasure is interrupted by the view of human bones mixed with those of animals. This spectacle, he tells the reader, is one that is, "on reflection, perhaps, rather disagreeable to a mind of delicate feelings and sensibility, since some of these objects recognize past transactions and events, perhaps not altogether reconcileable to justice and humanity" (263–64). The cautiousness of the formulation doubtless indicates a hesitation to criticize frontally the behavior of the colonizers in a period of consensus on the expansionist policies of the young nation.

Bartram also regularly "reads" the physiognomy of Indians he meets, seeing in their faces indications of moral qualities. His descriptions of visits to villages often begin with evocations of the physique of their inhabitants—sometimes that of the chief in particular—often focusing on faces. Thus, for example, he describes the Seminole village of Cuscowilla in East Florida by beginning, "The chief is a tall well made man, very affable and cheerful, about sixty years of age, his eyes lively and full of fire, his countenance manly and placid, yet ferocious, or what we call savage, his nose aquiline" (164). Describing another Seminole chief further on, the author insists that his appearance, similarly dignified, "is not the effect of vain supercilious pride, for his smiling countenance and his cheerful familiarity bespeaks magnanimity and benignity" (200–201). When in part 4 the author formulates generalizations about male Indians, it appears that Seminole chiefs are in fact representative of the norm: "The males ... are tall, erect, and moderately robust ... their features regular, and countenance open, dignified and placid; yet the forehead and brow so formed, as to strike you instantly with heroism and bravery.... Their countenance and actions exhibit an air of magnanimity, superiority and independence" (380).[51]

The correspondence between the physiognomic sketch of the Seminoles and that of male Indians whom Bartram encountered in the Southeast as a whole illustrates a tendency Bartram shares with most voyagers in Indian territories during that period. Though he does on occasion make statements about specific Indian nations and draws a few comparisons (Creeks and Seminoles: 181–83; Creeks and Cherokees: 380–81), the particularities are most often inconsequential. The essential traits are found in all the Indian communities known to the traveler. Likewise, while he notes in the more southerly regions signs of European influence (especially Spanish)—a village chief who displays a flag in front of his hut, a (non-Christianized) tribe that rests on Sundays (163, 362)—these components of a foreign culture are relatively superficial and do not compromise more fundamental Indian cultural patterns. In his commentary, then, Bartram concentrates on aspects of indigenous culture that are deeply rooted and shared by many different groups in the Southeast.

Finally, and crucially, despite the identification of Amerindians with Nature, as I mentioned earlier, Bartram insists on the organized—and in that sense "civilized"—character of Indian societies. In one passage, after using the stereotype "untutored savages," he corrects himself: "But I am afraid this is a common-phrase epithet, having no meaning, or at least improperly applied; for these people are both well-tutored and civil" (111).[52]

The portrait Bartram paints of these well-ordered Indian societies is a broad one, covering many of the features treated by the travelers already discussed. Yet Bartram's way of dealing with them is revelatory of his turn of mind. He takes Indian legends seriously, for example, and in his approach to them seems both sensitive to their evocative power as myths and at the same time concerned to understand them rationally and contextually. He relates one traditional Creek tale at some length; it involves an island lost in the middle of a huge marsh, inhabited by women of great beauty, "daughters of the sun." A band of Creek hunters who have gone astray in the marsh meet some of these women one day, and the women offer to help them. But soon they ask the hunters to flee so as to avoid being found by their husbands, who are ferociously cruel to strangers. In spite of this admonition the hunters try to reach the village of the mysterious beauties, which they see far off on a promontory. But the hunters become confused as they wander through "labyrinths," and as the village continually evades them they finally give up the quest. Back home, after they have told their story, other young warriors become enflamed with desire to conquer "so charming a country," but all their attempts to find the "enchanted land" meet with failure. At the conclusion of this narration, Bartram adds that the Creeks know another version of the tale, one that in all likelihood can account in real historical terms for the enigmatic human presence in the depths of the marsh. This version has it that the island was inhabited by the surviving remainder of the Yamasees, long ago decimated by the Creeks (47–48).

When Bartram takes up the religious beliefs of the Indians, he sees them as most essentially manifesting daily adoration of a Great Spirit disseminated throughout Nature. In this aspect Indian beliefs resemble his own Quaker faith, tinged as it is with pantheism. A further extension of this idea that resonates with Bartram's own idiosyncratic perspective—although he himself does not dwell on it—is the Amerindian tendency to consider humans as in no way superior to other elements of the universe. Unlike most traditional forms of Christianity, in native conceptions humanity is, as Jace Weaver points out, "undifferentiated from the rest of the created order."[53]

The magical conceptions and practices of the Indians are largely ignored by the author of *Travels*, for example those that gave rise to the rattlesnake incident mentioned earlier. In narrating this occurrence Bartram does not delve into the magical dimension of the mentality of the Indians that he helps rid of an unwanted taboo animal, presumably because in this area his perspective and theirs do not overlap. As for the festivals and rituals, sporting games and other recreations, which Bartram often participated in and shared the spirit of, he considers them mainly moments of intense tribal bonding. He is particularly interested in dance and music, the power of which he knows from experience. At times he has been aware of the creation, through singing, of a deep emotional unity: "there is then," he exclaims, "an united universal sensation of delight and peaceful union of souls throughout the assembly" (396).

But the Indians' community spirit is not exclusively nonrational. On the contrary, Bartram emphasizes the importance of "public" or "political" life,[54] describing the places in Creek villages—the public square or "areopagus," the council house for everyday affairs, the "rotunda" for more important ones—in which collective decisions are taken. He notes that women rarely take part in deliberations, but also stresses that male participation in council house discussions is largely egalitarian, the only hierarchy being based on age and experience. The "king," or "mico," is not feared. In the daily council he has the same position as the other elders, and outside the councils he is no more than an ordinary man (389).[55]

In addition to describing at length particular customs and institutions, Bartram pinpoints for discussion what he considers to be essential defining traits of Indian societies as he knows them, focusing on the egalitarian sharing of goods, mutual aid, and the absence of egoism, greed, and dissension (notably between men and women, adults and children). As for the first of these elements—from which he seems to intimate that the others might follow—Bartram gives precise indications meant to correct certain vague or erroneous reports about the absence of private property in Indian societies. In a Seminole or Creek tribe, he explains, there is a planting ground held in common, which is divided into segments corresponding to the size of each family. Everyone together plants and cultivates the ground as a whole, but each family harvests its own plot for its own consumption. From this harvest families donate, if they wish, a small quantity to a communal stock that is kept in case of need (170, 400–401). It appears that in dealing with Indian economy, which contrasts so fundamentally with that of European modernity, Bartram wanted to avoid any accusation of making fanciful, extravagant claims.[56]

Regarding war—the area of Indian life that might meet with incomprehension in a Quaker pacifist—Bartram's attitude is thoughtful and lucid. He contradicts the stereotype of the sanguinary savage in his explanation of the motives that incline Indians to warfare, arguing that some are analogous to and thus no worse than those of European nations: the establishment of territorial rights, revenge, and the cultivation of honor. Significantly none of their motives involves economic gain ("avarice of plunder"), an incentive that is found in European warfare and that Bartram seems to imply is especially barbarous (183, 315–16).[57] Bartram does not, on the other hand, confront the question of torture, except to insist that he never saw it being practiced during his travels. This phenomenon, had he encountered it, would of course have been a painful enigma for the sensitive Quaker that he was.

Though in the case of Indian warfare Bartram simply reserves judgment, he unreservedly admires most aspects of Indian culture that he points out and discusses. He appreciates the ancient Indian ruins or traces he encounters, both for their beauty—still visible, or imagined in their earlier state—and for the grandeur of the past civilizations that they hint at (e.g., 56). The Indian societies of the present, on the other hand, are seen as manifesting a peerless moral grandeur, however materially reduced they may be in relation to those of the past. Many facets of the daily life of Indians are praised in *Travels*: their corporeal beauty (206), the emotional depth of their singing (207), the dexterity of their dancers (299), the fine artisanship of paintings and wood sculptures (361).[58] But the author's most essential evaluation of Amerindians concerns their social ethics.

In one passage Bartram formulates with particular clarity the general conclusion toward which his more specific commentaries point. Muscogulge society, Bartram claims—and it seems clear that for him the same would apply to the other Indian groups he has cognizance of—is organized in such a way as to make "natural" and almost universal the achievement of virtues that only some individuals attain with great effort in European societies: "For, however strange it may appear to us, the same moral duties which with us form the amiable, virtuous character, so difficult to maintain there, without compulsion or visible restraint, operates like instinct, with a surprising harmony and natural ease, insomuch that it seems impossible for them to act out of the common high road to virtue" (182).

For Bartram, then, Indian lifeways create the necessary social conditions for the generalization of virtue, that is, of the very qualities that (traditional) European civilization defined as virtue. In other words, as he concludes in part 4, the Indians "put in practice those beautiful lectures delivered to us by the ancient sages and philosophers, and recorded for our instruction" (386). There the author also explicitly draws the logical conclusion to which this perspective leads—a conclusion that puts him at odds with most of his contemporaries and clashes with his statement of intention in the introduction: "As moral men they certainly stand in no need of European civilization" (385). In effect, by maintaining "friendly intercourse one with another, without any restraint of ceremonious formality, as if they were even insensible of the use or necessity of associating the passions or affections of avarice, ambition or covetousness," their mode of life has produced "a society of peace and love" (388).[59]

Bartram was aware of the reaction that such statements were likely to provoke in many of his readers, and at one point, after the characterization of Muscogulge society cited above, followed by an equally flattering portrait of the Seminoles, he responds in advance to anticipated objections: "I doubt not but some of my countrymen who may read these accounts of the Indians ... will charge me with partiality or prejudice in their favour. I will, however, now endeavour to exhibit their vices, immoralities, and imperfections" (183). The annotated list of "vices" that follows is anything but convincing, however, and only reinforces the demonstration of Bartram's sympathy. Aside from the fact that it takes up a single page as against dozens of pages of enthusiastic admiration, this negative side of the balance sheet is in no way seriously condemning. The vices are immediately attenuated, shown to be at least no worse than the European equivalent (war, adultery) or to be caused by European influence (overhunting of deer and bear). And in one case the "vice" mentioned is presented in such a way as not to constitute a serious fault: "They are fond of games and gambling, and amuse themselves like children, in relating extravagant stories, to cause surprise and mirth" (184). Although gambling might indeed be judged a vice by some readers, the other activities with which it is associated render it innocuous.[60] Clearly Bartram cannot bring himself to truly attack the Indian mode of living, and the indictment against them finally contributes to the case made in their defense.

RADICAL BARTRAM

In his study of the historical context of Bartram's voyage, Edward Cashin cites the passage in the manuscript text, "Some Hints and Observations," in which the author proclaims his hope that the newly adopted Constitution will make of the United States a universal model: "I forsee the Magnificent structure and would be instrumental in its advancement."[61] According to Cashin, the writer's contribution to that cause is the travel account itself. It depicts an Edenic America and takes up the cause of the Indians so as to convince his fellow citizens, and the new government, to treat them more humanely and stimulate their integration into the "Magnificent structure" of the United States as it is being born. If the nation could create itself while at the same time respecting the environment and the Indians, it could fully accomplish its emancipatory mission.[62] What emerges from Cashin's account, then, is the profile of a *liberal* Bartram, one who identifies with the national project but wishes to reform it from the inside. In this view Bartram's primary hope for the Indians is that they be included in the "civilization" of the new nation.

It is true that some passages, in *Travels* and elsewhere, might seem to bear out this idea. In his travel account the author on occasion uses formulas that suggest an association of Indians with the patriots of the Revolution, as when the Seminoles are called "sons of liberty" (64). Also, as already mentioned, examples of "prospective vision" and praise of planters are to be found in the text, which might be taken as favorable to colonization. Bartram's silences can also be seen to be significant. As Cashin notes, Bartram in one place writes of a new plantation he has seen, without mentioning that its owners are illegal squatters on Indian land.[63] Finally, there is the civilizing plan proposed in the introduction to *Travels*. Indeed in "Some Hints and Observations" Bartram goes so far as to assert that no steps would be more worthy of praise "than the introduction [among the Indians] of our Language, System of legislation, Religion, Manners, Arts and Sciences."[64]

It would be a mistake, however, to conclude that these formulations reflect a truthful image of the writer, or even that they reveal in him some deep-seated ambivalence. In *Travels* the passages are isolated ones that contrast with what surrounds them. In the manuscript versions one finds no such jarring elements, and so it is plausible that editorial modifications by another hand played a role. But more important, even supposing that the heterogeneous material in *Travels* is attributable to Bartram—as it clearly is in "Some Hints and Observations"—in my view there is no reason to believe that Bartram's was a divided or ambivalent consciousness nor that he hesitated between the advantages of his own society and that of the Indians.

Rather it would seem that a number of factors can account for Bartram's contradictions. First, there was the extreme pressure of the hegemonic discourse. In eighteenth-century British America, and a fortiori in Philadelphia, one of its primary urban centers, the pressure of the dominant ideology—utilitarian, expansionist, technologically manipulative—was intense. In this context, which was also that of a highly volatile, transitional period, many or perhaps even most intellectual productions were rife with unresolved tensions. Second, particularly true perhaps in the case of "Some Hints and Observations"—written at a time when there was an imminent danger of military action against the Creeks[65]—Bartram clearly sought a way of dealing with the "Indian problem" that would save them from annihilation, and the "civilizing" approach appeared to provide that. His temperament, which was tender and eschewed conflict, also probably played a role, predisposing him to seek reconciliation of situations and points of view, even though opposed and incompatible. Bartram seems to have attempted to convince himself that colonization and commercial development could coexist with Indian societies, that he could through persuasion bring his fellow citizens to change their attitudes about Indians, and that the latter could become part of the United States without losing their identity.

In reading *Travels* one does sometimes sense, as Thomas Hallock maintains, a "desire to evade"—to evade confrontation with intractable, unpleasant realities.[66] Bartram was unwilling finally to acknowledge the irreconcilable nature of the two cultures confronting each other in North America, and his hopes for accommodation proved chimerical. In spite of the evasion, though, Bartram remained faithful to his deeper convictions. Rather than be drawn into participation in the society he felt estranged from as it developed after the Revolution, he chose to withdraw, becoming a kind of internal exile in the botanical garden at Kingsessing. He received visits from some of the founding fathers of the United States, but it was they who came to him. He stayed away from Philadelphia and did not accept the offers of positions and honors, even, or perhaps especially when they involved governmental expeditions into the western Indian territories.

Far from being that of a reformer, then, the essential vision of William Bartram is a radical one. It includes a passionate identification with the Other of his own society and expresses a romantic revolt against the modernity that he was convinced had drawn away from the authentically human. Bartram's identification with the Indian Other is founded on a deep affinity (though he never attempted to "become" an Indian) with peoples he felt were both in harmony with the natural world and creators of social structures that allowed the best human qualities to flourish.

CHAPTER EIGHT

Fur Traders
Alexander Mackenzie and Jean-Baptiste Trudeau

Two travel accounts from the very end of the eighteenth century involve a specific category of traveler: the fur trader. Several of these works have already made an appearance in this book, but only episodically. In several places I have cited in passing *History of the American Indians* by James Adair, trader among the Chickasaws and other southeastern Indians from the 1730s to 1770s. In chapter 4 I dealt with the travel narrative of a fur trader who operated farther north and west after the French and Indian War: Alexander Henry (the Elder). But I analyzed as textualized "adventure" only the fragment that involved Henry's capture and time as a captive of Indians, rather than his longer career in trade with them. In this chapter I discuss full texts by fur traders.

As a general rule, since they were engaged in a commercial activity the aim of which was to generate profits and which employed Indians to that end as providers of the raw material of the trade, fur traders were surely not among those most likely to fulfill the travel genre's potential of "recognition." But as a plethora of research over the past half-century has demonstrated, the practice of the fur trade in North America was highly diversified, as were those who engaged in it.[1] There were many significant differences among fur traders—most important, from the perspective of my exploration, in terms of their relation to the culture of modernity. Some traders were principally businessmen, of differing degrees of wealth; some were motivated to a greater or lesser extent by various nonmercantile interests; others were employees of those who reaped most of the profits. Some lived for more or less lengthy periods in Indian communities, in many cases marrying Indian women and thereby becoming a part of indigenous kin and clan structures; in many instances such traders and their progeny could be said to manifest what one historian has called "biculturalism."[2] Clearly, then, there is no single profile of the fur trader in eighteenth-century North America.

The diversity of fur trading is reflected in the travel accounts that I take up here. One of the trader-authors is British, while the other is French Canadian, and although there was much variety of temperament and perspective among traders of each national group, this difference in national culture is doubtless one relevant factor in accounting for the divergences in their accounts of encounter experiences. While the first stands in sharp opposition—at the other end of the scale of recognition of the Other—to the exemplary figure of William Bartram, the second shows far greater complexity and ambiguity, similar to travelers I looked at earlier.

THE FUR TRADE

Alexander Mackenzie's historically important expeditions in search of the Northwest Passage and the travel account that came out of them are best understood in the context of the northwestern fur trade and his role in it. In North America the fur trade and exploration were from the start often linked. For a long period much of the exploratory effort in pursuit of a practicable route across North America that would give easier access to the Orient came from the French. Starting in the late seventeenth century *coureurs de bois*, adventurers, and officially sponsored leaders of expeditions attempted to penetrate beyond the Mississippi. One of their goals was to reach the Pacific, and China beyond. Often these forays were related to the fur trade. The motives of those who took part in the expeditions were usually mixed, though. In addition to the prospect of profitable commercial endeavors—whether through furs, discovery of precious metals, dealings with the Spanish, or a route to the Orient—many other factors could come into play: curiosity or scientific interest, imperial strategy (to contain the English and the Spanish), missionary zeal, a taste for unconstrained living or for personal glory, and the allure of Indian women.[3] As for the fur trade itself, Richard White has emphasized that, as practiced by the French—who dominated it as well as western exploration in the early period—it was never ruled entirely by the profit motive. French traders were still to some extent guided by the idea of "just price," and the need to maintain political alliances with Indians was paramount in the exchange of furs.[4]

Starting in the early 1760s, with the conquest of New France, the British participation in the fur trade in the North and West dramatically increased and the trade came to be significantly transformed. Since the late seventeenth century the Hudson's Bay Company had operated a trade monopoly in the Far North, but with the arrival of new British traders in Montreal there developed intense competition between rival companies and a strong impulse to expand production. This meant finding new fur-bearing territories farther west, since the animals, notably beaver, were increasingly depleted in the older areas of exploitation farther east. In the period following the Conquest, there was also increased intensity in the search for a route to the Pacific that might open up vast outlets for the goods in the Orient. Hence the strong thrust toward exploration and "discovery" in the Northwest.

ALEXANDER MACKENZIE

Like a great many of the British fur traders, Alexander Mackenzie was a Scotsman.[5] Born in Stornoway in the Hebrides in 1764, he was brought to New York by his father as an adolescent, then sent to Montreal in 1778 to get him away from the revolutionary conflict. After several years as a clerk in a small fur-trading establishment, he became a partner and moved out into the fur territory west of Lake Superior to supervise operations. In 1787 his firm merged with the larger North West Company. Under the influence of Peter Pond, another trader and explorer in that company, he conceived the plan, which was tacitly accepted but not actively sponsored by the company, of attempting to reach the Pacific by river (thereby establishing the existence of a Northwest Passage), starting from Lake Athabasca, nearly the farthest point north and west that had hitherto been reached by fur traders.[6]

Mackenzie made not one but two trips with this purpose in mind, because the first, from June to September 1789, took him to the Arctic Ocean instead of the Pacific. He therefore saw this first attempt as a failure, though he was the first European to explore the large river that runs from Great Slave Lake, above Lake Athabasca, into the Arctic, and which was later named after him by the British. (The Dene Indians of the region have continued to call it Dehcho.) Mackenzie undertook the second trip several years later (1793–94), taking off from another river running out of Lake Athabasca, the Peace, going more directly west. He succeeded this time in reaching the Pacific but did not find a continuous water passage. The expedition portaged across the Rockies, found what later came to be called the Frazer River, then made another overland trek and finally connected with the Bella Coola River, which took them to the coast. On both trips Mackenzie traveled by canoe and on foot, with a crew of French *voyageurs* as well as with several Indians who served as hunters and interpreters. They took on other Indians as guides as they went along. On both trips the travelers experienced extreme hardships of various kinds, and often both the crew and the accompanying Indians wanted to abandon the expedition.

When he set out on his expeditions Mackenzie seems to have had three aims in mind, all of which were mercenary: to earn the reward offered by the British Crown for finding the Passage, to make contact with new Indian tribes that could be brought into the fur trade, and, most important, to take the first steps toward setting up a western trade route to the Orient. According to Mackenzie's plan, the Russians, who had established several posts on the coast, were potential intermediaries with the Chinese. Mackenzie met no Russians, however, when he finally reached the Pacific in July 1793. Partly because he encountered some apparently hostile or unmanageable Indians (unidentified in the text, but possibly Kwakiutl) and partly because the traveling season was too far advanced, instead of going farther along the coast he returned to Lake Athabasca. He left there several months later for Montreal and never returned. He did not leave the fur trade, though, but continued to be involved in business dealings and maneuvers in Montreal until he finally returned to Britain in 1805. During this period he also attempted to convince British colonial officials to establish bases on the northwest Pacific coast as relays in a trade route to the Orient—a project that, as one commentator points out, "neatly conjoined imperial interest and private enterprise"[7]—but without any success.

Although a noncritical, often heroizing approach has tended to predominate in writing about Mackenzie,[8] several studies have made more lucid appraisals and painted a less glorious picture. First of all it seems clear, as James K. Smith points out, that Mackenzie's two journeys in search of the Passage, far from being defining moments, were "minor episodes" for the man who made them, in a long career otherwise fully focused on the fur trade.[9] It was commerce indeed, and not exploration, that molded and defined Mackenzie's character. Unlike his cousin Roderick, who found himself ill suited to the northwestern fur trade and longed to leave it, Mackenzie was a master of it and thrived in its environment—the environment of competitive business, that is, for Mackenzie was largely indifferent to the natural surroundings of the particular kind of trade in which he was engaged. Barry Gough, author of his most recent biography, espouses this view of Mackenzie; rather than devotion to imperial aims, a yen for discovery, or love of the outdoors, Gough claims, the crux of Mackenzie's being was commerce. He feels that earlier biographers on the whole have "failed to appreciate one fundamental fact—that his life in the wilderness was dedicated to one grand purpose, the making of money," and he argues, "In Mackenzie's business activities are to be found the secret to his motivations, to his aspirations for the British Empire in northern latitudes and on northern seas, and to his future hopes.... The wilderness offered him a place for profitable speculation, and he mastered it to fulfill his private aims of personal wealth."[10] The exploratory journeys were in a sense a parenthesis in a life mainly devoted to business, but they were also part of a larger commercial ambition to create an international trade network.

Mackenzie's book itself was in a real sense a part of his campaign to promote this project. For although he called on a ghostwriter to edit the original manuscript[11]—with the purpose of increasing its appeal to a broad public—he also clearly aimed at colonial administrators and traders who might be convinced that his ideas were feasible. The book appeared only in 1801, in London, under the (typically long) title *Voyages from Montreal on the River St. Laurence through the Continent of North America to the Frozen and Pacific Oceans in the Years 1789 and 1793, with a preliminary account of the rise, progress, and present state of the fur trade of that country.*

This title is curiously inaccurate, since the travel narratives themselves start from Lake Athabasca, as already mentioned, and not Montreal. Milo Quaife, editor of the Lakeside Press edition of Mackenzie's account of the 1793 voyage, notes the inaccuracy of the original title without attempting to elucidate it.[12] A possible explanation, however, is that in the preliminary account of the fur trade referred to in the title, there is a detailed description of the route habitually followed by the annual fur-trading expeditions from and to Montreal. The text, then, includes a kind of essay on the fur trade, as well as accounts of the two voyages. This structure corresponds to the familiar pattern in travel literature of the diachronic account of a trip being accompanied by a synchronic, synthesizing section. Moreover within Mackenzie's synchronic section, though it is mainly devoted to the fur trade, one finds another kind of synthesis more typical of works involving travel in Indian territories: extended treatment of the mode of life of two major Indian groups he encountered on his travels, the Knisteneaux (or Crees) and the Chipewyans.

The work went through several editions and translations in the years immediately following its first appearance, achieving considerable success. But as it contained, for its more targeted audience, much detailed factual material such as miles covered, compass directions, and astronomical readings, later nineteenth-century editions were often abridged.[13]

In the preface to *Voyages*, Mackenzie opens by linking his explorations both to commerce and to the discovery of the Northwest Passage. "I was led," he informs the reader somewhat complacently, "at an early period of life, by commercial views, to the country north-west of Lake Superior... and being endowed by nature with an inquisitive mind and enterprising spirit... contemplated the practicability of penetrating across the continent of America."[14] Immediately following this preface that frames the work comes the long introductory section on the fur trade. That the first part of a book purporting to recount voyages of exploration should open in this way makes clear that for the author not only are the two kinds of activity closely bound, but the fur trade takes precedence. It provides necessary context for the voyages, which are in a sense subsumed under it.

Although entitled "A General History of the Fur Trade from Canada to the North-West," and though there is some material on the early French trade, most of the first part concerns the recent British period, giving a close description of the constitutive elements and modus operandi of the trade in the present. The author's treatment shows the fur trade in its contemporary form to be a modern commercial industry—organized for efficiency, profit maximizing, hierarchical, and competitive. Mackenzie fully identifies with this industry, animated as it is by the same "spirit of enterprise" that he proclaimed in the preface to characterize both his own makeup and the collective ethos of Britain. In discussing those who are in one way or another connected with the trade, the author always measures categories of people in terms of their usefulness to those who direct and profit from it. The French *coureurs de bois*, who continue to work for British employers, are deemed "extremely useful to the merchants" in spite of their dissolute ways, and they are praised for their respectfulness and sense of subordination (10, 52). Similarly the missionaries who often accompanied exploratory ventures into new areas are said to have been "of great service to the commanders who engaged in those distant expeditions, and spread the fur trade" (13).

The Indians—those other workers who provide the furs[15]—are of course of the greatest service of all, and Mackenzie's account of the functioning of the fur trade in the region shows how the native providers of the pelts were submitted to the logic of commercial transaction and sometimes confronted by difficult choices put to them by competing firms. In discussing the competition between the Hudson's Bay Company, which obliged the Indians to bring the furs to their trading posts, and the North West Company, which sent canoes out to the Indian villages, Mackenzie explains that though the Indians had to pay much higher prices to the North West Company they were increasingly willing to do so because they spent most or all of what they earned from the Hudson's Bay Company to buy the very ammunition used up in hunting while on their way to the company's posts (20, 97). No matter whether they chose one or the other company, the author contends, the Indians were caught in the meshes of the trade, since they were compelled to "exchange their furs for such European articles as were now become necessary to them" (88). The text acknowledges that this situation has in some cases led to conflict and violence between natives and traders, as the bitter competition has done between traders (17, 21).

This assessment of the predicament of the area's Indians—mainly Crees and various subgroups of Denes—without a doubt underestimates, or underplays considerably, the extent to which natives exercised a strong counterforce in trading situations (bargaining, playing companies off against each other, refusing to cooperate, etc.) due to their irreplaceability as skilled hunters. Nevertheless they too could be pitted against each other by traders, and the growing dependency on European consumer items that Mackenzie points to was in many instances an undeniable reality.

The author offers no expression of moral judgment concerning this state of affairs. His only source of concern is that the trade as he describes it is enormously costly for the traders because of the lengthiness and difficulty of transportation of the goods. Profit margins are often small, and returns are at risk. Hence the need to find a new conduit to the west, which explains Mackenzie's interest and engagement in the search for the Passage in the first place and the voyages of which the narrative is to follow. As Smith nicely puts it, "Mackenzie, an exceedingly profit-minded Scot, was determined to lessen the tremendous imbalance between expenditure and income in the Northwest trade. His first attempt to do so was his voyage of 1789."[16]

I will now turn to the narratives of travel themselves. I will first of all examine the way Mackenzie portrays himself on the expeditions—the persona he constructs. Second, I will look at the kinds of relations this persona has with others—most importantly the Indians—and, beyond that, with the environment.

The authorial persona is in the first place defined as the absolute prime mover of the explorations, their sole instigator—since Peter Pond, the true initiator of the project, has been eliminated from the picture—and only leader. In depicting these undertakings, Mackenzie sidelines to a large extent his status as trader and brings to the fore the more glorified role of explorer and discoverer, under the aegis of the imperial power of Britain. (He has told the reader in the preface that he will be "unfolding countries hitherto unexplored, and which I presume, may now be considered as a part of the British dominions" [7–8].) The explorer's main goal in this instance is to cover terrain and reach a destination, and this is significantly different from the author's habitual aims and activities. Yet strikingly Mackenzie applies many facets of the trader's mentality to the new task.

When circumstances permit, Mackenzie does in fact engage in some trading on the side, and when they do not, he tries on occasion to set up future trading possibilities (207, 234). The trading thus never entirely ceases, and the reader is periodically reminded of Mackenzie's enduring zeal for dealing in peltries. But the main thrust of Mackenzie's energies is now directed toward the objective of reaching the Pacific ocean, an objective that, as he presents it, he alone has determined to achieve and pursues single-mindedly, even obsessively.

Repeatedly the author emphasizes the extreme urgency of this goal for him personally. It is "the project on which my heart was set, and in which my whole mind was occupied"; when the goal comes tantalizingly near he calls it his "darling project." At just this point, though, seemingly insurmountable obstacles loom, and he avers that the prospect of having to turn back produces in him "sensations little short of agony" (308, 364, 368).

This intensity of purpose leads Mackenzie to focus on time. Time is of the essence in achieving the projected goal, and the author often signals either satisfaction at not having wasted time or anxiety at having done so. Consulting his watch regularly is of great importance, and he notes with wonder in his journal, "I was so busily employed in collecting intelligence from our conductors that I last night forgot to wind up my timepiece, and it was the only instance of such an act of negligence since I left Fort Chepewyan" (389–90; see also 174, 204). As Kathleen Venema has demonstrated in a close linguistic analysis, Mackenzie dramatizes "temporal crisis" throughout his narrative.[17] For Venema this "thematization" of time is part of a larger discourse of imperial mastery, but the preoccupation with time and its efficient management is characteristic of commercial dealings as well.

In the quotation concerning his watch, the author excuses his "negligence" by the fact that he was "busily employed" in attempting to gain information. This points to another aspect of Mackenzie's self-portrayal in the text. He is described as almost continually applying himself, through thought and action, to achieving his purpose. He not only steadily applies energy but directs that energy rationally. He disciplines and controls himself so as to attain maximum efficiency, reining in any impulsive desires or emotions that might get in the way. In the narrative these impulses appear almost exclusively in others, while he, as he has already told the reader in the preface, "had . . . the passions and fears of others to control and subdue" (6). When he occasionally lapses, temporarily losing his calm, making an impetuous gesture or an imprudent decision, as he judges it with hindsight, the author takes himself severely to task, recognizing that in those cases he might have jeopardized his mission. In one passage, for instance, he tells of his "very painful mortification" at having committed "an act of indiscretion which might have put an end to the voyage that I had so much at heart" (301; see also 278, 368, 442). In so doing he underscores for the reader his overall seriousness of purpose and total commitment to his objective.

Mackenzie's fixation on accomplishing his aim at whatever cost also results in systematically instrumentalizing those who were in any way associated with the trip, both Europeans and Indians—among the latter both those who were members of the party and those encountered along the way. Moreover Mackenzie's overweening sense of self leads him often to belittle and subordinate the selves of others. Two categories of Europeans were part of the expeditions: other traders like himself and the crews of French Canadian *voyageurs*.[18]

The case of the other traders is instructive. On both of the trips another fur trader was present: on the first, a French Canadian named Le Roux, who went on only the first leg of the journey, and on the second another Scotsman, named Mackay, who made the entire trip. Le Roux, as we know from other sources,[19] was in fact at the time an important trader in the North West Company who had already played a role in expanding to the north of Lake Athabasca—he had built a fort on Great Slave Lake in 1786—and who was going to engage in his own mission once he left Mackenzie's party. Yet Mackenzie only very briefly mentions him and calls him a "clerk," emphasizing the fact that he is not a partner in the enterprise (136). As for Mackay on the second trip, he too is sparingly mentioned, and never as someone who plays a significant role in the venture.[20] In the few references to him, he is criticized, given an order, or ignored. Ironically it is only Indians on the Bella Coola River who recognize his superior hierarchical position in relation to the rest of the crew, since the narrative reports that both Mackenzie and MacKay were treated to a whole salmon on one occasion, while the other members of the expedition were given smaller portions (411; see also 332, 361, 366).

The crew of French Canadians is of course considered subordinate and inferior by Mackenzie, who, while paying homage to their physical prowess sees it mainly as a tool for the accomplishment of his aims. He drives his crew very hard, calculating the limit beyond which he cannot go without breaking them. When they complain of the pace or declare it would be madness to go on, Mackenzie cannily responds in some cases by listening, soothing, or giving temporary respite, and in others by ordering, rebuking, and ridiculing, depending on the technique that most promises to get them to perform as he wants. He seems to have been charismatic enough to command respect for much of the trip, but in some passages the distrust and resentment of the crew is alluded to in different ways. In one instance, when Mackenzie directs them to set out over a threatening set of rapids (earlier they had narrowly escaped disaster on other rapids), saying that he will walk beside the river so as to lighten the canoe, they refuse unless he comes on board as well (322).

Another, later incident particularly well illustrates Mackenzie's calculating, tactical approach to dealing with his men. He has heard rumblings of discontent and has understood that the men do not wish to continue. So as they grudgingly prepare a canoe for departure, he singles out one of the crew, who

> though a good man, was remarkable for the tardiness of his operations.... I therefore took this opportunity of unfolding my sentiments to him, and thereby discovering to all around me the real state of my mind, and the resolutions I had formed for my future conduct. After reproaching him for his general inactivity, but particularly on the present occasion ..., I mentioned the apparent want of economy, both of himself and his companions, in the article of provisions. I informed him that I was not altogether a stranger to their late conversations.... I concluded, however, by assuring them, that whatever plan they had meditated to pursue, it was my fixed and unalterable determination to proceed.... The man was very much mortified at my addressing this remonstrance particularly to him; and replied that he did not deserve my displeasure more than the rest of them. My object being answered, the conversation dropped, and the work went on. (373–74)

In this passage Mackenzie displays the managerial acumen with which he has defused the threat of insubordination by making a breach in the men through the focus on one alone.

In the narrative we are thus given some revealing glimpses of the master-servant dynamic as it worked itself out over these extraordinarily arduous voyages. A master-servant—or employer-employee—relation it certainly was, and apparently remained to the end, in spite of the extreme experiences shared, experiences of a kind that in many cases create strong ties. Mackenzie never reports fraternizing amicably with his *voyageurs* during the journeys, and he maintained no further contact with any of them after the journeys were completed.[21]

In his dealings with the Indians, as they are delineated in the text, Mackenzie is equally at pains to exercise control and assert superiority, to make the natives submit to the imperatives of his expedition and, when the occasion arises, to assure that they will carry out their functions properly in projected future fur trading. As with his crew, though, and to a much larger degree, Mackenzie encounters from the natives different forms of resistance to these impositions.

The Indians accompanying him on the trips as hunters and interpreters are continually ordered about, pressured to perform faster and do more, and they clearly find the regimen prescribed for them harder to accept than the *voyageurs* generally do theirs (e.g., 160, 223, 304). That they complain of fatigue and often wish to turn back or leave the expeditions are obvious indicators of disinterest in Mackenzie's goals, since when their own objectives were at stake it is well known that Indians were indefatigable. Even the Chipewyan chief, referred to by the author as the "English Chief,"[22] who is engaged to accompany the first trip and who has had considerable previous experience collaborating with whites, grumbles, resists complying, and threatens to leave on several occasions. Mackenzie makes no attempt to develop a collaborative relationship with him. Instead he treats the indigenous leader as an inferior who can be dictated to. When, for instance, the Chipewyans led by the English Chief do not immediately respond to Mackenzie's command to pursue a group of natives who have fled,[23] Mackenzie reprimands the chief as he might a subordinate director:

> I rebuked the English Chief with some severity for his conduct, and immediately ordered him, his young men, and my own people, to go in search of the fugitives.... The English Chief was very much displeased at my reproaches, and expressed himself to me in person to that effect. This was the very opportunity which I wanted, to make him acquainted with my dissatisfaction for some time past. I stated to him that I had come a great way, and at a very considerable expense, without having completed the object of my wishes, and that I suspected he had concealed from me a principal part of what the natives had told him respecting the country, lest he should be obliged to follow me.... These suggestions irritated him in a very high degree, and he accused me of speaking ill words to him.... His harangue was succeeded by a loud and bitter lamentation; and his relations assisted the vociferations of his grief.... As I could not well do without them, I was at length obliged to sooth it, and induce the chief to change his resolution, which he did, but with great apparent reluctance. (225–26)

As with his French crew, Mackenzie tactically adjusts his approach to obtain the performance he wishes from the Indians he has engaged for the trip, in this case through the intermediary of their chief.

Other Indians are temporarily brought into the traveling parties to serve as guides to the area as far forward on the itinerary as their knowledge of the terrain warrants. They too are almost always very reluctant to join the explorers, sometimes changing their minds and wishing to withdraw even before the expedition gets under way to the next destination. In many cases they are simply compelled by Mackenzie to come on board, and later to remain with the party if they appear to want to leave. They are for all practical purposes held prisoner, and Mackenzie is obliged continually to watch them—personally, because the others seem less enthusiastic about keeping guides against their will. In one of the rare passages with a hint of humor, Mackenzie recounts that the only method he has found to keep one such guide from escaping during the night is to share his bed. The strategy works, but the odor of fish oil and red earth from the man's hair and paint keeps Mackenzie awake until his great fatigue gets the better of him (386; see also 164, 169, 173).

As for the native tribes encountered along Mackenzie's route, they are approached principally with an eye to what they can do for the expeditions (mainly information, directions, and food). In some cases, though, as already mentioned, Mackenzie attempts to create a new trade link or to put an old one back on track. In these instances—which occur in the early phases of the trips, before the party has entered hitherto unknown territories—Mackenzie sometimes "lectures" the Indians, like a father to children. In one place not far out on the second trip, Mackenzie rebukes a band's recent "misconduct" in the trade, informing them that they will be treated well only if they "deserve it." Otherwise he would be "equally severe if they failed in those returns which I had a right to expect from them" (246–47).[24] While Mackenzie speaks here in a condescending and authoritarian manner, the situation he is addressing well illustrates the inability of traders often to effectively control the behavior of their native suppliers.

In trying to obtain the aid of tribes farther out on the journeys, Mackenzie generally must adopt a more conciliatory tone since his small group is isolated in uncontrolled Indian territory. He sometimes holds out the promise of the benefits of future trade (in particular the lure of guns and ammunition), but he also uses the usual tool of gifts—many kinds of European products, but importantly including rum (e.g., 242, 243). This item is made use of despite the fact that the author has shown in the fur trade essay that he is aware of the devastating effects of alcohol on native populations.

Mackenzie is also careful regularly to demonstrate his power as a white European. To do so he employs several means: firing guns to impress natives who have had little or no contact with whites, and also proclamation and dramatization of the power of European knowledge. At one point a native asks why Mackenzie is seeking information when whites claim to know everything. Mackenzie answers that indeed they do know everything in general; the only help Indians can give them is with local details. "Thus," he concludes, "I fortunately preserved the impression in their minds, of the superiority of white people over themselves" (360; see also 178, 352). Here, however, the author's bravado probably masks an anxious awareness of the tenuous or even illusory nature of white domination in this context. The question asked by his native interlocutor, in the terms reported by the author, seems clearly ironic, if not openly mocking.

Another form of knowledge-as-power that Mackenzie attempts to wield is medical, but the results are likely to appear comical to the present-day reader. Being far from well versed in European medical science, each time he wishes to impress the natives by making a cure he uses "Turlington's balsam," a well-known eighteenth-century patent medicine claiming multifarious curative powers. Unsurprisingly a patient who did not seem very sick in the first place gets better, and one who was gravely ill dies (237, 423).

All of these techniques are brought to bear—and are duly highlighted in the text—as devices serving in the effort to reach Mackenzie's all-absorbing goal. The Indians—like the others, but most crucially of all—are instrumentalized in multiple ways in an endeavor that is commercial at its heart. But one further dimension of Mackenzie's relations with Indians should be mentioned, as repeatedly manifesting his commercial trader's temperament over the course of the journeys. For he encounters in the

Indian groups along the way a mentality entirely foreign to his in regard to property and exchange. Their communal and gift-giving cultures clash with his own thoroughly mercantile one. Although Mackenzie too gives gifts, he does so to achieve specific purposes, and they can be seen as a kind of payment for which he expects a return. The concept of "honest payment" recurs often in the text. Mackenzie is happily surprised in the few cases when a native seems to be respecting the notion of private ownership, and he insists on paying for objects taken from Indians, even when no payment is asked for. In this sense, throughout the voyages cultural misunderstanding is rife, with little effort to achieve a middle ground on Mackenzie's part (e.g., 196, 320, 339, 474).

Several passages highlight this dissonance between value systems. On the first voyage Mackenzie reports an incident that occurred soon after they left the Arctic Sea to return, in which the Indians of his party, coming upon some (unidentified) native lodges, "found several articles which they proposed to take; I therefore gave beads and awls to be left as the purchase of them; but this act of justice they were not able to comprehend, as the people themselves were not present" (213). Mackenzie considers that what he terms the "justice" of payment should be applied regardless of circumstances, whereas presumably for the Indians giving something "in return" would make sense only in the context of a face-to-face ceremonial gift exchange.

Another illustration occurs early on the second expedition, while the explorer's party is wintering on the Peace River:

> There was a lodge of Indians here, who were absolutely starving with cold and hunger. They had lately lost a near relation, and had according to custom, thrown away every thing belonging to them ... in order, as I presume, to get rid of every thing that may bring the deceased to their remembrance. They also destroy every thing belonging to any deceased person, except what they consign to the grave.... We had some difficulty to make them comprehend that the debts of a man who dies should be discharged, if he left any furs behind him. (258)

Although he does not directly say so, it is evident that Mackenzie wonders at these Indians' behavior, so completely at odds with their self-interest, that is, with the promotion of their material prosperity. What is explicitly articulated is his conviction that the commercial concept of debt should override any traditional customs based on honoring the dead.

The misfit between Mackenzie's set of values and that of the Indians is also illustrated in the ethnological remarks made in the course of the narration as well as in the section included within the fur trade essay. As Parker Duchemin observes in his perceptive analysis of the treatment of Indians in *Voyages*, its author almost exclusively concentrates on the material culture of the various indigenous populations he came into contact with, showing virtually no interest in their spiritual life—essential, of course, to understanding them. Although clearly curious about some of their primitive techniques, Mackenzie ultimately judges them inferior. Since spiritual wealth is ignored, this view leaves the Indians leading "narrowly limited" lives, providing ideological justification for the European "commercial agenda" in North America.[25]

Blindness to their spirituality also could produce drastic misreadings of natives encountered and probable outrage to them. Mackenzie relates one incident on the second trip, soon after the expedition has reached the Bella Coola River and is descending it toward the sea, in which he is convinced he has acted for the best but has in all likelihood caused major offense. A group of Indians met earlier have decamped, leaving behind some belongings:

> On my return, I found my people indulging their curiosity in examining the bags and baskets which the natives had left behind them. Some of them contained their fishing tackle ... others of a smaller size were filled with a red earth, with which they paint themselves. In several of the bags there were also sundry articles of which I did not know the use. I prevented my men from taking any of them; and for a few articles of mere curiosity, which I took myself, I left such things in exchange as would be much more useful to their owners. (339)

These articles, which Mackenzie did not know the use of and took from "mere curiosity," were almost surely objects of religious significance and ritual usage for the Indians from whom they were taken, and for whom "more useful" objects would be no replacement.

A final angle from which to observe Mackenzie's mental makeup—one that also sharply contrasts it with the Indians' ethos—is his relation to the natural environment through which he passes on the trips, as well as that which has been his habitat as a fur trader since leaving Montreal and coming west. Both are areas of rugged forest terrain, defined as wilderness by Europeans though inhabited by indigenous groups. The author feels on the whole either indifferently or negatively toward this natural setting. In the narrative of the journeys Mackenzie for the most part treats natural phenomena as obstacles (steep mountains, dangerous rapids, etc.) or sources of discomfort (insects especially). Animals mentioned that are not pests are generally considered simply as sources of food. In one exceptional passage where the author pauses in the narration to comment on animal life, the beaver is unsurprisingly singled out. (The expedition has just passed through a region of higher concentration of them.) Here the treatment is positive, but precisely because the beaver exemplifies a quality prized by the trader: industry. The author exclaims with admiration that "the time which these wonderful creatures allot for their labours, whether in erecting their curious habitations, or providing food, is the whole of the interval between the setting and the rising sun" (296). The beaver has value, then, both as the raw material of trade and as an incarnation of a cardinal virtue for traders.

The description of landscape is usually presented with a technical or scientific framing: indications of numbers of miles between one point and another, readings of points on the compass, and locations of longitude and latitude. Very rarely the author admits to being impressed by the beauty of a scene, but the descriptions that follow are wooden and conventional. In one instance the attempt is cut short with the avowal that "no expressions of mind are qualified to describe" those scenes (267). In fact Mackenzie seems to have been wholly insensitive to scenes of wild nature, and the few admiring sketches of them are most likely the result of the ghostwriter's embellishments. A description of this kind, which occurs in the fur trade essay, has been analyzed by Ian MacLaren as incorporating Mackenzie's commercial vision as a subtext. This passage, clearly rewritten by the ghostwriter, portrays, in terms largely borrowed from the picturesque genre, the prospect of the watershed between the Hudson Bay and Arctic drainage basins, at the end of a long portage. A close analysis of the passage suggests that the rewriting of the scene translates Mackenzie's thoroughly mercantile perception into artistic prose, subliminally "selling," as it were, Mackenzie's projects for future development.[26]

In my discussion of Mackenzie's encounter with Indians as delineated in *Voyages*, I have focused on the ways its author's thoroughly commercial mentality—coming out of a total involvement in the British fur trade as practiced in the Northwest at the end of the eighteenth century—led his interactions with indigenous peoples to be coercive, manipulative, and instrumentalizing in the extreme. Rather than dialogues, they are monologues in which he attempts to impose his will. In the context of such interaction, understanding and evaluation—the two other parameters of the encounter experience—hardly come into play at all. Driven singlemindedly by his objectives—succeeding in the fur trade more generally and finding the Northwest Passage in his travel account—Mackenzie has little desire to understand Indians beyond the minimum that might serve these objectives. A monomaniacal devotion to commerce stretches the gap of otherness to the limit, repeatedly producing misunderstanding or severely truncated understanding. As for evaluation, it requires a modicum of interest, and that Mackenzie seems largely to have lacked. His work thus represents in almost every respect the reverse image or inversion of Bartram's. Rather than approaching fulfillment of the potential of the travel encounter, his narrative approaches its point of failure and shows that the travel account also can in some cases portray the zero degree. Mackenzie, like Bartram, though, constitutes an extreme case; as I will show, some fur traders share the complexities of other travelers in Indian territories.

WEST OF THE MISSISSIPPI

I will begin by sketching in the larger context for Jean-Baptiste Trudeau's travel account: the "trans-Mississippi West" and travel in the eighteenth century in that vast region below the far-northern scene of Mackenzie's operations. During that century diverse conceptions of what constituted "the West" held sway. In the Anglo-American sphere, because the settled colonies had for so long been limited to the east coastal strip, the West was often thought of as the region west of the Allegheny Mountains, extending to the Mississippi River—the area into which settlers were increasingly moving. This notion is reflected in the title of an influential work by the land speculator Gilbert Imlay, published in 1792, *A Topographical Description of the Western Territory of North America*, which deals with the Anglo-American frontier areas, particularly in the newly added state of Kentucky. But for the French, who had laid claim to huge, ill-defined domains in the heart of the continent, from the beginnings of Louisiana in the late seventeenth century "the West" meant west of the Mississippi. In the late eighteenth century the term came increasingly to take on this meaning for the British and the Americans as well, as they penetrated farther west themselves.

Like the Anglo-American frontier west of the Alleghenies, this trans-Mississippi West, although claimed variously by the French and the Spanish, was still effectively "Indian territory" in the sense of being inhabited mainly by indigenous groups and communities, and to a large extent controlled de facto by them.[27] Moreover the Amerindians in this "far west" had for the most part considerably less direct contact with whites than those of the trans-Allegheny West. Outside of a limited number of Spanish missions and towns in New Mexico and Texas, there were no European settlements, only a few scattered, small posts, with fur traders and explorers traveling through the region, sometimes living in Indian communities. Throughout the century extensive areas west of the Mississippi remained little known to Europeans and the subject of fantastic speculations, as is attested by maps of the period.[28] At the same time, nonetheless, indirect contact with Europeans had spread virtually everywhere through the mediated transmission of trade goods and disease.[29]

Travelers west of the Mississippi were almost exclusively French in the first six decades of the eighteenth century. The Spanish generally remained close to their southwestern settlements, and the British were still confronting the French farther east, in trans-Allegheny zones. But starting in the early 1760s Anglo-American traders and explorers began to move into the western areas. Many French traders remained, nonetheless, and continued their activities. Also, French *voyageurs* often joined Anglo-American exploratory or trading ventures as employees. Other Frenchmen joined the Spanish, who were bequeathed western Louisiana by the French in an effort to stymie British advance westward. In fact when the Spanish began to send out their own expeditions near the end of the century in an attempt to consolidate their control of the area, it was often Frenchmen in their service who carried them out. There were British as well who hired themselves out to the Spanish, so the travelers often exhibited shifting, transnational allegiances.[30]

In the trans-Mississippi West the fur trade was first dominated by the French, then later by the British, in competition with the Spanish. Two "systems" of that trade—the Canadian, coming out of Montreal and Hudson's Bay, and the Louisianan, out of New Orleans and St. Louis—overlapped and came into conflict on the Northern Plains and around the Missouri River.[31] As already mentioned, during the French regime there was considerable diversity of motive in trade and travel; this contrasts with the later period, after the arrival of the British, who were more sharply focused on business.

Like the travel itself, narratives of it and of European encounters with Amerindians were sparse for areas west of the Mississippi compared to farther east. Such as they are these narratives are often rather rudimentary—unelaborated journals, diaries, or reports to superiors, not intended for publication and not worked up into the classic form of the account of travel in Indian territory. In other cases the trans-Mississippi West usually constituted only a small part of their itineraries. In a few cases the travel is imaginary, and in several others the fruits of the travel are reported in another genre.[32]

In the first half of the eighteenth century the accounts are French and generally report journeys conceived in the characteristic French mode. Patronized or directed by the colonial administration, the expeditions aimed both to extend the French imperium and to develop trade. It should be added, though, that this series of prosaic French accounts was preceded by the Baron de Lahontan's maverick (and possibly apocryphal) narration of his trip in 1688 up the "Rivière longue," which may have been either the Minnesota or the Missouri River. Later accounts by French officers and agents were neither as personal and philosophical nor as fully elaborated as Lahontan's, generally being restricted to factual matters of interest to the superiors to whom they were addressed and espousing the latter's aims.[33]

These include Bénard La Harpe's journals of travel up the Red River in 1719 and the Arkansas in 1721–22; Véniard de Bourgmont's third-person narration in diary form of an expedition in 1724 up the Missouri and then overland onto the Plains; and the accounts of exploration by the La Vérandrye family, a father and three sons, who started in the Canadian North in the early 1730s but turned south to visit the Mandans on the upper Missouri in 1738.[34] In 1742–43, after their father was obliged to return to Montreal, two of the sons made further progress west from the Mandans, reaching the Black Hills and perhaps the Big Horn Mountains, encountering tribes that had hitherto been unknown to the French. Until his return east, the father chronicled these voyages in letters to his sponsors; the final trip was reported by one of the sons. Although the son's account contains some sympathetic and admiring passages on Indians encountered, and Bourgmont's account includes a few pages descriptive of the mode of life of Padouca Indians (Comanche or Apache), commentary on Indian lifeways is generally scanty in these texts.[35]

From the 1760s on, in a number of more fully adumbrated narratives Anglo-American travelers also cover areas west of the Mississippi, but only in a small portion of their accounts. Jonathan Carver's *Travels* includes a section on his stay with a group of Dakota Sioux at a spot somewhere along the Minnesota River (then called the St. Peter), though its exact location is not known. Scholars have disagreed, situating it anywhere from a few miles from the river's mouth on the Mississippi to its far upper reaches.[36] It was Peter Pond, the onetime associate of Mackenzie, who originally suggested that Carver went only a short distance up the Minnesota, fourteen miles, in an account of his own expedition up the same river in 1774, which claimed that he found the hut where Carver had wintered. Pond wrote a memoir at the end of his life that contains this account.[37] The manuscript of the memoir covering the period after 1774 was accidentally thrown away, so the section on his trip up the Minnesota is the only narration of Pond's own experiences in areas beyond the Mississippi that has survived. Pond claims that he proceeded hundreds of miles up the Minnesota beyond what he thought was Carver's hut to trade with a band of Sioux that had never been visited by European traders. He describes his treatment by them and some of their customs and beliefs.[38]

Like Carver's book, Alexander Henry's *Travels and Adventures in Canada* involves trans-Mississippi territories only in a small part of the narrative. At the end of his chronicle he relates an excursion in 1775–76 that began in Canada but finally led him southward onto the Plains. He tells of his sojourn there with a tribe of Assiniboin, with whom he traded, and makes some observations on their behavior and practices. Similarly David Thompson, a famous trader and explorer whose forays were largely in "Rupert's Land" and the Far Northwest, and mainly at the beginning of the nineteenth century, kept a journal on an early, lesser-known trip to the Mandans in 1797–98. Thompson had just joined the North-West Company, which sent him to establish trade relations. He stayed with the Hidatsas and Mandans just ten days, but claims that he spent much time conversing with the Indians on varied topics, observing them and participating in their festivities. These materials are only alluded to in the original journal but are presented in synthesized form in a memoir of his life written much later.[39]

Mention should be made, finally, of a work that illustrates the element of illusion that persisted throughout the century in regard to the region. In 1788 a book was published in Boston entitled *New Travels to the Westward, or, Unknown Parts of America* by Don Alonzo Decalves. Though the author identifies himself as a Spaniard, the text is in English and the name is evidently a pseudonym. The travels recounted take the author and several companions from New Orleans up the Mississippi, then west at some undesignated point, across the "Sublime mountains," and eventually to a vast lake that suggests the imagined and much sought-for "Sea of the West." Along the way the travelers find monstrous beasts in several places, and on a river beyond the lake they come across highly civilized "white" Indians—a probable reference to the legend of the medieval Welsh prince Madoc, who was thought to have established a community in the Far West. Though the first readers of this popular work—it went through many editions into the early nineteenth century—doubtless read it as a true account, its fictitious nature is beyond doubt today. In peopling the Far West with chimerae, this text published near the end of the century points up how much remained mysterious in the trans-Mississippi West at that time, despite the real explorations and their narrations that I have mentioned.[40]

JEAN-BAPTISTE TRUDEAU

Jean-Baptiste Trudeau's account of his expedition on the Missouri River at the end of the century has recently been published in a scholarly edition as *Voyage sur le Haut-Missouri, 1794–1796* (Journey on the Upper Missouri, 1794–1796).[41] It is of particular interest in a number of ways. Of the narratives dealing with trans-Mississippi travel this work is by far the longest and most amply developed. It shares many characteristics with full-fledged, published accounts of travel in Indian territory in the period, yet since it did not go through reworking by editors, as the others often did, it is perhaps closer to the original perceptions of its author. It also stands out as the work of a French Canadian, in the period following the fall of New France, which was dominated by Anglo-American travel and narration. Above all, Trudeau's account reveals in a particularly instructive way the complexities of the encounter with Amerindians in the West and, molded by commercial purposes though it is, significantly transcends them in its representation of the Indian Other.

Our knowledge of Trudeau's life is sketchy outside of the two years (1794–96) on the Missouri recorded in his account. He was born in Montreal in 1748 and sent to school at the Seminary of Quebec, where he acquired at least the rudiments of a classical—and Catholic—education. He seems to have moved to St. Louis in 1774, some five years after beginning work in the fur trade. He continued in that pursuit after the move, so that when he set out in 1794 he had been in the trade for some twenty-five years. For part of that time, possibly for most or all of it, Trudeau was a *voyageur* or *engagé*, that is, an employee rather than a partner or trader on his own account. While much of his experience of the trade was in the Illinois country, some was also west of the Mississippi, especially on the lower Missouri. After the 1794–96 expedition Trudeau surprisingly changed profession altogether, becoming a schoolteacher in St. Louis, though he maintained contact with other traders and probably joined one exploratory expedition in 1802. He died in St. Louis in 1827.[42]

During the first decades of the Spanish regime in Louisiana very little exploration and development of trade networks was carried out, while the British and Americans made increasing incursions from the Northeast. In response to this threat to their hegemony, the Spanish authorities, in conjunction with St. Louis merchants, finally created the Company for the Discovery of Nations on the Upper Missouri in May 1794, and Trudeau was quickly chosen to undertake its first probe up the river. Thus Trudeau made his voyage as an agent of the Company, under a precise set of orders: to travel as far upriver as the Mandan villages and set up trade relations with them, to put an end to the illicit trade activities of the English on the upper Missouri, to cultivate good relations with all Indian tribes in the area and promote peace among them (a measure that would facilitate trade), to gather information if possible about Indians farther west, even beyond the Rockies, and—the order that gave rise to the account itself—to keep a journal and send copies back at regular intervals.

Setting off in early June, Trudeau almost immediately encountered difficulties. Various nations on parts of the lower Missouri resisted his attempts to reach those farther up the river, and he was obliged to spend the winter of 1794–95 with the Omahas, about halfway to the Mandans. Thereafter he was able to continue on to the Arikara settlements, but though he sent envoys forward to them he never himself reached the Mandans. After spending the winter of 1795–96 with the Arikaras and becoming increasingly embroiled in tensions and conflicts among upper Missouri tribes, British traders, and his own party, he retreated home, via the Omahas, arriving in St. Louis in June 1796. From the point of view of the commercial objectives of the company, Trudeau's trip was a failure. What remains, though, is the travel account, which provides us with a telling portrayal of a situation and a set of encounters.[43]

There is no evidence that Trudeau ever intended his account to reach a larger audience than the members of the company by whom the trip was commissioned and to whom the account is addressed. If he ever thought of publishing his writing, we have no trace of such an intention. Though English translations of a few short excerpts were published during his lifetime, he may well have been unaware of their appearance, according to the editor of the full original text published by Septentrion in 2006.[44] In the first half of the twentieth century several longer fragments were published, most in English translation as well, but it was only with the Septentrion edition that the complete work, in the original French, was finally made available to the reading public.[45]

Although not brought into general circulation by its author, the work nonetheless came to the attention of several select readers and thereby exercised a tangible influence. First, Trudeau seems to have shown the manuscript to François-Marie Perrin du Lac, whose 1802 excursion up the Missouri he probably joined, since there are indications of plagiarism from it in Perrin du Lac's later published account of his own travels.[46] Second, an important part of Trudeau's journal at least came into the hands of Thomas Jefferson, who transmitted an English translation to Meriwether Lewis in preparation for his upcoming expedition.

The structure of Trudeau's work is that which characterized many published accounts: a narrative of the journey followed by a separate section with general observations and comments on the natives encountered. Similar also to many publications in the genre, the barrier between the two parts of the account is often breached, and elements of one invade the other. The narration is interrupted to present generalizing material, and the exposition on Indian communities and modes of living is interspersed with the telling of incidents. Both forms of discourse are intertwined, interrelated, and finally inseparable.

The author recounts his journey upriver, and then very succinctly the return, in a kind of modified diary presentation that mixes present and past tenses and shows signs of at least partial composition or recomposition after the trip was over. As the narrative moves with the traveler through the itinerary of the voyage, from relations with tribes lower on the river to those higher up, there is both contrast and continuity. The tribes farther up the Missouri have generally had less contact with Europeans, and Trudeau is struck, as were many travelers in Indian territories, by the differences. But at the same time all have been in crucial ways affected by Europeans, and tribes have also been displaced, so that some problems described by the author permeate the whole.

In the first months of travel Trudeau successively passes by a number of lower Missouri Indian settlements—that of the Otos, who are absent, to Trudeau's relief, then of the Omahas (called Mahas at the time) and the Poncas, both of whom he avoids by subterfuge. All of these nations have already had substantial trading relations with Europeans, and his orders are to develop new ones upstream. He knows that the lower Missouri nations will try to keep him from doing that. However, as he nears the Arikaras, the first of the upriver tribes he wishes to visit, he runs into a band of roving Sioux and is forced into a first encounter. They are on the opposite side of the river, and, knowing that they also will attempt to hold him back, Trudeau holds a cross-river conversation. They identify themselves as Yancton Sioux, and it turns out that not only has Trudeau had earlier relations with them, but, "since I had lived for a long period in their village on the Desmoines river, they regarded me as a man of their own nation."[47]

Trudeau remains suspicious but agrees to cross the river. His mistrust is partially confirmed when he reaches the other shore, since they have neglected to tell him that among them are also Titon (Teton) Sioux, displaced from the western Plains. The Tetons are extremely hostile, reject his attempt to make them acknowledge the Spanish governor as "Father," and insist that for them no chief is paramount over others (52). The situation becomes more and more tense, and the Yancton men, after first defending Trudeau, seem to abandon him. When it looks as if Trudeau and his crew will be attacked by the Tetons, though, Trudeau is warned and given advice, to his surprise, by elderly Yancton women. Though he acknowledges that he had known them earlier on the Desmoines River, in explaining their concern and aid he ungraciously supposes that "it was perhaps in gratitude for the knives and awls I was forced to distribute to them the day before" (58).

Trudeau finally escapes with his men and proceeds upriver. When he reaches an Arikara camp they are not there—as the Sioux had told him. Then, in fear of again falling into the hands of the Sioux, Trudeau returns downriver and winters with the Omahas. There he engages in conversations and negotiations with first a secondary chief, then the principal chief of the Omahas, Toangarest. During his stay he also speaks with several Ponca chiefs who visit, and continues these palavers when he stops at their village in the early spring before making a second attempt to reach the upper tribes.

Trudeau's reactions to these first encounters and his attitudes toward the peoples and chiefs he deals with are generally negative. In addition to resenting their resistance to his plans, he is irritated by the hard bargaining in trade, and in some cases the pillaging, that the lower tribes engage in. He reserves his strongest condemnation for the Teton Sioux, who had thwarted him most fiercely, calling them "brutes" and "ferocious beasts" (51, 53). But the Yancton also are treated disparagingly as "rascals" (*coquins*). He applies this term to the Omahas as well, calling Toangarest "the greatest rascal of all" (70). Behind the appellation is the idea that these Indians regularly dissemble and lie, although in several instances Trudeau admits that he and other Frenchmen do so as well in their dealings with Indians. As for the Poncas, they are "narrow-minded" (*bornés*) and "malicious" (*méchants*) because their superstitious credulity leads them to fear he is a sorcerer (86). He is obliged to write his journal at night so as to avoid encouraging their suspicions (88).

In spite of this categorical reprobation, though, Trudeau at the same time repeatedly shows that he is aware of the reasons for the behavior of the tribes that have had sustained contacts with Europeans already. The Omahas, whom he tells the company he has studied especially because of their potentially pivotal role in future trade upriver, have learned the tricks of the trade from *coureurs des bois*. Having learned that English merchandise is better and cheaper, and having been taken advantage of by French traders in the past, they have become as "sharp and cunning" as the European traders. Toangarest has become a master of trade stratagem, beating the traders at their own game, and apparently accruing undue tribal power to himself as well (67, 70, 73, 78). The Poncas, although they have had fewer and more recent dealings with traders, already have learned to act in similar ways to the nearby Omahas, but since they are upriver they are in a weaker, dependent position (83, 85). In general the tribes downstream are able to obtain arms and merchandise more easily, which explains their "policy" (*politique*) of trying to keep the Europeans from going farther upriver (42). As for the Sioux, Trudeau knows that the Yanctons, who have had much European contact, have been badly treated recently by some French traders (47), whereas the Tetons, who have not, have been forced to emigrate from the Far West because the animals on their usual hunting grounds have been decimated (51).

Trudeau leaves the Poncas in early April 1795 for his second try at visiting the upper nations. In mid-May he successfully reaches the Arikara settlement. They are there this time, and with them are bands of Cheyennes and Sioux. While Trudeau is there, several other bands of Sioux arrive, and he travels a short distance to see two other Cheyenne groups. The Sioux are all Teton subdivisions, and in one of them he recognizes some of the Indians who had threatened and pillaged him earlier (130). All of these tribal groups are in highly unstable relations among themselves and with tribes both up and downriver. Trudeau, following his orders, attempts repeatedly to settle conflicts and reestablish peace, but new discords continually break out. He never feels that the situation is sufficiently stabilized for him to leave, and therefore is never able to travel on to the Mandans and Gros Ventres (Hidatsas). He only indirectly gets information about them—and the Crows from farther west who are visiting them—through an envoy he sends and a French trader already there who comes downriver.

In addition to engaging in arduous peacekeeping as a prerequisite for trade, while with the Arikaras Trudeau also tries energetically to set the trade in motion. In the process he is caught in a web of tensions and contradictions that finally degenerate to the point where he must flee. He pushes the various tribes to go out and hunt beaver, although only the Sioux are accustomed to this type of hunting for trade. When some Arikaras embark on a hunting expedition and several are killed by Sioux in an unspecified dispute, Trudeau is held to blame, since, as he notes,

Indians hold responsible a person who has pressured others to take an action (128). Trudeau also at one point withholds arms from the Indians until he has received additional supplies. At another he refuses to exchange merchandise with them to his disadvantage, and insists on selling according to the French and Spanish price scale when the Indians he is bartering with get news from upstream and downstream of English traders offering a better deal. In all this Trudeau claims to be simply adhering to his directives, but he chafes under them and in several passages bitterly criticizes the company director and the St. Louis merchants who have a monopoly and make outrageous profits. He compares them to pirates of the high seas (*corsaires*; 119, 121, 133–34, 161). In this situation the Indians become increasingly hostile and turbulent. He is supported by only one chief, and finally resorts to paying him to continue his support. In the end Trudeau decamps precipitously, narrowly escaping with his life (138–40).

Despite his incessant frustrations and final rout at the hands of these upper Missouri tribes, the author of *Voyage* is strikingly less negative in his attitude toward them than he was toward those lower down. Aside from a few mocking comments on certain "ridiculous" or "absurd" superstitions (167, 202), he generally demonstrates his understanding of the Indians' predicament and expresses (qualified) admiration for their way of life.

When Trudeau interrupts the narrative portion of his work to insert a descriptive passage on the Arikaras, he insists, as he had previously regarding the Omahas, that understanding them is essential since they hold the "key" to future trade on the Missouri (95). He explains the discord that reigns among them and the tribes surrounding them by the regroupings occasioned by smallpox epidemics, as well as the competition for arms. And in a series of passages he shows that he has come to grasp certain general principles of Indian-European dynamics. He begins by noting that the Arikaras are "the mildest and most favorable to us" of all tribes he has encountered so far (95), but then adds that according to those who have gone farther west this is the case even more so with tribes out there—in particular the Mandans and Hidatsas (97). Though he finds at first that the Arikaras trade peacefully without contesting prices, Trudeau later discovers that this is not entirely true. His first impression was produced by contrast with the Omahas and others lower down. In the same way those who know the tribes farther up the Missouri find the Arikaras difficult by comparison. There seems to be a progression whereby those tribes with the least contact are the most amenable to easy trade relations; paradoxically, though, they are the ones with the least to offer in trade. They are not used to hunting beaver, "no one having yet incited them to" (127; also 103). Trudeau thus points to some important contradictions at the heart of the process: inciting Indians to hunt for trade and providing arms to do so produces heightened conflict among Indian groups, and the more dependent on trade Indians become, the more fiercely they struggle, using it to get what they need.

In these comments Trudeau is concerned principally to understand Indians and their situation with a view to the further development of trade relations sought by his patrons, though his implicit conclusions are decidedly pessimistic. Beyond this pragmatic assessment, though, he is at pains to understand the indigenous culture of Indians, as it was before and remains to a large extent in spite of the corrupting influence of whites. Though in early parts of the journal involving the lower Missouri tribes Trudeau throws out a few summary, negative stereotypes—on the "trickery and deceitfulness" (50) and "thirst for plunder" (54) of Indians in general—once with the upper nations he undertakes some relatively elaborate, subtle analysis that is broadly appreciative of Indian culture and critical of that of Europeans. His first exposition of this kind in the journal is presented as a portrait of the "character" of the Arikaras, but in the second part of the work, "Description abrégée du haut Missouri" (Abridged Description of the Upper Missouri), what begins with reference to several specific upper Missouri nations soon slides into a generalized treatment, Trudeau's version of the *mœurs des sauvages* (customs of the natives) genre.

In his character sketch of the Arikaras inserted into the journal, Trudeau announces the more general theme. The native peoples who have had little or no commerce with us, he claims, are the most "sincere" and "humane" (*humanisés*) because they follow "in their way of living only the laws and customary practices that reason, nature and humanity dictate to them" (97). He goes on to say that if these people we term savages and barbarians knew the true nature of the whites they sometimes deify—their lack of charity, the contemptible actions and even crimes they commit to accumulate wealth and power—they would certainly apply the same terms to them, and rightly so (98). A few pages further on the author asserts that Indians in their native state never act out of self-interest and share things equally in such a way that "what belongs to one belongs to the other"; unlike the state of affairs in "civilized" societies (*nations policées*), "in which one is only a man and only has a position of honor to the extent one is rich, to be a man and a well-esteemed one in their societies one must be decent, courageous, free-spirited, charitable and of good counsel" (101).

In the "Description" further on, under the heading, precisely, of "Mœurs des Sauvages du Haut-Missouri," Trudeau further develops and extends these reflections. Indian societies, he maintains, are strongly egalitarian, without "subordination" or "distinctions," and free of the constraints of religious or civil law (171). Several pages on he returns to these ideas to clarify them, specifying that when he had written "without law" he did not mean without norms (176), and when he had written "without distinctions" he had meant "frivolous" distinctions, not distinctions of any kind (177). This clarification seems intended to avoid being identified with those who have glorified the Indian as a culture-less "child of nature." For Trudeau, Indians have ordered cultures, but ones that are radically different from and ultimately more "noble" than those of present-day Europeans. As a follow-up on these passages the author indeed quotes a poem by Boileau on nobility (178–79) and in the closing pages of the work associates Indians with ancient Greek virtues (especially 218). This is not to say that his admiration is unconditional. He is shocked by some of their sexual mores (102, 189) and, as already mentioned, sharply disparages their superstitions. Yet these are considered secondary matters, and as regards the second, Trudeau points out that the Indians know very well how to reason, contrary to what has often been claimed (173). He knows this from experience, he declares, because he has learned some of their languages and has "reasoned with them" (175).

These broadly synthesizing and sympathetic remarks—along with some ambivalences and contradictions—situate Trudeau's account in the tradition of the other travel narratives of Indian encounter I have discussed, both French and Anglo-American. But the parallels are especially striking with Lahontan. Although there is no reference to Lahontan in Trudeau's writing, the echoes in many passages of *Voyage* are sufficient to suggest that its author had at least read and assimilated Lahontan, if not actually used his work in preparing his own text. Unlike Lahontan, Trudeau was a fur trader, and we have seen how his encounters were molded by the commercial imperatives of the trade. But we have also seen how Trudeau's account goes beyond and problematizes them, and in this it stands out in relation to the rest of the trans-Mississippi literature of this type.

Trudeau was not an "enlightened" aristocrat like Lahontan, but several aspects of his life may have contributed to his critical distance from the commercial nexus and affinity with Lahontan. First, Trudeau descended from one of the oldest Canadian families, a kind of local aristocracy. Second, his fur trading was largely undertaken as an employee, whose interests were not identical with those of employers. And third, drawing on his educational resources and interests he left the trade for school teaching. Whatever the case may be, the connection is there—with Lahontan's critical acumen and identification with Indians as a foil to the ills of his own society. It would seem that, though the river was—perhaps—a different one, Trudeau might well have epitomized his trip as Lahontan did his own: "The farther I went up the river, the more reasonable the natives seemed to me."[48]

With this bridge between two French writers at opposite ends of the temporal span covered by my study, we come full circle, after having passed through a variegated range of accounts throughout the eighteenth century—accounts that in spite of their diversity are united by many thematic strands as well.

Epilogue
Into the Nineteenth Century—George Catlin

At the opening of the nineteenth century, and especially after the War of 1812, the historical configuration that I have explored entered a new phase. This phase had already begun to manifest itself, though in a less pronounced form, in the decades following the American Revolution and before what has sometimes been called the second war of independence. As regards the development of modernity and capitalism, it was characterized by the growth of industry, technological innovation, large-scale financial institutions and corporations, and more efficient means of transportation to accelerate and facilitate commerce. Along with these developments the mentality oriented toward expansion and the accumulation of private wealth spread more widely than ever before and reinforced its hegemony. These tendencies continued to evolve during the nineteenth century, from the Jacksonian period to the Gilded Age that followed the Civil War. What was involved, though, was not a change in the nature of the society that had come into being in eighteenth-century Anglo-America—the fundamental structures were already in place—but rather the unfolding of its logic and potentialities. In the process of creation of the United States, according to a historian who has studied the first generation born after the Revolution, the new nation became not an "imagined community," as elsewhere, but an "imagined entreprise."[1]

In this era of increased industrialization and mechanization one trend inherited from the earlier period continued to play a key role: the expropriation of Indian lands and enlargement of territories under the control of whites, held as private property, commercially exploited and subject to financial speculation. But in this conflict with Native Americans for possession of land, a new chapter opened at the turn of the century. Already severely weakened by the Revolution and by several decisive defeats in the 1790s, by the early nineteenth century the Indians east of the Mississippi River had to a large extent lost their power, autonomy, and cultural coherency. With the failure of the movement led by Tecumsah, at the end of the War of 1812 the last resistance of the eastern Indians was overcome. With one exception: the Seminoles of Florida carried on a series of armed struggles throughout the first half of the nineteenth century and were definitively vanquished only in the years preceding the Civil War. Most of the other southeastern Indians underwent the forced displacement to the west in the 1830s called the Trail of Tears.

In terms of the confrontation of modernity with its indigenous Other, then, a geographical shift takes place. Indian territory, in the sense in which I have used the term, exists only west of the Mississippi in the nineteenth century, and the same dynamic of progressive shrinkage works itself out there over the course of the century. Consequently encounters of all kinds between the two sociocultural entities—skirmishes and wars, settler incursions, captivities, and travel in Indian territory—continue to happen, but only in the West, that immense and nebulously defined region called the Louisiana Territory when Lewis and Clark in 1804–6 and, less famously, Zebulon Montgomery Pike in 1805–7 began to explore and lay the first foundations for domination of the area by the United States.[2]

In this context a new literature developed, but in some ways the literature of the eighteenth century also continued to live on. First, some authors and works span the two centuries. Crèvecoeur, Freneau, and Bartram all lived on into the opening decades of the nineteenth century, and Freneau at least continued to publish well into the new century. Alexander Henry's

Travels and Adventures, although dealing with a period that ends in 1776, was published only in 1809. The memoirs of the "white Indian" John Tanner, who was captured by Ojibwes around 1790 and returned to white society in 1817, follow the author's life up to the end of the 1820s. The account of the life of Mary Jemison, carried off by Shawnees in 1758, is even more importantly tied to the nineteenth century. It was written and published in 1824 by James Everett Seaver, a man who was only thirteen years old in 1800 and who gave his recollection and interpretation of what Jemison had told him a year earlier, while adding a section of his own composition. In the numerous editions of Jemison's life story that followed later in the century, many further additions and rewritings were introduced.[3]

When eighteenth-century works were reedited in the nineteenth, publishers often did not hesitate to make changes meant to make them fit better with the supposed expectations of new publics. The case of the captivity accounts first published in 1783 by Brackenridge is interesting in this regard. The publication was twice reprinted in the nineteenth century, in 1843 in Nashville and 1867 in Cincinnati.[4] The original, rather neutral title *Narratives of a Late Expedition against the Indians* became *Indian Atrocities: Narratives of the perils and sufferings of Dr. Knight and John Slover, among the Indians during the revolutionary war*.[5] Moreover, although the accounts themselves were reproduced without changes, Brackenridge's peripheral essay, in which he calls for the elimination of Indians altogether, was truncated. The justification of extermination on the basis of the Indians' inhuman practice of torture was kept, but not the further step taken by Brackenridge in the first edition, in which he decrees that even if they abandon their violent practices the Indians must be exterminated because of their essentially vicious nature. This was perhaps a racist credo with which the nineteenth-century editors preferred not to associate themselves, at least insofar as it was applied to Indians. The title of the new editions insisted instead on the horror of Indian deeds, seemingly geared to the titillation of a broad public in a period when the eastern Indians no longer constituted a threat.

As for the major travel accounts, they were less often reedited, and their authors sometimes came to be partially forgotten. This was true, notably, of William Bartram and his *Travels*. In the case of Jonathan Carver, though after 1813 only one full edition of his book was published in the nineteenth century (New York, 1838), the work appeared many times in an abridged form aimed at young readers. Between 1845 and 1870, for example, a series of nine editions of excerpts in French translation appeared in the collection "Library of Christian schools, approved by Monseigneur the Bishop of Nevers," under the title *Aventures de Carver chez les sauvages de l'Amérique septentrionale* (Carver's Adventures with Savages in North America).[6] This kind of edition presented a selection from the original that highlighted adventure as well as educational and moral values.

In addition to these prolongations of the earlier literature into the nineteenth century, there was a proliferation of new works, both about the American modernity that was triumphantly moving forward and the continuing encounter with its Other—the "wild" Indians still beyond the control of "civilized" forces in the trans-Mississippi West. Often the most perceptive commentaries on the new nation, seen as different from all other nations but also as a prefiguration of their future, came from outside, in accounts by visitors. Notable among these were British travelers, now themselves foreigners in the United States, but also French and other Europeans. In the literature destined for a foreign public we find a continuation of the genre that offered advice or encouragement for the potential immigrant. Some of these works were quite detailed and nuanced.[7] But especially interesting are the accounts by literary writers, which view the young nation through a cultivated, often highly critical lens. Among the best known of the English visitors were Frances Trollope, whose acerbic *Domestic Manners of the Americans* (1832) created a scandal in the United States;[8] the antislavery author Harriet Martineau (*Society in America*, 1837); and Charles Dickens, whose *American Notes* was published upon his return—deeply disillusioned—from his first visit to the United States in 1842. But the nineteenth-century visitor whose analyses of American society are deservedly the most famous is the French aristocrat Alexis de Tocqueville (*De la démocratie en Amérique* [On Democracy in America], 1835–40).[9]

Astute critical viewpoints were not lacking from within the United States as well, of course, including some of the most important nineteenth-century literary voices: Emerson and Thoreau, Hawthorne and Twain, to name only a few. And at the end of the century, in 1899, as sociology began to develop as an intellectual discipline, Thorstein Veblen provided perhaps the first major analysis of American consumerism, *Theory of the Leisure Class*.

On the side of encounter with the Other we find examples, sometimes in abundance, of most of the previous century's genres that I have discussed: historical works (Thomas L. McKenney, *History of the Indian Tribes of North America*, 1833–44, 3 vols.); "customs" of the Indians (P. S. Ogden, *Traits of American Indian Life and Character*, 1853); and especially numerous accounts of captivity and travel in Indian territory.[10] Many of the accounts of new captivities in the West made intensive use of sensationalist literary effects, projecting monstrous images of bloodthirsty savages. Collections of these "atrocity" stories were also published to impress readers all the more forcefully. At the same time, though, one finds in the literature examples of "white Indians" who became members of their captors' communities and made common cause with them.[11] Moreover, according to one study of the genre, these nineteenth-century captivities—as they were written up and published in the East, where the Indian no longer threatened— often presented the encounter in a largely positive light, emphasizing the heroism of the pioneers and identifying their Indian antagonists as part of the national heritage.[12]

Accounts of travel in Indian territory, however, like their eighteenth-century predecessors, often involved a greater cultural implication with Indians. As in the earlier period the origins and profiles of the travelers were diverse: foreigners and Americans, scientists and missionaries, bourgeois and aristocrats.[13] A novelty in the nineteenth century was the presence of a significant number of artists who took the Indian as their principal subject. Before the early nineteenth century there was little illustration in texts involving encounter with North American Indians. Even Bartram did very few drawings of Indian subjects. This has meant that modern-day publishers of the earlier accounts, in search of enticing visuals, have sometimes resorted to using John White's exceptional set of drawings of sixteenth-century Virginia natives to illustrate texts involving other times and places.

The situation changed radically in the first half of the nineteenth century. Although Lewis and Clark had no artist on their expedition, soon thereafter many travelers who wrote about sojourns in Indian territories either were artists themselves or were accompanied by one. In addition, with the multiplication of visits to Washington by Indian delegations, many portraits of Indians were carried out there. The best known of the sedentary portraitists is Charles Bird King. Of the traveling artists, and travelers with artists accompanying them, some were Americans and some foreign visitors, usually noblemen with scientific interests. Many of the foreigners were Prussian or Swiss German. The two best known traveler-artists are the American George Catlin and the Swiss German Karl Bodmer.[14] While Catlin wrote a travel account to go along with his paintings, Bodmer only painted, accompanying Maximilian, Prince of Wied, the author of the account of their voyage.[15]

Later in the century photographers increasingly replaced painters. The most celebrated was E. S. Curtis, who began his work only at the close of the century, in 1899. Another new kind of traveler in Indian territory was the anthropologist. Lewis Henry Morgan was a pioneer of the discipline in America; after studying the Iroquois on reservations in the East, he visited and lived with some western tribes between 1859 and 1862.[16]

It should also be mentioned that in the nineteenth century, far more than in the eighteenth, the Indian becomes a significant literary figure: in fiction (James Fenimore Cooper's *Leatherstocking Saga*), poetry (Henry Wadsworth Longfellow's *Hiawatha*), and theater (*Metamora*, the tragedy of "King Philip").[17] A plethora of popular literature also thrived, which took the West and its Indians as one of its favorite subjects. This occurred not only in the United States but also abroad, notably in Germany, with Karl May's best-selling novels whose protagonist is Winnetou, an Apache warrior.

At least equally as important as this entry of Indian portraiture, often in stereotyped or culturally biased form, into mainstream Anglo-American and European literature was the burgeoning of written self-expression and representation by Native Americans themselves. The Mohegan Methodist missionary Samson Occom was the first American Indian to publish a work by himself—a short autobiographical text that appeared in 1772. But until the 1820s published writings by Indians were sparse and mainly limited to Christian converts. In 1828 Elias Boudinot initiated a secular trend of

Indian journalism by creating the *Cherokee Phoenix*, and a year later the mixed-blood Pequot William Apess published his important book-length autobiography. Although Apess, like Occom, was a Christian minister, in his autobiography and other writings he mounts an ironic critique of white society and a defense of the Amerindian cause. Later in the nineteenth century Indian writing—largely nonfiction and principally journalistic and autobiographical—proliferated, allowing for the articulation of Indian voices in a new way, directed toward both Indian and non-Indian publics.[18]

As for nineteenth-century writing by non-Indians about Indians, in spite of its diversity one defining feature differentiates it crucially from that of the eighteenth: the conviction that the natives of North America were condemned—in the more or less short term—to disappear. After the victory of whites over indigenous peoples east of the Mississippi, the march of "civilization" westward to the Pacific Ocean came to be seen as inevitable, and with it the destruction of the North American Indian. Attitudes toward this conviction were quite variable, however. Some—first and foremost those who would profit most from it—welcomed the perspective, but others, particularly those who can be associated with the cultural current of romanticism, saw it as a historical tragedy. In the United States, though, the most widespread point of view was situated in an ambiguous, intermediary zone: a sense of melancholy at the waning of an admirable culture, but at the same time a recognition that it must give way to a civilization that in the final analysis was superior. At any rate, whatever the stance adopted, the nineteenth century assumed that the outcome of the struggle between the two forces had been decided in advance. Consequently, even if an "Indian territory"—a territory of the Other—continued to exist on half of the continent, the way of seeing that Other by those who lived in modernity, and with it the nature of the encounter, had irremediably changed.

GEORGE CATLIN

An account of travel among western Indians by George Catlin (1796–1872) reveals the kinds of developments and transformations undergone in the nineteenth century by the dynamic of modernity and its Other.

Although his principal subject matter is thoroughly American, Catlin was in fact a transatlantic figure in the sense that he spent more than half of his adult life in England, France, and Belgium, presenting the Indians of the American West whom he had visited, painted, and written about earlier, as well as continuing to produce pictorial and textual representations of them there. After a brief period as a society portrait painter in Philadelphia and New York in the 1820s, Catlin decided to devote himself single-mindedly to the visual and verbal preservation of what he, like many others, saw as a "vanishing race." A period of travels in the trans-Mississippi West followed in the 1830s, during which Catlin painted western Indians of a wide variety of tribal affiliations, and their environment, made voluminous notes, and collected artifacts. These activities culminated in a series of lectures and exhibitions of his "Indian Gallery" in major cities on the East Coast at the end of the decade. After initial public interest in his work waned, though, and after failing to persuade the U.S. Congress to buy his Gallery, Catlin left for Europe in 1839, hoping to better his fortunes there. From late 1839 to 1845 he was based in London, lecturing, showing his paintings, and producing "spectacles" of Indian life. When the popularity of his productions subsided there as well, he moved them to Paris, then Brussels. In the following twenty-five years, hounded by chronic insolvency, he transferred the stage of his various activities—all involving the American Indian—back and forth between London, Paris, and Brussels, though according to his own accounts he interrupted his European sojourn with a series of travels in South America, and more briefly on the West Coast of North America, in the 1850s.[19] Catlin did not return to the United States to settle until 1871, the year before his death.[20]

Catlin's work generated a growing interest, both scholarly and popular, after World War II. During the 1950s and 1960s the books that appeared on him concentrated mainly on the paintings and were largely celebratory in tone, presenting the artist as a superb visual chronicler of the American West and its native inhabitants.[21] As a sign of a shift of interest, in the 1970s there appeared two editions, one a reprint of the original and the other an edited text for a wider public, of what is probably Catlin's best and most significant piece of writing: *Letters and Notes on the Manners, Customs, and*

Conditions of the North American Indians.[22] That travel account of his years with the western Indians in the 1830s is my main point of interest here.

Several publications at the end of the 1970s signaled a willingness to study not just the paintings, and isolated ones at that, as had often been the case before, but also the writings, the Indian Gallery, and Catlin's career as a whole.[23] That trend expanded and diversified thereafter, particularly beginning in the 1990s, as publications of all sorts on Catlin multiplied. Further collections and exhibition catalogues have appeared, notably the Smithsonian publication already cited, based on an exhibition in 2002, and a new edition of Catlin's *Letters and Notes* was published by Penguin.[24] Excerpts of his writing have appeared in anthologies of environmentalist texts.[25]

But most important, a significant number of scholarly works have begun to take a more critical view of Catlin, bringing into their analyses all aspects of his career. Their authors have explored from different vantage points the ways in which Catlin participated in the very evils—the wanton destruction of nature and its Indian inhabitants—he wished to denounce and combat. Among these critics one finds different emphases and approaches and disagreements on specific points, but there is broad consensus that Catlin's work is to the highest degree paradoxical, contradictory, and ambivalent.[26]

Although the recent studies have often drawn extensively on Catlin's published travel accounts, these accounts have generally not been treated as travel literature per se, as part of the genre of accounts of travel in Indian territory that I have explored in this study. During his own lifetime Catlin was in fact no less well known as a writer in this genre than as a painter of Indians and producer of Indian shows. In what follows I discuss *Letters and Notes*, the first of his accounts,[27] from this perspective, and stress the close linkage in it between text and image.

CATLIN'S TRAVELS IN THE 1830S

The long subtitle to the first edition of *Letters and Notes* is *written during eight years' travel amongst the wildest tribes of Indians in North America, in 1832, 33, 34, 35, 36, 37, 38, and 39*. This seemingly precise delineation of the scope of the travels does not entirely correspond to the itineraries and chronologies of Catlin's trips in the 1830s. Although the subtitle enumerates the years one by one, as if to emphasize that he was traveling among "wild Indians" during each of them, this was not the case. In 1833 and from 1837 to 1839, the year in which he left for England, Catlin did not travel in the West but was completing his paintings and organizing and carrying out lectures and exhibitions in the East. He thus inflated his dating, claiming eight years among the "wildest tribes" when what was involved was a number of trips of several months each during a six-year period, only some of which were among "wild" tribes.

Of these, three were particularly important: in 1832 a trip from St. Louis far up the Missouri River by steamboat, as far as Fort Union in Assiniboin, Crow, and Cree country (near the present-day North Dakota–Montana border), and the return trip by canoe, including a prolonged stay at Fort Clark (North Dakota), near the Mandan settlements; in 1834 a trip from New Orleans up the Mississippi and Arkansas rivers, and then, starting from Fort Gibson (Oklahoma), on foot and horseback accompanying an expedition of dragoons into Comanche territory (Texas); in 1836 a trip through the Great Lakes, up the Mississippi to Fort Snelling (near the present Wisconsin-Minnesota border), and then west to a sacred pipestone quarry in Sioux territory (Minnesota).[28]

These trips, as well as the general period of Catlin's travels and dealings with Indians before publication of *Letters and Notes*—starting in 1830, when he met Gen. William Clark, then superintendent of Indian Affairs in the West, in St. Louis—have significant historical contexts in terms of evolving relations among indigenous tribes, whites, and the U.S. government. The 1830s was a decade in which crucial developments occurred in this respect. Trappers, traders, and settlers moved into and through the trans-Mississippi West in greatly increasing numbers (the Santa Fe and Oregon trails were both open and active by 1830), and there were repeated conflicts between these encroachers and Indian tribes resisting them from the Dakotas and Montana in the North to Texas in the South. In Illinois in 1831–32 the Sauk leader Black Hawk waged a fierce though short-lived war that was a prelude to many others west of the Mississippi later in the century. The 1830s was a period in which the U.S. Army invested unprecedented resources in building roads and forts in the West and engaging in various kinds of military action. At the same time President Jackson's removal policy for the Indians east of the Mississippi was being applied, from the time of its passage into law in 1830 through to the arrival in Oklahoma of the last remnants of the Trail of Tears in 1838. The Seminoles of Florida continued to violently resist removal throughout the decade and beyond, though the capture of their leader Osceola in 1838 was a major blow to their struggle.[29]

One commentator sees *Letters and Notes* as a whole as "parallel[ling] the removal campaign of Indian peoples in the 1830s,"[30] and indeed each volume of the work is preceded by a map of the trans-Mississippi West, the first before and the second after the removal of the eastern Indians, with the southwestern territories created for them drawn in on the second map. But there are also specific links between the historical background I have alluded to and the principal trips Catlin recounts in the book. The 1832 trip up the Missouri was made on the maiden voyage of a steamboat of the American Fur Company, which was the spearhead of U.S. commercial exploitation of the upper Missouri. The 1834 overland trek from Fort Gibson on the Arkansas River was undertaken with dragoons who were attempting to make a show of force in the area through which the Santa Fe Trail passed.[31] Moreover, when in Fort Gibson, Catlin painted a number of Indians from tribes "removed" from the East.[32] The 1836 trip to the pipestone quarry relates more generally to the continuing history of white intrusion on Indian sacred grounds.

LETTERS AND NOTES

Catlin's *Letters and Notes* has a good deal in common with earlier accounts of travel in Indian territory, and he certainly drew on the tradition, perhaps unconsciously, in writing his account. His differs from eighteenth-century accounts, however, by the presence of abundant pictorial illustration, and in this way its author is part of the larger early nineteenth-century trend. Yet Catlin's work is unique among the artist-travelers of the period in its extremely close-knit relation between text and visual representation.

Not only are the artist and the writer one and the same, but also the two elements of the work are conceived of as equal parts of an indissoluble whole, with a systematic cross-referencing of the two.

Though Catlin's work differs from earlier accounts in this important pictorial aspect, it otherwise resembles previous examples of the genre in certain general ways. Like them, it provides information and analysis, value judgments, and representations of interaction. It also characteristically includes both diachronic and synchronic elements. These latter elements appear in two different configurations, separated from the travel narrative and inserted as blocks of text within it. Catlin interrupts the narrative line in many places to make lengthy comments on the way of life of tribes encountered but also generalizes more broadly in his last letter.

Indeed, as indicated by the title, the author adopts the epistolary convention. The novelty in the case of Catlin is that his letters are addressed not to imaginary persons but to the reader. Letter 1 begins, "The following pages have been hastily compiled, at the urgent request of a number of my friends, from a series of Letters and Notes written by myself during several years' residence and travel [among wild Indians]," and the author goes on to beg his readers to understand that he must dispense with a preface and begin with his opening remarks.[33] In this way letter 1 suggests the artificiality of the epistolary mode, since the authorial persona refers to letters written during the trip. At the end of letter 2 and beginning of letter 3 the pretense of an actual letter is introduced, and it is maintained in many subsequent ones. Letter 3 opens, "Since the date of my former Letter, I have been so much engaged in the amusements of the country, and the use of my brush, that I have scarcely been able to drop you a line until the present moment" (1:17). The correspondent is never given a name or the slightest indication of identity. In fact Catlin had originally published some of the material as a series of open letters to several New York newspapers.[34] Yet strangely this origin is entirely erased, never mentioned in the book. Since in the letters that subdivide it the author continually addresses himself to his readers, imagining what they may think or feel, readers can only conclude that the letters are metaphorical and are addressed to them.

"Notes" are also referred to, both in the title of the book and in the opening sentence of letter 1. Occasionally later the author speaks of a notebook that he carried with him, making entries in it as he went along (e.g., 1:66, 2:97). At certain points in the so-called letters Catlin even transcribes passages from the notebook verbatim, or claims to do so. From time to time he also transcribes long dialogues and stories he has been told. A final element of composition is the footnote, which comments on the text from the perspective of a later date, shortly before publication. All of these elements can be found in some form or other in earlier travel accounts, but nowhere else are they so fully subordinated to what is the main structural feature of Catlin's book: a direct address by the author to the reader (or to his collective readers; sometimes the singular, sometimes the plural is used). All the other compositional elements seem to be manipulated in a way that is calculated to create effects in the reader.

This applies, in addition, to Catlin's method of chronological organization of his material. When the travel narrative per se begins in letter 2, after the introductory material of letter 1, it starts not with the departure from St. Louis on the 1832 excursion but with the arrival three months later of the steamer at its ultimate destination, Fort Union, the farthest it would penetrate into Indian country. The intent to catch the reader's interest from the outset seems clear. But this organizational decision obliges Catlin to introduce material relating to what occurred on the way upriver at points in the account of the trip downriver where (or near where) the earlier events took place. The procedure—which is repeated elsewhere later on—is convoluted and clumsily executed, leading to a good bit of confusion and repetition. This explains the decision of the Penguin editors to reorganize and condense. Paradoxically, in the interest of gaining the attention of the twenty-first-century reader, they undo a construction that was aimed at seducing the nineteenth-century reader.

An overriding concern with the reader is reflected also in the style and tone of the work. There is tremendous variety in these, running from the intensely serious, lyrical, or even quasi-mystical to the broadly comic, the burlesque, and the coy. But in all its modulations Catlin's style seems motivated mainly by the desire to establish a rapport with his reading public—to involve them, to instruct and entertain them. Here also the gap between his immediate, intended public and that of our own time is evident. Many of Catlin's literary effects strike the modern reader as overblown, unconvincing, even ridiculous. There are numerous patches of purple prose, tiresome repetitions to hammer home a point, hyperbole, and heavy-handed humor. In one passage Catlin plays on the words *sticks* and *Styx* (1:18); in another he winks at the reader, noting that in the place where he is next visiting he'd better watch out for his scalp (1:59). The Penguin edition eliminates much of this material. Whatever its failings may appear to be to the modern reader, though, Catlin's prose is clearly meant to be a kind of virtuoso performance before the audience of his contemporaries.

As for the illustrations, there were over three hundred of them in the original edition. They took the form of line cuts from the paintings that Catlin made while on his journeys, since the more sophisticated forms of reproduction available at the time, lithograph and aquatint, would have taken much time and expense to prepare. In the Dover edition most of the line cuts have been replaced by photographic reproductions of the corresponding oil paintings, presumably as Catlin would have wished if the technology had been available. The illustrations fall into several broad categories: posed portraits of Indians (some full length, some from the waist up); scenes of Indian life (dances, ceremonies, buffalo hunting); drawings of objects used by Indians in their daily life (Catlin collected many of these, and they are often presented as part of his collection); landscapes, with little or no human presence; and scenes in which Catlin himself appears, sometimes also with the two *voyageurs* who did the canoe paddling on his first trip (Baptiste and Bogard).

As mentioned earlier, there is a continual cross-referencing between the text and these illustrations. They are intended as a visual complement to or extension of the text, the latter continually referring to different numbered plates and in some cases commenting on them at length. The most extended of these cross-references involves the Mandan chief Four Bears (or Matotopé), to whom an entire letter is devoted (1:145–54) and who is illustrated by a portrait, a drawing of the author being honored by him at a feast, and another of his buffalo robe, with a detailed analysis of the meaning of the figures on it.[35] Thus the pictorial and the written are closely intertwined.

TEXTUAL INCONGRUITIES

There is a main thread running through the long written text, supported by many of the images. Repeated again and again, in different tonalities but always passionate ones, is the conviction that North American Indians, highly admirable in their native or "classic" state,[36] are being or will soon be corrupted and exploited by whites, particularly traders, and are almost surely doomed to extinction. One of Catlin's major purposes is to correct misconceptions and prejudices concerning Indians commonly held by "civilized" whites—his potential readers—whose only contact with Indians, if any, has been with those in the frontier areas, where they have already been severely degraded by white influence. The contrast between Indians in their own culture and those debased by white contact is the subject of one of his best known paintings. An Assiniboine Indian named Wi-Jun-Jon is pictured "before and after": in the left-hand panel, resplendent in full tribal regalia before a trip to Washington as a delegate, and in the right-hand panel, after his return home, in an awkward, mismatched outfit of assorted Anglo-American clothing, with a bottle of liquor protruding from a back pocket.[37]

Catlin is often at pains to explain (and justify, up to a point) Indian customs and practices that he knows will appear bizarre, absurd, revolting, or objectionable to his readership. Thus he presents his work first and foremost as a celebration of the "wild" Indian and a criticism of the cupidity of white society, which is destroying the "savage" (undoubtedly a noble one, for Catlin). Sometimes his awareness of what is happening and his condemnation of white America become intensely bitter, as in the very last lines of the book, where he prophesies, "For the Nation, there is an unrequited account of sin and injustice that sooner or later will call for *national retribution*" (2:256).

The message seems clear and straightforward and might appear to associate Catlin with a form of romanticism. But a closer look at the text reveals greater complexities and some surprising contradictions. First, although Catlin's main theme regarding Indians is situated on the moral plane, this dimension alternates with the aesthetic and the "scientific," which, if not necessarily contradictory, at least coexist uneasily with it. In many passages Indians are treated not as beings with a morally interesting culture in a morally distressing predicament but as purely aesthetic objects. Beautiful bodies, perfect subjects for the painter, they are "picturesque" (a word he uses often, in reference to Indians as well as to landscapes; e.g., 1:23, 192).[38] Numerous other passages put the Indian under quasi-scientific scrutiny, speaking of Indian individuals as well as their clothes and other accoutrements as "specimens"—another word that recurs regularly (e.g., 1:22, 193). This ambiguity in the textual material is reflected in the illustrations as well: beside portraits that are strongly individualized and seem to project inner qualities, we find those that place emphasis on plastic beauty and stunning costume and also many catalogued arrangements of ethnological phenomena.

Another area in which an ambiguity exists, if not an outright contradiction, involves the place of the author in the work. In principle the Indian is the hero and the focus in *Letters and Notes*, yet at times it seems as if Catlin himself has taken over that role. Many passages foreground the author, in his thoughts, feelings, and actions, making the Indians recede into his shadow. We see the author both dramatized and glorified in various roles in the text, and some of these are represented visually in the category of illustration in which the artist puts himself in view: Catlin as artist (painting Indians),[39] as adventurer (hunting buffalo, alone on a plain with wolves in the distance), as friend of the Indian (being feted by a chief). In both text and image Catlin's courage, on the one hand, and good faith toward the Indians, on the other, are the characteristics most often insinuated or asserted. This focus on the (admirable) self of the author-traveler can be found to a certain extent in earlier accounts, but Catlin takes the tendency considerably further.[40]

These aspects of the work complicate the seeming simplicity of the primary message but are not necessarily problematic in themselves. As the work progresses, however, it becomes clear that Catlin is inhabited by some very stark, glaring contradictions, ones shared by many other Americans of the period. These raise more serious questions and finally negate any romantic critique of modernity that some passages might seem to point to. Although parts of the text treat—or show the author-protagonist treating—Indians and Indian customs with respect and sensitivity, other parts reveal a tendency toward condescension and ethnocentrism. On the one hand, for instance, concerning the strange (for his culture) burial customs of the Mandans, Catlin comments that the traveler who comes to "study and learn" can "draw many a deduction that will last him through life" (1:89). In another instance, when treated to a feast of dog meat by the Sioux, he willingly accepts it in the spirit in which it is offered (though, as he says, other visitors often react with disgust and ridicule), and explains to the reader the sacrificial nature of the custom, related to the role of dogs in Indian societies (1:230).

On the other hand, elsewhere the author himself ridicules Indian practices, particularly shamanistic ones, which are dismissed as "hocus-pocus" or "laughable farce," often with a wink to the reader (e.g., 1:35, 111, 134). The text creates a bond of cultural superiority between author and reader at the expense of the "benighted" savage. Several tribes that Catlin visits believe that his painting, of a realistic kind they have never seen before, is "medicine," a manifestation of sacred power. Catlin quickly discovers that this can give him leverage with his hosts and uses the awe that he inspires in ways that are sometimes manipulative. He informs the reader in one passage that he purposely made some gestures to suggest magical operations, in effect playing at being a shaman, and enjoying it (1:109).

More than this, in pursuing his own purposes Catlin is often prepared to engage in actions that are anathema to the Indians in terms of their belief systems, and using his own culture as a standard. He continually tries to buy for his collection sacred objects or irreplaceable, highly valued ones (such as a warrior's robe with his deeds painted on them), and after a first refusal he often wheedles in an attempt to have his way. (The Mandan chief Four Bears finally copies for Catlin the figures from his robe onto another, thereby making a replica; 1:148.) Perhaps the most striking case of this cultural insensitivity took place on the third of Catlin's major excursions, when he set out to discover the location of a fabled pipestone quarry (stone for the making of the calumet), common to many tribes of the region, which he had been told of on earlier trips. When he reached it, he was stopped by a party of Sioux, who at the time controlled access to it and who told him that he should not continue onto the site because it was sacred ground. He continued on anyway. Once there he painted the site, took samples of the rock, and later wrote an article on it for a scientific journal.[41] In *Letters and Notes* he builds reader curiosity about this visit early on, and when he recounts the incident proudly extols his achievement and attempts to discredit the Sioux who opposed him (1:31, 234, 2:166–68, 172–76, 201–2).

Most crucially of all, Catlin contradicts the very celebration of wildness that appears to be at the heart of his message, recognizing, implicitly or explicitly, the need for wild Indians to acquire the blessings of civilization, to become sedentary agriculturalists, adopt Christianity, and give up some of their "ignorant" superstitions and "disgusting" customs. (One such passage comes after a description of the "o-kee-pa," a key ceremony in Mandan culture that includes self-torture; 1:183).[42] In the same way Catlin sometimes bewilderingly takes the very opposite tack from his common theme of criticism of white encroachment on Indian land and condemnation of the cupidity that motivates it. The passages that make this shift appear mainly in volume 2, which concerns the later period of travels, generally among "semi-civilized" Indians farther east, therefore perhaps coming after the intensity of his first response to the wild tribes has worn off. The contradiction is nonetheless breathtaking. In one passage the author urges "the enterprising capitalists of the North" to come and prosper in Pensacola, a highly promising location now that a railroad is projected to reach it (2:34). In another he enthuses about the new town of Dubuque on the Mississippi, promising that "[a] visit of a few days to Dubuque will be worth the while of every traveller; and for the speculator and man of enterprize, it affords the finest field now open in our country"; with its nearby mines, Catlin claims, "it is to be the mint of our country" (2:149). Another passage describes the author's "sublime contemplations" of civilized man advancing joyfully farther west and sings the praises of the pioneer as the true American, though all the while expressing deep regret at the coming demise of the Indian (2:157–59). Given such passages in *Letters and Notes*, it is perhaps not surprising that in the late 1840s, when living abroad, Catlin wrote a pamphlet encouraging immigration to the frontier, and even touted the Gold Rush.[43]

Catlin appears to be blind to these discrepancies and unaware that those whites he willingly associates himself with on his travels—and he himself to a certain extent—are participants in the process of invasion and conquest that is under way. On his first excursion he travels up the Missouri on a steamboat of the American Fur Company that is penetrating deeper than ever before into Indian territory, enabling further extension of the trade in buffalo hides. Catlin reports that when it arrives at Indian encampments it fires its cannon as a means of impressing fear and awe in the natives. Yet he reports their reactions only with amusement (1:20).[44] On the second excursion he joins dragoons whose purpose is to lay the bases for the extension of U.S. government control in Comanche territory. He opens his account of that journey in volume 2 by commenting, "The *natives* are again 'to be astonished,' and I shall probably again be a witness to the scene," but he assures the reader, "I care not how badly we frighten them, provided we hurt them not, nor frighten them out of *sketching distance*" (2:37). Later he uneasily reports on the brutality of the officers' treatment of the Pawnees (encountered before his expedition reaches the Comanches; 2:47), but the issue is quickly dropped, and in the end the author has only praise for the commanders (2:84). On the third major trip, as already mentioned, Catlin was imperturbably prepared to desecrate what, from the native point of view, was a sacred site. Looking to the future, he approvingly sees the day when the quarry will be the domain of the geologist rather than the Indian (2:202).

A final instance might be mentioned. Although he elsewhere harshly criticizes whites for creating the conditions for the extinction of the buffalo on which the Plains Indians rely and discusses the reverent attitude of the Indians toward the animals they hunt, Catlin tells the reader he merely wanted a trophy when he went hunting. He describes how he delayed delivering the coup de grâce to a wounded buffalo so that he could make a dramatic sketch, close up, of its agony (1:26–27).

Such, then, are some of the ambiguities and contradictions that emerge from a reading of *Letters and Notes*. Their presence, in an extreme form, in this text produced during the 1830s would tend to support John Hausdoerffer's contention in *Catlin's Lament* that, contrary to a common interpretation of his European period as a betrayal of an earlier purity of mission, there is an essential continuity of conflicted vision throughout Catlin's life.[45] In this context some important aspects of his travel account, and of his larger life's work seen as a unified whole, can be linked to cultural trends already developing in early nineteenth-century America but destined to take on added importance later in the century. Three of these connections seem most significant: ethnological show business, ethnology and its collections and museums, and the development of tourism.

THE SHOW, THE MUSEUM, AND THE TOUR

The history of exhibition of "savage" or "primitive" peoples to audiences in "civilized" countries goes far back in time, as does that of displays of "abnormal" creatures or "freaks," with which the former kind of exhibition has significant similarities. In the case of American natives, such spectacles date back as far as the discovery of the New World. But in the nineteenth century they proliferate and are transformed by growing commercialism and consumerism in Europe and North America. Ethnological displays become a part of the early development of show business. Their impresarios are submitted to the pressures of competition and make extensive use of advertising to attract profitable publics. In Europe in the early nineteenth century—particularly in London but also in some continental capitals—a series of shows involving primitive peoples were put on: from the "Hottentot Venus" of the 1810s and "Eskimos" of the 1820s, to "Bushmen" in the 1840s and "Zulu Kaffirs" in the 1850s. Catlin's Indian shows in Europe fall within this series. His productions at first used whites, including himself, dressed in Indian garb and playing Indian roles, but later added live performances by actual, imported Indians (Ojibwes and Iowas) who danced, enacted ceremonies, and mimed the gestures of their daily life.[46]

In the second half of the nineteenth century and into the early twentieth this kind of ethnological show was carried to a further level of development, becoming a "major form of public entertainment" as a crucial component of wild west shows, circuses, world's fairs, and colonial expositions.[47] In relation to this later period, Catlin's Indian shows bear the strongest resemblance to Buffalo Bill's Wild West of the last two decades of the nineteenth century and first decade of the twentieth. Like Catlin, Buffalo Bill Cody produced his shows first in the United States and then in Europe, and both men focused on dramatizing western Indians in their western habitat. In spite of differences—Cody's shows achieved greater popularity than Catlin's by creating grand spectacle and enacting conflict— there was much continuity between the two. That this continuity extends beyond Buffalo Bill to the movie western is suggested by Paul Reddin in his comprehensive study of wild west shows, which devotes the first two chapters to Catlin, the middle three to Cody, and the concluding ones to later shows and their relation to the western film.[48]

Catlin the showman was thus an important early exponent of a nineteenth-century trend, and this aspect of his career is directly linked in several ways to the travel account. In addition to including materials also used in it, *Letters and Notes* is a kind of *advertisement* for Catlin's show.[49] Throughout the text we find references to a production called the "Indian Gallery," which the author is preparing, though when the travel account was published in 1841 the Gallery had already been running for some years. The book announces the show as a coming attraction, giving a preview to the reader through text and sketches, creating interest and curiosity, often suggesting that it is impossible to convey fully in words what the spectator at the Gallery will be able to see with his or her own eyes. This form of enticement includes some sensationalist appeals, such as notifying the reader in a note that the author has obtained the knife wrested by Four Bears from a Cheyenne warrior in the mortal combat that is recounted in the text. The knife still has blood on it, blood that has not been removed so that spectators may see for themselves (1:153–54).

But if the publication was an ad for the show, the converse was true as well, since copies of *Letters and Notes* were available for purchase at the entrance to Catlin's London productions.[50] Finally, it would not be too much to say that the travel account itself, through its rhetorical flourishes, takes on the character of a show, with the author as an impresario opening the curtain to reveal the curiosities, the wonders, and sometimes the horrors or grotesqueries of what he has witnessed in Indian territory—a "grand spectacle," as he calls it in several places, in which the Indians themselves are the main actors and "supernumeraries" (1:165). In addition to presenting the native denizens of the West as metaphorical players, in several passages Catlin describes Indians living close to white settlements as actually performing for visitors, sometimes for money (e.g., 1:237). It seems plausible that Catlin first had the idea of employing Indian actors after observing these entertainments.[51]

Like ethnological shows, ethnographic discourse and collections of artifacts of "primitive" human groups had a long history, especially in the form of travel accounts and the souvenirs brought back in the baggage of travelers, before they became institutionalized into a discipline and a kind of museum. This institutionalization occurred for the most part only in the second half of the nineteenth century. The American Ethnological Society and the Ethnological Society of London date from 1842 and 1843, respectively, the Smithsonian Institution from 1846, and Harvard's Peabody Museum from 1856; Henry Schoolcraft and Lewis Henry Morgan published works on North American Indian ethnology in the middle of the century. The era of anthropological theorization, as well as of intense collecting of primitive artifacts and art objects—in particular those of North American Indians—began somewhat later, in the last quarter of the nineteenth century.[52]

The scientific approach to the study of primitive societies and the constitution of museums documenting their material existence were thus in their earliest stages in the period when Catlin wrote *Letters and Notes* and developed his Gallery. Yet both of these works had strongly scientific pretensions, aiming to instruct as much as to divert. When Catlin set out on his travels in the early 1830s he had in mind from the outset to collect data and artifacts of Indian life as much as to represent it pictorially. He amassed large quantities of both in the following years and integrated them into the book and the exhibition. The text of *Letters and Notes* contains many long descriptions of customs, practices, and beliefs, with interpretations of their meanings in quasi-ethnological terms, while a considerable number of the book's illustrations offer systematically organized visual representations of artifacts. As for the Gallery, at least in part it had the aspect of a museum. On display one often found as a centerpiece a full-size tepee, as well as arranged specimens of Indian weapons, domestic and ritual objects, costumes, buffalo robes painted with scenes of battle, and more. Since *Letters and Notes* presents many drawings of these same materials, presented in the manner of scientific illustration, it also sometimes takes on a museum-like quality.

Both *Letters and Notes* and the Gallery, then, are hybrid mixes of the museum and the show. In this respect Catlin's work prefigures crosses between the two that came later in the century, most famously—or notoriously—in the ethnological exhibits at world's fairs and universal exhibitions.

A final connection, but one that has been less often noted, is with the early development of tourism. Defined as an organized form of travel, following a prescribed path and facilitated by relatively speedy and comfortable transportation, comfortable lodging at one's destination, and cultural framing in the form of a specialized travel literature, tourism had already developed to some extent in Europe in the eighteenth century. In the United States, however, it came somewhat later and took a specific form. The first manifestations of American tourism appeared in the 1820s, in the Hudson River Valley and west to Niagara Falls, following the introduction of the steamboat and the construction of the Erie Canal. Later, tourism extended to other northeastern destinations and moved progressively farther west, as settlement, industrialization, and modernization proceeded westward. Paradoxically, while tourism in the United States was always linked to these phenomena it often focused on natural sites. As several studies have emphasized, tourism played a crucial role in the young republic as part of the creation of a national identity, and the predominant image defining its singularity was that of "nature's nation."[53]

By the end of the 1820s the rudiments of tourism had already burgeoned on the Mississippi River, but it was only in the second half of the nineteenth century that the trans-Mississippi West became an object of the developing tourist industry, in parallel with pacification, settlement, and economic growth in the region.[54] Catlin's *Letters and Notes* represents a significant cultural intervention in both of these moments of western tourism.

In volume 2, when the author is reporting on an excursion with his wife up the Mississippi River, he writes concerning a group of "semi-civilized" Sioux encamped near the Falls of Saint Anthony, "[They] are assembled here at this time, affording us, who are visitors here, a fine and wild scene of dances, amusements, etc. They seem to take great pleasure in 'showing off' in these scenes, to the amusement of the many fashionable visitors, both ladies and gentlemen, who are in the habit of reaching this post, as steamers are arriving at this place every week in the summer from St. Louis" (2:132). The area, then, is already a relatively busy tourist stop in the mid-1830s, but Catlin attempts to promote it further, wishing to upgrade its reputation as a tourist experience and increase its frequentation by making it the ultimate destination of a well-defined western tour that will compete with eastern ones. He expresses the hope that a circuit starting in St. Louis, by steamboat up the river to the Falls of Saint Anthony, then returning east via Mackinaw, which he elsewhere calls a "summer's paradise" (2:161), might become "the next 'Fashionable Tour,'" adding, "This Tour would comprehend but a small part of the great 'Far West'; but it will furnish to the traveller a fair sample, and ... [is] so easily accessible to the world ... the only part of it to which *ladies* can have access" (2:130).[55]

Catlin's text reveals that the Sioux living in the area around the Falls of Saint Anthony are already adjusting to the tourist mode, performing for whites on tour. He seems to be entirely comfortable with this form of relationship between native and visitor. During an earlier sojourn in Sioux territory, while making portraits of a band, he had paid them to dance for him, persuading the head chiefs to join the dance, a departure from their usual practice (1:237). During the later visit to the Falls of Saint Anthony, in an unconsciously ironic gesture he initiated and organized an Indian ball game on the Fourth of July (2:135).

In these passages from volume 2 Catlin is simply reinforcing a trend already under way—the opening of the Mississippi and Great Lakes to tourism—but he also treats the trans-Mississippi West prospectively in a similar way. He calls his first excursion up the Missouri a "Tour" (1:20), and after describing a particularly "picturesque" landscape near one of the Mandan villages—a vista of bluffs called the "Grand Dome" (1:77)—he speaks of the green turf that protects them from erosion so that they may "be gazed upon with admiration, by the hardy voyageur and the tourist, for ages and centuries to come" (1:78). Here he seems to envisage a later period when not just the select "hardy voyageurs" but the more numerous group of "tourists" will be attracted to an area rarely visited by whites in the past.[56]

In recounting his travels in far western lands inhabited by "wild" Indians, Catlin often uses words such as *fun, amusement,* and *diversion* to characterize the experience, and his animated, enthusiastic descriptions of itineraries and landscapes often take on the accents of a guidebook or promotional brochure. All in all, in spite of Catlin's awareness that the encroachment of "civilization" will destroy the lands and peoples that were still largely "wild" when he visited them, *Letters and Notes* seems to call its readers to become future tourists in the Far West. As for the Indians in this imagined future, in a passage that has been much quoted and glossed Catlin proposes the creation by the U.S. government of "a magnificent park, where the world could see for ages to come, the native Indian in his classic attire, galloping his wild horse, with sinewy bow" (1:261).

As my discussion of *Letters and Notes* makes apparent, Catlin's work is rife with contradictions and manifests a radically split sensibility. On the one hand we find the articulation of a passionate affinity for "primitive" indigenous peoples and the natural wilds in which they live, mourning for the imminent destruction of both, and fierce criticism of the forces of "civilization" that are carrying it out. The authorial voice that expresses these themes in the work might appear to be a romantic one, similar to that of Bartram. Yet a decidedly antiromantic voice speaks from the text as well, one that praises, encourages, and takes part in entrepreneurship and the pursuit of profit, science as a desacralizing force, and the imperial spread westward of "American progress."

The two outlooks do not, however, have an equal status in Catlin's intellectual and artistic makeup. Ultimately it is the second of the two that dominates. Catlin's text in fact reveals a personality thoroughly permeated by the modern ethos, especially by the entrepreneurial impulse. As his recent biographer emphasizes, from the beginning Catlin resembled his father in his fixation on wealth and vulnerability to "get-rich-quick schemes,"[57] and he never seems to have been torn between the noncommercial values of art and the imperatives of the market, as many nineteenth-century artists were. Nowhere in his praise of "primitive" Indian life, moreover, do we find a searching critique of the mercantile civilization such as was articulated by Bartram. Consequently any incipient romantic tendency in Catlin's temperament remains marginal and is entirely co-opted. Entrepreneurship finally provides the organizing framework within which his "romantic" vision of the Indian expresses itself, and the net effect is the transformation of that vision into a commodity. That constitutes a radical paradox, since an essential feature of the romantic sensibility is protest against commodification in the modern world.

Conclusion

In this study I have taken eighteenth-century North America as an exemplary site from which to view the confrontation of two radically opposed social formations in close proximity and interpenetration, bringing to bear on the discussion two areas of study that are usually compartmentalized: the socioeconomic history of the colonies and the ethnohistory of Amerindians in their relations with colonists. But by examining writings from the period rather than engaging in historical analysis, I have explored this dual subject from the angle of memory rather than history per se—the collective memory of Europeans as they experienced, through their varied perspectives, the clash of the two civilizational forms.

Linkages between the two objects of scrutiny have appeared through continual overstepping of the boundaries of the two parts of the study. The textual materials I have looked at in each of them focus on one or the other of the two poles of the dichotomy. Yet they regularly overlap, the one type secondarily broaching themes that are dominant in the other. The texts often pointedly do this. Crèvecoeur has his "frontier man" dream of fleeing the colonies convulsed and corrupted by the revolutionary struggle to take refuge in an Indian village; Freneau has Indian protagonists judge white society; and many travelers among Indians, Lahontan and Bartram especially, highlight the contrast between qualities found in Indian groups and perceived evils of their own societies. The two broad social formations are often envisaged in relation to each other—two divergent models presented as mirror images that can appear to be a kind of philosophical-social choice.

Looking at the whole range of writings I have examined in detail, it is clear that there are many concordances between them on essential points; at the same time they are strongly inflected by the specific configuration of each author, both in their observations and analyses and in the attitudes toward the phenomena they bring to light. Regarding attitudes, what is most striking is the prevalence—although expressed in very different ways and to differing degrees—of ambivalence and hesitation, ambiguity and contradiction.

The testimony brought to bear by Crèvecoeur and Freneau on the development of capitalist modernity in the period before, during, and after the American Revolution reveals a society in continual expansion, ruled by the market and the power of money. Crèvecoeur shows that in the period preceding the Revolution activities as different as Nantucket whaling and frontier farming were determined by the same commercial logic; they were "speculations" as much as those of the British factory owner. In the Revolution itself Crèvecoeur sees the rise of a class of newly rich who use the patriot cause to accumulate possessions and impose their authority, though he never links this behavior with commercial dealings before the war. Freneau portrays a postrevolutionary society that, in spite of the republican political goals of the upheaval, is highly inegalitarian and dominated by those who ceaselessly pursue financial gain: commercial farmers in New England, Scottish merchants in Virginia, the "man in business" in Philadelphia.

These authors—and also Saint-Méry, the Creole outsider who visited the country at the end of the century—make apparent in their writings some dire human consequences of this burgeoning new society: at the most fundamental level the subversion of other values by the primacy of exchange value, the distortion and dissolution of bonds of community, and the alienation of human beings from the natural environment. Bartram echoes these themes as well, as do some of the other travelers in Indian territory, to a greater or lesser degree. Both Crèvecoeur and Freneau—though not Saint-Méry, who had no experience with Indians—point to the fact that from within such a society the Amerindian mode of life can be a tempting alternative: Crèvecoeur through the narrative voice that recognizes its "singular charm" and the flattering portraits of Indians in his French writing; Freneau through poems and prose pieces that celebrate the Indian and life in the forest, sometimes in schematic, oversimplified ways. Yet the stance of each toward modernity displays decided ambiguities. (By virtue of his outsider status and the relative brevity of his immersion in American society, Saint-Méry's hesitations in regard to it are minor by comparison.)

In the case of Crèvecoeur, alongside his critique of the dark side of Anglo-American society hidden by official and promotional discourses one undeniably finds many expressions of admiration for that society as well. An impulse to idealize it is to be found not only in his nostalgic look backward at the period before the Revolution but also in his view of postrevolutionary reality when he returns as French consul. Nothing better illustrates Crèvecoeur's unwillingness to abandon the model of British colonial society than the anxiety of the "frontier man" as he contemplates moving his family to an Indian village. Fearing that they will "go native" and lose touch with the monetary principle of their own culture, he finally decides he must calculate the profits of each member's farming work while there, to be paid upon return to "civilization." As for Freneau, his ambivalence takes a form that approaches ideological schizophrenia: as a romantic he is a severe critic of white colonial society and a partisan of the Indian; as a whiggish man of the Enlightenment he celebrates "progress," the limitless extension of commercial and urban development.

How can these contradictions be explained? In Crèvecoeur's work the most important factor seems clearly to be his split identity—involving both class and national culture, inextricably entwined—whereas in Freneau's case the crux of the matter is doubtless to be located in the vicissitudes of his political commitments. In both writers also the presence of conventional side by side with more subversive points of view is a further indication of the compelling power of a certain ideology in British America at the time. Whatever the case may be, there is nothing to keep the reader from reading these authors at least partially against the grain—against the beliefs and intentions they sometimes proclaim.

Part 2, dealing with the other side of the polarity, begins with the "zero degree" of encounter, but it quickly becomes apparent that this ultimate point—in its pure form, at any rate—is rarely reached. It turns out that in representations of violence and adventure that cast the Indian mainly as a danger, an aggressor, and an enemy complexity and ambivalence are to be found as well—as they are in the putative responses of readers, divided between horror and fascination, repugnance and admiration. Hugh Henry Brackenridge, with his call for the extermination of Indians, is in fact an isolated figure among the authors who come into the discussion of the negative encounter. His genocidal call comes in a text appended to the two captivity accounts he published to support his argument, yet paradoxically the narrator of one of them, John Slover, illustrates the condition of being *in between* the two cultures. For he tells how, after having been adopted into a tribe following an Indian raid when he was a boy, and later redeemed by the colonials against his will, he was reproached for his treachery by a member of his old tribe when he was captured again while lending his services to an anti-Indian campaign. Mary Jemison, another victim of Indian captivity, chose in spite of the horrendous circumstances of her capture to remain in a Seneca community until the end of her life. Even the professional Indian fighter Robert Rogers shows surprising understanding and sympathy for his former enemies in his (literally mediocre) tragic drama that takes Pontiac as its hero.

It is noticeable also that narratives couched in the form of "adventure"—that mode of writing that tends to eliminate the subjectivity and culture of the Indian—rarely come unalloyed. Even that of Captain Morris, which maintains the register of adventure almost to the end, offers in conclusion some remarks that demonstrate the author's understanding of the political situation of the Indian groups federated around Pontiac, and argues in support of the more flexible approach the French have taken in dealing with them. But this mixture of adventure with nonadventure is most striking in Alexander Henry's work, which, following the thrilling tale of capture, turns into a proto-ethnological essay when the author becomes assimilated into an Ojibwe family, and then into a travel account with virtually no adventure element when he returns to being a trader. Henry's evocation of the period of his back-and-forth movement between two worlds describes from the inside the kind of vacillation that Slover only alludes to in passing. During his time as an adopted Indian Henry is tempted by the life of simple pleasures he is leading, centered on hunting and easily provided for through barter. But he continues to experience his new condition at a distance, conscious of living "among savages," and finally chooses to return to his former life, again becoming a merchant.

Despite these complexities, the literature of the military and captivity account, as well as many histories and literary productions, remain focused on violence and hostility and contain germs of Brackenridge's absolute rejection of the Indian Other. Moreover Brackenridge was giving written expression to feelings harbored by a growing number of his compatriots as the United States came into being. In contrast to this zero degree of the encounter, however, I have shown how the account of free travel in territories controlled by Indians often stages meaningful contact on the sociocultural plane. Although violence and adventure are sometimes present, they are generally subordinated to sociocultural discovery.

Readings of the travel accounts have revealed many inflections of the overall patterns of the genre, coming out of significant aspects of the travelers' makeup. Due to the different relationships of the two nations and their colonies to the development of modernity, the division between voyagers of French and British culture is crucial. Lahontan, Charlevoix, and Trudeau all come out of a common matrix in the widest sense, one that includes the relative weakness of market relations, the dominance of the aristocracy, and the power of the state and Catholic Church. But within that overarching context their affiliations and commitments diverge: Lahontan and Charlevoix share the same class background, but their positions in relation to Church and state stand totally opposed. As for Trudeau, he differs from both by being French Canadian rather than French, and a fur trader for a considerable part of his career. The broad French perspective is also highly modulated in the ways it informs the writings on British America of Freneau, Crèvecoeur, and Saint-Méry, discussed in part 1.

The British and British American travelers—Lawson, Carver, Bartram, and Mackenzie—were conditioned in a developing, market-driven society, Protestantism, and a more diffuse political power often in the service of economic interests. But the positions of each within it are markedly diverse. Lawson and Mackenzie are closely identified with the primary thrust of economic development, one as a colonizer and speculator, the other as an aggressively competitive fur trader; Carver is linked to it as well, though in a more mediated way, as a militiaman and explorer in the service of the Crown. Bartram stands apart from them all in having entirely noncommercial goals, in spite of his father's efforts to make a merchant of him. And while Lawson's brand of Protestantism coexists, albeit uncomfortably to some extent, with thoroughly mercantile motivations, Bartram's radical (and eccentric) form of Quaker belief does not.

These factors throw light on some particularities of the accounts. Lahontan participates in Amerindian life mainly through hunting, a preferred activity of the rural nobility in France, but as a freethinker engages Indians in much discussion as well. Hunting is an activity that Carver also shares with the Naudowessies, since it was assiduously practiced by Anglo-Americans near the frontiers, but as a soldier Carver equally enjoys trading war stories. Charlevoix and Lawson seem to have had limited relations with Indians, at least as reported in their accounts; the first kept his distance in his role as a church official, while the second apparently entertained mostly instrumentalizing relations with the Carolina natives. Instrumental relations are the only ones chronicled by Mackenzie, while Trudeau recounts mainly ones that are intended to help carry out his mission: negotiations and peacemaking efforts among tribes. As for Bartram, his participation in the life of southeastern tribes he visited was particularly rich, undertaken in a spirit of friendship and respect conditioned by his form of Quakerism.

As regards knowledge of the natives encountered, the different profiles of the travelers influence the areas of Indian societies that are highlighted, underplayed, or ignored, and inflect their interpretations as well. Lahontan is interested in native religions because they appear close to deism; Bartram is drawn to them because of their resonances with his pantheistic sensibilities. For Charlevoix, on the other hand, the only important question about Indian beliefs is whether Catholicism can readily supplant them. Lahontan's intellectual rationalism leads him to leave aside consideration of Indian myth and magic, while Lawson's Anglo-Saxon pragmatism induces him to ridicule them and treat them as lies; at the same time the latter's Protestant faith encourages him to try his hand at proselytizing. Lahontan enumerates only "reasonable" motives for Indians going to war, while the Catholic perspective of Charlevoix more easily admits irrational impulses (for both good and evil).

Lawson's firm anchorage in the English commercial habitus brings him often to interpret Indian behavior through his own culture's conceptual and linguistic framework, while Mackenzie frequently misreads and diminishes it through his. The greater openness of Carver, and even more so that of Bartram, allow for a shift of point of view that seeks to understand the Other in the Other's own terms. Lahontan, the *déclassé* nobleman who sees himself as a "world citizen," exhibits this openness to a higher degree than Charlevoix, faithful missionary of the Society of Jesus (and servant of his king). Trudeau, although constrained by the trader's perspective and the imperatives of his mission, has independent cultural resources that allow him to approach the kind of critical freedom exercised by Lahontan.

Lahontan and Bartram, the most strongly predisposed to the encounter among the travelers I have discussed, have in common the posture of renegade and critic of their respective societies. Since these differ significantly, though, the Indian that Lahontan perceives is the Other of an authoritarian French society, while the one appearing to Bartram stands opposed to Anglo-American modernity. Lahontan emphasizes the lack of compulsion and hierarchy in Indian culture, while Bartram highlights harmonious community bonds and intimacy with nature.

The two angles of approach are not contradictory, however; Lahontan also recognizes the importance of social solidarity, and Bartram that of freedom, in Indian societies. The two writers do not disagree at the most basic level, and the same could be said more generally about the other travelers I have dealt with. Beyond differences of nuance and emphasis regarding particular aspects of native lifeways, and in spite of the fact that they refer to a wide variety of groups in diverse geographical areas, there is near universal agreement when it comes to defining the most fundamental characteristics of Amerindian culture. Each traveler focuses on a certain number of traits and practices that flow from several underlying principles: community (sharing, hospitality, generosity, friendly, nonaggressive relations), libertarian equality (the absence of social ranks and the noncoercive nature of power—in public life, the waging of war, family relations, etc.), and moral elevation (individual pride, honor as a key motivating factor).

The travelers also largely agree in their overall judgment of Indian culture. What is striking is the near unanimity of praise meted out by the travelers I have looked at, independently of their sociocultural profiles and of the prejudices they may have had at the outset. Charlevoix admits to the reader that he felt obliged in spite of himself to recognize the virtues of "pagan" Indians; Carver notes that he left on his trip with a negative image of Indians but quickly came to see that it was false; Lawson acknowledges that in the final analysis the natives are better than the colonists; and in the end Trudeau comes to admire those tribes farthest up the river that remain truest to themselves. Only Mackenzie is largely unimpressed by Indian cultures.

Each expresses it in his own terms, but in the course of their encounter all (except Mackenzie) become aware of a radical paradox. Lahontan formulates the paradox sharply but is untroubled by it: the "savages" are in fact more "civilized" than those who designate themselves as such. The baron identifies himself (ironically but unambiguously) with savages as already civilized but does not explicitly question his compatriots' plans to "civilize" Indians in the sense of making them like the French. Charlevoix, however, defines the paradox in a different way and ends up contradicting himself. The Indians collectively accomplish the principal virtues espoused by Christianity (as well as other, aristocratic ones)—thus "civilized" virtues—without even considering them to be virtues, through an internalized and institutionalized ideology. As a man of the church and servant of the French state Charlevoix cannot but wish for the Christianization and *francisation* of the Indians, but he also knows that they lose their generalized "virtue" in the exact measure that this plan succeeds—due to the spirit of egotism, self-interest, and greed to be found in French and French Canadian society. Trudeau is aware of the same contradiction as it impacts trade relations with Indians: the more the Indians are brought into the fur trade, the more they act like traders themselves and become less profitable to trade with. But he also views the process in terms of loss on the moral plane.

On the Anglo-American side, Lawson experiences the paradox as a Protestant Christian, and with him it corresponds also to an internal contradiction. While he has a thoroughly commercial turn of mind, he takes seriously some traditional Christian values that clash with it. The devoutly Christian part of him, then, is led to declare at the end of his account that in spite of the religion and the education from which his countrymen have benefited, the Indians are superior to them in carrying out the very precepts taught by that religion and education. Lawson seems entirely unaware, however, of the contradiction between this affirmation and his full adherence, in the same conclusion, to the goal of "civilizing" the natives. Carver exhibits a similar incoherency, for he raises the Naudowessies, who live far from white influence, to a more or less ideal status, recognizes the degradation that inevitably follows contact with whites, and yet is willing to participate in that process himself (partly, at least, for personal advantage).

Bartram's case is different. Among the travelers, he understands the paradox perhaps most deeply, seeing the customs and institutions of Indian societies as a "royal road of virtue," which puts the lessons of the philosophers of antiquity into practice. This formulation could be said to point to the crux of the paradox. Most fundamentally what is involved in fact is a contradiction internal to European culture (and of which Lawson's internal conflict is a reflection)—the contradiction between its present and its past, between the quantitative, commercial values of its modernity and the qualitative, moral values of its traditional heritage. In this perspective, when Bartram simply states that the Indians have no need of European civilization, he would mean that, having brought to fruition the European civilization of the past—the carrier of true values, for Bartram—they do not need to have this civilization inculcated into them (since they possess it already), but neither do they need to be corrupted by the modern values increasingly replacing the older European civilization. With this declaration Bartram unambiguously takes his position on the question of the need to civilize the Indians. Only due to his intellectual isolation and a pressing desire to find a peaceful resolution to the conflict between Indians and whites is he led in some texts to back away from this viewpoint and support the civilizing thesis.

Returning to the study as a whole, there is one aspect of the discussions that has not yet been mentioned: the Enlightenment and romantic perspectives or worldviews as they impinge on the encounter I have explored. These two broad sensibilities and intellectual frameworks are present, separately or intermingled, in a number of these authors and texts. In both Crèvecoeur and Freneau the two visions appear together—clearly marked and alternating in Freneau, more indistinct and partially mixed in Crèvecoeur. Among the travelers in Indian territory, Lahontan is a precocious—and pure—representative of the French Enlightenment spirit, while traces of an Enlightenment viewpoint can be found in Carver as well. Bartram, on the other hand, has a strongly romantic sensibility, although as a botanist he shares some partial elements of Enlightenment thought. The other travelers do not fit easily into either of the categories. But Brackenridge draws explicitly and assertively on a form of Enlightenment perspective.

What conclusions can be drawn from these diverse expressions of the two worldviews in relation to the encounter of modernity and its Other in eighteenth-century North America? First, there is clearly a special link—an "elective affinity"—between romanticism and openness toward the Amerindian in that context, since the romantic current of sensibility in its many variations articulates a protest against the civilization of capitalist modernity in the name of premodern values. This "structure of feeling," to use Raymond Williams's term, is present to some degree in Crèvecoeur's writing, is forcibly expressed by one of Freneau's two authorial personae, and permeates Bartram's work as a whole.

As for the Enlightenment point of view, the situation is considerably more complex. While in Lahontan's writing this stance leads to criticism of some aspects of modernity and admiration of the Indian as its antithesis, Freneau in his Enlightenment frame of mind takes the exactly opposite tack, and Brackenridge, from the point of view of a certain species of Enlightenment, carries rejection of the Indian to its ultimate consequences. These dissonances provide perhaps one more illustration of the "dialectic of Enlightenment" famously analyzed by Horkheimer, Adorno, and the Frankfurt school of social theory. The Enlightenment in the eighteenth century—and beyond—is without doubt a multifarious, unstable, and contradictory configuration in its relation to modernity; on the one hand it includes a rationalist tendency critical of modernity (as well as of vestiges of an oppressive past) in the name of some of its own principles, and on the other it has a whiggish tendency that accepts modernity in toto and wishes to eliminate all that impedes its progress. In the encounter with Amerindians, then, the Enlightenment can express itself at both ends of the spectrum of attitudes. That this philosophical tendency could give rise to such heterogeneous positions in the context I have been studying, and that it could be found in such jarring admixture with romanticism, is further testimony to the extreme ideological mobility of the period.

In the nineteenth century the context changes crucially, and although for much of the time there continue to be vast areas west of the Mississippi that remain Indian territory in the fullest sense—occupied and controlled by native groups—a process is under way that fundamentally alters perception of the encounter. As settlers, with the support of the army, penetrate and disseminate farther and farther west under the banner of Manifest Destiny, the conviction that the Indians are doomed to disappear becomes consensual. In the light of this perception the quality of the encounter shifts significantly. Now travelers in Indian territory like George Catlin see the encountered Other as a fast-fading remnant of the past. The case of Catlin is emblematic more generally in demonstrating the increasing potency of modernity's dissemination in that century. For although his travel account, accompanied by his illustrations, follows some familiar patterns and articulates some of the previous themes, it is informed at the most basic level by a logic that makes of the Indian a commodity and a museum piece. In Catlin's work, it would seem, whiggish Enlightenment does not coexist with romanticism, but rather undermines and ultimately negates it.

At the end of the century, with the "closing" of the frontier and elimination of spaces still not controlled by the U.S. Army, with the containment of native populations on reservations, their display as entertainment in the wild west show, and their forced acculturation in special schools, a decisive step is taken and a new period opens. In the twentieth century, and into the twenty-first, capitalist modernity thoroughly pervades and dominates the United States as a whole. In this period, while Indian peoples have survived, have engaged in cultural renewal—including the creation of a vibrant literature—and have initiated movements of revolt against their condition, they have done so from within the belly of the whale, so to speak. In this sense the subtitle of a collection of essays published in 2001, *Encounters in Indian Country, 1850 to the Present*,[1] deflects the original meaning of the phrase onto the metaphorical plane. Already threatened in the nineteenth century, the confrontation between an inside and an outside of modernity—in its strongest, fullest sense—no longer exists. It is in the context of this loss that eighteenth-century North America appears to be a unique, bygone historical moment and that its retrieval through memory—in the form of textual testimony—takes on all its value.

APPENDIX
Chronology of Historical Events, Travels, and Publications

1683–93   Period spent by Baron de Lahontan in North America

1688–89   Baron de Lahontan's travels west of the Great Lakes and in the upper Mississippi River region

1700   Arrival of John Lawson in Charles Town (Charleston, South Carolina)

1700–1701   John Lawson's excursion in the back country of Carolina

1702   Publication of Baron de Lahontan's two-volume travel account, *Nouveaux Voyages de M. le Baron de Lahontan dans l'Amérique septentrionale* (New Voyages of M. le Baron de Lahontan in North America) and *Mémoires de l'Amérique septentrionale* (Memoirs of North America)

1703   Publication of Baron de Lahontan's *Dialogues de M. le Baron de Lahontan et d'un sauvage* (Dialogues of the Baron de Lahontan with a Savage)

1705   Publication of *The History and Present State of Virginia* by Robert Beverley

1705	Trip from Boston to New York of Sarah Kemble Knight, recounted in *The Journal of Madam Knight*
1705–9	François-Xavier de Charlevoix's first stay in Canada, at a Jesuit school in the town of Quebec
1709	Publication of John Lawson's *A New Voyage to Carolina*
1711	Death of John Lawson, captured and tortured by Tuscarora Indians
1720	Charlevoix returns to New France to carry out an exploratory expedition "by order of the King"
1721–22	Charlevoix's journey in the Great Lakes area and down the Mississippi River (account appears in 1744)
1724	Publication of Joseph-François Lafitau's *Mœurs des sauvages américains comparées aux mœurs des premiers temps* (Customs of the American Savages Compared to the Customs of Antiquity)
1727, 1747	Publication in two parts of *History of the Five Indian Nations* by Cadwallader Colden
1744	Publication of Charlevoix's *Journal d'un voyage fait par ordre du Roi dans l'Amérique Septentrionale* (Journal of a Voyage in North America, Made by Order of the King)
1754–60	Seven Years' War (or French and Indian War) between the French and the English in North America
1757	Edict by the General Court of Massachusetts that promises a bounty of three hundred pounds for each scalp of an "enemy Indian"
1758	Beginning of the captivity of Mary Jemison, who subsequently becomes a "white Indian" in a Seneca community
1759	Under General Montcalm the French are defeated in the battle of the Plains of Abraham by the British under General Wolfe; the town of Quebec is taken by the British; Crèvecoeur, a soldier in the French Army, leaves Canada for the British colonies

1760–76	Period of travels and "adventures" of the fur trader Alexander Henry (account appears in 1809)
1763	Treaty of Paris: France cedes all of its possessions east of the Mississippi to the English
1763–64	"Pontiac's rebellion"
1763	Massacre at Fort Michilimackinac, witnessed by Alexander Henry
1764	Expedition of Col. Henry Bouquet against the Indians of the Ohio region
1764	Mission of Capt. Thomas Morris in the Illinois country (account appears in 1791)
1765	Publication of *Memoirs of Lieut. Henry Timberlake (Who Accompanied the Three Cherokee Indians to England in the Year 1762)*
1765	Publication of the *Journals* of Robert Rogers, militia leader in the Seven Years' War
1765–66	Journey of John and William Bartram in East Florida, in the area of the St. John's River
1766	Anonymous publication in London of *Ponteach: Or the Savages of America. A Tragedy* by Robert Rogers
1766–68	Period of Jonathan Carver's travels in the Great Lakes and upper Mississippi River area
1767	Crèvecoeur travels beyond the Allegheny Mountains, as far as the Mississippi River
1768	Appearance in a Boston newspaper of an appeal for subscriptions to finance publication of a travel account by Jonathan Carver
1772	Philip Freneau and Hugh Henry Brackenridge publish together a long poem entitled "The Rising Glory of America"

1773–77	Period of William Bartram's travels in North and South Carolina, Georgia, and East and West Florida (account appears in 1791)
1774–83	American Revolution and War of Independence
1775	Publication of James Adair's *History of the American Indians*
1778	Publication of Jonathan Carver's *Travels through the Interior Parts of North America In the Years 1766, 1767, and 1768*
1782	First edition, published in London, of Crèvecoeur's *Letters from an American Farmer*
1783	Publication by H. H. Brackenridge, in Philadelphia, of *Narratives of a Late Expedition against the Indians*
1784, 1787	Publication, in Paris, of two successive French versions of *Letters from an American Farmer*, both entitled *Lettres d'un cultivateur américain*
1786	Publication of a second version of "The Rising Glory of America," signed by only Philip Freneau
1789	Beginning of the captivity in an Ojibwe tribe of John Tanner, who later becomes a "white Indian"
1789	William Bartram, at the request of a university professor friend, writes *Observations on the Creek and Cherokee Indians*
1789	Alexander Mackenzie's first excursion in search of the Northwest Passage, in which he reaches the Arctic Ocean instead of the Pacific
1790	Publication of Philip Freneau's poem "The Rising Empire"
1791	First edition of William Bartram's *Travels* published in Philadelphia
1793–94	Alexander Mackenzie's second excursion in search of the Northwest Passage, taking him to the Pacific Ocean
1793	Moreau de Saint-Méry escapes the Terror in France on board a ship bound for the United States

1794–98	Moreau de Saint-Méry's travels in the United States and long residence in Philadelphia
1794–96	Fur trader Jean-Baptiste Trudeau's travels on the Missouri River
1795	Publication of Philip Freneau's "Tomo Cheeki, a Creek Indian in Philadelphia" in serial form in the newspaper *Jersey Chronicle*
1799	Publication of La Rochefoucauld-Liancourt's *Voyage dans les Etats-Unis d'Amérique, fait en 1795, 1796, et 1797* (Voyage in the United States of America in 1795, 1796, and 1797)
1801	Thomas Jefferson elected president of the United States
1801	Publication of Alexander Mackenzie's *Voyages from Montreal on the River St. Laurence through the Continent of North America to the Frozen and Pacific Oceans in the Years 1789 and 1793*
1801	Publication of Crèvecoeur's *Voyage dans la haute Pensylvanie et dans l'état de New-York* (Voyage in Upper Pennsylvania and the State of New York)
1804–6	Lewis and Clark expedition in the trans-Mississippi West
1809	Publication of Alexander Henry's *Travels and Adventures in Canada and the Indian Territories between 1760 and 1776*
1810	The Indian leader Tecumsah initiates a movement calling for a return to traditional values
1812–15	The War of 1812 between the United States and England
1832–36	Period of George Catlin's travels among Indians of the Far West
1841	Publication of George Catlin's *Letters and Notes on the Manners, Customs, and Conditions of the North American Indians*

NOTES

PREFACE

1. Sayre, *La modernité et son autre*.
2. Fixico, "Ethics and Responsibilities in Writing American Indian History," 94.
3. Calloway, "2008 Presidential Address," 198.

INTRODUCTION

1. Polanyi, *The Great Transformation*, 75.
2. Weber, *The Protestant Ethic*, 53; Wallerstein, *Historical Capitalism*, chap. 1.
3. Degler, *Out of Our Past*, chap. 1. See also, for example, Hacker, *American Capitalism*, 10.
4. See especially Carson et al., *Of Consuming Interests*.
5. For a summary of the debates around the question, see "The Transition to Capitalism"; Merrill, "Putting 'Capitalism' in Its Place."
6. Henretta, *The Origins of American Capitalism*, 256. For another important contribution in this area, one that also provides a useful summary of discussions involving the question of the "transition to capitalism," see Kulikoff, *The Agrarian Origins of American Capitalism*.
7. See Merrill, "Putting Capitalism in Its Place," 317, 323. Merrill himself, however, is in partial disagreement with the majority position. For a broad overview of the economic historiography, see the chapter "Economy" by Margaret Newell in Vickers, *A Companion to Colonial America*, esp. 177–80.

8. With the development of an "Atlantic world" dominated by British commerce, the eighteenth century is a crucial step in the evolution of a capitalist "world-system." See Wallerstein, *The Modern World-System III*.
9. This point is emphasized in "Puritanism and Capitalism in Early Massachusetts" by Stephen Innes, who took a minority position in the debate over the "transition to capitalism." Without going so far as to support completely the thesis that capitalism arrived in the first ships, Innes points to significant aspects of Puritan society that already have a capitalist dimension; according to him that society could be characterized as "communal capitalism."
10. Quoted in Hofstadter, *America at 1750*, 138.
11. Quoted in Henretta, *The Evolution of American Society*, 99.
12. Henretta, *The Origins of American Capitalism*, 294.
13. Wood, "Inventing American Capitalism," 49. A recent special issue of *Early American Studies* titled "Markets and Morality" points to a complex though marked evolution, starting from the late seventeenth century but accelerating in the postrevolutionary period, in which philosophers and religious leaders increasingly justified the market system of values, finally rendering "self-interest . . . morally neutral" (Matson, "Markets and Morality," 480). Christopher Clark, a participant in the "transition to capitalism" debate that had largely played itself out by the mid-1990s, when Wood wrote his *New York Review of Books* article, points out in his contribution to the special issue that a great deal of historiography in the past several decades "has come to treat markets as benign, or unproblematic." In his conclusion he calls for a reconsideration of the issue ("A Wealth of Notions," 675, 683).
14. See especially Hoxie, "Retrieving the Red Continent"; Hixson, *American Settler Colonialism*.
15. See Calloway, *The American Revolution in Indian Country*. See also Bergmann, "A 'Commercial View of This Unfortunate War.'"
16. Trigger and Washburn, *The Cambridge History of the Native Peoples of the Americas*, 1:453.
17. Taylor, "Continental Crossings," 183.
18. Du Val, *The Native Ground* (the Arkansas valley); Hämäläinen, *The Comanche Empire* (New Mexico and the Southwest); Witgen, *An Infinity of Nations* (Great Lakes and upper Mississippi valley).
19. Roy Harvey Pierce comments that the sovereignty of the United States was won in this war, not only against the British but also against the Indians (*Savagism and Civilization*, 55). The Seminoles were an isolated exception to the subjugation of the eastern Indians after the war; they continued to resist, in a series of armed conflicts, up to the Civil War.

20. One recent study, for instance, has shown the decisive power—and impact on colonial powers in the area—exercised by Indian raiders in the Southwest in the 1830s and 1840s: DeLay, *War of a Thousand Deserts*.
21. The most influential Puritan ministers of seventeenth-century Boston, Increase and Cotton Mather, were violently hostile toward Indians but shared specific beliefs with them, such as the efficacy of magic in rain making: see Jennings, *The Invasion of America*, 50.
22. See, for example, Hallam and Street, *Cultural Encounters*.
23. See Washburn, "The Clash of Morality in the American Forest"; Axtell, *The European and the Indian*, chap. 3. According to Axtell, many scholars studying relations between the English and the Indians in this period ignore the radical otherness of the latter in relation to the former (274).
24. In *A Strange Likeness*, Nancy Shoemaker argues that beyond the oppositions there were significant similarities between European and Amerindian cultures and societies in that period. She acknowledges and explores many important differences, however, and locates the congruences she discusses at a high level of generality, such that they would apply to most if not all human societies (see, for example, p. 39, regarding "political structure").
25. This, for example, is the position taken by Donald Fixico: see "Ethics and Responsibilities in Writing American Indian History," 89.
26. See the table of contrasts drawn up by Annie Jacob in "L'Indien des Anglais, l'Indien des Français," 217–18. Wilcomb Washburn paints a general portrait of the North American Indian based on the conviction that in spite of differences and changes in Indian cultures, "it is possible to isolate unifying and consistent patterns of behavior" (*The Indian in America*, xv–xvi, and see chapters 2 and 3). For Eastern Indians more particularly, see Axtell, *The Indian Peoples of Eastern America*. Comparisons between individual Indian nations and the Europeans they were in contact with also usually focus on much the same traits as those that generalize more widely; see, for example, Calloway, *The Shawnees and the War for America*, xxvii–xxx, xxxvii, 14, 18.
27. According to the Jesuit Joseph Lafitau, who lived for five years among the Iroquois, honor was the predominant motive determining their behavior; see White, *The Middle Ground*, 100. The idea of the integrated economy is the "substantivist" position (vs. the "formalist") on the nature of premodern societies, as represented notably by Marshall Sahlins (*Stone Age Economics*); see Martin, "A Better Way to Write Indian History," 30. Karl Polanyi is also associated with the substantivist position, and although his analyses have been much debated, they continue to be used by many ethnohistorians; see Ray, *Indians in the Fur Trade*, xii, xvii, xviii.
28. For an analysis of family relations among Indians, see Coontz, *The Social Origins*

of *Private Life*, chap. 2. On the importance of gift-giving and sharing in Huron society, see Delâge, *Le Pays renversé*, 64–65, 70.

29. On the dialectic of conflict and solidarity during the colonial period, within the family unit and among these units, see Vickers, "Competency and Competition."
30. See White, "Indian Peoples and the Natural World," 89.
31. Shepard Krech III's *The Ecological Indian: Myth and History*, synthesized much that had come before and developed its own theses, becoming the focus of intense debate and controversy following its publication.
32. In Harkin and Lewis, *Native Americans and the Environment*, a collection of essays by a range of specialists which assesses Krech's *The Ecological Indian* and the questions raised by it, Krech himself points out, in an article in which he addresses the criticism his book has received, that he and his critics agree on at least one thing: "Whatever the impact of Indians on land and resources, it didn't hold a candle to the long-term impact of people of European descent" (11). For a perspective on Amerindians' ecology in relation to their belief systems, see Hughes, *North American Indian Ecology*.
33. See Cronon, *Changes in the Land*, 40–51.
34. In Cronon's view the "economic relations of production" of the colonists were as a whole "ecologically self-destructive": *Changes in the Land*, 169.
35. The political and spiritual leader Tecumsah called his fellow Indians to return to this earlier perspective in 1810; see his oration in Hurtado and Iverson, *Major Problems in American Indian History*, 170–71.
36. Cronon, *Changes in the Land*, 75. Allan Greer has argued in a recent article, "Commons and Enclosure in the Colonization of North America," that the initial point of conflict between Indian and Anglo-American uses and conceptions of land, preceding the imposition of commercialized private property but already initiating the process of dispossession, was the incursion of settler commons—mainly through livestock grazing and foraging—on Indian commons devoted to hunting.
37. Weber, *The Vocation Lectures*, 13, 30.
38. Marx and Engels, *The Communist Manifesto*, 82.
39. Vickers, "Competency and Competition," 19. *Moral economy* is the term used by the English historian E. P. Thompson to designate the premodern mentality founded on the qualitative value of "fair price"—a mentality shared by many sectors of the English working classes during the transition to capitalism. See especially *The Making of the English Working Class* (1963) and *Customs in Common* (1991).
40. Aron, "The Significance of the Frontier in the Transition to Capitalism," 271.
41. See Delâge, *Le Pays renversé*.
42. For example, the quasi-talismanic nature of certain objects used in Catholic worship, the preternatural aspect of the legends of saints, the "magic" of miracles, relics.

Indeed for Weber Catholicism does not go as far as Protestantism in the process of rationalization and the elimination of magic; see *The Protestant Ethic*, 117. Michael Löwy has explored this theme by analyzing the scattered references to Catholicism in Weber's work. See Löwy, "Catholic Ethics and the Spirit of Capitalism."

43. See Axtell, *Beyond 1492*, chap. 6.
44. Griffiths and Cervantes, *Spiritual Encounters*, 15. See also 17, 19; Murray, "Spreading the Word," 44, 51.
45. Quoted in Calloway, *Dawnland Encounters*, 79.
46. See Calloway, *Dawnland Encounters*, 78, 81, 83. Father Rasles's murder by torture was very probably the work of Indians allied with the English.
47. At certain times and places conflicts of this kind did occur, though; see, for example, Walthall and Emerson, *Calumet and Fleur-de-lys*, 10.
48. A plethora of recent publications have studied the colonial French in the Mississippi River valley and "Illinois country": see, notably, Ekberg, *French Roots in the Illinois Country*; Morgan, *Land of Big Rivers*; Englebert and Teasdale, *French and Indians in the Heart of North America*.
49. White, *The Middle Ground*, 115. For more on the fur trade and differences between its practice by the French and the English, see chapter 8.
50. The differences in relation to the English were far from absolute, though, and tensions between Indians and *coureurs des bois* did arise: see White, *The Middle Ground*, 27, 29.
51. Recent research on immigration patterns to New France suggests, however, that a significant portion of immigrants, perhaps more than half, came from cities and towns; see Taylor, *American Colonies*, 366, 370; Havard and Vidal, *Histoire de l'Amérique française*, 204–16; Greer, "Comparisons," 478.
52. Bourguet, "Le Sauvage, le colon et le paysan," 218.
53. For further discussion of New France, see chapter 5.
54. For a comparison between French and English attitudes toward Indians, see Jacob, "L'Indien des Anglais, l'Indien des Français." For a comprehensive treatment of the French in early North America, see Havard and Vidal, *Histoire de l'Amérique française*. For a broad comparative overview of historiographies of the main colonial and native spheres of influence in the Americas, see Vidal and Ruggiu, *Sociétés, colonisations et esclavages dans le monde atlantique*. See also Edward Watts's study of the ways Anglo-Americans perceived French colonial culture: *In This Remote Country*.
55. On the travel account in relation to the novel, see Adams, *Travel Literature and the Evolution of the Novel*. On the travel account in the eighteenth century, see Batten, *Pleasurable Instruction*; Vivies, *Le récit de voyage en Angleterre au 18e siècle*.
56. Quoted in Edwards, *The Story of the Voyage*, 3.

57. On the American travel account in English and in French, see, respectively, Franklin, *Discovers, Explorers, Settlers*; Berthiaume, *L'Aventure américaine au dix-huitième siècle*.
58. Friedrich Wolfzettel gives the following minimal definition of the genre: "a personal discourse (most often in the first person) recounting an experience of encounter with the Other, that is, of a real voyage" (*Le discours du voyageur*, 5).
59. These distinctions should be tempered, though. Some prisoners, for example, were well treated and became acclimated to their captivity; in many cases they were ultimately adopted into a tribe. Also some historical works, though not formally structured as travel accounts, were based on personal travel and sojourns with Indians (e.g., Adair, *The History of the American Indians*, 1775). Moreover the lines of demarcation between the different genres were often blurry.
60. In his study of late eighteenth- and early nineteenth-century travel writing Nigel Leask also refuses to treat all travelers of European origin as fitting into a single "imperialist" mold and insists on the need to particularize and contextualize each traveler being analyzed (*Curiosity and the Aesthetics of Travel Writing*, introduction).
61. See Pearce, *Savagism and Civilization*; Berkhofer, *The White Man's Indian*.
62. In France the work of Henri Lefebvre was foundational. See his *Critique de la vie quotidienne*, especially 2:234ff, and *Introduction à la modernité*, in which he develops a distinction between modernity and premodernity that is similar to the one I am using here. For an important application of praxis-based analysis to indigenous societies of the Americas, see Clastres, *La société contre l'état*.
63. For a discussion of some of these questions, see Gohard-Radenkovic, "'L'altérité' dans les récits de voyage," especially 84–86.
64. Pagden, *The Fall of Natural Man*.
65. Pagden, *European Encounters with the New World*, 184.
66. Pagden, *European Encounters with the New World*, 10.
67. See the commentaries on this subject by Washburn and Axtell: Washburn, "The Clash of Morality in the American Forest," 336; Axtell, *The Indian Peoples of Eastern America*, xviii.
68. See Montaigne, *Essais*, 1:31.
69. Adair, *The History of the American Indians*.
70. Washburn, "James Adair's 'Noble Savages.'" The travel account of John Lawson has also been analyzed in the framework of this concept; see Diket, "The Noble Savage Convention as Epitomized in John Lawson's *A New Voyage to Carolina*."
71. Washburn, "James Adair's 'Noble Savages,'" 91.
72. Axtell, *After Columbus*, 12. Gordon Sayre espouses a similar point of view, though formulated differently, with his notion of the "dialectical Noble Savage," which incorporates negative elements (*Les Sauvages Américains*, 123–24, 126–27).
73. Vizenor, *Manifest Manners*, 174.

74. Coulthard, *Red Skin, White Masks*. See especially chapter 1.
75. See Ricoeur, *La mémoire, l'histoire, l'oubli*.
76. See Sayre and Löwy, *Romanticism against the Tide of Modernity* and "Romanticism and Capitalism."
77. Richter, *Facing East from Indien Territory*. Two other works adopt, each in its own way, a similar vantage point: Wright, *Stolen Continents*; Calloway, *The World Turned Upside Down*.
78. On this approach, see Fixico, *Rethinking American Indian History*. In defense of the use of oral history and its importance, see Fixico, "Methodologies in Reconstructing Native American History"; Wilson, "Power of the Spoken Word." White, "Indian Peoples and the Natural World," especially 92, points to some of its problems.
79. H. David Brumble's *American Indian Autobiography* includes a section on "preliterate traditions." On Indian writing, see Warrior, *Tribal Secrets* and *The People and the Word*; Vizenor, *Survivance*. On earlier Indian writing more specifically, see Round, *Removable Type*, esp. chap. 2; Lopenzina, *Red Ink*. In *A Strange Likeness*, Shoemaker notes a growing dependence on writing as a means of extratribal communication among Indians in the eighteenth century. By the end of the century Indians who themselves knew how to write began to replace whites writing for them (73, 80).

1. CRÈVECOEUR

1. For British America as a whole, see Butler, *Becoming America*. For the northern colonies, using the example of Connecticut, see Bushman, *From Puritan to Yankee*; for the South, exemplified by Virginia, see Isaac, *The Transformation of Virginia*.
2. Examples of these are Grant, *Memoirs of an American Lady*; Carter, *The Diary of Colonel Landon Carter of Sabine Hall*; Eddis, *Letters from America*.
3. On the promotional tract see Schramm, "Promotion Literature"; Greene, *Selling a New World*; Saur, "A Dialogue between a Newcomer and a Settler in Pennsylvania." An example of modern chorography is Beverley, *The History and Present State of Virginia*. On the genre of chorography, see Shapiro, *A Culture of Fact*, chap. 3. According to Shapiro, in the early modern period chorography was "a rather peculiar ... genre that combined history, geography, topography, natural history, antiquities, and genealogy with socioeconomic, political, and cultural description of a particular region. Typically, it followed a preexisting pattern of topics ... and ... tended to focus on the description of 'things' available to the eye both of human and natural origin" (65).
4. "The History of the Dividing Line" and "The Secret History of the Line," which in spite of their titles are travel accounts, in Byrd, *The Prose Works of William Byrd of*

Westover; Hamilton, "The Itinerarium"; Kalm, *Peter Kalm's Travels in North America*; Chastellux, *Voyages de M. le marquis de Chastellux dans l'Amérique Septentrionale*.

5. "The Journal of Madam Knight," in Martin, *Colonial American Travel Narratives*. In several passages Knight also expresses a great contempt for Indians; see especially 63–64, 65. Another travel account, by an Antiguan merchant and ship captain, exhibiting a similar state of mind and offering commercial observations at midcentury is Birket, *Some Cursory Remarks Made by James Birket in His Voyage to North America*.

6. In the view of Katherine and Everett Emerson, Crèvecoeur was "one of the most knowledgeable people of his time concerning America and American civilization" (Emerson and Emerson, "Crèvecoeur, J. Hector St. John de," 729).

7. Chevignard, "St. John de Crèvecoeur." Moreover Chevignard severely criticizes a biography that had appeared the year before: Allen and Asselineau, *St. John de Crèvecoeur*. On the renewal of interest in Crèvecoeur in the early twentieth century, see Philbrick, *St. John de Crèvecoeur*, 163, 171.

8. Chevignard, *Michel Saint-John de Crèvecoeur*.

9. According to what he claimed many years later, but the exact date of his arrival in North America is not known with certainty. His mother's family were well-established members of the local aristocracy, but his father's was only of the judicial nobility (*noblesse de robe*); see Chevignard, *Michel Saint-John de Crèvecoeur*, 19–20.

10. On the basis of the available evidence, Chevignard believes that Crèvecoeur did not take part in the battle (*Michel Saint-John de Crèvecoeur*, 29).

11. But his position in this period was not clear even to those close to him; see Chevignard, "St. John de Crèvecoeur in the Looking Glass," 176–77.

12. Crèvecoeur, *Sketches of Eighteenth Century America*; Crèvecoeur, *More Letters from the American Farmer*. The latter edition is a more elaborated version of one prepared by Moore as a doctoral thesis (1990). In it Moore includes not only the materials that remained entirely unpublished but also the texts that had already appeared in *Sketches* and several that were published separately in journals in the 1920s. *More Letters* puts all of the texts into full conformity with the manuscripts, which was not always the case in the publications of the 1920s. Moore has more recently published a large selection of these texts, along with those of the original *Letters* of 1782, in a "regularized" form intended to make them more easily readable: Crèvecoeur, *Letters from an American Farmer and Other Essays* (see xxxiv).

13. For a detailed history of Crèvecoeur's publications, see Rice, *Le Cultivateur américain*.

14. Concerning these interests of the author, see Robert de Crèvecoeur, *Saint John de Crèvecoeur*, 11, 51; Allen and Asselineau, *St. John de Crèvecoeur*, 13, 16, 28.

15. This viewpoint is developed at length by Philbrick in his monograph *St. John de Crèvecoeur*. Philbrick sees a return to this reality, though, in *Voyage dans la haute Pensylvanie*.
16. Robinson, "Community and Utopia in Crèvecoeur's *Sketches*," 18.
17. According to the estimate made by the editor of a selective translation: Crèvecoeur, *Crèvecoeur's Eighteenth-Century Travels in Pennsylvania and New York*, xiv.
18. See Crèvecoeur, *Crèvecoeur's Eighteenth-Century Travels in Pennsylvania and New York*, xxxviii–xli.
19. See Dennis Moore's introduction to Crèvecoeur, *Letters from an American Farmer and Other Essays*, xii–xiii. An example of this kind of approach is Osborne, "American Antipathy and the Cruelties of Citizenship in Crèvecoeur's *Letters from an American Farmer*."
20. Chevignard, *Michel Saint-John de Crèvecoeur*, 58, 91.
21. Emerson and Emerson, "Crèvecoeur, J. Hector St. John de," 731. See also Carlson, "Crèvecoeur's *Letters from an American Farmer*," 553; Moore, introduction to Crèvecoeur, *Letters from an American Farmer and Other Essays*, xv.
22. This is arguably the case also for some of the letters in the 1782 edition. Nathaniel Philbrick points out that in the middle five letters, involving Nantucket, the narrative voice changes considerably, becoming more distant and seemingly "objective" ("The Nantucket Sequence in Crèvecoeur's *Letters from an American Farmer*," 414–15).
23. Crèvecoeur, *Letters from an American Farmer*, 61. All references to the *Letters* of 1782 are from this edition.
24. Crèvecoeur, *Sketches of Eighteenth Century America*, 104. All references to *Sketches* are from the original 1925 edition.
25. This is Chevignard's hypothesis in "St. John de Crèvecoeur in the Looking Glass," 181.
26. Norman Plotkin makes the point that the original publications, both in English and in French, were inflected by ideological pressures, but that the "discerning reader" can find in them "suggestions of the rigourous social criticism that remained unpublished for so long" ("Saint-John de Crèvecoeur Rediscovered," 403).
27. The fact that this letter is the almost exclusive choice for anthologization from Crèvecoeur's writing has considerably distorted general understanding of the author, since one finds elsewhere far more unflattering answers to the question posed in the title of the letter. See Robinson, "Community and Utopia in Crèvecoeur's *Sketches*," 31; Richards, "Revolution, Domestic Life, and the End of 'Common Mercy' in Crèvecoeur's 'Landscapes,'" 285. But a close examination of this text itself reveals a darker underside, as we will see further on.
28. The following commentary by the historian Daniel Vickers is relevant here: "Since

it was from the surplus of family production . . . that wealth and power flowed in the colonial Northeast, the creation of social and economic institutions that could attract immigrant families and nourish their mercantile interests was vital to the region's economic development" ("The Northern Colonies," 239).

29. Crèvecoeur returns to this analysis and develops it further in *Voyage dans la haute Pensylvanie*: "However the colonists do not all succeed. Here, as elsewhere, success does not crown all enterprises. . . . All do not bring with them the necessary aptitudes, nor the habits or astuteness required by this new way of life; all do not have the same degree of strength, courage or shrewdness." Some new settlers become "idlers," this being more frequent among "foreign colonists than among those who come from the Northern countries, whose acumen, industriousness and way of life are so worthy of praise" (*Crèvecoeur's Eighteenth-Century Travels*, 55–56).

30. Cf. Taylor, in *Writing Early American History*, 151: "A romantic mythology has miscast the common colonists as self-sufficient yeomen who produced all that they needed or wanted. Although most colonists did live on farms that produced most of their food and fuel and some homespun cloth, no household could produce everything that a family needed. And by no means did mere subsistence satisfy colonial desire. Consequently, colonial farms and plantations produced crops both for household use and for the external market."

31. According to Daniel Vickers, several institutions and cultural practices of this kind constituted a "celebration of neighborliness" necessary for the "preservation of local and family consensus": "Precisely because cooperation between families was at once so necessary and so difficult to reconcile with the pursuit of competency [of each family unit], it had to be clothed in a self-conscious spirit of community" ("Competency and Competition," 27).

32. Crèvecoeur himself visited John Bartram on his farm in 1765; see Chevignard, *Michel Saint-John de Crèvecoeur*, 80.

33. This text offers a remarkable contrast with "What Is an American?" in *Letters*. According to James Henretta, in the movement of settlement to the West, largely carried out by young people, the hierarchy of wealth that had been left behind in the East reproduced itself in the course of a few generations (*The Origins of American Capitalism*, 80–81).

34. Since James has slaves on his Pennsylvania farm, the North-South contrast he establishes can be seen to be self-serving and hypocritical. For an extended analysis that takes this tack, see Osborne, "American Antipathy and the Cruelties of Citizenship in Crèvecoeur's *Letters from an American Farmer*," 535–44. Crèvecoeur himself, however, had slaves on his New York farm, so the ambiguities of the narrative commentary are those of the author as well.

35. Respectively, "The English and the French before the Revolution" (*Sketches*), "Sketch

of a Contrast between the Spanish and the English Colonies" (*More Letters*), and "Sketches of Jamaica and Bermudas and Other Subjects" (*More Letters*).

36. For a general comparison of the English and French versions, see Béranger, "Un auteur, deux publics." Bernard Chevignard's unpublished doctoral thesis provides an exhaustive comparison between the versions: "Saint-John de Crèvecoeur: *Letters from an American Farmer* et *Lettres d'un cultivateur américain*."

37. Crèvecoeur, *Lettres d'un cultivateur américain*, 231. Note the similarity of the final phrase to "fraud against fraud" in the passage quoted earlier concerning the settler who succeeds (*Sketches* 78).

38. For the relationship between *Letters* and *Sketches* from this point of view, see Robinson, "Community and Utopia in Crèvecoeur's *Sketches*."

39. This rise of a new bourgeoisie is attested to by many social historians of the Revolution, starting with J. Franklin Jameson in *The American Revolution Considered as a Social Movement*, in which he writes of "new strata [brought] everywhere to the surface" and of "economic desires,... social aspirations [that] were set free by the political struggle" (16, 9). But see also, for example, Appleby, *Capitalism and a New Social Order*, 13.

40. The economic historian James Henretta argues that the Revolution is the culmination of a social evolution that accelerates through the revolutionary process and finds its justification in republican ideology (*The Evolution of American Society*, 169).

41. For a discussion of the texts involving the frontier, see Sayre, "L'expérience et l'interprétation de la crise chez Crèvecoeur."

42. This portrait shows a strong resemblance to the "ideal type" of the entrepreneur in the early stages of capitalist development, as defined by Weber in *The Protestant Ethic and the Spirit of Capitalism*: those who "have carried through this change" are "calculating and daring at the same time,... temperate and reliable, shrewd and completely devoted to their business," "[avoid] ostentation and unnecessary expenditure," exhibit a "formalistic, hard, correct character," and are thoroughly imbued with the Puritans' sense of moral superiority (69, 71, 166).

43. See Richards, "Revolution, Domestic Life, and the End of 'Common Mercy' in Crèvecoeur's 'Landscapes,'" 281–82; Philbrick, *St. John de Crèvecoeur*, 126–27.

44. This point is emphasized by Richards, "Revolution, Domestic Life, and the End of 'Common Mercy' in Crèvecoeur's 'Landscapes.'"

45. A slang term during the period for a rigid Calvinist. See Richards, "Revolution, Domestic Life, and the End of 'Common Mercy' in Crèvecoeur's 'Landscapes,'" 283.

46. Neither the date nor the location is conclusively established, however.

47. See Crèvecoeur, *Crèvecoeur's Eighteenth-Century Travels*, xv; Allen and Asselineau, *St. John de Crèvecoeur*, 21, 27–30, 48, 51; Chevignard, "St. John de Crèvecoeur:

A Case of Arrested Biographical Development," 324–25; Robert de Crèvecoeur, *Saint-John de Crèvecoeur*, 39–42; Rice, *Le Cultivateur américain*, 125–26.

48. Mandell, *Behind the Frontier*, 202, 203; see also 182, 197. Mandell later extended his study of Indians in the region both spatially and temporally—farther south, into Rhode Island and Connecticut, and beyond the Revolution through most of the nineteenth century: Mandell, *Tribe, Race, History*. In this work Mandell shows how in that later period the natives in the area both became part of the larger socioeconomic environment, joining poor whites and blacks in an "emerging proletariat," and on the remaining reservations—of the Narragansetts and Mohegans in Connecticut, for example—perpetuating some communitarian practices that made of them "reservoirs of antimarket traditions that drew poor whites and blacks threatened by an increasingly uncertain, impersonal economy" (1, 2; see also 10–15).

49. This asymmetry of attraction to the other's form of society was noticed by contemporaries of Crèvecoeur as well, and more recently has been analyzed by ethnohistorians such as Wilcomb Washburn, Francis Jennings, and James Axtell.

50. Crèvecoeur, *Lettres d'un cultivateur américain*, 2:381–400.

51. In the second edition of *Lettres* (1787) new texts are added that present Indians in a positive light to an even greater extent; see Rice, *Le Cultivateur américain*, 135.

52. Crèvecoeur, "Mémoire sur la région située à l'ouest des Montagnes d'Alleghany," 68–72. Chevignard emphasizes this aspect of the travel account in his paper on the manuscript text at the annual congress of the Association française d'études américaines, in Lyon, France, in 1996.

53. The only modern edition of the work in its entirety is an English translation: Crèvecoeur, *Journey into Northern Pensylvania and the State of New York*. A selective edition in French, with a preface by Chevignard, has only recently been published: Crèvecoeur, *Voyage dans la Haute Pensylvanie et dans l'Etat de New-York depuis l'année 1785 jusqu'en 1798*. The quotations below are from the original French edition, in my translation.

54. Crèvecoeur, *Voyage dans la haute Pensylvanie*, 1: 93, 7, chap. 7.

55. Allan Kulikoff notes the highly contradictory character of ideologies in general during the late eighteenth century and points out that several discrepant perspectives are often found to cohabit in a single person (*The Agrarian Origins of American Capitalism*, 114).

2. PHILIP FRENEAU

1. Jameson, *The American Revolution Considered as a Social Movement*, 9. See also a more recent reappraisal of Franklin's seminal work: Hoffman and Albert, *The Transforming Hand of Revolution*.

2. Among the economic historians, see especially Henretta, *The Origins of American Capitalism*, part 2; Kulikoff, *The Agrarian Origins of American Capitalism*, part 2. See also Appleby, *Capitalism and a New Social Order*; Wood, *The Radicalism of the American Revolution*.
3. Demos, *Circles and Lines*, 51.
4. An example of advice to the potential immigrant is an anonymous pamphlet that appeared in London in 1796, entitled *Look before You Leap*. It was a warning against immigration in the form of a series of letters from disappointed immigrants. As for "chorography" (the history and description of a region: see chapter 1, note 3), Thomas Jefferson's *Notes on the State of Virginia* (1786) falls within that genre.
5. Miranda, *The New Democracy in America*; Verme, *Seeing America and Its Great Men*.
6. Brissot's *Nouveau voyage dans les Etats-Unis* (Paris, 1791) appeared in English translation in London in 1792 and 1794 and in Boston in 1797. In 1788, the year of his visit, Brissot himself published an English translation of a letter rebuttal addressed to Chastellux, *A Critical Examination of the Marquis de Chastellux's Travels*. In another Frenchman's account of travel in 1791, the author reports hearing a discussion in a political club in Frederick, Maryland, in which Chastellux's work was bitterly denounced and Brissot's answer to it highly praised: Bayard, *Voyage dans l'intérieur des Etats-Unis*, 37.
7. It was called the College of New Jersey in that period.
8. It was published the following year and was Freneau's first publication.
9. The experience inspired a poem: "The British Prison Ship" (1781).
10. The poems such as they appeared in the initial newspaper publications—often in different versions than those of the later collections—have been republished in Freneau, *The Newspaper Verse of Philip Freneau*. The main collections that appeared during Freneau's lifetime are *The Poems of Philip Freneau* (Philadelphia, 1786); *Poems Written between the Years 1768 & 1794* (Monmouth NJ, 1795); *Poems Written and Published during the American Revolutionary War . . .* (Philadelphia, 1809, 2 vols.); *A Collection of Poems . . . Written between the Year 1797 and the Present Time* (New York, 1815, 2 vols.). The poems in their later, collected form have also been republished in several modern editions. My quotations will be taken from them, except where the first journal version is relevant to my discussion.
11. He was notably the editor in chief of the *National Gazette* (1791–93) and editor owner of the *Jersey Chronicle* (1795–96) and *The Time-Piece* (1797–98); see Freneau, *A Freneau Sampler*, introduction. On the growth of the independent press and its crucial role in postrevolutionary politics, see Daniel, *Scandal and Civility*. Daniel's study includes a chapter on Freneau.
12. For a work that puts "commitment" at the center of Freneau's life and work, see Elliott, *Revolutionary Writers*, chap. 4.

13. But the accusation was never proven: see Freneau, *A Freneau Sampler*, 13.
14. Leary, *That Rascal Freneau*. This work provides a very detailed bibliography. Other, partly biographical works are Marsh, *The Works of Philip Freneau*; Bowden, *Philip Freneau*.
15. On the *Aurora* and its first editor, B. F. Bache, see Tagg, *Benjamin Franklin Bache and the Philadelphia Aurora*, especially chap. 5. A collection of Freneau's essays in the *Aurora*, which is representative of his political ideas, appeared in Philadelphia in 1799 as *Letters on Various Interesting and Important Subjects*. A facsimile edition of the work has been published.
16. Among his poems are "To a Wild Honeysuckle," "The Indian Burying Ground," and "To the Memory of the Brave Americans." The recent Library of America anthology, Shields, *American Poetry: The Seventeenth and Eighteenth Centuries*, includes a somewhat larger and more varied selection. The only collection of the prose that has been published to date appeared many decades ago, printed in typescript by an artisanal publisher: Freneau, *The Prose of Philip Freneau*. Trodd, *American Protest Literature*, includes as its Freneau contribution a poem, one that concerns political (anti-British) rather than social protest.
17. The ambivalence that Freneau shares with Crèvecoeur applies to some extent in this area as well. In the poem coauthored with Brackenridge, who was a sworn enemy of the Indian, but also in several of his own late texts, Freneau reproduces a stereotyped, strongly pejorative image of the Indian; see, for example, "The Old Indian School Must Be Abandoned," *Aurora*, October 24, 1812 (in Freneau, *A Freneau Sampler*, 353–54). On Freneau texts that portray Indians in a negative light during and after the War of 1812, see Marsh, *The Works of Philip Freneau*, 162, 164, 166.
18. Eve Kornfeld focuses on this aspect in her largely negative evaluation of Freneau's treatment of Indians, "Encountering the 'Other.'" For a more general, and less critical, discussion of Freneau's representations of Indians, see Keiser, *The Indian in American Literature*, chap. 3.
19. Freneau also wrote poetry on Indian subjects, but in the poetic work the Indian is often treated at a distance, in the third person.
20. On the contradictory character of ideologies during the late eighteenth century, see Kulikoff, *The Agrarian Origins of American Capitalism*, 114.
21. For a study of this tradition that focuses on representations of Indian civilizations in the southern hemisphere and includes an analysis of Freneau, see Wertheimer, *Imagined Empires*.
22. See Sayre and Löwy, *Romanticism against the Tide of Modernity* and "Romanticism and Capitalism." For a more detailed treatment than will be presented here, see Sayre, "'Romantisme anti-capitaliste' et révolution chez Freneau." The article has

appeared more recently in a collection of essays with Michael Löwy: Sayre and Löwy, *Esprits de feu*.
23. "Ode to the Americans" (1798), in Freneau, *The Poems of Philip Freneau*, 3: 203–4.
24. "A Picture of the Times, with Occasional Reflections" (1782), in *Poems*, 2:166.
25. Freneau, *The Prose of Philip Freneau*, 257.
26. "Commerce," in Freneau, *The Poems of Philip Freneau*, 3:220. The poem was entitled "On the too Remote Extension of American Commerce" in its original newspaper publication. That version does not include the quoted phrase, which was added in the later, collected edition. See Freneau, *The Newspaper Verse of Philip Freneau*, 557–58.
27. Quoted in Bowden, *Philip Freneau*, 105. The Pilgrim is the eponymous fictional author of a series of essays by Freneau entitled "The Pilgrim," published in the *Freeman's Journal* between 1781 and 1783.
28. "The Hermit of Saba" (1788), in Freneau, *The Poems of Philip Freneau*, 2:366.
29. "Pennsylvania" (1790), in Freneau, *The Poems of Philip Freneau*, 3:14.
30. "American Liberty," in Freneau, *The Poems of Philip Freneau*, 1:152; "To a Republican with Mr. Paine's Rights of Man" (1795), in Freneau, *The Poems of Philip Freneau*, 3:91.
31. Freneau, *The Prose of Philip Freneau*, 227.
32. "American Liberty," in Freneau, *The Poems of Philip Freneau*, 1:152.
33. Freneau seems to associate Indians exclusively with the environment of the forest and to ignore the role that agriculture—albeit of a significantly different kind from that of Europeans—played in many Amerindian communities.
34. "Commerce," in Freneau, *The Poems of Philip Freneau*, 3:221.
35. See Freneau, *The Prose of Philip Freneau*, 335.
36. "Discovery" and "The Pictures of Columbus" on the discovery of the Americas, and "American Liberty" on its colonization.
37. For a more complete analysis of the themes of history and memory in Freneau, see Sayre, "Philip Freneau, poète et journaliste, ou la lutte contre l'oubli."
38. The Pattee edition of Freneau's poems includes both versions of "The Rising Glory of America," giving the first version in footnotes and identifying the authors of passages throughout. For a comparison of the two versions, see Wertheimer, "Commencement Ceremonies."
39. In this Freneau exemplifies a general tendency in British America to use the "Black Legend" of Spanish colonization to put the English settlements in the North in a better light by contrast. On this ideological utilization of the theme, see Marienstras, *Les Mythes fondateurs de la nation américaine*.
40. Freneau, *The Poems of Philip Freneau*, 1:62. References for all of the historical poems will be to this edition and will be cited parenthetically in the text.

41. "For the time has been here, (to the world be it known,) / When all a man sailed by, or saw, was his own" (Freneau, *The Poems of Philip Freneau*, 2:275.
42. 1792. See Freneau, *Newspaper Verse of Philip Freneau*, 500–501.
43. 1790. See Freneau, *The Poems of Philip Freneau*, 3:45–46.
44. As in Crèvecoeur's, the adjective appears quite often in Freneau's writing (for example in the title of a poem published in 1797, "A Modern Tale": *The Newspaper Verse of Philip Freneau*, 610–12), indicating the sense of living in a modernity that has its own specificity.
45. Most notably missing in the series is the backcountry, but Freneau never traveled, as Crèvecoeur did, in these territories.
46. Freneau, *The Prose of Philip Freneau*, 60. On stores, consumerism, and the credit system practiced by merchants, see "Reflections on Credit" (1789), in Freneau, *The Newspaper Verse of Philip Freneau*, 327–28.
47. 1788. Freneau, *The Newspaper Verse of Philip Freneau*, 110–11.
48. Freneau, *The Newspaper Verse of Philip Freneau*, 111–12.
49. 1793. Freneau, *The Newspaper Verse of Philip Freneau*, 297, 298.
50. 1785. Freneau, *The Newspaper Verse of Philip Freneau*, 239–40.
51. Freneau, *The Prose of Philip Freneau*, 271.
52. Freneau, *The Poems of Philip Freneau*, 3:53.
53. Freneau, *The Newspaper Verse of Philip Freneau*, 486–96.
54. Freneau, *The Poems of Philip Freneau*, 3:7.
55. Freneau, *The Poems of Philip Freneau*, 3:8.
56. Freneau, *The Poems of Philip Freneau*, 3:11. In the conclusion of the poem, however, Freneau attenuates his condemnation by affirming that the "avarice" motivating commercial activity does have the effect of dynamizing humanity.
57. Freneau, *The Poems of Philip Freneau*, 3:9–10.
58. Freneau, *The Poems of Philip Freneau*, 3:12–13. In his youth, when he was for a short period a schoolteacher, he lived on Long Island; see Marsh, *The Works of Philip Freneau*, 57.
59. Freneau, *The Poems of Philip Freneau*, 3:14 (from the original newspaper version, given in a footnote).
60. Freneau, *The Poems of Philip Freneau*, 3:18. Regarding Scots in the South, in his plea for a global approach to ethnohistorical study, Colin Calloway provides an illuminating gloss on Claudio Saunt's work showing the mercantile influence of Scottish traders on eighteenth-century Creek Indians (farther south than Virginia, cited in Freneau's poem), by pointing out that Scotland itself was being transformed at the same time: "On both sides of the Atlantic tribal lands were being turned into other people's property.... Highland Scots in America may have ridden the capitalist wave, and their Scots-Indian offspring injected

capitalist values into Creek society, but those values did not originate with them" ("2008 Presidential Address," 206–7). On the complex colonial history of Scots, especially Highlanders, North American Indians, and their interrelations, see Calloway, *White People, Indians, and Highlanders*.

61. See Freneau, *The Newspaper Verse of Philip Freneau*, 140–41, 509–10, 610–11.
62. Freneau, *The Newspaper Verse of Philip Freneau*, 140.
63. See especially "To an Author" (1788) and "To Memmius" (1795), in Freneau, *The Poems of Philip Freneau*, 2:332, 406–7.
64. See Freneau, *The Poems of Philip Freneau*, 2:8; Freneau, *The Prose of Philip Freneau*, 375–76.
65. Freneau, *The Newspaper Verse of Philip Freneau*, 164. There is an interesting variation between the first version of 1782 and the final version as it appeared in the 1786 collection. In the 1782 version a "timid race" gives "honours" to an "odious train," whereas in the 1786 version the former is a "sordid race"—a clear escalation in the condemnation of the present elite: Freneau, *The Poems of Philip Freneau*, 2:189.
66. Freneau, *The Newspaper Verse of Philip Freneau*, 301–3; Freneau, *The Poems of Philip Freneau*, 2:371–74.
67. Otaheite was the way the first "discoverers" of the island mistakenly transcribed the name given them by the Tahitians, not recognizing that the initial O was an article.
68. Freneau, *The Prose of Philip Freneau*, 143, 255, 256.
69. Freneau, *The Prose of Philip Freneau*, 333, 334.
70. Freneau, *The Prose of Philip Freneau*, 337, 346, 341.
71. Freneau, *The Prose of Philip Freneau*, 340, 344.
72. Crèvecoeur, *Voyage dans la haute Pensylvanie*, I, 93.
73. The character of Hezekiah Salem was first created by Freneau as the pseudonymous author of a series of newspaper essays in 1797. Later Freneau identified him as the author of some of the works collected in *Poems Written and Published during the American Revolutionary War* (1809). The Hezikiah who appears in "Elijah, the New England Emigrant," however, differs in some significant respects from the earlier authorial persona. See Lewis Leary's introduction to his collection of the Hezekiah Salem material in Freneau, *The Writings in Prose and Verse of Hezekiah Salem*.
74. Freneau, *The Last Poems of Philip Freneau*, 44, 45, 50.

3. MOREAU DE SAINT-MÉRY

1. For a thorough, annotated bibliography of accounts of travel in the United States by the French, see Monaghan, *French Travellers in the United States*.
2. See Chateaubriand, "Voyage en Amérique"; Louis-Philippe, *Diary of My Travels in America*; La Rochefoucauld-Liancourt, *Voyage dans les Etats-Unis d'Amérique*.

3. Dubois, *Avengers of the New World*, 10.
4. The major work published in France before his departure for America was *Lois et constitutions des colonies françaises sous le vent* (6 vols.; 1784–1790). The most important works produced during the Philadelphia period, and published in that city, were *Description topographique et politique de la partie espagnole de l'isle Saint-Domingue* (1796) and *Description topographique, physique, civile, politique et historique de la partie française de Saint-Domingue* (1797). An abridged English translation of the latter has been published as Saint-Méry, *A Civilization That Perished* (1985).
5. A colloquium on Saint-Méry held in Fort-de-France, Martinique, in September 2004 explored some of his contradictions and ambiguities. See *Moreau de Saint-Méry ou les ambiguïtés d'un créole des Lumières*.
6. Saint-Méry, *Voyage aux Etats-Unis de l'Amérique*.
7. Saint-Méry, *Moreau de Saint-Méry's American Journey*. The Roberts edition reprints the introduction by Stewart L. Mims to the original 1913 publication, which provides a brief account of Saint-Méry's life and works, in English. For more detail, see Elicona, *Un colonial sous la Révolution en France et en Amérique*. Roberts's best-known novel, *Northwest Passage* (1936), deals with Robert Rogers, the famous militia leader of the French and Indian War.
8. Saint-Méry, *Moreau de Saint-Méry's American Journey*, 1. All further references are to this translation, cited parenthetically in the text.
9. See Saint-Méry, *Voyage aux Etats-Unis de l'Amérique*, 4, 7, and then later, 292.
10. The author notes much further on, though, that when yellow fever broke out in Philadelphia fear took precedence and one-third of the city's population fled (236).
11. Names of French émigrés that appear in Saint-Méry's text include, in addition to his closer friends Liancourt and Talleyrand, Beaumetz, Blacon, Cadignan, Cazenove de Létombe, Champion, General Collot, la Colombe, Démeunier, Dupont de Nemours, Noailles, Talon, and Volney. François Furstenberg's recent historical study of this community in Philadelphia, *When the United States Spoke French*, focuses on five of them: Saint-Méry himself, Liancourt, Talleyrand, Noailles, and Volney.
12. Works by other émigrés include La Rochefoucauld-Liancourt's *On the Prisons of Philadelphia* (1796), of which an edition in French was published as well, and, also in 1796, Jean-Marie de Bordas's *Défense des colons de Saint-Domingue: ou examen rapide de la nouvelle déclaration des droits de l'homme, en ce qu'elle a particulièrement de relatif aux colonies*.
13. Saint-Méry considers attitudes and behaviors involving sex and marriage also to be crucial aspects of American character equally at odds with his Gallic and Creole sensibilities and treats this material with extreme candor and explicitness.

On this second thematics of Saint-Méry's narrative, see Sayre, "A French Creole Emigré in Late Eighteenth-Century Philadelphia."

14. Saint-Méry, *Voyage aux Etats-Unis de l'Amérique*, 289.
15. According to Saint-Méry's biographer, the French exiles in Philadelphia on the whole remained tenuously on the margins of the host society, subsisting through modest professional pursuits like teaching. Some did attempt to venture into the quintessential American activity of land speculation, but their efforts were usually unsuccessful and abortive. See Elicona, *Un colonial sous la Révolution en France et en Amérique*, 179–83.
16. See La Rochefoucauld-Liancourt, *Le Voyage en Amérique de La Rochefoucauld-Liancourt*, 426–27. I will cite parenthetically subsequent references to this modern, abridged edition of the original eight-volume work.
17. See Furstenberg, *When the United States Spoke French*, 320, 322.
18. See La Rochefoucauld-Liancourt, *Voyage dans les Etats-Unis d'Amérique*, 1:307 (the passage mentioning Brant is not included in the abridged edition of Liancourt's work.
19. La Rochefoucauld-Liancourt, *Voyage dans les Etats-Unis d'Amérique*, 1:303ff.
20. Volume 8 of the original edition.

4. THE ZERO DEGREE OF THE OTHER

1. The early Anglo-American presence in northern parts of the continent, however—in "Rupert's Land" around Hudson's Bay and more widely in Canada and the Northwest after 1763—was, like the French, organized mainly around the fur trade, which did not displace natives but rather employed them as providers and processors of the raw materials of the trade.
2. Harold E. Driver points out that "few indigenous peoples in the world at the same level of culture have fought so valiantly against European intruders as did the Indians east of the Rocky Mountains" (*Indians of North America*, 309).
3. See Slotkin, *Regeneration through Violence*; Bailyn, *The Barbarous Years*. On the theme of violence as regards early Spanish expeditions in North America, see Rabasa, *Writing Violence on the Northern Frontier*.
4. For a treatment of eighteenth-century Indian warfare that focuses on the mid-Atlantic region and highlights the significance of these conflicts in American historical development, see Silver, *Our Savage Neighbors*.
5. On these overall historical developments, see Washburn, *The Indian in America*; Horowitz, *The First Frontier*.
6. In his study of the Catawba Indians of the Carolina piedmont, James H. Merrell observes that they often aggressively sought out armed confrontation, and in this way "shared with Indians throughout Eastern North America a culture of

conflict" (*The Indians' New World*, 121). See also Driver, "Violence, Feuds, Raids, War," in *Indians of North America*. According to Driver, "On the Plains, Prairies, and the East, warfare was a more integral part of the total culture than in any other region of equal size north of Mexico.... [But] fights between whole tribes seem to have been rare before White contact.... The European demand for trade goods, especially furs, created a general economic competition which... vastly increased the number and size of armed conflicts" (320). See also "Savage War" in Francis Jennings's *The Invasion of America*, in which Jennings emphasizes the high level of violence in European societies of the period compared with that among Indians. Finally, see "Peace and War" in Axtell, *The Indian Peoples of Eastern America*. Axtell points out that the Indians were by no means perpetually at war, either with the colonists or among themselves, during the colonial period (160).

7. It was very common practice to make prisoners run through the middle of a crowd—composed largely of women and children armed with sticks or clubs—on entering the village in which they would finally either be adopted or killed and also villages passed through on the way.

8. See Driver, *Indians of North America*, 324: "The most distinctive feature of the warfare pattern in the East as compared with other areas north of Mexico was the emphasis on the torture of prisoners. Most instances of torture on the Plains and Prairies seem to have been derived from the East." See the collection of articles *Scalping and Torture*. Axtell's *The European and the Indian* includes two chapters on scalping.

9. This was the case in many newspaper articles and pamphlets produced during the French and Indian War, written in a style characterized by Peter Silver as "anti-Indian sublime" (*Our Savage Neighbors*, esp. 83, 85).

10. In the introduction to his *Decennium Luctuosum* (1699), a history of the Indian wars in New England between 1688 and 1698. See Lincoln, *Narratives of the Indian Wars*, 177.

11. Rogers, *Journals*, v. In the body of his journal Rogers inserts a short treatise on the rules of "frontier warfare" (60–69). On Rogers and the guerrilla combat carried on by him and other militiamen in the Seven Years' War, see Codignola, *Guerra e guerriglia nell'America coloniale*.

12. Smith, *Expedition against the Ohio Indians*.

13. Rogers, *Journals*, 48.

14. Rogers, *Journals*, 26. Several pages further on (31) more French scalps arrive in Rogers's camp.

15. Mary Rowlandson, *The Sovereignty and Goodness of God, Together with the Faithfulness of His Promises Displayed; Being a Narrative of the Captivity and Restoration*

of Mrs. Mary Rowlandson (1682). On the captivity genre, see Van Der Beets, *The Indian Captivity Narrative*; Derounian-Stodola and Levernier, *The Indian Captivity Narrative*.

16. Silver notes that journalistic literature practicing the "anti-Indian sublime" also "excelled at sweeping away contexts" (*Our Savage Neighbors*, 85).
17. See Calloway, *The Shawnees and the War for America*, 44.
18. The newspaper was the *Freeman's Journal*, April 30–May 21, 1783.
19. See Washburn, "The Clash of Morality in the American Forest," 343.
20. Brackenridge, *Narratives of a Late Expedition against the Indians*, 16, 30–31. This publication is an example of generic hybridity, since it concerns both military operations and captivities.
21. The Moravian missionary David Zeisberger reported being told by Shawnees—among the Indians who participated in the executions—that they had tortured to death all those they thought were involved at Gnadenhütten; see Calloway, *The Shawnees and the War for America*, 72. For a study of the Gnadenhütten events themselves that argues for and applies to that case a broadly contextualizing approach to the analysis of violence, see Harper, "Looking the Other Way."
22. Johnston, *A Narrative of the Incidents Attending the Capture, Detention, and Ransom of Charles Johnston*, 18.
23. Smith, *An Account of the Remarkable Occurrences in the Life and Travels of Col. James Smith*, 9–11. Smith later published a treatise on Indian warfare (1812). The Kahnawakes were Mohawks Christianized by the French who had left their Iroquois homeland to live in a community outside Montreal, but they continued to consider themselves Mohawks and to follow many of their practices. In his study of this group of Indians, Gerald R. Alfred finds that Smith's adoption ceremony "is indicative of the synthesis of autonomy and tradition in the formation of Kahnawake's identity at that time. Tradition is evident in the fact that the Kahnawake Mohawks were continuing the captive-adoption ritual. . . . But rather than being adopted into the Mohawk Nation per se, Smith is told that as a result of the ceremony 'every drop of White blood was washed out of your veins; you are taken into the Caughnewago nation.' . . . Clearly, the foundation of a new community not wholly divorced from the other Iroquois, but unique in many important ways, had been completed" (*Heeding the Voices of Our Ancestors*, 49).
24. Spencer, *Indian Captivity*, 40.
25. Brackenridge, *Narratives of a Late Expedition against the Indians*, 21.
26. Johnston, *A Narrative of the Incidents Attending the Capture, Detention, and Ransom of Charles Johnston*, 33, 65.
27. Beverley, *The History and Present State of Virginia*. On chorography, see chap. 1, note 3.

28. Loskiel, *History of the Mission of the United Brethren among the Indians of North America*, x.
29. Adair, *Adair's History of the American Indians*, 414–15.
30. Colden, *The History of the Five Indian Nations Depending on the Province of New-York in America*, 121.
31. Adair, *Adair's History of the American Indians*, 417.
32. Adair, *Adair's History of the American Indians*, 425.
33. See Keiser, *The Indian in American Literature*, 21–32.
34. The relevant letters are "Distresses of a Frontier Man"; "The Man of Sorrows"; "The Wyoming Massacre"; "History of Mrs. B"; "The Frontier Woman." See Sayre, "L'expérience et l'interprétation de la crise chez Crèvecoeur," 281–84.
35. Bissell, *The American Indian in English Literature of the Eighteenth Century*, 78–117.
36. *The Voyages of Captain Richard Falconer*. See Bissell, *The American Indian in English Literature of the Eighteenth Century*, 84–86.
37. This is the point of view of the heroine in *Lydia; or Filial Piety* (1755), by John Shebbeare, the English novel of the period in which the Indian figures most importantly; see Bissell, *The American Indian in English Literature of the Eighteenth Century*, 90.
38. Smollett, *The Expedition of Humphry Clinker*, 228. The title of the song, in Gaelic, refers to a type of cow.
39. Smollett, *The Expedition of Humphry Clinker*, 229.
40. Rogers, *Ponteach*, published anonymously in London in 1766. The first act of the play satirically portrays greedy British traders and hunters, willing to take any base action that will allow them to make money at the expense of the Indians, and British military officers who despise them and refuse to listen to their pleas. On the context for this acerbic depiction—the arrival of British traders in the Illinois territories after the French defeat, their introduction of more corrupt commercial practices threatening to replace the largely kin-based trade earlier exercised by the French, and the debate in the period in Britain over the need for increased regulation—see Colpitts, *North America's Indian Trade in European Commerce and Imagination*, 202–5.
41. Brackenridge, *Narratives of a Late Expedition against the Indians*, 20, 23–26.
42. See "The White Indians of Colonial America" in Axtell, *The European and the Indian*. For a study of the factors that favored or discouraged assimilation, see Heard, *White into Red*.
43. See his autobiographical account: Tanner, *A Narrative of the Captivity and Adventures of John Tanner*. John T. Fierst, who has studied Tanner and his narrative for many years and is preparing a scholarly edition of the work, claims that although Tanner told his story to the white doctor-naturalist Edwin James, who put it into

English and copiously annotated it, the work "is largely an Anishinaabe account" in content, perspective, and structure ("A 'Succession of Little Occurrences,'" 4). See also Fierst's much earlier article on the last period of Tanner's life, "Return to 'Civilization.'"

44. See the chapter on Mary Jemison in Namias, *White Captives*.
45. But it is not always possible to tell what was said by Mary Jemison herself and what was introduced into the written text by Seaver, whose perspective is clearly different.
46. Seaver, *A Narrative of the Life of Mrs. Mary Jemison*, 160.
47. Adair, *Adair's History of the American Indians*, 414.
48. Relating to this edict, see Seybolt, "Hunting Indians in Massachusetts." Silver cites a similar proclamation in Philadelphia the year before, that offered scalp bounties for the killing of Delaware Indians (*Our Savage Neighbors*, 161). In the dialogue between two English hunters near the beginning of Rogers's *Ponteach* (Act 1, scene 2), one of them calls the Indians "mere savage beasts! / They don't deserve to breathe in Christian Air, / And should be hunted down like other Brutes." His companion fully approves of this idea (184).
49. In *Decennium Luctuosum* (1699): see Lincoln, *Narratives of the Indian Wars*, 192, 196, 233.
50. Smith, *Expedition against the Ohio Indians*, 16. On a letter written by one officer to Bouquet, calling for this approach in the name of a consensus among his fellow officers, see Silver, *Our Savage Neighbors*, 132–33. See also Calloway, *The Shawnees and the War for America*, 36–37.
51. On this trend of opinion in the wake of the Revolution, see Calloway, *The American Revolution in Indian Country*, epilogue. According to Silver, before the 1780s ideas of this kind were largely confined to soldiers and, in smaller numbers, to the relatives of victims of Indian violence (*Our Savage Neighbors*, 129–30, 133, 264).
52. Hixson, *American Settler Colonialism*, viii; see also vii and ix. For a general discussion of the relationship between settler colonialism, the "logic of elimination," and "genocide," see Wolfe, "Settler Colonialism and the Elimination of the Native." Wolfe argues that "settler colonialism is inherently eliminatory but not invariably genocidal" (387).
53. Brackenridge, *Narratives of a Late Expedition against the Indians*, 32, 35.
54. Brackenridge, *Narratives of a Late Expedition against the Indians*, 36, 37. Silver contends that an attitude toward Indians develops after the Revolution that can appropriately be considered racist or proto-racist, though it is not based on skin color (*Our Savage Neighbors*, xxi, 264, 273, 295). For a discussion of some of the complexities of the evolving notion of race in eighteenth-century North America as it related to skin color, see Shoemaker, *A Strange Likeness*, chap. 6.

55. In his captivity account Johnston mentions the common practice of traders selling Indians bullets, tomahawks, and scalping knives, which could be used against whites (*A Narrative of the Incidents Attending the Capture, Detention, and Ransom of Charles Johnston*, 211). Rogers's protagonist Ponteach says disdainfully of the English, "Many of their own brave trusty Soldiers, / In hope of Gain, will give us their Assistance; / For Gain's their great Commander, and will lead them / Where their brave Generals cannot force their March" (*Ponteach*, 202).

56. The fur trade varied considerably in different circumstances, was practiced in quite different ways by the French and English, and was often adapted by Indian participants to their own (nonmodern) purposes.

57. In his study of the works of Brackenridge, *Hugh Henry Brackenridge*, Daniel Marder defines the point of view that informs the whole as that of the Enlightenment. Two years after the publication of his ideas on the Indian question, in 1785, Brackenridge became the defense lawyer in a case in which an Indian was accused of murder and later published an account of the trial. But in that same year he defended several participants in a riot that he found reprehensible, so it seems likely that his defense of the Indian was motivated by commitment to the right of legal representation—an aspect of his Enlightenment outlook—rather than by any change of heart concerning Indians. His written account, while showing some understanding of the mentality of his Indian client, is puzzlingly ambiguous. It is anthologized in Brackenridge, *A Hugh Henry Brackenridge Reader*.

58. See Sheehan, *Seeds of Extinction*; Wallace, *Jefferson and the Indians*. Calloway asserts, however, that in the case of the Ohio Shawnees "Jefferson . . . wanted to see [them] exterminated or driven from their lands" (*The Shawnees and the War for America*, 70). On Jefferson, see also 113–15.

59. For a discussion of colonists' conceptions and representations during King Philip's War, see Lepore, *The Name of War*.

60. Several titles including the term are *The History of the Life and Adventures of Mr. Anderson* (London, 1754); *The Adventures of Emmera; or, The Fair American* (Dublin, 1767); *The Female American; or, The Adventures of Unca Eliza Winkfield* (London, 1767). See Bissell, *The American Indian in English Literature of the Eighteenth Century*, chap. 4.

61. Smith, *Expedition against the Ohio Indians*, ix.

62. Smith was provost of the College of Philadelphia, ancestor to the University of Pennsylvania. He was also the author, however, of many unsigned pamphlets and newspaper articles that Silver sees as prime examples of the "anti-Indian sublime" (*Our Savage Neighbors*, 192–201).

63. Rogers, *Journals*, v–vi.

64. In the preamble Morris indicates that the original manuscript remained for years in a chest and then was submitted to the royal authorities in support of his petition for additional compensation for his military service. Still later a friend advised him to publish it, along with his literary productions, for the purpose of aiding his children through revenues from the sale of the book. One may suppose that the manuscript was rewritten at that point, so as to make it appeal to a wider public.
65. Morris, *Journal of Captain Thomas Morris*, iv, vi. All further references to Morris's journal will be cited parenthetically in the text.
66. The complex multitribal situation in that area and general period is analyzed in White, *The Middle Ground*, chap. 1.
67. The author of the work is usually referred to in this way to distinguish him from his nephew, Alexander Henry the Younger, who was also a trader, traveler, and author.
68. For an exhaustive study of the events and their context, see Widder, *Beyond Pontiac's Shadow*.
69. Henry, *Travels and Adventures in Canada and the Indian Territories*. References will henceforth be cited parenthetically in the text.
70. Although Henry only identifies him as a "Canadian," the person who took him in, albeit cautiously, was Charles-Michel Mouet de Langlade, a highly esteemed Métis leader, son of a French Canadian trader and an Ottawa woman. Like his Ottawa relatives, Langlade was favorable to the British and later played a key role in helping the survivors of the massacre and in creating the conditions for the return of the British to Michilimackinac. See Widder, *Beyond Pontiac's Shadow*, xxv, 137, 141–42, 147–54.
71. The Indian's decision to adopt Henry was perhaps made earlier, and the scene described would then have been a kind of ritual enactment of it. But typically for the adventure mode of narration, the author makes no attempt to comprehend or analyze the Indian's gesture.
72. Slotkin claims that the friendship between Henry and Wawatam, which develops after the adventure is over and Henry becomes a part of Wawatam's family, is a new departure in captivity literature: "Never before had the relationship between captor and captive been portrayed in this manner, outside of a few literary romances by Europeans" (*Regeneration through Violence*, 329).
73. In the same passage Henry also calls them "proprietors" of their land. In 1776 Henry suspended his fur trading travels and embarked on the first of a series of visits to Europe. In 1781 he settled in Montreal, where he continued to engage in business activities, partly connected with the fur trade. See his entry in *Dictionary of Canadian Biography*.

5. ACCOUNTS OF TRAVEL IN NEW FRANCE

1. For an overview of the relation between ethnography and travel literature, see Rubiés, "Travel Writing and Ethnography."
2. See, for example, Berthiaume, *L'aventure américaine au dix-huitième siècle*, 2, 234.
3. Wolfzettel, *Le discours du voyageur*, 5.
4. According to Gordon M. Sayre, for example, the travel account is a narrative that is linear in both the temporal and the spatial senses, and in which the traveler, the narrator, and the author are one and the same (*Les Sauvages Américains*, 84). More recent overall treatments of travel writing have sometimes followed Jan Borm in distinguishing texts of this kind—called "travel books" or "travelogues"—from "travel writing" more generally, seen as a broad thematic grouping rather than a genre. See Borm, "Defining Travel," 13, 17–19; Thompson, *Travel Writing*, chap. 2, esp. 23. But Tim Youngs does not make this differentiation, instead adopting the more limited, generic notion in *The Cambridge Introduction to Travel Writing*, esp. 4–5.
5. Campbell, *The Witness and the Other World*, 2–3. Sayre points out that, given the individual nature of the testimony in the travel account, the "relations" of the Jesuit and Récollet missionaries constitute a borderline case. Usually formulated as the expression of a collective voice, they may be considered as falling outside the limits of the genre (*Les Sauvages Américains*, 45–46).
6. See Berthiaume, *L'Aventure américaine au dix-huitième siècle*, 3. In chapter 6 I trace the process of transformation that took place between the original journal kept by Jonathan Carver and his final, published account.
7. Campbell, *The Witness and the Other World*, 11, 265, 6, 265. In a later article Campbell discusses the theoretical issues raised by the genre, surveying recent trends in the critical literature; see "Travel Writing and Its Theory," in Hulme and Youngs, *The Cambridge Companion to Travel Writing*.
8. Campbell, *The Witness and the Other World*, 262–65. A Spanish nobleman and soldier, Alvar Nunez Cabeza de Vaca took part in an expedition to conquer Florida in 1527 that rapidly met with disaster. Along with three other survivors, Cabeza de Vaca spent eight years with tribes along the Gulf of Mexico, first as a prisoner and slave, then as an adopted and revered shaman. When he finally found some of his Spanish compatriots, he had to a large extent taken on the mentality of the Indians with whom he had been living. See Cabeza de Vaca, *Cabeza de Vaca's Adventures in the Unknown Interior of America*.
9. This work has been republished in a modern edition: Lafitau, *Mœurs des sauvages américains comparées aux mœurs des premiers temps*.
10. Berthiaume, *L'Aventure américaine au dix-huitième siècle*, 228.
11. Since the early sixteenth century accounts of travel in Amerindian territories

have habitually included sections descriptive of both the native peoples and the fauna and flora of the country covered: see Sayre, *Les Sauvages Américains*, 99. On the coexistence of the two generic forms in travel literature, see also 24–25, 80, 83, 110–12, 121.

12. Concerning specific editorial problems posed by this kind of literature, see Warkentin, *Critical Issues in Editing Exploration Texts*, especially, for the process of authorship in travel texts, I. S. MacLaren, "The Metamorphosis of Travellers into Authors: The Case of Paul Kane."
13. On the development of the collection from the sixteenth century on, see Mancall, *Bringing the World to Early Modern Europe*, 4–7.
14. Wolfzettel, *Le discours du voyageur*, 239–40.
15. See Duchet, *Anthropologie et histoire au siècle des Lumières*, introduction.
16. In the preface to *Les Sauvages Américains* (xix), Sayre states his intention to treat the texts he will be dealing with "as literary [works]." However, with only a few exceptions he organizes his study thematically rather than textually.
17. Early scholarship on New France tended to concentrate on the Canadian Northeast, but the past thirty years has seen a strong development of study of the huge central area claimed by the French; see Englebert and Teasdale, *French and Indians in the Heart of North America*, introduction.
18. For W. J. Eccles (*The Canadian Frontier*, vi) there were convergences as well as differences between the two colonies. In the body of his book, however, the latter clearly predominate. For a more recent history of the French colonies that sees some parallels as well as many specificities, see Skinner, *The Upper Country*.
19. See Delâge, *Le pays renversé*, chap. 1; see also Trigger, *The Indians and the Heroic Age of New France*, 3; Trigger, *Natives and Newcomers*, 299–300.
20. See Eccles, *The Canadian Frontier*, vi, 94–101; Trigger, *Natives and Newcomers*, 322; Hamilton, *Feudal Society and Colonization*, 51, 53, 109.
21. Roberta Hamilton's *Feudal Society and Colonization* provides a critical synthesis of the historiography, bringing out the main trends. Hamilton herself argues that France and its colonies remained essentially feudal in both the seventeenth and the eighteenth centuries. At the other extreme, Leslie Choquette's *Frenchmen into Peasants* puts the main emphasis on the "modernity" of New France and its points in common with the English colonies. In *The Middle Ground* Richard White seems to adopt an intermediate position; see especially 51–52. On the historiographic debate, see also Greer, "Comparisons," 478–79.
22. This is the conclusion reached by Greer in *Peasant, Lord, and Merchant*, 175–76.
23. Michael Löwy has further developed this idea in "Catholic Ethics and the Spirit of Capitalism," basing his analysis on the scattered references to Catholicism in Weber's work.

24. Moogk, *La Nouvelle France*, chap. 9.
25. See Mathieu, *La Nouvelle France*, 162–63.
26. Bourguet, "Le sauvage, le colon et le paysan," 239–40.
27. See Ekberg, *French Roots in the Illinois Country*, 108–9, 239–40, 242–43, 250–51. Ekberg argues that the Illinois French communities were also similar to those of seventeenth-century Massachusetts, before enclosure and the development of more individualistic farming practices there. When Anglo-Americans arrived in large numbers in the Illinois country at the end of the eighteenth century, their methods of commercial farming clashed with those of the remaining French settlers, and land use began to shift toward their model.
28. See Eccles, *The Canadian Frontier*, chap. 1. For Daniel Richter the French frontier was complex and "plural," protecting the Indians from Anglo-American incursions for a certain time (*Facing East from Indian Country*, 187).
29. See Taylor, *American Colonies*, 384–90; Havard and Vidal, *Histoire de l'Amérique française*, 310–17.
30. The Récollet missionaries were, however, less tolerant from this point of view than the Jesuits, who replaced them as the dominant religious order in New France in 1625, when they were granted a monopoly on missions. On the differences of perspective between the two orders, see Trigger, *The Indians and the Heroic Age*, 16; Trigger, *Natives and Newcomers*, 316–17, 326, 331.
31. Greer, "Comparisons," 477.
32. See Delâge, "Indian-White Relations in New France," 282–83. A limited exception to this rule is the brutal retaliation carried out by the French for the uprising of the Natchez Indians in 1729. Alan Taylor also cites the war between the Chickasaws and the Choctaws, allies of the French, during which Bienville, then governor of Louisiana, came to believe by the mid-1730s that the total destruction of the Chickasaw nation was in the French interest (*American Colonies*, 393–94).
33. See White, *The Middle Ground*, 50–51. It is surely not by coincidence that the French anthropologist Pierre Clastres, in *La société contre l'état*, singles out the radical rejection of authoritarian hierarchy and state political structures as the prime distinguishing feature of "archaic" Amerindian societies (in the Americas as a whole).
34. See Bourguet, "Le sauvage, le colon et le paysan," 250–53.
35. See Eccles, *The Canadian Frontier*, 102.
36. Jacquin, *Les Indiens blancs*.
37. Jacquin, *Les Indiens blancs*, 203, 208–12. See also 9, 10, 188, 193, 198–201.
38. In the late seventeenth century the French authorities set up a system that issued a limited number of licenses (called *congés*) granting the right to engage in the fur trade. Under this system some *coureurs de bois* became salaried employees

of Montreal merchants ("bourgeois") who held licenses. Others remained independent (and illegal) small traders. Some moved between the two conditions. The employees were usually called *voyageurs*, though there was much overlap in terminological usage. For a thorough study of the *voyageurs* that focuses on the period after 1763, when the masters of the trade were British, see Podruchny, *Making the Voyageur World*.

39. For a "biographical dictionary" of the main authors, see Sayre, *Les Sauvages Américains*, 323–32. See also Sayre's bibliography, 352–66, and that of Duchet in *Anthropologie et histoire au siècle des Lumières*, 502–7. Among the most important works of the period: Louis Hennepin, *Description de la Louisiane* (1683) and *Nouvelle découverte d'un très grand pays* ... (1697); Chrestien Le Clercq, *Nouvelle Relation de la Gaspesie* (1691); Nicolas Perrot, *Mémoire sur les mœurs, coustumes, et relligion des sauvages de l'Amérique Septentrionale* (written in 1704–8); N. de Diéreville, *Relation du voyage du Port Royal* (1708); Bacqueville de la Potherie, *Histoire de l'Amérique septentrionale* (1722); Joseph-François Lafitau, *Mœurs des sauvages américains comparées aux mœurs des premiers temps* (1724); Antoine Simon Le Page du Pratz, *Histoire de la Louisiane* (1758); Jean-Bernard Bossu, *Nouveaux voyages aux Indes Occidentales* (1768) and *Nouveaux voyages dans l'Amérique Septentrionale* (1777).

40. Jacob, "L'Indien des Anglais, l'Indien des Français," 231.

41. See Hazard, *La Crise de la conscience européenne*, esp. 1:16–18, 33, 2:294–95.

42. Lahontan, *Œuvres complètes*. In addition to *Nouveaux Voyages*, *Mémoires*, and *Dialogues*, this edition contains the second part of vol. 3, "Voyages du Portugal et du Danemarc," as well as letters, memoirs, and a poem. Ouellet has since edited paperback publications of *Mémoires* and *Dialogues*, with new introductions: Lahontan, *Dialogues avec un sauvage*; Lahontan, *Mémoires de l'Amérique septentrionale*.

43. In *Le discours du voyageur*, Friedrich Wolfzettel considers Lahontan—like Robert Challe, a traveler to the East whose sensibility was similar to his—exemplary of the "contradictory discourse of the Enlightenment" (252–60). See also Ferland and Ouellet, "Les sauvages de Lahontan." A German monograph has recently appeared that studies Lahontan's work in the context of the "early Enlightenment" (*Frühaufklärung*): Dölling, "*Mes amis sauvages*."

44. The *Dictionary of Canadian Biography* points out, however, that there is no independent evidence either of his transatlantic passage at that date or of his being an officer when he arrived.

45. The authenticity of this trip has been questioned, notably by Charlevoix, who had ideological reasons, however, for wishing to discredit Lahontan. The controversy has continued up to the present. While some historians are convinced that the

voyage was at least partially invented (see, for example, Berthiaume, *L'aventure américaine au dix-huitième siècle*, 124–25), according to the Lahontan specialist Réal Ouellet, editor of his complete works, recent research would seem to indicate that it did in fact take place, that the "Long River" is the Minnesota River, and that the peoples encountered upstream were Dakota Sioux. See Lahontan, *Œuvres complètes*, 1:43. More recently another scholar has put forth the intriguing hypothesis that the river was not the Minnesota but the Missouri: Wood, "The Mysterious 1688 Journey of M. Lahontan." In *Encounters at the Heart of the World*, Elizabeth Fenn finds this thesis compelling, though unproven, and concludes that if true it would mean that the Indians farthest up the river were Mandans rather than Sioux (41–47).

46. See Lahontan, *Œuvres complètes*, 1:15.
47. For a biographical sketch of Lahontan, see *Œuvres complètes*, "chronologie" (1:209–38).
48. Lahontan never radically questioned the legitimacy of colonization. His "treason" as regards the French colony consisted in proposing his services to another colonial enterprise—that of England.
49. Several editions and issues of the work appeared in the year of its first publication.
50. The book being stepped on may be the Bible, although for some, including Michelet, who admired Lahontan's work, it is a book of legal codes: see Lahontan, *Dialogues avec un Sauvage*, 8.
51. A parallel to this dilemma can be found in the case of another French nobleman, whom Lahontan knew and mentions in *Nouveaux Voyages*: the Baron de Saint-Castin. He married the daughter of an Abenaki chief and lived as an Indian in the contested zone between Canada and New England. He also served as an agent for the French but kept a large measure of independence, carrying on commercial relations with Boston merchants. He is said to have once told an Englishman that he "had much rather be a subject of England than a slave to France." Yet he never emigrated to New England, preferring the Indian mode of living. And his role as informer for the French led him to be increasingly hated by the English authorities, who at one point attempted to kill him. See Calloway, *Dawnland Encounters*, 226, and more generally 223–27.
52. The elderly relative is clearly a fiction. The two volumes were almost surely written, or at the very least entirely reworked, in Europe.
53. On the unity of *Nouveaux voyages* and *Mémoires*, see Wolfzettel, *Le Discours du voyageur*, 254; Lahontan, *Œuvres complètes*, 1:29.
54. See Lahontan, *Œuvres complètes*, 1:44. Supposing the veracity of his trip up the "Long River," Lahontan would have met Dakota Sioux (or Arikaras and Mandans, if the Missouri River hypothesis is correct), among other tribes, during that excursion.

55. See Lahontan, *Mémoires de l'Amérique septentrionale*, 30, 22n. The dictionary of words from Algonquin languages that he includes at the end of *Mémoires* demonstrates real knowledge, though it remains elementary (*Œuvres complètes*, 1:732–71). See also appendix 8, "Lahontan et les langues amérindiennes" (2:1271–77).
56. For examples of cases where Lahontan himself highlights an interpretive issue, see *Œuvres complètes*, 1:409, 423. Henceforth page references to *Œuvres complètes*, vol. 1 (*Nouveaux voyages* and *Mémoires* are both included in this volume) will be cited in parentheses in the text. The translations of quotations are my own. When it seems useful for the reader to see the original French, short phrases will be placed in brackets within the translation, and longer passages will be set in a note. For a contemporaneous English translation of the works (1703), see the reprint edited by Reuben G. Thwaites: Lahontan, *New Voyages to North-America*. Ouellet indicates that this translation sometimes differs significantly from the original (Lahontan, *Dialogues avec un Sauvage*, 22).
57. On the role of hunting and the intensity of the bond created through it, see Ferland and Ouellet, "Les sauvages de Lahontan," 198–99. The authors point out that in his account of the first winter of hunting Lahontan alternately uses the pronouns "they" and "we."
58. Kondiaronk was one of the most prominent leaders of the pro-French Indian groups of the Great Lakes area in the late seventeenth century—a member of the the Petun, or Tionontati band of the Huron Confederacy at Michilimackinac. He was widely admired as a strategist ("Le Rat," the name given him by the French, referred to his political cunning), an orator, and a conversationalist. For details on his historical role, see his entry in the *Dictionary of Canadian Biography*.
59. See Ferland and Ouellet, "Les sauvages de Lahontan," 199–200.
60. An active relationship of another kind—the sex act—is referred to once, but only negatively, with the indication that it did not finally take place. Lahontan tells of how he and his companions were once invited to spend the night with some Indian women: "The temptation would have been stronger in other circumstances, [but] the offering was of no use to travelers weakened from exertion and lack of food and drink, *sine Cerere et Baccho friget Venus* (without Ceres and Bacchus, Venus cools)" (417).
61. "Plus je montois la Rivière, plus les Sauvages me paroissoient raisonnables."
62. "Empirical subjectivity" is Wolfzettel's expression (*Le discours du voyageur*, 259).
63. In this sense the register of *Mémoires* is to be located somewhere between the empiricism of *Nouveaux voyages* and the imaginary debate of the *Dialogues*.
64. See Lahontan, *Œuvres complètes*, 1:43. The editors also refer the reader to a 1979 doctoral thesis at the University of Toronto, by Judith Chamberlin Neave: "A Study of the Historical Veracity in the Works of the Baron de Lahontan."

65. Concerning the inhabitants of New France, see, for example, Choquette, *Frenchmen into Peasants*, 143, 272, 282. On the subject of the Indians, see Bailey, *The Conflict of European and Eastern Algonkian Cultures*, 84, 87, 134. More recently Nancy Shoemaker quotes Lahontan several times in *A Strange Likeness* (17, 55).
66. Referring to the work of Bruce Trigger, however, the ethnohistorian William B. Hart argues that while "we know that the *Jesuit Relations* contain embellished accounts, invented speeches, and inflated claims . . . it is not useful to assume that all that appears [there] is hyperbole and fabrication" ("'The Kindness of the Blessed Virgin,'" 66).
67. See Ferland and Ouellet, "Les sauvages de Lahontan," 201. Berthiaume (*L'aventure américaine au dix-huitième siècle*, 176) makes a similar remark regarding the descriptions of fauna and flora.
68. ". . . est l'ouvrage d'un principe supérieur en sagesse et en connoissance, qu'ils appellent le GRAND ESPRIT ou le Maître de la vie, & qu'ils adorent de la manière du Monde la plus abstraite. . . . L'Existence de Dieu étant inséparablement unie avec son Essence, il contient tout, il paroît en tout, il agit en tout, & il donne le mouvement à toutes choses. Enfin tout ce qu'on voit, & tout ce qu'on conçoit est ce Dieu. . . . Ce qui fait qu'ils l'adorent en tout ce qui paroît au monde."
69. Ethnohistorians have, however, pointed out that wars carried out for purposes of revenge allowed for the replacement, through prisoner adoption, of members of a tribe who had been killed.
70. See Lahontan, *Œuvres complètes*, 638nn503, 505, where the editors quote passages from other travelers and sojourners in New France—Lescarbot, Leclercq, Lejeune, Perrot, and Charlevoix—which emphasize the same characteristics.
71. Lahontan's perception of Indian rationality also prefigures twentieth-century anthropological perspectives, notably the conceptualizations of Claude Lévi-Strauss.
72. This statement is uncharacteristic of Lahontan, who usually takes pleasure in turning the stereotyped roles upside down and showing the Europeans to be the true savages.
73. ". . . que la Tradition est trop suspecte, inconstante, obscure, incertaine, trompeuse & vague, pour se fier à elle."
74. While Lahontan did not go down the Mississippi as far, he explored it higher up and, at least if he is to be believed, went higher up one of its tributaries than Charlevoix did.
75. On the life and travels of Charlevoix, see the introduction, by Pierre Berthiaume, to Charlevoix, *Journal d'un voyage fait par ordre du roi dans l'Amérique septentrionale*. For a brief treatment in English, see Savage, *Discovering America*, 38–42.
76. See Charlevoix, *Charlevoix (1682–1761)*, 10. The *Journal d'un voyage* takes up most of the third volume of the work. The reasons for this delay are not known.

In the introduction to the Bibliothèque du Nouveau Monde edition of *Journal d'un voyage*, Berthiaume mentions the hypothesis that an obstacle was created for political reasons but thinks it more likely that the onerousness of the research, and Charlevoix's other obligations, greatly slowed down the writing of the work. See Charlevoix, *Journal d'un voyage*, 1:50–58.

77. "Projet d'un corps d'histoires du Nouveau Monde," in Charlevoix, *Charlevoix (1682–1761)*, 19. Charlevoix more pointedly wants to sort through the published works so as to "extricate the truth from the monstrous heap of fabrications . . . shored up by a charming style and a pernicious seasoning of satire, licentiousness [*libertinage*] and free-thinking [*irreligion*]" (20). He seems to be aiming at Lahontan, among others, in this passage.

78. In addition to his history of New France, Charlevoix published histories of Japan (1736) and Paraguay (1756). He indicates in the first volume of *Histoire et description générale de la Nouvelle France* that the *Journal d'un voyage* is a "preliminary" to it. See Charlevoix, *Journal d'un voyage*, 1:41n170.

79. After having inserted one of these blocks of synthetic material, the author makes the following comment (at the end of Letter 13): "These notions seem necessary, Madame, to give you a complete knowledge of all that concerns the wars of the Savages, about which I will [continue to] speak in my letters, until I have exhausted the subject" (*Journal d'un voyage*, 1:472).

80. See Charlevoix, *Journal d'un voyage*, 1:63–64.

81. Trigger, *Natives and Newcomers*, 23. See, more generally, the section "The Charlevoix Tradition," 20–29.

82. Charlevoix, *Journal d'un voyage*, 1:241. Hereafter references to this work will be cited in parentheses in the text.

83. "Son air, le son de sa voix, & son action, quoiqu'il ne fît aucun geste, me parurent avoir quelque chose de noble & d'imposant, & il falloit que ce qu'il disoit, fût bien éloquent, puisque dépouillé dans la bouche de l'Interprete, qui étoit un Homme ordinaire, de tous les ornements du Langage, nous en fûmes tous charmés. Je vous avouë même que, quand il auroit parlé deux heures, je ne me serois pas ennuyé un moment."

84. Although Charlevoix does not identify them, the bodies were probably Fox warriors, or allies of theirs, since the Fox were at war in the area with the French and Indians affiliated with them.

85. In the context of their gift exchange mentality, and their understanding of the obligations of their French "father," the Indians allied to the French often felt the French were not generous enough in the presents they distributed. Charlevoix does not consider here that the Miamis may have taken things from the French as merely their due or as making up for the perceived meagerness of French largesse.

86. "Didactic fervor" is J. H. Kennedy's phrase, in *Jesuit and Savage in New France*, 182.
87. "... même eu bien de la peine à détromper sur cela les Chrétiens."
88. "Ce qui surprend infiniment dans des Hommes, dont tout l'extérieur n'annonce rien que de barbare, c'est de les voir se traiter entr'eux avec une douceur & des égards, qu'on ne trouve point parmi le Peuple dans les Nations les plus civilisées."
89. "Cela vient sans doute en partie de ce que le mien & le tien, ces paroles froides, comme les appelle SAINT CHRYSOSTOME, mais qui en éteignant dans nos cœurs le feu de la charité, y allument celui de la convoitise, ne sont point encore connus de ces Sauvages." On these ideas in Charlevoix's work, see Kennedy, *Jesuit and Savage in New France*, 155–59.
90. "Quant à ce qu'on appelle ... les qualités du cœur, les Sauvages ne s'en piquent pas ou pour mieux dire, elles ne sont point en eux des vertus: il semble même qu'ils ne les sçavent pas envisager sous ce point de vuë; amitié, compassion, reconnoissance, attache, ils ont quelque chose de tout cela, mais ce n'est point dans le cœur, & c'est moins en eux l'effet d'un bon naturel, que de la réflexion, ou de l'instinct.... [These qualities] ne sont pour eux qu'une suite de la persuasion, où ils sont, que tout doit être commun entre les Hommes."
91. See the introduction to Charlevoix, *History and General Description of New France*.
92. The so-called *petites nations*—small Indian nations in the vicinity of New Orleans—also regularly rendered services to the French and became adept at marketing them. Daniel Usner cites Charlevoix as commenting, in his account of a visit to one of these peoples in the village of Tunica, that the chief displayed entrepreneurial qualities and had mastered from the French "the art of laying up money" (Usner, *Indians, Settlers, and Slaves in a Frontier Exchange Economy*, 63).
93. The term *francisation* was long used to designate the goal of the state with regard to the natives in New France.
94. Charlevoix favors *francisation* before (or at the same time as) Christianization in a passage of *Journal d'un voyage* (1:250–51) and the contrary in *Histoire et description générale de la Nouvelle France* (see *Journal d'un voyage*, 1:251n26).

6. ANGLO-AMERICAN TRAVELERS

1. See Sayre, *Les Sauvages Américains*, chap. 1.
2. The accounts were not all published in the 1760s, however.
3. On these go-betweens who played a key role in relations between the colonies and the Indians beyond the frontier, see Merrell, *Into the American Woods*.
4. A recent study has explored the relationship between the Moravians' participation in the market economy and their missionary effort: Engel, *Religion and Profit*.
5. On Anglo-American travel literature in the colonial period, see (1) anthologies: Mereness, *Travels in the American Colonies*; Thwaites, *Early Western Travels*; (2)

annotated bibliography: Cole, *Travels in the Old South*; (3) collections of texts on Internet sites: *Early Encounters in North America: Peoples, Cultures, and the Environment* (University of Chicago, Alexander St. Press, 2001); *American Journeys: Eyewitness Accounts of Early American Exploration and Settlement* (Wisconsin Historical Society, 2003); *American Notes: Travels in America, 1750–1920* (Library of Congress, 2003). These sources also provide considerable French documentation.

6. See Mereness, *Travels in the American Colonies*: "Col. Chicken's Journal to the Cherokees, 1725," "Captain Fitch's Journal to the Creeks, 1725," "A Ranger's Report of Travels with Gen. Oglethorpe, 1739."
7. The three texts have been published together in a modern edition (though Evans's is fragmentary): Bartram et al., *A Journey from Pennsylvania to Onondaga in 1743*.
8. John Heckewelder, a Moravian missionary and the author of a treatise on Indian customs, a history of Moravian missions, and several travel accounts, was Post's assistant in the Ohio country in 1762. The works of Weiser, Crogan, and Post have been brought together in Thwaites, *Early Western Travels*, vol. 1.
9. First edition: New York, 1809.
10. First edition: London, 1765. A German edition appeared in 1796. The English Romantic poet Robert Southey drew on this text in his epic poem *Madoc* (1805). See Timberlake, *The Memoirs of Lieut. Henry Timberlake*, 16.
11. See Randolph, *British Travelers among the Southern Indians*, 78.
12. The best modern edition of the work, with a scholarly introduction and bibliography, is Lawson, *A New Voyage to Carolina*. All references are to this edition, cited parenthetically in the text.
13. The main problem confronted by biographers of the author of *A New Voyage*, insofar as his English period is concerned, is the commonness of both his first and last names in England at the time. For biographical information on Lawson, fragmentary though it is, see the introduction to the Lefler edition, the Lawson entries in *Dictionary of North Carolina Biography* and *American National Biography*; Hudson, "Among the Tuscarora"; and the digital exhibition on the Internet site *John Lawson: Imagining a Life*, Joyner Library, East Carolina University, 2003.
14. There seems to be no sure indication of the motives for Lawson's trip: see Randolph, *British Travelers among the Southern Indians*, 79n1.
15. The full title of the first edition is *A New Voyage to Carolina; Containing the Exact Description and Natural History of that Country: Together with the Present State thereof. And a Journal of a Thousand Miles, Travel'd thro' several Nations of Indians. Giving a particular Account of their Customs, Manners, etc.*
16. For a brief historical overview of these developments, see Fenn, *Natives and Newcomers*, 33–41, 43–49. For a more detailed social and political history of the area, see McIlvenna, *A Very Mutinous People*.

17. The two reprints, in 1714 and 1718, were entitled *The History of Carolina*, although the section containing the travel account was retained. Both German translations appeared in Hamburg, in 1712 and 1722.
18. In his dedication Lawson praises the English political principles on which their governance is based, while making it clear that these principles are applicable only to the colonists: "Those Charms of Liberty and Right, the Darlings of an English Nature, which Your Lordships grant and maintain, make you appear Noble Patrons in the Eyes of all Men, and we a happy People in a Foreign Country" (*A New Voyage to Carolina*, 4). A very different picture—involving tensions and tumultuous conflict between several settler factions, governors, and proprietors—appears in McIlvenna, *A Very Mutinous People*, chaps. 6 and 7.
19. The other parts are the travel narrative, a synthetic portrait of the Indians, and sections on fauna and flora.
20. Vizenor, *Manifest Manners*, 55. In Vizenor's view, identities "are created in stories, and names are essential to a distinctive personal nature, but memories, visions, and the shadows of heard stories are the paramount verities.... The shadows are active and intransitive, the visual memories that are heard as tribal stories; these memories are trusted to sacred names and tribal nicknames" (56). He further argues that translation of the tribal names as surnames "is the closure of tribal stories," constituting "misconstrued identities" (59).
21. This kind of terminology was apparently common among Indian traders. James H. Merrell, in his study of the indigenous peoples of the Carolina piedmont, cites a similar use of "landlord" and "landlady" by a trader at a later period (*The Indians' New World*, 63). Nancy Shoemaker points out that in eighteenth-century North America Indians and Europeans each tried to fit the other into their own nomenclature. In the context of colonial conquest, however, the functions of the practice were of a different nature on the two sides (*A Strange Likeness*, 39).
22. Although it is not named specifically in the text, Merrell identifies the Indian group with which the incident takes place as Waxhaws (*The Indians' New World*, 3).
23. Probably a forced marriage (editorial note in the Lefler edition).
24. The author also gives considerable attention to the Indians' sexual mores and comments on the beauty and sensuality of Indian women. See Randolph, *British Travelers among the Southern Indians*, 83.
25. On the subsequent career of "Enoe Will," whose strongly pro-English stance apparently angered some of his tribe to the point where they tried to poison him, and who subsequently left it to "[fall] into the limbo between two cultures, no longer fully a part of native society yet only a marginal member of colonial life," see Merrell, *The Indians' New World*, 43–44.
26. On the refusal of Indians in the area later in the century to reveal some beliefs

and practices held to be sacred, see Merrell, *The Indians' New World*, 131–32. Devon Mihesuah also indicates that in gathering contemporary oral histories, interviewers may discover that tribes do not wish to reveal all aspects of their cultures (*Natives and Academics*, 4).

27. In his introduction to *The Indians' New World*, Merrell poses the question of the range of reference in Lawson's general comments on Indians. He concludes that while Lawson surely knew best the Tuscaroras that lived near where he later settled in North Carolina, his comments plausibly apply to most of the fifteen-odd tribes he visited in the interior, which, while each was distinct, "shared certain fundamental similarities" (2–3).

28. This inability to step out of his "habitus" (Bourdieu) gives rise to many unresolved contradictions. In different passages, or even within the same passage, Lawson describes Indians as both lazy and vigorous, full of desire and passionless, thievish and generous, mercenary and disinterested, in most cases without attempting further explanation.

29. In at least one case it is a *positive* judgment that reflects the author's prejudices— those of the European male: "Amongst Women, it seems impossible to find a scold.... Would some of our *European* Daughters of Thunder set these *Indians* for a Pattern" (*A New Voyage to Carolina*, 43).

30. In *Les Sauvages Américains* Sayre proposes several hypotheses to account for similar discrepancies that he and other commentators have noted in texts containing the two generic forms. Remarkably, though, in the corpus to which he refers the positive-negative polarity does not always operate in the same direction (see 80, 112).

31. Two of these lexicons have been republished separately as part of a series of ethnographic materials: Lawson, "A Vocabulary of Tuscarora" and "A Vocabulary of Woccon."

32. One study of *A New Voyage to Carolina* treats it as an example of literary representation of the Noble Savage: Diket, "The Noble Savage Convention as Epitomized in John Lawson's *A New Voyage to Carolina*." I have attempted in this chapter to show that while that dimension is indeed present in Lawson's text, the image of the Indian in his work is considerably more complex. A more recent article has developed a related argument, according to which Carolina, as it appears in Lawson's account, is a paradisiacal New World Eden: Shields, "Paradise Regained Again." In my view Shields also oversimplifies Lawson's text, in particular by minimizing the author's utilitarian aim of encouraging future colonization.

33. Another objective aimed for by Rogers, who had been named commander of Fort Michilimackinac and governor of the region by the Board of Trade, was probably to develop fur trade relations, and perhaps also to prospect with an eye to future colonization.

34. "Naudowessie," as Carver wrote it, is a variant of "Nadouessioux," the shortened form of which is "Sioux." The origin and meaning of the term have not been definitively established, but one broadly accepted theory is that it derives from the name given this Indian group by the Ojibwes, their traditional enemies, as adopted by the French, who were allies of the Ojibwes. The Ojibwe name may have been pejorative, meaning "little snakes," but this interpretation has been questioned. For a discussion of the Sioux Nation, including its designations and subdivisions, by a Native American scholar (Oglala Lakota), see the entry for "Sioux" in Hoxie, *Encyclopedia of North American Indians*, 590–93.
35. Assuming that Lahontan's "Rivière Longue" refers to the same waterway, Carver's Naudowessies may have been descendants of Indians encountered by Lahonton some eighty years earlier.
36. On Carver's life and travels, see Carver, *The Journals of Jonathan Carver and Related Documents*, introduction; Carver, *Jonathan Carver's Travels through America*, introduction; and the entry on Carver in *American National Biography*, vol. 4.
37. On the activities and initiatives of Carver in London, particularly in the period 1773–75, see Parker, "New Light on Jonathan Carver."
38. For a bibliography of editions, see Lee, *A Bibliography of Carver's Travels through the Interior Parts of North America in the Years 1766, 1767, and 1768*; Lee, "Captain Jonathan Carver"; Carver, *The Journals of Jonathan Carver and Related Documents*, 38–56, appendix 3.
39. Carver, *Jonathan Carver's Travels through America*, 1.
40. On Carver's borrowings, see the introduction to *Jonathan Carver's Travels through America*, 47; Savage, *Discovering America*, 47–48; Williams, "Until They Are Contaminated by Their More Refined Neighbors," 191.
41. These documents are reproduced in Carver, *The Journals of Jonathan Carver and Related Documents*, 199–203.
42. Brief descriptions of this new material were first made by Lee in 1913, in "Captain Jonathan Carver," but the material itself did not appear in published form until 1976, in *The Journals of Jonathan Carver and Related Documents*.
43. For a discussion of typical textual stages in the process, which distinguishes preprint and print-era works, see MacLaren, "In Consideration of the Evolution of Explorers and Travellers into Authors."
44. In the Manuscript Department, listed as Additional Manuscripts 8949 and 8950.
45. Carver, *The Journals of Jonathan Carver and Related Documents*, 143.
46. See Carver, *The Journals of Jonathan Carver and Related Documents*, 31–32. There are indications that the "reviser" was Alexander Bicknell, a well-known hack of the period.
47. For a more detailed treatment of the genesis of this travel account, see Sayre, "From Journal to 'Travels.'"

48. Carver, *Jonathan Carver's Travels through America*, 62. All further references are to this edition, cited parenthetically in the text.
49. See Gelb's introduction to *Jonathan Carver's Travels through America*, 18.
50. The book also includes an appendix containing the author's reflections on future "commercial" colonization of North America: "The Probability of the Interior Parts of North America Becoming Commercial Colonies and the Means by Which This Might Be Effected."
51. The French officer Le Roy Bacqueville de la Potherie, in his *Histoire de l'Amérique Septentrionale* (1722), recounts how Ottawas received a friendly party of Potawatomis "in military fashion" on a visit around 1686. The Ottawas and their French allies fired a volley of blanks at the Potawatomis, who returned the same. After a second exchange of symbolic fire, the Ottawas carried the Potawatomi canoes onshore and "conducted the chiefs into their cabins, where the guests were regaled" (quoted in Kinietz, *The Indians of the Western Great Lakes*, 250–51).
52. The name in all probability designates him as the principal chief of the Ojibwes living in the region around the Sault Sainte Marie, the large waterfall between Lakes Huron and Superior. They were named "Saulteurs" by the French.
53. The ethnographic section is in fact scattered with diachronic fragments—anecdotes and short narratives—offered as illustrations of general themes.
54. Carver, *Journals of Jonathan Carver and Related Documents*, 120–21.
55. Was the encounter with the Grand Sautor invented or borrowed, for instance? Did the author fear for his life as the dancers approached, and was he told of their customs authoritatively or tentatively, during or after the event? All these questions remain unanswered.
56. The transcription of this speech also allows Carver to demonstrate the utility of his trip for the Crown, since in it he asks the Indians he is addressing (the Naudowessie), "Let me know if you are willing to acknowledge yourselves the children of my great master, the King of the English and other nations" (91). As for Carver's ability to compose and deliver the speech in Dakota, Raymond J. DeMallie concludes from an examination of the Dakota dictionary included by Carver in his work (but excised from the Gelb edition) that he did not have sufficient knowledge of the language to do so on his own (see Carver, *The Journals of Jonathan Carver and Related Documents*, 212).
57. Several pages further on (106), the author makes similar remarks about a story that was reported to him. In 1762 a rain the color of ink fell in the area of the fort at Detroit, shortly before the Indian wars began there. Generally Carver seems inclined to believe in the omens and magical practices of the Indians, without wanting explicitly to acknowledge that he does. However he ridicules the idea, held by some colonists, that the Indians call up the devil. He tells of having seen

the "Black Dance" performed when he was "in the interior parts," during which, though the dance was formidable, no demon appeared (141).

58. See Carver, *Travels through the Interior Parts of North America*, "An Address to the Public," unpaginated, following the dedication. Elizabeth Fenn cites several sources, including Peter Pond, as suggesting that the rattlesnake story was in fact a "tall tale" and that the French trader who told it to Carver was a certain Pennesha Gegare (Fenn, *Encounters at the Heart of the World*, 148–49, 377n49). See also *The Journals of Jonathan Carver and Related Documents*, 83. For Pond's allusion to the incident, in which he claims that the trader "imposed" on Carver, see Gates, *Five Fur Traders of the Northwest*, 38.

59. On Indian women in general, Carver notes that they "are of an amorous temperament and before they are married are not the less esteemed for the indulgence of their passions" (126). The statement is followed by the story of a Naudowessie woman who, honoring an old tradition, gives herself to forty warriors in a row, thereby gaining the admiration of the entire tribe. These considerations on Indian sexual mores make no pejorative associations with European courtesans or prostitutes.

60. Carver adds—unusually for European travelers—that the Indians "shew an equal degree of indifference for the productions of art" (128).

61. Awareness of the damaging effects of alcohol on the natives does not hinder Carver from providing them with it on occasion, nor of contemplating the construction of a distillery in Indian territory to facilitate the sale of alcohol for furs.

62. It is also corroborated in the letter sent by Carver to his wife from Michilimackinac in September 1767 and published subsequently in the *Boston Chronicle* (February 22, 1768). In the letter he insists that, with only one exception, he "never received any considerable insult during my voyage" (*Journals of Jonathan Carver and Related Documents*, 200).

63. Carver may not have fully understood the meaning of the Winnebago chief's gesture. One of the supernatural forces recognized by the Winnebagos (whose name for themselves is Ho-Chunk) is the "Water Spirit," and the "Water-Spirit clan" is one of the clans belonging to the "Earth" moiety. See the entry for the Winnebagos in Hoxie, *Encyclopedia of North American Indians*, 682–83. Kinietz refers to the practice by the neighboring Ojibwes of making propitiatory sacrifices to "the spirits of various objects, such as rocks, rapids, and lakes," and he cites a description of one such by Radisson (*The Indians of the Western Great Lakes*, 327–28).

7. TRAVELS OF WILLIAM BARTRAM

1. See Long, *Voyages and Travels of an Indian Interpreter and Trader*. Long's period of travel ran between 1768 and 1788. See Filson, *The Discovery, Settlement and*

Present State of Kentucke. Filson's work includes a ghostwritten "autobiography" of Daniel Boone, the beginning of Boone's career as a legend. For a collection of accounts of settlers moving west from 1775 to 1796, see Eslinger, *Running Mad for Kentucky*. See Smyth, *A Tour in the United States of America*; Weld, *Travels through the States of North America and the Provinces of Upper and Lower Canada*; Baily, *Journal of a Tour in Unsettled Parts of North America*.

2. The full title is *Travels through North and South Carolina, Georgia, East and West Florida, the Cherokee Country, the Extensive Territories of the Muscogulges or Creek Confederacy, and the Country of the Chactaws*.
3. See Cutting, *John and William Bartram, William Byrd II and St. John de Crèvecoeur*, x.
4. See Sayre, "William Bartram and Environmentalism."
5. See Campbell, *The Witness and the Other World*, 2–3, 5–6.
6. On the lives of John and William Bartram, with emphasis on their relationship, see Slaughter, *The Natures of John and William Bartram*. For a reflection on William's life and the father-son nexus, see also Waselkov and Braund, *William Bartram on the Southeastern Indians*, chap 1. The latter work provides a collection of William's writings on Amerindians.
7. See the introduction to the Beehive Press edition of *Travels*, which reproduces several of Fothergill's letters concerning Bartram's trip (xvi–xix). This edition is a facsimile of the first London edition (1792).
8. See Porter, "William Bartram's Travels in the Indian Nations," 434; Cashin, *William Bartram and the American Revolution on the Southern Frontier*, 51.
9. The so-called Creek confederacy was fluid and imprecisely defined and developed as a process over the course of the eighteenth century. On the ethnopolitical history of the Creek "nation," see Hahn, *The Invention of the Creek Nation*.
10. See Saunt, *A New Order of Things*. On the continuities in Creek culture in spite of change, see Braund, *Deerskins and Duffels*, 129–30. For an interesting memoir and travel account involving the Creeks in the period following Bartram's trip, see Milfort, *Chef de guerre chez les Creek* (original title: *Mémoire, ou Coup d'œil sur mes voyages parmi les peuplades sauvages de l'Amérique septentrionale*). On the transformations of Indian societies in the Southeast, see also Axtell, *The Indians' New South*.
11. Ethridge, *Creek Country*, 2.
12. In *William Bartram and the American Revolution on the Southern Frontier*, the historian Edward Cashin traces Bartram's itinerary and attempts to fill in the historical omissions. See also his article "The Real World of Bartram's *Travels*."
13. Tolles, *Meeting House and Counting House*.
14. Hallock and Hoffmann, *William Bartram*, 93.
15. See the introduction to the Beehive Press edition of *Travels*, xv.

16. Clarke, "The Quaker Background of William Bartram's View of Nature," 438–40.
17. See the introduction by Frederick Tolles to Woolman, *Journal of John Woolman and Plea for the Poor*.
18. According to the classicist Richard Gummere, William Bartram's view of nature has much in common with the pantheism of the Stoics: see Cutting, *John and William Bartram, William Byrd II and St. John de Crèvecoeur*, 65. Several scholars have discussed ways in which Bartram's approach to nature can be related to that of other figures of the radical subcurrent of Quakerism, including Anthony Benezet as well as Woolman. While seventeenth-century American Quakers shared to an extent Puritan attitudes toward Nature, in the eighteenth century this group developed a specifically Quaker ecological consciousness. These scholars acknowledge, however, that Bartram's stance was distinct—and original—in relation to theirs. See Kelley, "The Evolution of Quaker Theology and the Unfolding of a Distinctive Quaker Ecological Perspective in Eighteenth-Century America," 244, 248–49; Kelley, "Friends and Nature in America," 261–66; Walters, "The 'Peaceable Disposition' of Animals," 159–60, 162, 165, 167.
19. Regis, *Describing Early America*, 48.
20. William Bartram, "Thoughts on Morality," manuscript fragments without dates in the Bartram Papers, Pennsylvania Historical Society, Philadelphia. The texts of these documents have been transcribed in Hoffmann, "The Construction of William Bartram's Narrative Natural History," appendix C. The page numbers refer to this transcription and are cited parenthetically in the text. The fragments are also reproduced, in an altered form, in Hallock and Hoffmann, *William Bartram*, 348–58.
21. These images have not been mentioned, to my knowledge, in any other discussions of these manuscripts.
22. For further discussion of Bartram's views on animals, see Walters, "The 'Peaceable Disposition' of Animals."
23. For a discussion of this concept and its possible applications, see Löwy, "Le concept d'affinité élective en sciences sociales."
24. Critics have found traces of its influence also in works by P. B. Shelley, Dorothy Wordsworth, Charles Lamb, Emerson, and Thoreau. See Cutting, *John and William Bartram, William Byrd II and St. John de Crèvecoeur*, xi.
25. The influence of *Travels* on Coleridge (and secondarily on William and Dorothy Wordsworth) is studied exhaustively in Lowes, *The Road to Xanadu*. More recently Robin Jarvis discusses several romantic poets—including Coleridge and Wordsworth—in a broader context as readers of travel literature, notably of Bartram's work (*Romantic Readers and Transatlantic Travel*, chap. 4).
26. Charles Bédier and Gilbert Chinard treat in detail the influence of the work

on Chateaubriand (especially in *Les Natchez*). See Cutting, *John and William Bartram, William Byrd II and St. John de Crèvecoeur*, 47, 51.

27. Quoted in Cutting, *John and William Bartram, William Byrd II and St. John de Crèvecoeur*, 45. For Bartram's influence on the romantics, and the romanticism of Bartram, see also 41, 48–50, 52–53, 56–57, 61, 64, 70. Emerson's journals show that he had in fact already discovered Bartram's work years earlier (*Selected Journals*, 487).

28. See Hoffmann, "The Construction of William Bartram's Narrative Natural History," 6–7; Cashin, *William Bartram and the American Revolution on the Southern Frontier*, 64. The report to Fothergill was first published as "Travels in Georgia and Florida, 1773–74: A Report to Dr. John Fothergill" in *Transactions of the American Philosophical Society*. More recently it has been republished in Bartram, *Travels and Other Writings*.

29. This text is transcribed and carefully studied in Nancy Hoffmann's thesis, "The Construction of William Bartram's Narrative Natural History." A part of it (book 1), introduced by Hoffmann, is reproduced in Hallock and Hoffmann, *William Bartram*, 302–39.

30. See Hoffmann's introduction to book 1 of the manuscript, in Hallock and Hoffmann, *William Bartram*, 287.

31. See Hoffmann, "The Construction of William Bartram's Narrative Natural History," 3, 12, 27, 28, 31, 32.

32. Hoffmann, introduction to book 1 of the manuscript, in Hallock and Hoffmann, *William Bartram*, 292.

33. Several later editions introduced further modifications, reducing even more the emotive, philosophical, and social aspects of the text: see Cutting, *John and William Bartram, William Byrd II and St. John de Crèvecoeur*, 56–57.

34. See Hoffmann, "The Construction of William Bartram's Narrative Natural History," 37.

35. The treatment of flora, however, is different. The manuscript draft integrates botanical material into the flow of the narrative, while the published version periodically interrupts the narration with blocks of text giving enumerations and sometimes lengthy descriptions of plant life rather than concentrating them in a separate part of the work. See Hoffmann, "The Construction of William Bartram's Narrative Natural History," 5, 13–15; Hoffmann, introduction to book 1 of the manuscript, in Hallock and Hoffmann, *William Bartram*, 284–85.

36. See Waselkov and Braund, *William Bartram on the Southeastern Indians*, 200. Often the dates given by Bartram are also erroneous.

37. See Cashin, *William Bartram and the American Revolution on the Southern Frontier*, 54; Braund, *Deerskins and Duffels*, 54; Bartram, *Travels of William Bartram*, 53,

69, 291. All further references to *Travels* are to this edition and are cited parenthetically in the text.

38. In some places, though, tensions were less severe and the Indians were mainly concerned to reestablish relations of trade (100, 204).
39. In her study of European-Indian couples and their children in the Southeast Theda Perdue begins by citing a story recounted by Bartram in *Travels* that shows that the traders were not the only ones who gained from these unions, since for matrilineal Creeks and Seminoles—the latter being the tribe involved in Bartram's story—the property of the husband became that of the wife and her extended family (*"Mixed Blood" Indians*, 1–2). The trader might think that he owned some properties, while his wife and their family saw things differently. See also Braund, *Deerskins and Duffels*, 84–85.
40. Bartram also takes this position in an undated manuscript entitled "Some Hints and Observations, concerning the civilization of the Indians, or Aborigines of America." A transcription of it appears in Waselkov and Braund, *William Bartram on the Southeastern Indians*, and Hallock and Hoffmann, *William Bartram*.
41. Hallock, "'On the Borders of a New World,'" 112.
42. Iannini, *Fatal Revolutions*, 199.
43. In the introduction to the "Some Hints and Observations" manuscript in Hallock and Hoffmann, *William Bartram*, Kathryn Holland Braund comments that Bartram's "obvious desire to find a peaceful solution to the Indian problem blinded him to the flaws inherent in the belief that Native peoples would willingly abandon their basic cultural tenets" (363). *Travels* also makes some accommodation with the prevailing ethos in regard to slavery. Although Bartram dedicated the work to Thomas Mifflin, a Quaker leader known for his antislavery stance, and although he had clearly been incapable of acting as a slave master during his brief tenure as a planter, he never openly criticizes the system of slavery in his book, limiting himself to praise of one planter for his "good" treatment of his bondservants (255–57). Sometime in the late 1780s or 1790s, however, Bartram wrote a strong antislavery statement addressed to his countrymen, apparently meant to be published, though it never was. For the manuscript transcription and commentary on it, see Hallock and Hoffmann, *William Bartram*, 372–80.
44. The only incidents, relatively rare, that could be characterized as adventures in the usual sense are dangerous encounters with animals, particularly alligators (see e.g., 120).
45. See Cashin, "The Real World of Bartram's *Travels*," 6. Bartram also describes the meeting with "Cowkeeper" in a letter to his father dated March 27, 1775 (Hallock and Hoffmann, *William Bartram*, 112).
46. See also 295, where the author tells of his meeting with the "grand chief" of the

Cherokees, Ata-cul-culla. On this occasion Bartram identifies himself as being of the "tribe" of William Penn.

47. On the sexual freedom of unmarried Cherokee women, see Perdue, *Cherokee Women*, 56.
48. In 1789 Bartram wrote up another synthesis, independently of *Travels*, in the form of answers to written questions submitted to him by the naturalist Benjamin Barton Smith. The text was published for the first time only in 1853, in the *Transactions of the American Ethnological Society* (3, no. 1, 1–81). It has been republished more recently in Waselkov and Braund, *William Bartram on the Southeastern Indians*, and Bartram, *Travels and Other Writings*.
49. For a study that emphasizes the continuing influence of these precontact cultures on postcontact Creek society, see Wesson, *Households and Hegemony*.
50. Cf. *Observations on the Creek and Cherokee Indians*, 1: "History and Traditions of the Muscogulges"; 2: "Probable Origins and Relations" (Bartram, *Travels and Other Writings*, 527–32).
51. Cf. *Observations on the Creek and Cherokee Indians*, 7: "Physical Characteristics," (Bartram, *Travels and Other Writings*, 541–43). Anglo-American observers often noticed similar traits in other Indian groups. For the example of the Shawnees, see Calloway, *The Shawnees and the War for America*, 18–19.
52. It is interesting to compare this passage with the manuscript version. After "untutored savages" there is an additional adjective, "uncivilized," and in place of the following sentences a segment of text that has been heavily crossed out and is illegible. If the crossed-out words correspond to the sentences I have quoted in the published version, it seems plausible that the author thought they were problematic, since they so far-reachingly question received ideas of the period. Perhaps after first writing them Bartram crossed them out, but in the end again changed his mind and reinstated them. See Hoffmann, "The Construction of William Bartram's Narrative Natural History," 157.
53. Weaver, "From I-Hermeneutics to We-Hermeneutics," 20.
54. See part 4, chap. 2: "On Their Government and Civil Society."
55. On male and female roles and the position of the "mico" in Creek society, see Braund, *Deerskins and Duffels*, 14, 19–20, 22–23.
56. Cf. *Observations on the Creek and Cherokee Indians*, 10: "Tenure of Lands and Property," (Bartram, *Travels and Other Writings*, 548–53). On Creek property relations and how they were partially changed under white influence, see Braund, *Deerskins and Duffels*, 21, 130.
57. In the manuscript version of the passage involving warfare on page 183, Bartram included a sentence that was not retained in the published work: "I profess myself of the Christian Sect of the People called Quakers, & consequently am against

War and violence, in any form or maner whatever." Thus in the manuscript the author seems to have realized that he was appearing to be relatively understanding with regard to Indian warfare practices and wished to make clear his own point of view on the subject. See Hoffmann, "The Construction of William Bartram's Narrative Natural History," 268.

58. An exception to the rule is the author's lack of enthusiasm for the Indians' instrumental music (395–96).
59. As I have emphasized, though, this position on Indian versus European civilization was so marginal that Bartram inevitably was led to doubt his own perceptions and in some instances to adopt, tentatively, partially, or temporarily, the hegemonic perspective. On his continuing hesitation on the issue of the confrontation of the two cultures, see Waselkov and Braund, *William Bartram and the Southeastern Indians*, 202–4.
60. Although Bartram does not mention it in this passage, it should also be noted that Indian economic relations were such that losing in gambling did not have the disastrous effects that it often did in European societies. On gambling in Creek society, see Braund, *Deerskins and Duffels*, 17.
61. "Some Hints and Observations," quoted in Cashin, *William Bartram and the American Revolution on the Southern Frontier*, 4, 248.
62. Bartram's antislavery tract (which also remained in manuscript) dates from the same period. See Cashin, *William Bartram and the American Revolution on the Southern Frontier*, 249–50.
63. Cashin, *William Bartram and the American Revolution on the Southern Frontier*, 66.
64. Quoted in Cashin, *William Bartram and the American Revolution on the Southern Frontier*, 248–49.
65. See Waselkov and Braund, *William Bartram on the Southeastern Indians*, 188–90.
66. Hallock, "On the Borders of a New World," 130.

8. FUR TRADERS

1. The literature of research on the fur trade is far too vast to allow for anything other than a few cursory bibliographical indications. See, among others, the acts of a series of international conferences on the fur trade, running from the first, in 1965, to the seventh in 1995: Fiske et al., *New Faces of the Fur Trade*. For research and debates up to the mid-1980s, see Peterson and Anfinson, "The Indian and the Fur Trade." For the most recent period, see especially Sleeper-Smith, *Rethinking the Fur Trade*; Podruchny and Peers, *Gathering Places*.
2. See Frank, *Creeks and Southerners*.
3. See Havard and Vidal, *Histoire de l'Amérique française*, 102–46. On the motivations of the explorers, see esp. 103–4, 106, 120, 135, 145.

4. See White, *The Middle Ground*, chap. 3, esp. 97–98, 115.
5. For a thorough study of the presence of Scots as fur traders and explorers in the American Northwest, see Szasz, *Scots in the North American West*.
6. On the career of Mackenzie in the context of the British fur trade and exploration of the American Northwest, see Daniells, *Alexander Mackenzie and the North West*; Gough, *First across the Continent*; Newman, *Caesars of the Wilderness*, vol. 2; Woollacott, *Mackenzie and His Voyageurs*. For a recent, full-length biography of Pond, see Chapin, *Freshwater Passages*.
7. Smith, *Alexander Mackenzie, Explorer*, 154.
8. For example, Vail, *The Magnificent Adventures of Alexander Mackenzie*; Paton, *Adventuring with Boldness*.
9. Smith, *Alexander Mackenzie, Explorer*, 2. Roy Daniells also acknowledges that Mackenzie's explorations were only an "interlude" in a career in trade; see Mackenzie, *Voyages from Montreal on the River St. Laurence through the Continent of North America to the Frozen and Pacific Oceans*, ed. R. Daniells, vii.
10. Gough, *First across the Continent*, 3, 5. See also 108–9.
11. Hayes, *First Crossing*, 7.
12. Mackenzie, *Alexander Mackenzie's Voyage to the Pacific Ocean in 1793*, xxvii.
13. For a full bibliography of editions, see Mackenzie, *The Journals and Letters of Sir Alexander Mackenzie*.
14. Mackenzie, *Voyages*, Radisson Society edition, 4. The full title of the work is *Voyages from Montreal on the River St. Laurence through the Continent of North America to the Frozen and Pacific Oceans in the Years 1789 and 1793*. All subsequent references to *Voyages* are to this edition and are cited parenthetically in the text.
15. Harold Hickerson speaks of Indians involved in the fur trade as "a kind of vast forest proletariat" ("Fur Trade Colonialism and the North American Indians," 39).
16. Smith, *Alexander Mackenzie, Explorer*, 63.
17. Venema, "'He Never Harmed an Indian.'"
18. On the participation of the French on British expeditions after the Conquest, see Brouillette, *La Pénétration du continent américain par les Canadiens français*. For an excellent recent study of the *voyageurs* from an ethnological standpoint, see Podruchny, *Making the Voyageur World*.
19. See Gough, *First across the Continent*, 79–80; *Dictionary of Canadian Biography*, under "Laurent Leroux." Leroux subsequently left the fur trade to pursue various other business activities, including real estate investment, becoming one of the wealthier Canadian businessmen in the early nineteenth century.
20. On this North West Company trader, see *Dictionary of Canadian Biography*, under "Alexander MacKay" (he sometimes spelled his name McKay). At the beginning of the nineteenth century MacKay became a partner and then shareholder in the

company. He later joined the Pacific Fur Company and took part in the expedition that founded Astoria.

21. For the names, profiles, and later life of several of Mackenzie's crew, see Mackenzie, *First Man West*, 307.
22. The "English Chief" is one of two Indians who are actually named in Mackenzie's text; all the others remain anonymous. In both cases the names are those given them by whites. See Duchemin, "'A Parcel of Whelps,'" 70. On the "English Chief," who worked with the Hudson's Bay Company as a trading chief before and after collaborating with the North West Company, see *Dictionary of Canadian Biography*, under his native name, "Aw-Gee-Nah."
23. Presumably one of the Dene bands called "Slave" or "Slavey" Indians, living near Great Slave Lake.
24. The meeting occurs when Mackenzie first arrives at the place at which he is to winter before continuing on his exploratory probe. The natives are presumably "Beaver" Indians, a band the author discusses further on.
25. Duchemin, "'A Parcel of Whelps,'" 65. See also 63–64.
26. See MacLaren, "Alexander Mackenzie and the Landscapes of Commerce."
27. In his review essay of several recent studies of the early West, Allan Taylor points out that into the 1790s "most of North America remained Indian country" ("Continental Crossings, 183). More recently still, a number of important monographs have shown in detail how effective Indian agency and control operated in specific areas: Du Val, *The Native Ground* (the Arkansas Valley); Hämäläinen, *The Comanche Empire* (New Mexico and the Southwest); Witgen, *An Infinity of Nations* (Great Lakes and upper Mississippi Valley).
28. See Mapp, *The Elusive West and the Contest for Empire*, esp. 6–17; Berthier-Foglar, "À l'Ouest de la Louisiane," esp. 44–47. On the element of fantasy in conceptions of the West in the period, see Ronda, "Dreams and Discoveries," 148, and his introduction to the reedition of Nasatir, *Before Lewis and Clark*, xx–xxi.
29. See Taylor, "Continental Crossings," 183–84; Wood and Thiessen, *Early Fur Trade on the Northern Plains*, 5–6. For an excellent, chapter-length overview of the history of the Plains in the period concerned, see Taylor, *American Colonies*, chap. 17. For a broad, book-length history of the area from prehistoric times to 1800, see Colin Calloway's magisterial *One Vast Winter Count*.
30. On the history of eighteenth-century travel west of the Mississippi, especially on the Missouri River, see Nasatir's long introductory essay in *Before Lewis and Clark*.
31. See Wood and Thiessen, *Early Fur Trade on the Northern Plains*, 3.
32. Le Page du Pratz's three-volume *Histoire de la Louisiane* (1758) adopts the genre of colonial history rather than the travel account. Though it is mainly concerned

with areas east of and along the Mississippi, it does bring in several narratives of western journeys. In particular it recounts a purported expedition by the author himself onto the Plains, and the voyage of a Yazoo Indian in quest of his people's origins, all the way to the Pacific. The veracity of these accounts, however, remains open to question. On Le Page du Pratz and his work, with translations from *Histoire de la Louisiane*, see Gordon Sayre's webpage devoted to him: *Antoine-Simon Le Page du Pratz: The History of Louisiana / L'Histoire de la Louisiane (1758)*, http://darkwing.uoregon.edu/~gsayre/LPDP.html.

33. For an annotated bibliography of French accounts before the fall of New France, see Hubach, *Early Midwestern Travel Narratives*, chap. 2.
34. On the La Verandrye family and the Mandans, see Fenn, *Encounters at the Heart of the World*.
35. Excerpts from the journals of La Harpe and Bourgmont appear in Margry, *Découvertes et Établissements des Français dans l'Ouest et dans le Sud de l'Amérique Septentrionale*, vol. 6. Several pages of Bourgmont's earlier *Exacte Description de la Louisiane* very briefly describe Indian groups along and around the Missouri, drawing on a previous expedition in 1714. See the *American Journeys* website, http://www.americanjourneys.org/aj-093/. The full texts of the La Vérandrye accounts are in Burpee, *Journals and Letters of Pierre Gaultier de Varennes de la Vérendrye and His Sons*. A more recent edition of selected passages, with commentary, is Combet, *In Search of the Western Sea*.
36. On the question of the location of the Sioux settlement, see Carver, *The Journals of Jonathan Carver and Related Documents*, 16–17.
37. For a modern edition of the text, see Pond, "The Narrative of Peter Pond."
38. See Pond, "The Narrative of Peter Pond," 52–59.
39. The text of the original diary of the trip has been published in Wood and Thiessen, *Early Fur Trade on the Northern Plains*, 96–128. Thompson's later memoir was first published posthumously, in 1916, as Thompson, *David Thompson's Narrative of His Explorations in Western America*. The ethnological comments are in chap. 14. For a modern scholarly edition of Thompson's complete works, see Thompson, *The Writings of David Thompson*.
40. A facsimile edition of Decalves's work, along with other "apocryphal" accounts, was issued by Ye Galleon Press in 1996. For reference to another fictitious travel account published several years after Decalves's, see Wood and Thiessen, *Early Fur Trade on the Northern Plains*, 30. It might be pointed out also that Jonathan Swift chose to locate the Brobdingnag of *Gulliver's Travels* (1726) on the Pacific northwest coast, then unknown and therefore available for fantasy. For an annotated bibliography of western travel literature in the second half of the eighteenth century, see Hubach, *Early Midwestern Travel Narratives*, chaps 4–6.

41. See Trudeau, *Voyage sur le Haut-Missouri*. The text is accompanied by a CD-ROM that presents its multiple versions.
42. On Trudeau's life, see Trudeau, *Voyage sur le Haut-Missouri*, introduction by Fernand Grenier, 22–29.
43. When Trudeau's problems became apparent to the company, they sent out two other expeditions, which overlapped with Trudeau's. One collapsed almost immediately, while the other met with only a little more success than Trudeau's. The latter, carried out by two British men, James McKay and John Evans, gave rise to a journal account as well, but one much less extensive and significant than Trudeau's. McKay had in fact already visited the Mandans in 1787. For relevant excerpts from McKay's journals, see Nasatir, *Before Lewis and Clark*, 1:354–64, 2:490–99.
44. Trudeau, *Voyage sur le Haut-Missouri*, 28.
45. This edition is based on all of the extant manuscripts, one integral and two fragmentary. The book itself synthesizes them and modernizes the French minimally, while the attached CD-ROM collates the different original versions. Since the manuscript variations have no real significance for my commentary, I will refer only to the book version. All translations are mine. A complete, edited English translation of Trudeau's account is in press: Trudeau, *A Fur Trader on the Upper Missouri*. See the annotated bibliography appended to *Voyage sur le Haut-Missouri*; Hubach, *Early Midwestern Travel Narratives*, 33. Several fragments in English translation were included by Nasatir in *Before Lewis and Clark*.
46. François-Marie Perrin du Lac, *Voyage dans les deux Louisianes et chez les nations sauvages du Missouri, par les Etats-Unis, l'Ohio et les Provinces qui le bordent, en 1801, 1802 et 1803*, published in 1805.
47. Trudeau, *Voyage sur le Haut-Missouri*, 49–50. Hereafter citations from Trudeau's account are parenthetical in the text.
48. Lahontan, *Œuvres complètes*, 1:410: "plus je montois la Rivière, plus les Sauvages me paroissoient raisonnables." Peter H. Wood has hypothesized that the river Lahontan traveled up was in fact the Missouri—which would make it the same as Trudeau's—rather than the Minnesota, as has often been supposed; see Wood, "The Mysterious 1688 Journey of M. Lahontan." Elizabeth Fenn finds Wood's proposition persuasive (*Encounters at the Heart of the World*, 41–47). If Wood's identification of the river is correct, Lahontan would have visited the Arikaras and the Mandans more than a century before Trudeau's trip.

EPILOGUE

1. Appleby, *Inheriting the Revolution*, 56. The concept of the nation as an "imagined community" is elaborated by Benedict Anderson in *Imagined Communities*.

2. See Pike, *The Expeditions of Zebulon Montgomery Pike*.
3. On the transformations of Jemison's text over the course of the nineteenth century, see Namias, *White Captives*, chap. 5.
4. These editions are reproduced, respectively, in *The Garland Library of Narratives of North American Indian Captives*, vol. 12, and *Popular Culture in America, 1800–1925*.
5. The subtitle of the first edition does, however, include the phrase "with an account of the barbarous execution of Col. Crawford."
6. Published in Tours by A. Mame et Cie. They include, in addition to the excerpts, a "historical note" on the discovery and exploration of the New World and an introduction on Carver. For a bibliography of abridged editions of Carver's book in several languages, see Carver, *The Journals of Jonathan Carver*, 229–31.
7. For example, *Sketches of America*, by Henry Bradshaw Fearon, was published in London in 1818. Its long subtitle clearly summarizes its content: *A narrative of a journey of five thousand miles through the eastern and western states of America: containing in eight reports addressed to the thirty-nine English families by whom the author was deputed, in June 1817, to ascertain whether any, and what part of the United States would be suitable for their residence*. See the facsimile edition.
8. Her son, the novelist Anthony Trollope, visited the United States in 1861–62 and on his return published the voluminous *North America*, in two volumes.
9. On European visitors, see Billington, *Land of Savagery, Land of Promise*; Rose, *Unspeakable Awfulness*. On British visitors, see DeVine, *Nineteenth-Century British Travelers in the New World*. On French visitors, see Jullien, *Récits du Nouveau Monde*.
10. McKenney was superintendant of Indian affairs under the Monroe presidency. Ogden, a fur trader, bases his work on his experiences in and around the Rocky Mountains.
11. See, in particular, Hunter, *Memoirs of a Captivity among the Indians of North America* (London, 1824; Hunter lived with Kansas and Osage Indians); Lehmann, *Nine Years among the Indians, 1870–79* (Lehmann lived with Apaches and Comanches).
12. Derounian-Stodola and Levernier, *The Indian Captivity Narrative*, 31–37.
13. For a study that shows how European travelers in the period—both aristocrats and those who aspired to nobility—saw the Indian as a noble fellow figure, see Liebersohn, *Aristocratic Encounters*.
14. See *Artist Explorers of the 1830s*; Hartmann, *George Catlin und Balduin Möllhausen*; Hollmann, *Five Artists of the Old West*. One artist who, like Catlin, produced a travel account as well as artwork was Rudolph Friederich Kurz, *Journal of Rudolph Friederich Kurz*. Another was Paul Kane, a Toronto painter who traveled mainly among Canadian Indians. There are significant parallels between his career and the career of Catlin, by whom he was directly inspired;

see Kane, *Paul Kane's Frontier, including Wanderings of an Artist among the Indians of North America*, 13–14.
15. See Wied, *Travels in the Interior of North America during the years 1832–1834* (illustrations by Karl Bodmer).
16. Morgan, *The Indian Journals*.
17. See Lepore, *The Name of War*, chap. 8.
18. On Indian writing and publication to the end of the eighteenth century, see Lopenzina, *Red Ink*; in the nineteenth century: Konkle, *Writing Indian Nations*; and more generally: Jaskoski, *Early Native American Writing*; Warrior, *The People and the Word*; Round, *Removable Type*. In Gerald Vizenor's edited volume *Survivance: Narratives of Native Presence*, Arnold Krupat treats William Apess as an early, exemplary "storier of survivance" (chap. 6), and in his introductory essay Vizenor pays homage to the tradition of native journalism begun by Boudinot. In *The People and the Word*, Robert Warrior contends that although Apess "embraced a foreign religious tradition," it had "arguably become Pequot," and although he used "Western writing and the technology of the book . . . he was shaped by his experiences in the Native world of New England" (183).
19. According to a recent biography of Catlin, there is no independent documentation, outside of Catlin's own writings and iconography, to confirm that he in fact made any of these trips. While their authenticity cannot be entirely ruled out, there are substantial reasons to think that Catlin's presentation of them is partially or wholly fictional; see Eisler, *The Red Man's Bones*, 371–87.
20. On the European period of Catlin's career, see Christopher Mulvey, "George Catlin in Europe," in Gurney and Heyman, *George Catlin and His Indian Gallery*. For Catlin's life in the context of the artistic, intellectual, and sociopolitical milieu of the period, see Dippie, *Catlin and His Contemporaries*.
21. See for example McCracken, *George Catlin and the Old Frontier*.
22. The two editions are, respectively, Catlin, *Letters and Notes on the Manners, Customs, and Conditions of the North American Indians, Written during Eight Years' Travel (1832–1839) amongst the Wildest Tribes of Indians in North America* (Dover, 1973); and Catlin, *Letters and Notes on the North American Indians* (Potter, 1975).
23. Millichap, *George Catlin*; Truettner, *The Natural Man Observed*. Truettner's excellent, comprehensive treatment of Catlin's life and work laid the groundwork for later developments.
24. Gurney and Heyman, *George Catlin and His Indian Gallery*. The shortened, rearranged Penguin edition, retitled *North American Indians*, was edited by Peter Matthiessen; originally published in 1989, it was reissued in 1996 and 2004. In the same period a German-language edition also appeared: Catlin, *Die Indianer Nordamerikas*.

25. Branch, *Reading the Roots*; McKibben, *American Earth*.
26. Articles: John, "Cultural Nationalism, Westward Expansion and the Production of Imperial Landscape"; John, "Benevolent Imperialism." Chapters of books: "With a Colt, a Brush, and a Pen: George Catlin's Preservation of the Indian," in Cabanas, *The Cultural "Other" in Nineteenth-Century Travel Narratives*; "George Catlin, Te-ho-pe-nee Wash-ee," in Bellin, *Medicine Bundle*. Monograph: Hausdoerffer, *Catlin's Lament*. For discussion of the kind of criticism of Catlin that has been leveled by Native Americans themselves, see the introduction to Gurney and Heyman, *George Catlin and His Indian Gallery*, by the director of the National Museum of the American Indian, W. Richard West, himself a Cheyenne Arapaho.
27. Catlin's later travel accounts are *Notes of eight years' travel and residence in Europe with his North American Indian collection* (London, 1848); *Life amongst the Indians: A book for youth* (New York, 1857); *Last Rambles amongst the Indians of the Rocky Mountains and the Andes* (New York, 1867). None of these has been republished in its entirety in a modern edition. Short excerpts of the last two, rearranged thematically, have been published as *George Catlin: Episodes from Life among the Indians and Last Rambles*.
28. For a map that traces Catlin's western itineraries between 1832 and 1836, see Dippie, *Catlin and His Contemporaries*, 23.
29. For this background of conflict with Indians in the 1830s, see Osborn, *The Wild Frontier*, 180–83; Yenne, *Indian Wars*, 27–38; Nunnally, *American Indian Wars*, 72–82; Wooster, *The American Military Frontiers*, 78–95.
30. Cabanas, *The Cultural "Other" in Nineteenth-Century Travel Narratives*, 172.
31. See Wooster, *The American Military Frontiers*, 81. In *Catlin's Lament* (15–16), John Hausdoerffer indicates that it was because Catlin had "alienated" the American Fur Company by his criticisms of traders' activities in lectures and newspaper accounts after 1832 that he was obliged to attach himself to a military expedition in 1834.
32. See the introduction to the Dover edition of *Letters and Notes* by Marjorie Halpin, xi.
33. Catlin, *Letters and Notes* (Dover edition), 1:1. All subsequent references are to this edition and are cited parenthetically in the text.
34. See Bellin, *Medicine Bundle*, 22; Hausdoerffer, *Catlin's Lament*, 15; John, "Cultural Nationalism," 186.
35. This Mandan chief likewise impressed Maximilian von Wied and his accompanying artist, Karl Bodmer, who also painted Four Bears several times. Four Bears carefully observed the work of both Catlin and Bodmer and came to use some of their methods in his hide drawings. On these, and for the text of his "death speech," in which he expresses bitter disillusionment with whites, see Calloway, *Our Hearts Fell to the Ground*, chap. 4.

36. As used by Catlin, this term (see e.g., 1:60, 2:163) may denote excellence or typicality, or may possibly suggest identification with classical antiquity.
37. *Wi-Jun-Jon, Pigeon's Egg Head (The Light) Going to and Returning from Washington*, 1837, oil, Smithsonian. The line drawing of this painting that appeared in *Letters and Notes*, which I have included in the illustrations, has a slightly different title (*Wi-jun-jon, Pigeon's Egg Head, going to and returning from Washington*). Catlin had earlier painted a portrait of the same Assiniboine Indian as "a distinguished warrior" (1831, oil, Smithsonian: see Gurney and Heyman, *George Catlin and His Indian Gallery*, 201), and included it in the form of a line drawing in *Letters and Notes*. The text of the travel account discusses him at 1:56–57, 67.
38. Miguel Cabanas comments that, more generally, Catlin "makes the Indian into an aesthetic object to be consumed by Anglo-American and European audiences" (*The Cultural "Other" in Nineteenth-Century Travel Narratives*, 175).
39. As in the frontispiece of *Letters and Notes*.
40. Cabanas also emphasizes this aspect of *Letters and Notes*, claiming that the author's "narcissistic character controls the narrative" (*The Cultural "Other" in Nineteenth-Century Travel Narratives*, 173). See also 186.
41. Catlin was also fascinated by the artistry of calumets, made an extensive collection of them during his excursions, and later in life prepared a monograph on Indian pipes, which is held by the British Museum. It has been published, along with the text of a letter in which Catlin describes his trip to the quarry and confrontation with the Sioux; see Ewers, *Indian Art in Pipestone*. In *Medicine Bundle* (57), Joshua Bellin asserts that this is one of the rare instances in which Catlin portrays himself as an interloper in Indian territory. He does, however, acknowledge in other passages the distrust and hostility that Indians sometimes exhibited toward him.
42. For a description and discussion of the Okipa ceremony, which draws largely on Catlin as well as on other accounts, see Fenn, *Encounters at the Heart of the World*, 120–30.
43. See the "handbill advertisement for Catlin's London lecture titled 'Valley of the Mississippi,' April, 1850, Archives of American Art, Washington DC," in Gurney and Heyman, *George Catlin and His Indian Gallery*, 77.
44. Hausdoerffer comments that Catlin "is on the front lines of Manifest Destiny" in this situation but assumes his own innocence (*Catlin's Lament*, 66; see also 82).
45. See *Catlin's Lament*, chap. 4, esp. 131, 1n. Hausdoerffer's understanding of the roots of Catlin's contradictions is, however, somewhat different from my own.
46. See Lindfors, "Ethnological Show Business"; Altick, *The Shows of London*, 275–81. For a detailed discussion of Catlin's dealings with the Indians in his shows, with a focus on the Iowas, see Herring, "Selling the 'Noble Savage' Myth." See

also Mulvey, "Among the Sag-a-noshes." For two recent discussions that highlight how some of the natives involved in these performances, and others of the same type, reacted, resisted, and expressed their own perspectives, see Magubane, "Ethnographic Showcases as Sites of Knowledge Production and Indigenous Resistance"; Weaver, *The Red Atlantic*, 198–206.

47. Lindfors, "Ethnological Show Business," 207.
48. Reddin, *Wild West Shows*; see also Moses, *Wild West Shows and the Images of American Indians*, esp. introduction and chap. 1.
49. Joshua Bellin comments that "*Letters and Notes* seems to have been worked up by Catlin as both marquee and script for his traveling show" (*Medicine Bundle*, 22).
50. Altick, *The Shows of London*, 276.
51. See Reddin, *Wild West Shows*, 8.
52. See Berlo, "Introduction."
53. On these aspects of American tourism, see Gassan, *The Birth of American Tourism*, introduction; Brown, *Inventing New England*, chap. 1; Sears, *Sacred Places*, introduction.
54. See Smith, *River of Dreams*, chap. 3; Fifer, *American Progress*, introduction; Shaffer, *See America First*, introduction.
55. The first American "Fashionable Tour," sometimes also referred to as the "American Grand Tour," was the Hudson Valley, Saratoga Springs, Niagara Falls circuit.
56. One commentator points up Catlin's leading role, especially as a painter of landscape, in "[offering] a vision of the West that was exotic and inviting," to replace the prevailing earlier "Great American Desert" (Hyde, *An American Vision*, 29). See also Hyde's history of the West in the first six decades of the nineteenth-century: *Empires, Nations, and Families*.
57. See Eisler, *The Red Man's Bones*, 371.

CONCLUSION

1. Hoxie et al., *American Nations*.

BIBLIOGRAPHY

This bibliography is divided into two sections: primary sources and secondary sources. I include in the primary sources section publications of writings from the periods studied in this book. Included there are both original editions and later reprints and new editions, and collections of texts as well as single works. I have also included in the primary sources section bibliographies of texts from the periods under study. The secondary sources section, on the other hand, lists publications referenced in my book that analyze or provide context for understanding the various aspects of its subject matter.

PRIMARY SOURCES

Adair, James. *Adair's History of the American Indians.* 1775. Ed. Samuel C. Cole. New York: Promontory Press, 1930.

———. *The History of the American Indians.* Ed. Kathryn E. Holland Braund. Tuscaloosa: University of Alabama Press, 2005.

Axtell, James, ed. *The Indian Peoples of Eastern America: A Documentary History of the Sexes.* Oxford: Oxford University Press, 1981.

Baily, Francis. *Journal of a Tour in Unsettled Parts of North America in 1796 and 1797.* London: Baily Brothers, 1856.

Bartram, John, Lewis Evans, and Conrad Weiser. *A Journey from Pennsylvania to Onondaga in 1743.* Barre MA: Imprint Society, 1973.

Bartram, William. "Observations on the Creek and Cherokee Indians, 1789." Ed. Ephraim G. Squier. *Transactions of the American Ethnological Society* 3, part 1 (1853): 1–81.

———. "Thoughts on Morality." Bartram Papers. Vol. 1, folders 81, 83. Pennsylvania Historical Society, Philadelphia.

———. *Travels and Other Writings*. Ed. Thomas P. Slaughter. New York: Library of America, 1996.

———. "Travels in Georgia and Florida, 1773–74: A Report to Dr. John Fothergill." Ed. Francis Harper. *Transactions of the American Philosophical Society*, new series, 33, part 2 (November 1943): 134–71.

———. *Travels of William Bartram*. Facsimile of 1928 edition. New York: Penguin, 1988.

———. *Travels through North and South Carolina, Georgia, East and West Florida*. 1792. Facsimile edition. Savannah GA: Beehive Press, 1973.

Bayard, Ferdinand. *Voyage dans l'intérieur des Etats-Unis, à Bath, Winchester, dans la vallée de Shenandoha*. 2nd edition. Paris: Batilliot, 1798.

Beverley, Robert. *The History and Present State of Virginia*. 1722. Revised edition. Chapel Hill: University of North Carolina Press, 1979.

Birket, James. *Some Cursory Remarks Made by James Birket in His Voyage to North America 1750–1751*. New Haven CT: Yale University Press, 1916.

Brackenridge, Hugh Henry. *A Hugh Henry Brackenridge Reader, 1770–1815*. Ed. Daniel Marder. Pittsburgh PA: University of Pittsburgh Press, 1970.

———, ed. *Indian Atrocities: Narratives of the perils and sufferings of Dr. Knight and John Slover, among the Indians during the revolutionary war*. 1843. In *Indian Atrocities: Captivities of Knight and Slover*. New York: Garland, 1978.

———, ed. *Indian Atrocities: Narratives of the perils and sufferings of Dr. Knight and John Slover, among the Indians during the revolutionary war*. 1867. In *Popular Culture in America, 1800–1925: Captivity Tales*. New York: Arno Press, 1974.

———, ed. *Narratives of a Late Expedition against the Indians*. 1783. In *Indian Atrocities: Captivities of Knight and Slover*. New York: Garland, 1978.

Branch Michael P., ed. *Reading the Roots: American Nature Writing before Walden*. Athens: University of Georgia Press, 2004.

Brissot de Warville, Jacques-Pierre. *A Critical Examination of the Marquis de Chastellux's Travels*. Philadelphia: Joseph James, 1788.

———. *Nouveau voyage dans les Etats-Unis de l'Amérique septentrionale, fait en 1788*. Paris: Buisson, 1791.

Burpee, Lawrence J., ed. *Journals and Letters of Pierre Gaultier de Varennes de la Vérendrye and His Sons*. Toronto: Champlain Society, 1927.

Byrd, William. *The Prose Works of William Byrd of Westover*. Ed. L. B. Wright. Cambridge MA: Harvard University Press, 1966.

Calloway, Colin G., ed. *Dawnland Encounters: Indians and Europeans in Northern New England*. Hanover NH: University Press of New England, 1991.

———, ed. *Our Hearts Fell to the Ground: Plains Indian Views of How the West Was Lost*. Boston: Bedford/St. Martin's, 1996.

———, ed. *The World Turned Upside Down: Indian Voices from Early America*. Boston: Bedford/St. Martin's, 1994.

Carter, Landon. *The Diary of Colonel Landon Carter of Sabine Hall, 1752–1778*. Ed. J. P. Greene. Richmond: Virginia Historical Society, 1987.

Carver, Jonathan. *Jonathan Carver's Travels through America 1766–1768: An Eighteenth-Century Explorer's Account of Uncharted America*. Ed. Norman Gelb. New York: John Wiley & Sons, 1993.

———. *The Journals of Jonathan Carver and Related Documents, 1766–1770*. Ed. John Parker. St Paul: Minnesota Historical Society Press, 1976.

———. *Travels through the Interior Parts of North America, in the Years 1766, 1767, and 1768*. Facsimile of 3rd edition. Minneapolis MN: Ross and Haines, 1956.

Catlin, George. *Die Indianer Nordamerikas: Abenteuer und Schicksale*. Stuttgart: Erdmann, 1994.

———. *George Catlin: Episodes from Life among the Indians and Last Rambles*. Ed. Marvin C. Ross. Civilization of the American Indian Series. Norman: University of Oklahoma Press, 1959.

———. *Letters and Notes on the Manners, Customs, and Conditions of the North American Indians, Written during Eight Years' Travel (1832–1839) amongst the Wildest Tribes of Indians in North America*. 2 vols. New York: Dover, 1973.

———. *Letters and Notes on the North American Indians*. Ed. Michael Macdonald Mooney. New York: Charles N. Potter, 1975.

———. *North American Indians*. Ed. Peter Matthiessen. New York: Penguin, 2004.

Charlevoix, François-Xavier de. *Charlevoix (1682–1761)*. Ed. Léon Pouliot. Montreal: Fides, 1959.

———. *History and General Description of New France*. 6 vols. Chicago: Loyola University Press, 1962.

———. *Journal d'un voyage fait par ordre du roi dans l'Amérique septentrionale*. 2 vols. Ed. Pierre Berthiaume. Montreal: Presses de l'Université de Montréal, Bibliothèque du Nouveau Monde, 1994.

Chastellux, Marquis de. *Voyages de M. le marquis de Chastellux dans l'Amérique Septentrionale: Dans les années 1780, 1781 et 1782*. Paris: Chez Prault, 1786.

Chateaubriand, François-René de. "Voyage en Amérique." In *Œuvres romanesques et voyages*. Paris: Gallimard, 1969.

Colden, Cadwallader. *The History of the Five Indian Nations Depending on the Province of New-York in America*. Ithaca NY: Cornell University Press, 1958.

Cole, T. D., ed. *Travels in the Old South: A Bibliography*. 2 vols. Norman: University of Oklahoma Press, 1956.

Combet, Denis. *In Search of the Western Sea: Selected Journals of La Vérendrye. À la recherche de la mer de l'Ouest: Mémoires choisis de La Vérendrye*. Winnipeg: Great Plains/Éditions du Blé, 2001.

Crèvecoeur, St. John de. *Crèvecoeur's Eighteenth-Century Travels in Pennsylvania and New York*. Ed. Percy G. Adams. Lexington: University of Kentucky Press, 1961.

———. *Journey into Northern Pennsylvania and the State of New York*. Ed. Clarissa S. Bostelmann. Ann Arbor: University of Michigan Press, 1964.

———. *Letters from an American Farmer*. New York: Signet, 1963.

———. *Letters from an American Farmer and Other Essays*. Ed. Dennis D. Moore. Cambridge MA: Harvard University Press, 2013.

———. *Lettres d'un cultivateur américain*. Geneva, Switzerland: Slatkine Reprints, 1979.

———. "Mémoire sur la région située à l'ouest des Montagnes d'Alleghany." 84 pp. Marine, 3JJ274,32. Archives Nationales, Paris.

———. *More Letters from the American Farmer: An Edition of the Essays in English Left Unpublished by Crèvecoeur*. Ed. Dennis D. Moore. Athens: University of Georgia Press, 1995.

———. *Sketches of Eighteenth Century America: More "Letters from an American Farmer."* Ed. Henry L. Bourdin, Ralph H. Gabriel, and Stanley T. Williams. New Haven CT: Yale University Press, 1925.

———. *Voyage dans la Haute Pensylvanie et dans l'Etat de New-York depuis l'année 1785 jusqu'en 1798*. Ed. Françoise Plet. Saint-Denis: Presses Universitaires de Vincennes and XYZ éditeur, 2002.

———. *Voyage dans la haute Pensylvanie et dans l'état de New-York, par un membre adoptif de la nation Onéida*. 3 vols. Paris: Maradon, 1801.

Dickens, Charles. *American Notes*. 1842. New York: Modern Library, 1996.

Eddis, William. *Letters from America*. Ed. A. C. Land. Cambridge MA: Harvard University Press, 1969.

Emerson, Ralph Waldo. *Selected Journals 1820–1842*. New York: Library of America, 2010.

Eslinger, Ellen, ed. *Running Mad for Kentucky: Frontier Travel Accounts*. Lexington: University Press of Kentucky, 2004.

Fearon, Henry Bradshaw. *Sketches of America*. 1818. Facsimile edition. New York: Benjamin Blom, 1969.

Filson, John. *The Discovery, Settlement and Present State of Kentucke*. Wilmington DE: James Adams, 1784.

Freneau, Philip. *A Freneau Sampler*. Ed. Philip M. Marsh. New York: Scarecrow Press, 1963.

———. *The Last Poems of Philip Freneau*. Ed. Lewis Leary. New Brunswick NJ: Rutgers University Press, 1945.

———. *Letters on Various Interesting and Important Subjects*. Ed. H. H. Clark. New York: Scholars' Facsimiles & Reprints, 1943.

———. *The Newspaper Verse of Philip Freneau: An Edition and Bibliographical Survey*. Ed. Judith R. Hiltner. Troy NY: Whitston, 1986.

———. *The Poems of Philip Freneau*. Ed. F. L. Pattee. 3 vols. New York: Russell & Russell, 1963.

———. *The Prose of Philip Freneau*. Ed. Philip M. Marsh. New Brunswick NJ: Scarecrow Press, 1955.

———. *The Writings in Prose and Verse of Hezekiah Salem*. Ed. Lewis Leary. Delmar NY: Scholar's Facsimiles and Reprints, 1975.

The Garland Library of Narratives of North American Indian Captives. Vol. 12. New York: Garland, 1978.

Gates, Charles M., ed. *Five Fur Traders of the Northwest*. St. Paul: Minnesota Historical Society, 1965.

Grant, Anne. *Memoirs of an American Lady, with sketches of manners and scenes in America as they existed previous to the Revolution*. New York: Dodd, Mead, 1903.

Greene, Jack P., ed. *Selling a New World: Two Colonial South Carolina Promotional Pamphlets*. Columbia: University of South Carolina Press, 1989.

Hallock, Thomas, and Nancy E. Hoffmann. *William Bartram: The Search for Nature's Design: Selected Art, Letters and Unpublished Writings*. Athens: University of Georgia Press, 2010.

Hamilton, Alexander. "The Itinerarium." In *Colonial American Travel Narratives*, ed. Wendy Martin. Harmondsworth, UK: Penguin, 1994.

Henry, Alexander. *Travels and Adventures in Canada and the Indian Territories, between the Years 1760 and 1776*. 1809. Readex Microprint, 1966.

Hubach, Robert R. *Early Midwestern Travel Narratives: An Annotated Bibliography 1634–1850*. Detroit: Wayne State University Press, 1961.

Hunter, John Dunn. *Memoirs of a Captivity among the Indians of North America*. 1824. Ed. R. Drinnon. New York: Schocken, 1973.

Johnston, Charles. *A Narrative of the Incidents Attending the Capture, Detention, and Ransom of Charles Johnston*. New York: J. J. Harper, 1827.

Kalm, Pehr. *Peter Kalm's Travels in North America: The English Version of 1770*. Ed. A. B. Benson. 1937. New York: Dover, 1964.

Kane, Paul. *Paul Kane's Frontier, including Wanderings of an Artist among the Indians of North America*. Ed. J. Russell Harper. Austin: University of Texas Press, 1971.

Kurz, Rudolph Friederich. *Journal of Rudolph Friederich Kurz: An Account of His Experiences among Fur Traders and American Indians on the Mississippi and the*

Upper Missouri Rivers during the Years 1846 to 1852. Ed. J. N. B. Hewitt. Lincoln: University of Nebraska Press, 1970.

Lafitau, Joseph-François. *Mœurs des sauvages américains comparées aux mœurs des premiers temps.* 1724. 2 vols. Paris: La Découverte, 1983.

Lahontan, Baron de. *Dialogues avec un sauvage.* Ed. Réal Ouellet. Montreal: Lux, 2010.

———. *Mémoires de l'Amérique septentrionale.* Ed. Réal Ouellet, Montreal: Lux, 2013.

———. *New Voyages to North-America.* 1703. 2 vols. Ed. Reuben G. Thwaites. New York: Burt Franklin, 1970.

———. *Œuvres complètes.* 2 vols. Ed. Réal Ouellet. Montréal: Presses de l'Université de Montréal, 1990.

La Rochefoucauld-Liancourt, Duc de. *Voyage dans les Etats-Unis d'Amérique, fait en 1795, 1796, et 1797.* Paris: DuPont, Buisson, Pougens, 1799.

———. *Le Voyage en Amérique de La Rochefoucauld-Liancourt, 1794–1798.* Ed. Daniel Vaugelade. Paris: Editions de l'Amandier, 2010.

Lawson, John. *A New Voyage to Carolina.* Ed. H. T. Lefler. Chapel Hill: University of North Carolina Press, 1967.

———. "A Vocabulary of Tuscarora." American Language Reprints, vol. 6. Southampton PA: Evolution, 1998.

———. "A Vocabulary of Woccon." American Language Reprints, vol. 7. Southampton PA: Evolution, 1998.

Lee, John Thomas. *A Bibliography of Carver's Travels through the Interior Parts of North America in the Years 1766, 1767, and 1768.* Proceedings of the State Historical Society of Wisconsin for 1909, 1910, 143–83.

Lehmann, Herman. *Nine Years among the Indians, 1870–79.* Ed. J. M. Hunter. Albuquerque: University of New Mexico Press, 1993.

Lincoln, Charles H., ed. *Narratives of the Indian Wars, 1675–1699.* New York: Scribner's, 1913.

Long, John. *Voyages and Travels of an Indian Interpreter and Trader.* London: Printed for the author, 1791.

Loskiel, George Henry. *History of the Mission of the United Brethren among the Indians of North America.* 1788. London: Brethren's Society for the Furtherance of the Gospel, 1794.

Louis-Philippe. *Diary of My Travels in America.* New York: Delacorte Press, 1977.

Mackenzie, Alexander. *Alexander Mackenzie's Voyage to the Pacific Ocean in 1793.* Ed. Milton Quaife. Chicago: R. R. Donnelley and Sons, 1931.

———. *First Man West: Alexander Mackenzie's Journal of His Voyage to the Pacific Coast of Canada in 1793.* Ed. Walter Sheppe. Berkeley: University of California Press, 1962.

———. *The Journals and Letters of Sir Alexander Mackenzie.* Ed. W. Kaye Lamb.

Published for the Hakluyt Society. Cambridge, UK: Cambridge University Press, 1970.

———. *Voyages from Montreal on the River St. Laurence through the Continent of North America to the Frozen and Pacific Oceans*. 1801. Facsimile edition. Ed. Roy Daniells. Edmonton, Canada: M. G. Hurtig, 1971.

———. *Voyages from Montreal on the River St. Laurence through the Continent of North America to the Frozen and Pacific Oceans in the Years 1789 and 1793*. 1801. Toronto: Radisson Society of Canada, 1927.

Margry, Pierre, ed. *Découvertes et Établissements des Français dans l'Ouest et dans le Sud de l'Amérique Septentrionale (1614–1754)*. 6 vols. Paris: Maisonneuve, 1879–88.

Martin, Wendy, ed. *Colonial American Travel Narratives*. Harmondsworth, UK: Penguin, 1994.

Martineau, Harriet. *Society in America*. 1837. New York: AMS Press, 1966.

McKenney, Thomas. *History of the Indian Tribes of North America*. 1833–44. Ed. Frederick Webb Hodge. Totowa NJ: Rowman and Littlefield, 1972.

McKibben, Bill, ed. *American Earth: Environmental Writing since Thoreau*. New York: Literary Classics of the United States/Penguin Putnam, 2008.

Mereness, N. D., ed. *Travels in the American Colonies*. New York: Macmillan, 1916.

Milfort, Louis. *Chef de guerre chez les Creek*. Ed. Christian Buchet. Paris: France-Empire, 1994.

Miranda, Francisco de. *The New Democracy in America: Travels of Francisco de Miranda in the United States, 1783–84*. Ed. J. S. Ezell. Norman: University of Oklahoma Press, 1963.

Monaghan, Frank. *French Travellers in the United States: 1765–1932*. New York: New York Public Library, 1933.

Morgan, Lewis Henry. *The Indian Journals, 1859–62*. Ed. L. A. White. New York: Dover, 1993.

Morris, Thomas. *Journal of Captain Thomas Morris*. Ann Arbor MI: University Microfilms, 1966.

Nasatir, A. P., ed. *Before Lewis and Clark: Documents Illustrating the History of the Missouri 1785–1804*. 1952. Norman: University of Oklahoma Press, 2002.

Nunez Cabeza de Vaca, Alvar. *Cabeza de Vaca's Adventures in the Unknown Interior of America*. Albuquerque: University of New Mexico Press, 1983.

Ogden, P. S. *Traits of American Indian Life and Character*. 1853. New York: Dover, 1995.

Pike, Zebulon Montgomery. *The Expeditions of Zebulon Montgomery Pike*. 2 vols. Ed. E. Coues. New York: Dover, 1987.

Pond, Peter. "The Narrative of Peter Pond." In *Five Fur Traders of the Northwest*, ed. Grace Lee Nute. Minneapolis: University of Minnesota Press, 1933.

Popular Culture in America, 1800–1925: Captivity Tales. New York: Arno Press, 1974.

Rogers, Robert. *Journals.* 1765. Ann Arbor MI: University Microfilms, 1966.
———. *Ponteach: or the Savages of America. A Tragedy.* Chicago: Caxton Club, 1914.
Saint-Méry, Moreau de. *A Civilization That Perished: The Last Years of White Colonial Rule in Haiti.* Ed. Ivor D. Spencer. Boston: University Press of America, 1985.
———. *Moreau de Saint-Méry's American Journey.* Eds. and trans. Kenneth Roberts and Anna M. Roberts. Garden City NY: Doubleday, 1947.
———. *Voyage aux Etats-Unis de l'Amérique, 1793–1798.* Ed. Stewart L. Mims. New Haven CT: Yale University Press, 1913.
Saur, Christoph. "A Dialogue between a Newcomer and a Settler in Pennsylvania." In *Early American Writings,* edited by Carla Mulford. Oxford: Oxford University Press, 2002.
Seaver, James E. *A Narrative of the Life of Mrs. Mary Jemison.* 1824. In *Women's Indian Captivity Narratives,* edited by Kathryn Z. Derounian-Stodola. Harmondsworth, UK: Penguin, 1998.
Shields, David S., ed. *American Poetry: The Seventeenth and Eighteenth Centuries.* New York: Library of America, 2007.
Smith, James. *An Account of the Remarkable Occurrences in the Life and Travels of Col. James Smith.* Lexington KY: John Bradford, 1799.
Smith, William. *Expedition against the Ohio Indians.* Ann Arbor MI: University Microfilms, 1966.
Smollett, Tobias. *The Expedition of Humphry Clinker.* 1771. Ed. Angus Ross. Harmondsworth, UK: Penguin, 1967.
Smyth, J. F. D. *A Tour in the United States of America.* 2 vols. London, 1784.
Spencer, O. M. *Indian Captivity: A True Narrative of the Capture of the Rev. O. M. Spencer by the Indians, in the Neighborhood of Cincinnati.* Washington PA: G. W. Brice, Printer, 1835.
Tanner, John. *A Narrative of the Captivity and Adventures of John Tanner (U.S. Interpreter at the Saut de Ste. Marie), during thirty years residence among the Indians in the interior of North America.* Ed. Edwin James. 1830. Minneapolis MN: Ross and Haines, 1956.
Thompson, David. *David Thompson's Narrative of His Explorations in Western America, 1784–1812.* Ed. J. B. Tyrrell. Toronto: Champlain Society, 1916.
———. *The Writings of David Thompson.* Vol. 1. Ed. William E. Moreau. Montreal: McGill-Queen's University Press, 2009.
———. *The Writings of David Thompson.* Vol. 2. Ed. William E. Moreau. Montreal: McGill-Queen's University Press, 2015.
Thwaites, Reuben G., ed. *Early Western Travels: 1748–1846.* Cleveland OH: Arthur H. Clark, 1904.
Timberlake, Henry. *The Memoirs of Lieut. Henry Timberlake.* New York: Arno Press, 1971.

Tocqueville, Alexis de. *De la démocratie en Amérique*. 1835–40. Paris: J. Vrin, 1990.
Trodd, Zoe, ed. *American Protest Literature*. Cambridge MA: Harvard University Press, 2006.
Trollope, Frances Milton. *Domestic Manners of the Americans*. 1832. New York: Penguin, 1997.
Trudeau, Jean-Baptiste. *A Fur Trader on the Upper Missouri: The Journal and Description of Jean-Baptiste Truteau*. Ed. Douglas R. Parks, Raymond J. DeMallie, and Robert Vézina. Trans. Mildred Mott Wedel, Raymond J. DeMallie, and Robert Vézina. Lincoln: University of Nebraska Press, in press.
———. *Voyage sur le Haut-Missouri, 1794–1796*. Ed. Fernand Grenier and Nilma Saint-Gelais. Québec: Éditions du Septentrion, 2006.
Verme, Francesco dal. *Seeing America and Its Great Men: The Journal and Letters of Count Francesco dal Verme, 1783–84*. Charlottesville: University Press of Virginia, 1969.
Waselkov, Gregory A., and Kathryn E. Holland Braund, eds. *William Bartram on the Southeastern Indians*. Lincoln: University of Nebraska Press, 1995.
Weld, Isaac. *Travels through the States of North America and the Provinces of Upper and Lower Canada, during the Years 1795, 1796, and 1797*. London: J. Stockdale, 1798.
Wied, Maximilian, Prince of. *Travels in the Interior of North America during the years 1832–1834*. Illustrations by Karl Bodmer. Köln, Germany: Taschen, 2001.
Wood, W. Raymond, and Thomas D. Thiessen, eds. *Early Fur Trade on the Northern Plains: Canadian Traders among the Mandan and Hidatsa Indians, 1738–1818*. Norman: University of Oklahoma Press, 1985.
Woolman, John. *Journal of John Woolman and Plea for the Poor*. Secaucus NJ: Citadel Press, 1961.

SECONDARY SOURCES

Adams, Percy G. *Travel Literature and the Evolution of the Novel*. Lexington: University Press of Kentucky, 1983.
Alfred, Gerald R. *Heeding the Voices of Our Ancestors: Kahnawake Mohawk Politics and the Rise of Native Nationalism*. Oxford: Oxford University Press, 1995.
Allen, Gay Wilson, and Roger Asselineau. *St. John de Crèvecoeur: The Life of an American Farmer*. New York: Viking Penguin, 1987.
Altick, Richard D. *The Shows of London*. Cambridge MA: Harvard University Press, 1978.
Anderson, Benedict. *Imagined Communities: Reflections on the Origin and Spread of Nationalism*. London: Verso, 1983.
Appleby, Joyce. *Capitalism and a New Social Order: The Republican Vision of the 1790s*. New York: New York University Press, 1984.
———. *Inheriting the Revolution: The First Generation of Americans*. Cambridge MA: Harvard University Press, 2000.

Aron, Steven. "The Significance of the Frontier in the Transition to Capitalism." In "The Transition to Capitalism in America: A Panel Discussion." *History Teacher* 27, no. 3 (1994): 263–88.

Artist Explorers of the 1830s: George Catlin, Karl Bodmer, Alfred Jacob Miller. Omaha NE: Joslyn Art Museum, 1963.

Axtell, James. *After Columbus: Essays in the Ethnohistory of Colonial North America.* New York: Oxford University Press, 1988.

———. *Beyond 1492: Encounters in Colonial North America.* Oxford: Oxford University Press, 1992.

———. *The European and the Indian: Essays in the Ethnohistory of Colonial North America.* Oxford: Oxford University Press, 1981.

———. *The Indians' New South: Cultural Change in the Colonial Southeast.* Baton Rouge: Louisiana State University Press, 1997.

Bailey, Alfred G. *The Conflict of European and Eastern Algonkian Cultures 1504–1700: A Study in Canadian Civilization.* 2nd edition. Toronto: University of Toronto Press, 1969.

Bailyn, Bernard. *The Barbarous Years: The Peopling of British North America. The Conflict of Civilizations, 1600–1675.* New York: Knopf, 2012.

Batten, Charles L., Jr. *Pleasurable Instruction: Form and Convention in 18th-Century Travel Literature.* Berkeley: University of California Press, 1978.

Bellin, Joshua David. *Medicine Bundle: Indian Sacred Performance and American Literature, 1824–1932.* Philadelphia.: University of Pennsylvania Press, 2008.

Béranger, Jean. "Un auteur, deux publics: Étude des versions françaises et anglaises des *Lettres d'un cultivateur américain* de St. John de Crèvecoeur." In *La Révolution américaine et l'Europe.* Paris: Editions du CNRS, 1979.

Bergmann, William H. "A 'Commercial View of This Unfortunate War': Economic Roots of an American National State in the Ohio Valley, 1775–1795." *Early American Studies* 6, no. 1 (2008): 137–64.

Berkhofer, Robert F., Jr. *The White Man's Indian: Images of the American Indian from Columbus to the Present.* New York: Random House, 1978.

Berlo, Janet Catherine. "Introduction: The Formative Years of Native American Art History." In *The Early Years of Native American Art History*, ed. J. C. Berlo. Seattle: University of Washington Press, 1992.

Berthiaume, Pierre. *L'Aventure américaine au dix-huitième siècle: Du voyage à l'écriture.* Ottawa: Presses universitaires d'Ottawa, 1990.

Berthier-Foglar, Susanne. "À l'Ouest de la Louisiane: Les frontières de Quivira." In *La France en Amérique: Mémoire d'une conquête*, ed. S. Berthier-Foglar. Chambéry, France: Presses de l'Université de Savoie, 2009.

Billington, Ray Allen. *Land of Savagery, Land of Promise: The European Image of the*

American Frontier in the Nineteenth Century. Norman: University of Oklahoma Press, 1981.

Bissell, Benjamin. *The American Indian in English Literature of the Eighteenth Century.* New Haven CT: Yale University Press, 1925.

Borm, Jan. "Defining Travel: On the Travel Book, Travel Writing and Terminology." In *Perspectives on Travel Writing*, ed. G. Hooper and T. Youngs. Aldershot, UK: Ashgate, 2004.

Bourguet, Marie-Noëlle. "Le Sauvage, le colon et le paysan." In *Figures de l'Indien*, ed. Gilles Thérien. Montreal: Typo, 1995.

Bowden, Mary Weatherspoon. *Philip Freneau.* Boston: Twayne, 1976.

Braund, Kathryn E. Holland. *Deerskins and Duffels: The Creek Indian Trade with Anglo-America, 1685–1815.* Lincoln: University of Nebraska Press, 1993.

Braund, Kathryn E. Holland, and Catherine M. Porter, eds. *Fields of Vision: Essays on the Travels of William Bartram.* Tuscaloosa: University of Alabama Press, 2010.

Brouillette, Benoît. *La Pénétration du continent américain par les Canadiens français, 1763–1846: Traitants, explorateurs, missionaires.* Montréal: Granger Frères, 1939.

Brown, Dona. *Inventing New England: Regional Tourism in the Nineteenth Century.* Washington DC: Smithsonian Institution Press, 1995.

Brumble, H. David. *American Indian Autobiography.* Lincoln: University of Nebraska Press, 1988.

Bushman, Richard L. *From Puritan to Yankee: Character and the Social Order in Connecticut, 1690–1765.* Cambridge MA: Harvard University Press, 1967.

Butler, Jon. *Becoming America: The Revolution before 1776.* Cambridge MA: Harvard University Press, 2000.

Cabanas, Miguel A. *The Cultural "Other" in Nineteenth-Century Travel Narratives.* Lewiston NY: Edwin Mellen Press, 2008.

Calloway, Colin G. *The American Revolution in Indian Country: Crisis and Diversity in Native American Communities.* Cambridge, UK: Cambridge University Press, 1995.

———. *One Vast Winter Count: The Native American West before Lewis and Clark.* Lincoln: University of Nebraska Press, 2003.

———. *The Shawnees and the War for America.* New York: Viking, 2007.

———. "2008 Presidential Address: Indian History from the End of the Alphabet; And What Now?" *Ethnohistory* 58, no. 2 (2011): 197–211.

———. *White People, Indians, and Highlanders: Tribal Peoples and Colonial Encounters in Scotland and America.* Oxford: Oxford University Press, 2008.

Campbell, Mary B. *The Witness and the Other World: Exotic European Travel Writing, 400–1600.* Ithaca NY: Cornell University Press, 1988.

Carlson, David J. "Crèvecoeur's *Letters from an American Farmer*." In *The Oxford*

Handbook of Early American Literature, ed. Kevin J. Hayes. Oxford: Oxford University Press, 2008.

Carson, Cary, Ronald Hoffman, and Peter J. Albert, eds. *Of Consuming Interests: The Style of Life in the Eighteenth Century*. Charlottesville: University Press of Virginia, 1994.

Cashin, Edward. "The Real World of Bartram's *Travels*." In *Fields of Vision: Essays on the* Travels *of William Bartram*, ed. K. E. Holland Braund and Catherine M. Porter. Tuscaloosa: University of Alabama Press, 2010.

———. *William Bartram and the American Revolution on the Southern Frontier*. Columbia: University of South Carolina Press, 2000.

Chapin, David. *Freshwater Passages: The Trade and Travels of Peter Pond*. Lincoln: University of Nebraska Press, 2014.

Chevignard, Bernard. *Michel Saint-John de Crèvecoeur*. Paris: Belin, 2004.

———. "St. John de Crèvecoeur: A Case of Arrested Biographical Development." *Early American Literature* 23, no. 3 (1988): 319–27.

———. "St. John de Crèvecoeur in the Looking Glass: *Letters from an American Farmer* and the Making of a Man of Letters." *Early American Literature* 19, no. 2 (1984): 173–90.

———. "Saint-John de Crèvecoeur: *Letters from an American Farmer* et *Lettres d'un cultivateur américain*. Genèse d'une œuvre franco-américaine." 3 vols. Dissertation, University of Lille, 1989.

Choquette, Leslie. *Frenchmen into Peasants: Modernity and Tradition in the Peopling of French Canada*. Cambridge MA: Harvard University Press, 1997.

Clark, Christopher. "A Wealth of Notions: Interpreting Economy and Morality in Early America." *Early American Studies* 8, no. 3 (2010): 672–83.

Clarke, Larry R. "The Quaker Background of William Bartram's View of Nature." *Journal of the History of Ideas* 46, no. 3 (1985): 435–48.

Clastres, Pierre. *La société contre l'état: Recherches d'anthropologie politique*. Paris: Editions du Minuit, 1974.

Codignola, Luca. *Guerra e guerriglia nell'America coloniale: Robert Rogers e la Guerra dei Sette Anni, 1754–1760*. Venice: Marsilio, 1977.

Colpitts, George. *North America's Indian Trade in European Commerce and Imagination, 1580–1850*. Leiden: Brill, 2014.

Coontz, Stephanie. *The Social Origins of Private Life: A History of American Families, 1600–1900*. London: Verso, 1988.

Coulthard, Glen Sean. *Red Skin, White Masks: Rejecting the Colonial Politics of Recognition*. Minneapolis: University of Minnesota Press, 2014.

Crèvecoeur, Robert de. *Saint John de Crèvecoeur: Sa vie et ses ouvrages*. Paris: Librairie des bibliophiles, 1883.

Cronon, William. *Changes in the Land: Indians, Colonists and the Ecology of New England*. New York: Hill & Wang, 2003.
Cutting, Rose-Marie. *John and William Bartram, William Byrd II and St. John de Crèvecoeur: A Reference Guide*. Boston: G. K. Hall, 1976.
Daniel, Marcus. *Scandal and Civility: Journalism and the Birth of American Democracy*. Oxford: Oxford University Press, 2009.
Daniells, Roy. *Alexander Mackenzie and the North West*. London: Faber and Faber, 1969.
Degler, Carl N. *Out of Our Past: The Forces That Shaped Modern America*. New York: Harper & Brothers, 1959.
Delâge, Denys. "Indian-White Relations in New France." In *The Encyclopedia of North American Indians*, ed. Frederick E. Hoxie. Boston: Houghton Mifflin, 1996.
——— . *Le Pays renversé: Amérindiens et européens en Amérique du nord-est, 1600–1664*. Montreal: Boréal, 1985.
DeLay, Brian. *War of a Thousand Deserts: Indian Raids and the U.S.-Mexican War*. New Haven CT: Yale University Press, 2008.
Demos, John. *Circles and Lines: The Shape of Life in Early America*. Cambridge MA: Harvard University Press, 2004.
Derounian-Stodola, Kathryn Z., and James A. Levernier. *The Indian Captivity Narrative, 1550–1900*. New York: Twayne, 1993.
DeVine, Christine, ed. *Nineteenth-Century British Travelers in the New World*. Farnham, UK: Ashgate, 2013.
Diket, A. L. "The Noble Savage Convention as Epitomized in John Lawson's *A New Voyage to Carolina*." *North Carolina Historical Review* 43, no. 4 (1966): 413–29.
Dippie, Brian W. *Catlin and His Contemporaries: The Politics of Patronage*. Lincoln: University of Nebraska Press, 1990.
Dölling, Corinne M. *"Mes amis sauvages": Die Reiseberichte Louis-Armand de Lahontans als Dokumente der Frühaufklärung*. Munich: Akademische Verlagsgemeinschaft München, 2013.
Driver, Harold E. *Indians of North America*. Chicago: University of Chicago Press, 1969.
Dubois, Laurent. *Avengers of the New World: The Story of the Haitian Revolution*. Cambridge MA: Harvard University Press, 2004.
Duchemin, Parker. "'A Parcel of Whelps': Alexander Mackenzie among the Indians." In "Native Writers and Canadian Writing." Special issue of *Canadian Literature* 124–25 (Spring-Summer 1990): 49–74.
Duchet, Michèle. *Anthropologie et histoire au siècle des Lumières*. Paris: Albin Michel, 1995.
Du Val, Kathleen. *The Native Ground: Indians and Colonists in the Heart of the Continent*. Philadelphia: University of Pennsylvania Press, 2006.
Eccles, William J. *The Canadian Frontier, 1534–1760*. Albuquerque: University of New Mexico Press, 1974.

Edwards, Philip. *The Story of the Voyage: Sea Narratives in 18th-Century England.* Cambridge, UK: Cambridge University Press, 1994.

Eisler, Benita. *The Red Man's Bones: George Catlin, Artist and Showman.* New York: Norton, 2013.

Ekberg, Carl J. *French Roots in the Illinois Country: The Mississippi Frontier in Colonial Times.* Urbana: University of Illinois Press, 1998.

Elicona, Anthony Louis. *Un colonial sous la Révolution en France et en Amérique: Moreau de Saint-Méry.* Paris: Jouve, 1934.

Elliott, Emory. *Revolutionary Writers: Literature and Authority in the New Republic, 1725–1810.* New York: Oxford University Press, 1982.

Emerson, Katherine, and Everett Emerson. "Crèvecoeur, J. Hector St. John de." In *American National Biography.* New York: Oxford University Press, 1999: 729–33.

Engel, Katherine Carté. *Religion and Profit: Moravians in Early America.* Philadelphia: University of Pennsylvania Press, 2009.

Englebert, Robert, and Guillaume Teasdale, eds. *French and Indians in the Heart of North America, 1630–1815.* East Lansing: Michigan State University Press, 2013.

Ethridge, Robbie. *Creek Country: The Creek Indians and Their World.* Chapel Hill: University of North Carolina Press, 2003.

Ewers, John C., ed. *Indian Art in Pipestone: George Catlin's Portfolio in the British Museum.* Washington DC: Smithsonian Institution Press, 1979.

Fenn, Elizabeth A. *Encounters at the Heart of the World: A History of the Mandan People.* New York: Hill and Wang, 2014.

———. *Natives and Newcomers: The Way We Lived in North Carolina before 1770.* Chapel Hill: University of North Carolina Press, North Carolina Department of Cultural Resources, 1983.

Ferland, Rémi, and Réal Ouellet. "Les sauvages de Lahontan: Enfants de la nature ou porte-parole des 'Lumières'?" In *Figures de l'Indien,* ed. Gilles Thérien. Montreal: Typo, 1995.

Fierst, John T. "Return to 'Civilization': John Tanner's Troubled Years at Sault Ste. Marie." *Minnesota History* 50, no. 1 (1986): 23–36.

———. "A 'Succession of Little Occurrences': Scholarly Editing and the Organization of Time in John Tanner's Narrative." *Scholarly Editing: The Annual of the Association for Documentary Editing* 33 (2012): 1–29.

Fifer, J. Valerie. *American Progress: The Growth of the Transport, Tourist, and Information Industries in the Nineteenth-Century West.* Chester CT: Globe Pequot Press, 1988.

Fiske, Jo-Anne, Susan Sleeper-Smith, and William Wicken, eds. *New Faces of the Fur Trade: Selected Papers of the Seventh North American Fur Trade Conference, Halifax, Nova Scotia, 1995.* East Lansing: Michigan State University Press, 1998.

Fixico, Donald. "Ethics and Responsibilities in Writing American Indian History."

In *Natives and Academics: Researching and Writing about American Indians*, ed. Devon A. Mihesuah. Lincoln: University of Nebraska Press, 1998.

———. "Methodologies in Reconstructing Native American History." In *Rethinking American Indian History*, ed. Donald L. Fixico. Albuquerque: University of New Mexico Press, 1997.

———, ed. *Rethinking American Indian History*. Albuquerque: University of New Mexico Press, 1997.

Frank, Andrew K. *Creeks and Southerners: Biculturalism on the Early American Frontier*. Lincoln: University of Nebraska Press, 2005.

Franklin, Wayne. *Discovers, Explorers, Settlers: The Diligent Writers of Early America*. Chicago: University of Chicago Press, 1979.

Furstenberg, François. *When the United States Spoke French: Five Refugees Who Shaped a Nation*. New York: Penguin, 2014.

Gassan, Richard H. *The Birth of American Tourism: New York, the Hudson Valley, and American Culture, 1790–1830*. Amherst: University of Massachusetts Press, 2008.

Gohard-Radenkovic, Aline. "'L'altérité' dans les récits de voyage." *L'Homme et la Société* 134, no. 4 (1999): 81–96.

Gough, Barry. *First across the Continent: Sir Alexander Mackenzie*. Norman: University of Oklahoma Press, 1997.

Greer, Allan. "Commons and Enclosure in the Colonization of North America." *American Historical Review* 117, no. 2 (2012): 365–86.

———. "Comparisons: New France." In *A Companion to Colonial America*, ed. Daniel Vickers. Oxford: Blackwell, 2003.

———. *Peasant, Lord, and Merchant: Rural Society in Three Quebec Parishes 1740–1840*. Toronto: University of Toronto Press, 1985.

Griffiths, Nicholas, and Fernando Cervantes, eds. *Spiritual Encounters: Interactions between Christianity and Native Religions in Colonial America*. Lincoln: University of Nebraska Press, 1999.

Gurney, George, and Therese Thau Heyman, eds. *George Catlin and His Indian Gallery*. New York: Norton, Smithsonian American Art Museum, 2002.

Hacker, Louis M. *American Capitalism*. New York: Van Nostrand Reinhold, 1957.

Hahn, Steven C. *The Invention of the Creek Nation, 1670–1763*. Lincoln: University of Nebraska Press, 2004.

Hallam, Elizabeth, and Brian V. Street, eds. *Cultural Encounters: Representing "Otherness."* London: Routledge, 2000.

Hallock, Thomas. "'On the Borders of a New World': Ecology, Frontier Plots, and Imperial Elegy in William Bartram's 'Travels.'" *South Atlantic Review* 66, no. 4 (2001): 109–33.

Hämäläinen, Pekka. *The Comanche Empire*. New Haven CT: Yale University Press, 2008.

Hamilton, Roberta. *Feudal Society and Colonization: The Historiography of New France.* Gananoque, Canada: Langdale Press, 1988.

Harkin, Michael E., and David Rich Lewis, eds. *Native Americans and the Environment: Perspectives on the Ecological Indian.* Lincoln: University of Nebraska Press, 2007.

Harper, Rob. "Looking the Other Way: The Gnadenhütten Massacre and the Contextual Interpretation of Violence." *William and Mary Quarterly* 64, no. 3 (2007): 621–44.

Hart, William B. "'The Kindness of the Blessed Virgin': Faith, Succour, and the Cult of Mary among Christian Hurons and Iroquois in Seventeenth-Century New France." In *Spiritual Encounters: Interactions between Christianity and Native Religions in Colonial America*, ed. Nicholas Griffiths and Fernando Cervantes. Lincoln: University of Nebraska Press, 1999.

Hartmann, Horst. *George Catlin und Balduin Möllhausen: Zwei Interpreten der Indianer und des Alten Westens.* Berlin: D. Reimer, 1963.

Hausdoerffer, John. *Catlin's Lament: Indians, Manifest Destiny and the Ethics of Nature.* Lawrence: University Press of Kansas, 2009.

Havard, Gilles, and Cécile Vidal. *Histoire de l'Amérique française.* Paris: Flammarion, 2003.

Hayes, Derek. *First Crossing: Alexander Mackenzie, His Expedition across North America, and the Opening of the Continent.* Vancouver: Douglas and McIntyre, 2001.

Hazard, Paul. *La Crise de la conscience européenne (1680–1715).* 2 vols. Paris: Boivin, 1935.

Heard, J. Norman. *White into Red: A Study of the Assimilation of White Persons Captured by Indians.* Metuchen NJ: Scarecrow Press, 1973.

Henretta, James. *The Evolution of American Society, 1700–1850: An Interdisciplinary Analysis.* Lexington MA: Heath, 1973.

———. *The Origins of American Capitalism: Collected Essays.* Boston: Northeastern University Press, 1991.

Herring, Joseph B. "Selling the 'Noble Savage' Myth: George Catlin and the Iowa Indians in Europe, 1843–45." *Kansas History*, Winter 2006–7, 226–45.

Hickerson, Harold. "Fur Trade Colonialism and the North American Indians." *Journal of Ethnic Studies* 1, no. 2 (1973): 15–44.

Hixson, Walter. *American Settler Colonialism: A History.* New York: Palgrave Macmillan, 2013.

Hoffman, Ronald, and Peter J. Albert, eds. *The Transforming Hand of Revolution: Reconsidering the American Revolution as a Social Movement.* Charlottesville: University Press of Virginia, 1996.

Hoffmann, Nancy Everill, ed. "The Construction of William Bartram's Narrative Natural History: A Genetic Text of the Draft Manuscript for *Travels through North and South Carolina, Georgia, East and West Florida*." PhD dissertation, University of Pennsylvania, 1996.

Hofstadter, Richard. *America at 1750: A Social Portrait*. New York: Knopf, 1971.

Hollmann, Clide. *Five Artists of the Old West: George Catlin, Karl Bodmer, Alfred Jacob Miller, Charles M. Russell and Frederic Remington*. New York: Hastings House, 1965.

Horowitz, David. *The First Frontier: The Indian Wars and America's Origins 1607–1776*. New York: Simon and Schuster, 1978.

Hoxie, Frederick E., ed. *Encyclopedia of North American Indians*. New York: Houghton Mifflin, 1996.

———. "Retrieving the Red Continent: Settler Colonialism and the History of American Indians in the U.S." *Ethnic and Racial Studies* 31, no. 6 (2008): 1153–67.

Hoxie, Frederick E., Peter C. Mancall, and James H. Merrell, eds. *American Nations: Encounters in Indian Country, 1850 to the Present*. London: Routledge, 2001.

Hudson, Marjorie. "Among the Tuscarora: The Strange and Mysterious Death of John Lawson." *North Carolina Literary Review* 1, no. 1 (1992): 62–82.

Hughes, J. Donald. *North American Indian Ecology*. 2nd edition. El Paso: Texas Western Press, 1996.

Hulme, Peter, and Tim Youngs, eds. *The Cambridge Companion to Travel Writing*. Cambridge, UK: Cambridge University Press, 2002.

Hurtado, Albert L. and Peter Iverson, eds. *Major Problems in American Indian History: Documents and Essays*. Lexington MA: D. C. Heath, 1994.

Hyde, Anne Farrar. *An American Vision: Far Western Landscape and National Culture, 1820–1920*. New York: New York University Press, 1990.

———. *Empires, Nations, and Families: A History of the North American West, 1800–1860*. Lincoln: University of Nebraska Press, 2011.

Iannini, Christopher P. *Fatal Revolutions: Natural History, West Indian Slavery, and the Routes of American Literature*. Chapel Hill: University of North Carolina Press, 2012.

Innes, Stephen. "Puritanism and Capitalism in Early Massachusetts." In *Capitalism in Context: Essays on Economic Development and Cultural Change*, ed. John A. James and Mark Thomas. Chicago: University of Chicago Press, 1994.

Isaac, Rhys. *The Transformation of Virginia, 1740–1790*. Chapel Hill: University of North Carolina Press, 1982.

Jacob, Annie. "L'Indien des Anglais, l'Indien des Français: Images comparées." In *Figures de l'Indien*, ed. Gilles Thérien. Montreal: Editions Typo, 1995.

Jacquin, Philippe. *Les Indiens blancs: Français et Indiens en Amérique du Nord (XVIe–XVIIIe siècle)*. Paris: Payot, 1987.

Jameson, J. Franklin. *The American Revolution Considered as a Social Movement*. Boston: Beacon Press, 1956.

Jarvis, Robin. *Romantic Readers and Transatlantic Travel: Expeditions and Tours in North America, 1760–1840*. Farnham, UK: Ashgate, 2012.

Jaskoski, Helen, ed. *Early Native American Writing: New Critical Essays.* Cambridge, UK: Cambridge University Press, 1996.

Jennings, Francis. *The Invasion of America: Indians, Colonialism, and the Cant of Conquest.* Chapel Hill: University of North Carolina Press, 1975.

John, Gareth E. "Benevolent Imperialism: George Catlin and the Practice of Jeffersonian Geography." *Journal of Historical Geography* 30 (2004): 597–617.

———. "Cultural Nationalism, Westward Expansion and the Production of Imperial Landscape: George Catlin's Native American West." *Ecumene* 8, no. 2 (2001): 175–203.

Jullien, Dominique. *Récits du Nouveau Monde: Les voyageurs français en Amérique, de Chateaubriand à nos jours.* Paris: Nathan, 1992.

Keiser, Albert. *The Indian in American Literature.* New York: Oxford University Press, 1933.

Kelley, Donald Brooks. "The Evolution of Quaker Theology and the Unfolding of a Distinctive Quaker Ecological Perspective in Eighteenth-Century America." *Pennsylvania History* 52, no. 4 (1985): 242–53.

———. "Friends and Nature in America: Toward an Eighteenth-Century Quaker Ecology." *Pennsylvania History* 53, no. 4 (1986): 257–72.

Kennedy, John H. *Jesuit and Savage in New France.* New Haven CT: Yale University Press, 1950.

Kinietz, W. Vernon. *The Indians of the Western Great Lakes, 1615–1760.* Ann Arbor: University of Michigan Press, 1965.

Konkle, Maureen. *Writing Indian Nations: Native Intellectuals and the Politics of Historiography, 1827–1863.* Chapel Hill: University of North Carolina Press, 2004.

Kornfeld, Eve. "Encountering the 'Other': American Intellectuals and Indians in the 1790s." *William and Mary Quarterly*, 3rd series, 52, no. 2 (1995): 287–314.

Krech, Shepard, III. *The Ecological Indian: Myth and History.* New York: Norton, 1999.

Kulikoff, Allan. *The Agrarian Origins of American Capitalism.* Charlottesville: University Press of Virginia, 1992.

Leary, Lewis. *That Rascal Freneau: A Study in Literary Failure.* New Brunswick NJ: Rutgers University Press, 1941.

Leask, Nigel. *Curiosity and the Aesthetics of Travel Writing, 1770–1840.* Oxford: Oxford University Press, 2002.

Lee, John Thomas. "Captain Jonathan Carver: Additional Data." *Proceedings of the State Historical Society of Wisconsin for 1912,* 1913, 87–123.

Lefebvre, Henri. *Critique de la vie quotidienne.* 2 vols. Paris: L'Arche, 1958.

———. *Introduction à la modernité.* Paris: Editions du Minuit, 1962.

Lepore, Jill. *The Name of War: King Philip's War and the Origins of American Identity.* New York: Knopf, 1998.

Liebersohn, Harry. *Aristocratic Encounters: European Travelers and North American Indians*. Cambridge, UK: Cambridge University Press, 1998.

Lindfors, Bernth. "Ethnological Show Business: Footlighting the Dark Continent." In *Freakery: Cultural Spectacles of the Extraordinary Body*, ed. Rosemarie Garland Thomson. New York: New York University Press, 1996.

Lopenzina, Drew. *Red Ink: Native Americans Picking Up the Pen in the Colonial Period*. Albany: SUNY Press, 2012.

Lowes, John Livingston. *The Road to Xanadu: A Study in the Ways of the Imagination*. Princeton NJ: Princeton University Press, 1927.

Löwy, Michael. "Catholic Ethics and the Spirit of Capitalism: The Unwritten Chapter in Max Weber's Sociology of Religion." In *Max Webers Religionssoziologie in interkultureller Perspektive*, ed. H. Lehmann and J.-M. Ouédraogo. Göttingen, Germany: Vandenhoeck & Ruprecht, 2003.

———. "Le concept d'affinité élective en sciences sociales." *Critique internationale* 2 (Winter 1999): 42–50.

MacLaren, Ian S. "Alexander Mackenzie and the Landscapes of Commerce." *Studies in Canadian Literature* 7, no. 2 (1982): 141–50.

———. "In Consideration of the Evolution of Explorers and Travellers into Authors: A Model." *Studies in Travel Writing* 15, no. 3 (2011): 221–41.

Magubane, Zine. "Ethnographic Showcases as Sites of Knowledge Production and Indigenous Resistance." In *Contesting Knowledge: Museums and Indigenous Perspectives*, ed. Susan Sleeper-Smith. Lincoln: University of Nebraska Press, 2009.

Mancall, Peter, ed. *Bringing the World to Early Modern Europe: Travel Accounts and Their Audiences*. Leiden: Brill, 2007.

Mandell, Daniel R. *Behind the Frontier: Indians in Eighteenth-Century Eastern Massachusetts*. Lincoln: University of Nebraska Press, 1996.

———. *Tribe, Race, History: Native Americans in Southern New England, 1780–1880*. Baltimore: Johns Hopkins University Press, 2010.

Mapp, Paul W. *The Elusive West and the Contest for Empire, 1713–1763*. Chapel Hill: University of North Carolina Press, 2011.

Marder, Daniel. *Hugh Henry Brackenridge*. New York: Twayne, 1967.

Marienstras, Elise. *Les Mythes fondateurs de la nation américaine*. Paris: Éditions Complexe, 1992.

Marsh, Philip. *The Works of Philip Freneau: A Critical Study*. Metuchen NJ: Scarecrow Press, 1968.

Martin, Calvin. "A Better Way to Write Indian History." In *Major Problems in American Indian History*, ed. Albert L. Hurtado and Peter Iverson. Lexington MA: D. C. Heath, 1994.

Marx, Karl, and Friedrich Engels. *The Communist Manifesto*. Harmondsworth, UK: Penguin, 1967.

Mathieu, Jacques. *La Nouvelle France: Les Français en Amérique du Nord XVI–XVIII siècle*. Paris: Belin/Presses de l'Université Laval, 1991.

Matson, Cathy. "Markets and Morality: Intersections of Economy, Ethics, and Religion in Early North America." In "Markets and Morality," ed. Cathy Matson. Special issue of *Early American Studies* 8, no. 3 (2010): 475–81.

McCracken, Harold. *George Catlin and the Old Frontier*. New York: Dial Press, 1959.

McIlvenna, Noeleen. *A Very Mutinous People: The Struggle for North Carolina, 1660–1713*. Chapel Hill: University of North Carolina Press, 2009.

Merrell, James H. *The Indians' New World: Catawbas and Their Neighbors from European Contact through the Era of Removal*. Chapel Hill: University of North Carolina Press, 1989.

———. *Into the American Woods: Negotiators on the Pennsylvania Frontier*. New York: Norton, 1999.

Merrill, Michael. "Putting 'Capitalism' in Its Place: A Review of Recent Literature." *William and Mary Quarterly* 52, no. 2 (1995): 315–26.

Mihesuah, Devon A., ed. *Natives and Academics: Researching and Writing about American Indians*. Lincoln: University of Nebraska Press, 1998.

Millichap, Joseph R. *George Catlin*. Western Writers Series, no. 27. Boise ID: Boise State University Press, 1977.

Moogk, Peter N. *La Nouvelle France: The Making of French Canada–A Cultural History*. East Lansing: Michigan State University Press, 2000.

Moreau de Saint-Méry ou les ambiguïtés d'un créole des Lumières. Fort-de-France, Martinique, September 2004. Fort-de-France: Société des amis des archives, 2006. Online.

Morgan, M. J. *Land of Big Rivers: French and Indian Illinois*. Carbondale: Southern Illinois University Press, 2010.

Moses, Lester G. *Wild West Shows and the Images of American Indians, 1883–1933*. Albuquerque: University of New Mexico Press, 1996.

Mulvey, Christopher. "Among the Sag-a-noshes: Ojibwa and Iowa Indians with George Catlin in Europe, 1843–1848." In *Indians and Europe: An Interdisciplinary Collection of Essays*, ed. Christian F. Feest. Aachen, Germany: Edition Herodot, 1987.

Murray, David. "Spreading the Word: Missionaries, Conversion and Circulation in the Northeast." In *Spiritual Encounters: Interactions between Christianity and Native Religions in Colonial America*, ed. Nicholas Griffiths and Fernando Cervantes. Lincoln: University of Nebraska Press, 1999.

Namias, June. *White Captives: Gender and Ethnicity on the American Frontier*. Chapel Hill: University of North Carolina Press, 1993.

Newman, Peter C. *Caesars of the Wilderness: Company of Adventurers.* 2 vols. New York: Viking, 1987.
Nunnally, Michael L. *American Indian Wars: A Chronology of Confrontations between Native Peoples and Settlers and the United States Military, 1500s–1901.* Jefferson NC: McFarland, 2007.
Osborn, William M. *The Wild Frontier: Atrocities during the American-Indian War from Jamestown Colony to Wounded Knee.* New York: Random House, 2000.
Osborne, Jeff. "American Antipathy and the Cruelties of Citizenship in Crèvecoeur's *Letters from an American Farmer.*" *Early American Literature* 42, no. 3 (2007): 529–53.
Pagden, Anthony. *European Encounters with the New World: From Renaissance to Romanticism.* New Haven CT: Yale University Press, 1993.
———. *The Fall of Natural Man: The American Indian and the Origins of Comparative Ethnology.* Cambridge, UK: Cambridge University Press, 1982.
Parker, John. "New Light on Jonathan Carver." *American Magazine and Historical Chronicle* 2, no. 1 (1986): 4–17.
Paton, Bruce C. *Adventuring with Boldness: The Triumph of the Explorers.* Golden CO: Fulcrum, 2006.
Pearce, Roy Harvey. *Savagism and Civilization: A Study of the Indian and the American Mind.* 2nd edition. Baltimore: Johns Hopkins University Press, 1965.
Perdue, Theda. *Cherokee Women: Gender and Culture Change, 1700–1835.* Lincoln: University of Nebraska Press, 1998.
———. *"Mixed Blood" Indians: Racial Construction in the Early South.* Athens: University of Georgia Press, 2003.
Peterson, Jacqueline, and John Anfinson. "The Indian and the Fur Trade: A Review of Recent Literature." In *Scholars and the Indian Experience: Critical Reviews of Recent Writing in the Social Sciences,* ed. W. R. Swagerty. Bloomington: Indiana University Press, 1984.
Philbrick, Nathaniel. "The Nantucket Sequence in Crèvecoeur's *Letters from an American Farmer.*" *New England Quarterly* 64 (1991): 414–32.
Philbrick, Thomas. *St. John de Crèvecoeur.* New York: Twayne, 1970.
Plotkin, Norman A. "Saint-John de Crèvecoeur Rediscovered: Critic or Panegyrist?" *French Historical Studies* 3, no. 3 (1964): 390–404.
Podruchny, Carolyn. *Making the Voyageur World: Travelers and Traders in the North American Fur Trade.* Lincoln: University of Nebraska Press, 2006.
Podruchny, Carolyn, and Laura Peers, eds. *Gathering Places: Aboriginal and Fur Trade Histories.* Vancouver: University of British Columbia Press, 2010.
Polanyi, Karl. *The Great Transformation: The Political and Economic Origins of Our Time.* Boston: Beacon Press, 2001.

Porter, Charlotte M. "William Bartram's Travels in the Indian Nations." *Florida Historical Quarterly* 70, no. 4 (1992): 434–50.
Pratt, Mary-Louise. *Imperial Eyes: Travel Writing and Transculturation*. London: Routledge, 1992.
Rabasa, José. *Writing Violence on the Northern Frontier: The Historiography of Sixteenth-Century New Mexico and Florida and the Legacy of Conquest*. Durham NC: Duke University Press, 2000.
Randolph, J. Ralph. *British Travelers among the Southern Indians, 1660–1763*. Norman: University of Oklahoma Press, 1973.
Ray, Arthur. *Indians in the Fur Trade*. Toronto: University of Toronto Press, 1998.
Reddin, Paul. *Wild West Shows*. Urbana: University of Illinois Press, 1999.
Regis, Pamela. *Describing Early America: Bartram, Jefferson, Crèvecoeur, and the Rhetoric of Natural History*. DeKalb: Northern Illinois University Press, 1992.
Rice, Howard C. *Le Cultivateur américain: Etude sur l'œuvre de Saint John de Crèvecoeur*. Paris: Champion, 1933.
Richards, Jeffrey H. "Revolution, Domestic Life, and the End of 'Common Mercy' in Crèvecoeur's 'Landscapes.'" *William and Mary Quarterly*, 3rd series, 55, no. 2 (1998): 281–96.
Richter, Daniel K. *Facing East from Indien Territory: A Native History of Early America*. Cambridge MA: Harvard University Press, 2001.
Ricoeur, Paul. *La mémoire, l'histoire, l'oubli*. Paris: Seuil, 2000.
Robinson, David M. "Community and Utopia in Crèvecoeur's *Sketches*." *American Literature* 62, no. 1 (1990): 17–31.
Ronda, James P. "Dreams and Discoveries: Exploring the American West, 1760–1815." *William and Mary Quarterly* 46, no.1 (1989): 145–62.
Rose, Kenneth D. *Unspeakable Awfulness: America through the Eyes of European Travelers, 1865–1900*. London: Routledge, 2014.
Round, Philip H. *Removable Type: Histories of the Book in Indian Country, 1663–1880*. Chapel Hill: University of North Carolina Press, 2010.
Rubiés, Joan Pau. "Travel Writing and Ethnography." In *The Cambridge Companion to Travel Writing*, ed. Peter Hulme and Tim Youngs. Cambridge, UK: Cambridge University Press, 2002.
Sahlins, Marshall. *Stone Age Economics*. New edition. London: Routledge, 2004.
Saunt, Claudio. *A New Order of Things: Property, Power, and the Transformation of the Creek Indians, 1733–1816*. Cambridge, UK: Cambridge University Press, 1999.
Savage, Henry, Jr. *Discovering America, 1700–1875*. New York: Harper and Row, 1979.
Sayre, Gordon M. *Les Sauvages Américains: Representations of Native Americans in French and English Colonial Literature*. Chapel Hill: University of North Carolina Press, 1997.

Sayre, Robert Woods. "L'expérience et l'interprétation de la crise chez Crèvecoeur." *Revue Française d'Études Américaines* 64 (May 1995): 279–87.

———. "A French Creole Emigré in Late Eighteenth-Century Philadelphia: Moreau de Saint-Méry." In *La France en Amérique: Mémoire d'une conquête*, ed. Susanne Berthier-Foglar. Chambéry, France: Presses de l'université de Savoie, 2009.

———. "From Journal to 'Travels': Jonathan Carver's 18th-Century Voyage into Indian Country." In *Seuils et Traverses: Enjeux de l'écriture du voyage*, vol. 2, ed. J. Borm and J.-Y. Le Disez. Brest: Presses de l'Université de Bretagne Occidentale, 2002.

———. *La modernité et son autre: Récits de la rencontre avec l'Indien en Amérique du Nord au XVIIIe siècle*. Bécherel, France: Editions Les Perséides, 2008.

———. "Philip Freneau, poète et journaliste, ou la lutte contre l'oubli." *Études Anglaises* 48, no. 1 (1995): 12–24.

———. "'Romantisme anti-capitaliste' et révolution chez Freneau." *Revue Française d'Études Américaines* 40 (April 1989): 175–86.

———. "William Bartram and Environmentalism." *American Studies* 54, no. 1 (2015): 67–87.

Sayre, Robert Woods, and Michael Löwy. *Esprits de feu: Figures du romantisme anti-capitaliste*. Paris: Éditions du Sandre, 2010.

Sayre, Robert Woods, and Michael Löwy. *Romanticism against the Tide of Modernity*. Durham NC: Duke University Press, 2001.

Sayre, Robert Woods, and Michael Löwy. "Romanticism and Capitalism." In *A Companion to European Romanticism*, ed. Michael Ferber. London: Blackwell, 2005.

Scalping and Torture: Warfare Practices among North American Indians. Ohswegen, Canada: Irocrafts, 1985.

Schramm, Karen. "Promotion Literature." In *The Oxford Handbook of Early American Literature*, ed. Kevin J. Hayes. Oxford: Oxford University Press, 2008.

Sears, John F. *Sacred Places: American Tourist Attractions in the Nineteenth Century*. New York: Oxford University Press, 1989.

Seybolt, Robert Francis. "Hunting Indians in Massachusetts: A Scouting Journal of 1758." *New England Quarterly* 3, no. 3 (1930): 527–31.

Shaffer, Marguerite S. *See America First: Tourism and National Identity, 1880–1940*. Washington DC: Smithsonian Institution Press, 2001.

Shapiro, Barbara. *A Culture of Fact: England 1550–1720*. Ithaca NY: Cornell University Press, 2000.

Sheehan, Bernard. *Seeds of Extinction: Jeffersonian Philanthropy and the American Indian*. Chapel Hill: University of North Carolina Press, 1973.

Shields, E. Thomson, Jr. "Paradise Regained Again: The Literary Context of John Lawson's *A New Voyage to Carolina*." *North Carolina Literary Review* 1, no. 1 (1992): 83–97.

Shoemaker, Nancy. *A Strange Likeness: Becoming Red and White in Eighteenth-Century North America*. New York: Oxford University Press, 2004.

Silver, Peter. *Our Savage Neighbors: How Indian War Transformed Early America*. New York: Norton, 2008.

Skinner, Claiborn. *The Upper Country: French Enterprise in the Colonial Great Lakes*. Baltimore: Johns Hopkins University Press, 2008.

Slaughter, Thomas P. *The Natures of John and William Bartram*. New York: Vintage, 1996.

Sleeper-Smith, Susan, ed. *Rethinking the Fur Trade: Cultures of Exchange in an Atlantic World*. Lincoln: University of Nebraska Press, 2009.

Slotkin, Richard. *Regeneration through Violence: The Mythology of the American Frontier, 1600–1860*. Middletown CT: Wesleyan University Press, 1973.

Smith, James K. *Alexander Mackenzie, Explorer: The Hero Who Failed*. Toronto: McGraw-Hill, 1973.

Smith, Thomas Ruys. *River of Dreams: Imagining the Mississippi before Mark Twain*. Baton Rouge: Louisiana State University Press, 2007.

Szasz, Ferenc Morton. *Scots in the North American West, 1790–1917*. Norman: University of Oklahoma Press, 2000.

Tagg, James. *Benjamin Franklin Bache and the Philadelphia Aurora*. Philadelphia: University of Pennsylvania Press, 1991.

Taylor, Alan. *American Colonies*. New York: Viking, 2001.

———. "Continental Crossings." *Journal of the Early Republic* 24, no. 2 (2004): 182–88.

———. *Writing Early American History*. Philadelphia: University of Pennsylvania Press, 2004.

Thompson, Carl. *Travel Writing*. London: Routledge, 2011.

Thompson, Edward Palmer. *Customs in Common*. New York: Norton, 1991.

———. *The Making of the English Working Class*. London: V. Gollancz, 1963.

Tolles, Frederick. *Meeting House and Counting House: The Quaker Merchants of Colonial Philadelphia. 1682–1763*. New York: Norton, 1948.

"The Transition to Capitalism in America: A Panel Discussion." *History Teacher* 27, no. 3 (1994): 263–88.

Trigger, Bruce G. *The Indians and the Heroic Age of New France*. No. 30. Ottawa: Canadian Historical Association, 1977.

———. *Natives and Newcomers: Canada's "Heroic Age" Reconsidered*. Kingston, Canada: McGill-Queens University Press, 1985.

Trigger, Bruce G., and Wilcomb E. Washburn, eds. *The Cambridge History of the Native Peoples of the Americas*. Vol. 1. Cambridge, UK: Cambridge University Press, 1996.

Truettner, William H. *The Natural Man Observed: A Study of Catlin's Indian Gallery*. Washington DC: Smithsonian Institution Press, 1979.

Usner, Daniel H., Jr. *Indians, Settlers, and Slaves in a Frontier Exchange Economy: The Lower Mississippi Valley before 1783*. Chapel Hill: University of North Carolina Press, 1992.

Vail, Philip. *The Magnificent Adventures of Alexander Mackenzie*. New York: Dodd, Mead, 1964.

Van Der Beets, Richard. *The Indian Captivity Narrative: An American Genre*. New York: University Press of America, 1984.

Venema, Kathleen. "'He Never Harmed an Indian': Ethnographic Consequences of Alexander Mackenzie's Heroic Narrative." *Mosaic* 35, no. 3 (2002): 89–107.

Vickers, Daniel, ed. *A Companion to Colonial America*. London: Blackwell, 2003.

———. "Competency and Competition: Economic Culture in Early America." *William and Mary Quarterly*, 3rd series, 47, no. 1 (1990): 3–29.

———. "The Northern Colonies: Economy and Society, 1600–1775." In *The Cambridge Economic History of the United States*, Vol. 1: *The Colonial Era*, ed. Stanley L. Engerman and Robert E. Gallman. Cambridge, UK: Cambridge University Press, 1996.

Vidal, Cécile, and François-Joseph Ruggiu, eds. *Sociétés, colonisations et esclavages dans le monde atlantique: Historiographie des sociétés américaines des XVIe–XIXe siècles*. Bécherel, France: Les Perséides, 2009.

Vivies, Jean. *Le récit de voyage en Angleterre au 18e siècle: De l'inventaire à l'invention*. Toulouse, France: Presses universitaires du Mirail, 1999.

Vizenor, Gerald. *Manifest Manners: Postindian Warriors of Survivance*. Hanover NH: University Press of New England, 1994.

———, ed. *Survivance: Narratives of Native Presence*. Lincoln: University of Nebraska Press, 2008.

Wallace, Anthony F. C. *Jefferson and the Indians: The Tragic Fate of the First Americans*. Cambridge MA: Harvard University Press, 1999.

Wallerstein, Emmanuel. *Historical Capitalism, with Capitalist Civilization*. London: Verso, 1995.

———. *The Modern World-System III: The Second Era of Great Expansion of the Capitalist World-Economy, 1730–1840s*. San Diego: Academic Press, 1989.

Walters, Kerry S. "The 'Peaceable Disposition' of Animals: William Bartram on the Moral Sensibility of Brute Creation." *Pennsylvania History* 56, no. 3 (1989): 157–76.

Walthall, John A., and Thomas E. Emerson, eds. *Calumet and Fleur-de-lys: Archaeology of Indian and French Contact in the Midcontinent*. Washington DC: Smithsonian Institution Press, 1992.

Warkentin, Germaine, ed. *Critical Issues in Editing Exploration Texts*. Toronto: University of Toronto Press, 1995.

Warrior, Robert Allen. *The People and the Word: Reading Native Nonfiction.* Minneapolis: University of Minnesota Press, 2005.

———. *Tribal Secrets: Recovering American Indian Intellectual Traditions.* Minneapolis: University of Minnesota Press, 1995.

Washburn, Wilcomb. "The Clash of Morality in the American Forest." In *First Images of America: The Impact of the New World on the Old*, vol. 1, ed. Fredi Chiappelli. Berkeley: University of California Press, 1976.

———. *The Indian in America.* New York: Harper & Row, 1975.

———. "James Adair's 'Noble Savages.'" In *The Colonial Legacy, Vol. 3: Historians of Nature and Man's Nature*, ed. Lawrence H. Leder. New York: Harper & Row, 1973.

Watts, Edward. *In This Remote Country: French Colonial Culture in the Anglo-American Imagination, 1780–1860.* Chapel Hill: University of North Carolina Press, 2006.

Weaver, Jace. "From I-Hermeneutics to We-Hermeneutics: Native Americans and the Post-Colonial." In *Native American Religious Identity: Unforgotten Gods*, ed. J. Weaver. Maryknoll NY: Orbis, 1998.

———. *The Red Atlantic: American Indigenes and the Making of the Modern World, 1000–1927.* Chapel Hill: University of North Carolina Press, 2014.

Weber, Max. *The Protestant Ethic and the Spirit of Capitalism.* New York: Dover, 2003.

———. *The Vocation Lectures.* Ed. David Owen and Tracy B. Strong. Trans. Rodney Livingstone. Indianapolis IN: Hackett, 2004.

Wertheimer, Eric. "Commencement Ceremonies: History and Identity in *The Rising Glory of America*, 1771 and 1786." *Early American Literature* 29, no. 1 (1994): 35–58.

———. *Imagined Empires: Incas, Aztecs, and the New World of American Literature, 1771–1876.* Cambridge, UK: Cambridge University Press, 1999.

Wesson, Cameron B. *Households and Hegemony: Early Creek Prestige Goods, Symbolic Capital, and Social Power.* Lincoln: University of Nebraska Press, 2008.

White, Richard. "Indian Peoples and the Natural World: Asking the Right Questions." In *Rethinking American Indian History*, ed. Donald Fixico. Albuquerque: University of New Mexico Press, 1997.

———. *The Middle Ground: Indians, Empires and Republics in the Great Lakes Region, 1650–1815.* Cambridge, UK: Cambridge University Press, 1991.

Widder, Keith R. *Beyond Pontiac's Shadow: Michilimackinac and the Anglo-Indian War of 1763.* East Lansing: Michigan State University Press, 2013.

Williams, Daniel E. "Until They Are Contaminated by Their More Refined Neighbors: The Images of the Native Americans in Carver's 'Travels through the Interior' and Its Influence on the Euro-American Imagination." In *Indians and Europe: An Interdisciplinary Collection of Essays*, ed. Christian F. Feest. Aachen, Germany: Ed. Herodot, Rader Verlag, 1987.

Wilson, Angela Cavender. "Power of the Spoken Word: Native Oral Traditions in

American Indian History." In *Rethinking American Indian History*, ed. Donald L. Fixico. Albuquerque: University of New Mexico Press, 1997.

Witgen, Michael. *An Infinity of Nations: How the Native New World Shaped Early North America*. Philadelphia: University of Pennsylvania Press, 2012.

Wolfe, Patrick. "Settler Colonialism and the Elimination of the Native." *Journal of Genocide Research* 8, no. 4 (2006): 387–409.

Wolfzettel, Friedrich. *Le discours du voyageur: Le récit de voyage en France, du Moyen Age au XVIIIe siècle*. Paris: Presses Universitaires de France, 1996.

Wood, Gordon S. "Inventing American Capitalism." *New York Review of Books* 41, no. 11 (9, 1994): 44–49.

———. *The Radicalism of the American Revolution*. New York: Knopf, 1992.

Wood, Peter H. "The Mysterious 1688 Journey of M. Lahontan." *Georgia Workshop in Early American History and Culture*, 2007. Online.

Woollacott, Arthur P. *Mackenzie and His Voyageurs, by Canoe to the Arctic and the Pacific, 1789–93*. London: J. M. Dent & Sons, 1927.

Wooster, Robert. *The American Military Frontiers: The United States Army in the West, 1783–1900*. Albuquerque: University of New Mexico Press, 2009.

Wright, Ronald. *Stolen Continents: The Americas through Indian Eyes Since 1492*. Boston: Houghton Mifflin, 1992.

Yenne, Bill. *Indian Wars: The Campaign for the American West*. Yardley PA: Westholme, 2006.

Youngs, Tim. *The Cambridge Introduction to Travel Writing*. Cambridge, UK: Cambridge University Press, 2013.

INDEX

Abenaki Indians, 11–12
Adair, James, 18, 109, 114, 186, 235
Adams, Abigail, 30
Adams, John, 66
"adventure" with Indians, 22, 101–2, 117–29, 160, 187, 188, 190–94, 221, 223, 272, 298–99
agriculture: European and Anglo-American, 8, 12, 35, 37, 39–40, 53, 73, 138, 296, 322n30; Indian, 8, 51, 53, 55, 76–77
alcohol, 52, 184–85, 199, 249, 352n61
Algonquin Indians, 145, 148
alienation, 24, 206, 212, 296
American character, 85–87, 91–92, 94, 95
American Revolution, 29, 44–50, 57, 62, 65–66, 96, 208, 232, 269, 296
anthropology, 16, 134, 290
Apess, William, 275, 364n18
Arikara Indians, 25, 259, 261–62, 264–65

aristocracy, 12–13, 22–23, 31, 33, 47, 53, 63, 81, 83, 139, 140, 142–43, 146, 150, 165, 267, 299, 300, 302
artefacts, 290–91
artist-travelers, 273–74, 284
Assiniboin Indians, 257, 278, 283

Bache, Benjamin Franklin, 60
back country. *See* frontier
Baltimore, 74, 82, 88
banking, 72
Banks, Joseph, 186
barter, 65, 128, 264, 299
Bartram, John, 23, 40, 169, 206, 209
Bartram, William, 23–24, 34, 203, 205–34, 236, 253, 270, 271, 293, 296, 300, 301, 303–4
Bermuda, 43–45. *See also* Caribbean islands
Beverley, Robert, 108, 319n3

Black Hawk (Sauk chief), 278
Bodmer, Karl, 274
Boudinot, Elias, 274, 364n18
Bouquet, Henri, 104, 115, 119, 335n50
Bourgmont, Véniard de, 256
Brackenridge, Hugh Henry, 59, 61, 66–69, 107, 115–16, 141, 153, 271, 298–99, 304–5, 336n57
Braddock, Edward, 107
Bradstreet, John, 120, 128
Brant, Joseph, 95
Brissot de Warville, Jacques-Pierre, 58
British colonies, 34–45, 66–70, 166
Buffalo Bill Cody, 289
Byrd, William, II, 30

Cabeza de Vaca. *See* Nunez Cabeza de Vaca, Alvar
Cabot, John, 70
Canada, 22, 43, 94, 136, 142, 152, 154, 241. *See also* New France
capitalism, xiv, 1–4, 29, 57, 64, 101, 136–37, 269, 304, 314n9. *See also* "transition to capitalism"
captivity accounts, 15, 22, 105–8, 119, 124–28, 270, 271, 273, 298, 299
Caribbean islands, 38, 59, 82, 137
Carlyle, Thomas, 212, 213
Carver, Jonathan, 23, 34, 156, 170, 183–202, 222, 223, 225, 256–57, 271–72, 301, 302, 303, 304
Catawba Indians, 173, 331n6
Catholicism, 11–12, 137, 139, 144, 149, 154, 159, 161, 163, 299, 316n42
Catlin, George, 25, 269, 274, 275–94, 305–6
Charlevoix, François Xavier de, 22–23, 131, 153–66, 183, 186, 299, 300, 301, 302, 345n78
Chastellux, Marquis de, 30, 58

Chateaubriand, François-René de, 81, 212
Cherokee Indians, 24, 107, 109, 168, 169, 207, 214–15, 222, 224, 225, 227
Cheyenne Indians, 263, 289
Chickasaw Indians, 18, 109, 235
Chipewyan Indians, 240, 247
Chippewa Indians. *See* Ojibwe Indians
Choctaw Indians, 24, 109, 207, 214–15, 216, 223
chorography, 30, 133, 319n3, 325n4
Christianization, 148, 165, 302, 346n94
Christianized Indians, 139, 156–58, 162, 165, 227, 333n23
cities, 65, 71, 72, 76, 77–78
"civilization" and Indians, 95, 96, 116, 153, 210, 211, 213, 219, 220, 227, 230–31, 232, 233, 266, 302, 303–4, 357n52
Clark, William, 278
Colden, Cadwallader, 4, 109
Coleridge, Samuel Taylor, 212
Columbus, Christopher, 69, 70
Comanche Indians, 278, 287
commerce, 66, 73
community, 161, 180, 301, 302, 322n31
competitiveness, 2, 29, 36
Congaree Indians, 173
Connecticut, 70, 73
"consumer revolution," 3, 10
conversion of Indians, 149, 159, 162, 165, 176–77, 182, 301
Cooper, James Fenimore, 274
coureurs des bois, 12, 140, 236, 241, 262, 317n50, 340n38. *See also* fur trade; traders; *voyageurs*
Crawford, William, 106, 113, 364n5
Cree Indians (Killistinoe), 184, 197, 198, 240, 242, 278
Creek Indians (Muscogulge), 24, 76, 168, 207–8, 214–15, 225, 227–28, 229, 230, 233, 328n60, 353n9

398 · *Index*

Crèvecoeur, St. John de, 13, 21, 29, 31–55, 60, 78, 111, 270, 295, 296, 297, 300, 304
Croghan, George, 55, 169
Crow Indians, 263, 278
Curtis, Edward S., 274
customs of Indians, 95, 108, 133, 180–81, 188, 195, 214, 257, 265–66, 283, 284–86, 290, 303

Dakota Indians. *See* Sioux Indians: Dakota (Naudowessie)
Decalves, Don Alonzo, 257
deism, 149, 300
Delaware Indians (Lenape), 75, 106, 107, 115, 122
Démeunier, Jean-Nicolas, 92
Dene Indians, 238, 242
destruction of Indians, 96, 114–16, 117, 141, 153, 298, 335n48, 335n51. *See also* genocide
Detroit, 125, 128, 156, 157, 165
devil, 162, 177, 192, 351n57
Dickens, Charles, 272
"disenchantment of the world" (Weber), 9, 137, 139
Drake, Francis, 70
Duane, William, 60
Dutch in the Americas, 70, 74, 92, 136

"ecological Indian," 7–8, 316n32
ecology, 217, 316n32
egoism, 63, 94, 166, 229
Emerson, Ralph Waldo, 213, 272
encyclopedists, 33, 134
Enlightenment, 25, 61, 62–66, 82, 83, 93, 116–17, 134, 142, 153, 200, 297, 304–6, 341n43
Enoe Indians, 175, 176, 178, 348n25
equality, 150, 151, 161, 200, 202, 229, 266, 296, 302

ethnohistory, xi–xii, xiv, 20, 295
ethnological displays and shows, 25, 288–90
ethnology. *See* anthropology
Evans, Lewis, 169
The Expedition of Humphry Clinker (Smollett), 111
exploration, 17, 154, 202, 236–37, 239, 241, 243, 254, 300

farming. *See* agriculture
Federalist Party, 60
Filson, John, 205
Fixico, Donald, xi, xiii
forests, 65, 77, 145, 297
Fothergill, John, 207, 209, 213
Fox, George, 210
Fox Indians (Ottagaumie), 145, 146, 159, 184, 201, 202
francisation, 166, 302, 346n93
fraternity, 161, 200
freedom, 148–49, 150, 151, 153, 161, 164, 181–82, 200, 218, 266, 301
French and Indian War. *See* Seven Years' War
French character, 87, 92–93, 94
French Creoles, 81, 84, 85, 89, 91, 92, 93
French in North America. *See* New France
French Revolution, 62, 65–66, 81, 82, 83; émigrés from, 81, 82, 83, 87, 89, 93; values of, 142, 151, 200
French West Indies, 82. *See also* Caribbean islands
Freneau, Philip, 13, 21, 58–79, 110, 116, 270, 295–96, 297, 300, 304–5
Frontenac, Comte de, 109, 143, 147
frontier, 41, 45, 52, 65, 68, 96, 104, 111, 286, 297; French "frontier," 138, 340n28

Index · 399

fur trade, 11, 12, 24, 116, 136, 137, 235–37, 239–41, 246, 254, 303. See also *coureurs des bois*; traders; *voyageurs*

generosity, 165, 198, 302
genocide, 116, 298, 335n52
genres of accounts: of encounters with Indians, 22, 103, 124, 129, 141, 318n59; of travel in Indian territory, 131–35, 167, 188, 277, 338n5
gift-giving, 7, 151, 161, 177, 194, 250, 345n85
Gnadenhütten. *See* massacre: at Gnadenhütten
golden age, 63
Graffenried, Baron von, 171–72
Greco-Roman antiquity, comparison with, 155, 200–201, 266, 303
greed, 46, 63, 70, 90, 166, 180, 211, 229, 303

habitants, 140
habitus, 15, 349n28
Hamilton, Alexander (Maryland doctor), 30
Hamilton, Alexander (statesman), 60
Hawthorne, Nathaniel, 272
Heckewelder, John, 347n8
Henry, Alexander, the Elder, 124–29, 142, 169, 205, 235, 257, 270–71, 299, 337n73
Hidatsa Indians (Gros Ventre), 257, 263, 264
hierarchy, 138, 151, 166, 175, 210, 212, 218, 228, 229, 245, 301
histories: of colonies, 15, 22; of Indian nations, 15, 108–10
honor, 6, 7, 12, 116, 160, 164, 199, 229, 302, 315n27
hospitality, 7, 35, 39–40, 74, 94, 177, 198, 199, 302

Hudson, Henry, 70
Hudson's Bay Company, 237, 241–42
hunting, 12–13, 53, 128, 145–46, 149, 195, 263, 265, 299, 300. *See also* fur trade
Huron Indians, 122, 142, 145, 148, 156, 165; "Petun" Hurons, 146, 157

"ideal type" (Weber), 9, 323n42
Illinois country, 120, 123, 136, 138, 158–59, 163, 259, 334n40, 340n27
Imlay, Gilbert, 254
immigrants, 36–38, 44, 71, 272, 317n51, 321n28, 325n4
Indians, North American: diversity, 6; general characteristics, 7–9, 315n26
individualism, 2, 29, 57, 117
industry, 66, 73, 269, 270, 291
Iowa Indians, 288
Irish in North America, 38, 44, 49, 71
Iroquois Indians, 109, 142, 146, 147, 169, 274

Jacksonian period, 269
Jamaica, 43–45. *See also* Caribbean islands
Jefferson, Thomas, 60, 64, 66, 78, 79, 117, 260, 336n58
Jemison, Mary, 113, 271, 298
Jesuits, 11, 139, 140, 141, 147, 153, 154, 155, 163, 340n30
Johnston, Charles, 107–8

Kalm, Pehr, 30
Kane, Paul, 363n14
Kentucky, 107, 113, 254
Keyauwee Indians, 175, 176
Kickapoo Indians, 122
King, Charles Bird, 274
King Philip's War, 114, 274
Knight, Sarah Kemble, 30

Kondiaronk (Huron chief), 142, 146, 149, 343n58
Kwakiutl Indians, 238

Lafitau, Joseph-François, 133, 155–56, 163, 315n27
La Harpe, Bénard, 256
Lahontan, Louis-Armand de Lom d'Arce, baron de, 22–23, 131, 141–53, 165, 186, 255–56, 267, 296, 299, 300–302, 304, 341n45
Langlade, Charles-Michel Mouet de, 126, 337n70
La Rochefoucauld-Liancourt, Duc de, 21–22, 81, 83, 89, 93–96
La Vérandrye family, 256
Lawson, John, 23, 168, 170–82, 198, 225, 300, 301, 302, 303
lawyers, 48, 72, 74, 82
legends, 152, 178, 197, 227–28. *See also* myth
Lenape Indians. *See* Delaware Indians
Le Page du Pratz, Antoine-Simon, 360n32
Leroux, Laurent, 245, 359n19
Letters from an American Farmer (Crèvecoeur), 32, 33, 34–35, 36
Lettres persanes (Montesquieu), 76
Lewis, Meriwether, 260
Lewis and Clark expedition, 270, 273
linguistic aspect of encounter, 145, 157, 175, 181, 195
literary works on Indians, 110–12, 118
Long, John, 205
Longfellow, Henry Wadsworth, 274
Loskiel, George Henry, 108
Louisiana, 136, 254, 255, 270
Louis XIV, 138
Louis-Philippe, 81
luxury, 70, 74, 211

Machapunga Indians, 178
MacKay, Alexander, 245, 359n20
Mackenzie, Alexander, 24, 205, 235–53, 256, 300, 302
Madison, James, 59, 65, 78
Madoc, Prince, 257–58
magic, 9, 137, 140, 151, 162, 197, 228, 301, 315n21, 316n42. *See also* marvelous; supernatural
Mandan Indians, 25, 147, 256, 257, 259, 263, 264, 278, 285, 286
Manifest Destiny, 305, 366n44
maps, 173, 184, 201–2, 254, 279
market society. *See* capitalism
Maryland, 70, 74
Martineau, Harriet, 272
Martinique, 81, 82. *See also* Caribbean islands; French West Indies
marvelous, 9, 137, 139, 140
Massachusetts, 70, 73
massacre, 68, 69, 215; at Gnadenhütten, 106, 115, 333n21; at Michilimackinac, 124–27
Mather, Cotton, 103–4, 114
Matotopé (Four Bears, Mandan chief), 282, 285, 289, 365n35
May, Karl, 274
McKay, James, 362n43
McKenney, Thomas L., 273, 363n10
medicine, Indian, 152, 178
memory, collective, xiii, 19, 20, 21, 295, 306
Menominee Indians, 152, 198, 202
Metacomet (Wampanoag chief), 54, 274
métissage, 140
Miami Indians, 111, 112, 122, 123, 145, 158
Michilimackinac, 124, 127, 128, 129, 142, 183, 184. *See also* massacre
"middle ground," 9
military accounts, 15, 22, 103–5, 119–23, 299. *See also* war with Indians

Index · 401

Mingo Indians, 115
mining, 129, 174–75, 184, 286
missionaries, 11, 108, 139, 148, 151, 162, 168, 197, 241, 273
modernity, xii, 1–4, 9–10, 62, 93, 97, 101, 115, 136, 212, 236, 269, 305–6
Mohawk Indians, 95, 121; Kahnawake Mohawks, 107, 333n23
money, 4, 49, 70, 72, 77, 94, 95, 172, 174, 239, 296; for Indians, 150, 153, 177, 179, 199
Monroe, James, 59, 78
Montaigne, Michel de, 17
Montreal, 237, 239, 240, 255
Moravians, 106, 108, 115, 168, 169
Morgan, Lewis Henry, 274, 290
Morris, Thomas, 119–23, 298
myth, 9, 152, 178, 197, 227, 301. *See also* legends

naming, 175, 195, 202, 222, 348n20, 360n22
Nantucket, 38–39, 41, 51–52
Napoleon Bonaparte, 66
Natchez Indians, 138
Native American studies, xiii
naturalists, 168, 205, 209
nature, relation to: of Europeans and Anglo-Americans, 8–9, 64–65, 252; of Indians, 7–8, 76, 211, 218–19, 228, 234, 301
Naudowessie Indians. *See* Sioux Indians: Dakota (Naudowessie)
New France, 11–13, 22–23, 31, 43, 131, 136–39, 144, 148, 166, 339n21, 340n32; writers and travelers in, 139–41, 143, 154, 155
New York, 72, 76, 82
Niagara, 128
noble savage theme, 17–18, 55, 142, 283

North Carolina, 171, 348n18
North West Company, 237, 242, 245, 257
"Northwest Passage," 24, 154, 183, 238, 239, 240, 242
novels with Indian themes, 15, 22
Nunez Cabeza de Vaca, Alvar, 132, 338n8

Occom, Samson, 20, 274
Oglethorpe, James, 168
Ohio country, 104, 106, 107, 108, 113, 115, 119
Ojibwe Indians, 113, 125, 127–28, 129, 145, 190–94, 199–200, 202, 271, 288, 299, 352n63
Omaha Indians (Maha), 25, 259, 261–65
Oneida Indians, 51
Osceola (Seminole chief), 279
the "Other," 6, 10, 13, 20, 101, 117, 132, 234, 270, 275; evaluation of, 135, 151, 180, 199–200, 230–31, 253, 302; interaction with, 135, 156, 175, 188, 189, 196, 220–25, 253; knowledge or understanding of, 16–17, 135, 160, 177–79, 196, 198, 225, 253, 301; "recognition" of, 17, 18, 235, 236
Oto Indians, 261
Ottawa Indians, 113, 120, 121, 125, 127, 145, 157, 184, 190, 192

Padouca Indians, 256
Paine, Thomas, 60
"pan-indian" movements, 52
paradise lost, 47, 63. *See also* utopia
Pawnee Indians, 287
peasantry, 12, 139, 140
Pennsylvania, 74
Penn, William, 75
Pequot Indians, 275
Perrin du Lac, François-Marie, 260
Petiver, James, 170, 171

Philadelphia, 37, 72, 77, 81, 82, 83, 87, 89–92
physiocratic ideal, 64–65
Pike, Zebulon Montgomery, 270
pioneers, 36, 68, 71, 273, 286. *See also* frontier
poetry with Indian themes, 15
Polanyi, Karl, 2, 315n27
Ponca Indians, 261–63
Pond, Peter, 237, 243, 256–57, 352n58
Pontiac, 112, 120, 121, 124, 298
Post, Christian Frederick, 169
Potawatomi Indians, 145, 152, 157, 158
poverty, 72
praxis-based analysis, 16, 318n62
precapitalism, 3, 12, 62, 78, 116, 151, 304
pre-Columbian, 68–69
premodern. *See* precapitalism
progress, 63, 66, 297
promotional tract, 30
property arrangements: of Europeans and British, 8–9, 38–39, 316n36; of Indians, 8–9, 150, 199, 229, 250
"prospective vision," 172, 219, 232
The Protestant Ethic and the Spirit of Capitalism (Weber), 2, 38, 209, 323n42
Protestantism, 38, 137, 139, 168, 209, 300, 301, 303
publics, 14, 103, 118, 119, 124, 181, 188, 271
puritanism, 6, 46–47, 70, 117, 314n9, 315n21

Quakerism, 24, 38, 40, 49, 50, 58, 74; William Bartram in relation to, 206, 207, 208–10, 212, 221–22, 229–30, 354n18
Quebec (City), 142–43, 145, 147, 154, 156

racism, 116, 271, 335n54
Radisson, Pierre-Esprit, 140
Raleigh, Sir Walter, 132

Rasles, Father, 11–12
rationalism, calculating. *See* utilitarian reason
rationality, 147, 150, 151, 152, 178, 211, 212, 266, 301, 305, 344n71
reader response, 102, 103, 104, 109–10, 118, 122, 127, 128, 190, 281–82, 298
Récollets, 140, 340n30
religion, 23, 29, 46–47, 49–50, 68, 69, 105, 108, 110; of Indians, 129, 149, 178, 196–97, 228, 251
Republican Party, 60, 66
revenge, 149–50, 160, 164, 221, 229, 344n69
Revolution. *See* American Revolution and French Revolution
Rhode Island, 70, 73
Rogers, Robert, 104, 112, 120, 183, 184, 187, 298, 330n7
romanticism, 19, 24, 33, 212, 214, 234, 275, 283, 284, 293–94; and Enlightenment, 25, 61–66, 297, 304–5
Rousseau, Jean-Jacques, 32, 33, 200
Rowlandson, Mary, 105
ruins, Indian, 225, 230
Rupert's Land, 136, 257, 331n1

the sacred, 7, 129, 278, 279, 285–86, 287, 293, 348n20, 348n26
Saint-Castin, baron de, 342n51
Saint-Domingue, 21, 81, 82, 155, 330n4. *See also* Caribbean islands; French West Indies
Saint-Méry, Moreau de, 13, 21, 81–94, 296, 297, 300
Santee Indians, 175
Saponi Indians, 173
Sauk Indians, 125, 152, 184, 201, 202, 278
Sault Sainte Marie, 125
scalping, 104–5, 107, 336n55

Schoolcraft, Henry, 113, 290
Scots in North America, 30, 36–38, 74, 237, 242, 296, 328n60
Seaver, James Everett, 113, 271
selfishness, 40
Seminole Indians, 24, 207, 214, 219–23, 226–27, 229, 231, 232, 270, 279
Seneca Indians, 113–14, 298
"settler colonialism," 5, 12, 97, 101, 115, 335n52
settlers, 41–42, 96, 115, 220, 226, 270, 278, 322n29, 322n33
Seven Years' War, 104, 112, 114, 124, 167, 169, 183
sexuality, 163, 176, 177, 224, 266, 330n13, 348n24, 352n59
Shakori Indians, 178
shamanism, 11, 178, 197, 285. *See also* magic
Shawnee Indians, 107, 112, 115, 271
sharing, 7, 150, 161, 180, 199, 229, 266, 302
Sioux Indians: Dakota (Naudowessie), 147, 184, 185, 190, 195–97, 201–2, 256–57, 278, 285–86, 292, 303, 350n34; Teton, 261–63; Yancton, 261–63
Sketches of Eighteenth-Century America (Crèvecoeur), 32, 33, 36
slavery, 40, 41, 70, 74, 76, 82, 95, 356n43
Slover, John, 107, 112–13, 298, 299
Smith, James, 107
Smith, William, 119
Smollett, Tobias, 111–12
Spanish in North America, 11, 43, 227, 237, 254–55, 257, 259, 261, 264
Spanish in South America, 67, 69
speculation, 38, 41, 74–75, 90, 171, 239, 296; on land, 8, 75, 96, 106, 107, 168, 205, 215, 270, 300
Spencer, Oliver M., 107
the state, 12, 138, 139, 144, 148, 299

stereotypes, 16, 76–77, 106–7, 151, 199, 201, 265, 274
subordination, 13, 139, 150, 153, 164, 166
supernatural, 9, 178, 197. *See also* magic
superstition, 63, 137, 24, 264, 266, 286

Talleyrand, Charles Maurice de, 89
Tammany (Tamanend, Delaware chief), 75
Tanner, John, 113, 271, 334n43
Tecumseh (Shawnee chief), 102, 270, 316n35
Thompson, David, 257
Thoreau, Henry David, 272
Ticonderoga, 111
Timberlake, Henry, 169
time, 179, 243–44
Toangarest (Omaha chief), 262–63
Tocqueville, Alexis de, 272
Tomo Cheeki, 76–78
Tories, 46, 48–50
torture, 103, 105–7, 109–12, 116, 121, 123–24, 147, 160–61, 181, 200, 230, 271; practiced mainly in East, 332n8
tourism, 25, 288, 291–93, 367n55
traders: British, 12, 123, 124, 174, 216–18, 221, 259, 264, 334n40; French Canadian, 255–56, 258–59, 262–63, 301. *See also coureurs des bois;* fur trade; *voyageurs*
Trail of Tears, 270, 279
"transition to capitalism," 3–4, 10, 136, 314n13. *See also* capitalism
trans-Mississippi West, 5, 253–58, 276, 278, 291, 292
travel accounts, 13–16; in British colonies, 30, 81; editing of, 134, 186–87, 192, 213–14, 220, 232, 240, 252–53; ethnographic, 15–16, 22, 131–36, 193–94, 196; manuscripts of, 186–88, 190, 193–94, 201–2, 210, 213–14, 220, 232,

404 · Index

240, 357n52, 357n57; method of study of, 134–36; publics of, 14, 172, 185, 187–89, 194, 196–97, 205–6, 213–14, 240, 281–82; tradition of, 279–80
Treaty of Paris, 102, 104
Trollope, Frances, 272, 363n8
Trudeau, Jean-Baptiste, 25, 235, 258–67, 299, 300, 301, 302, 303
Tuscarora Indians, 95, 171, 172, 178
Twain, Mark, 272

utilitarian reason, 2, 64, 75, 90
utopia, 39, 45, 201–2, 219. *See also* paradise lost

Veblen, Thorstein, 273
violence, 22, 101–17, 211, 222, 271, 298, 299. *See also* war among Indians; war with Indians; "zero degree" of encounter
Virginia, 70, 74, 108, 296; Norfolk, city in, 88, 90
Vizenor, Gerald, xi, 18, 175, 364n18
voyageurs, 159, 238, 244, 246, 247, 255, 258, 282, 340n38. *See also coureurs des bois*; fur trade; traders

war among Indians, 102–3, 108–9, 149, 160, 164, 200, 229–30, 301, 331n6
War of 1812, 5, 78, 102, 269, 270, 314n19
War of Independence, 29, 45–50, 60, 62, 81, 102, 104–5, 111, 113, 115, 202
war with Indians, 102, 103, 114, 270, 278–79
Washington, George, 60, 106
Waxhaw Indians, 175
Weber, Max, 2, 9, 38, 137, 209, 323n42
Weiser, Conrad, 169
the "West," 253–54. *See also* trans-Mississippi West
whaling, 38, 41, 51, 73, 296
whiggism, 61, 66, 78, 297, 305, 306
Whigs, 47, 50
White, John, 273
"white Indian," 113, 128, 271, 273
Wied, Maximilian, Prince of, 274
wilderness, 14, 65, 68, 96, 131, 239, 252
Winnebago Indians, 184, 201, 202, 352n63
Woolman, John, 210
Wordsworth, William, 212
Wyandot Indians, 106, 107

Yamasee Indians, 228
Yankee, 73, 79

"zero degree" of encounter, 22, 101–29, 112, 114, 116–17, 118, 141, 253, 298–99

OTHER WORKS BY ROBERT WOODS SAYRE

*Solitude in Society: A Sociological Study
in French Literature* (1978)

*La Modernité et son autre: Récits de
la rencontre avec l'Indien en Amérique
du Nord au XVIIIe siècle* (2008)

*La Sociologie de la littérature: Histoire,
problématique, synthèse critique* (2011)

WITH MICHAEL LÖWY

*Révolte et mélancolie: Le romantisme à
contre-courant de la modernité* (1992)

*Romanticism against the Tide of
Modernity* (2001, a revised, expanded
translation of *Révolte et mélancolie*)

*Esprits de feu: Figures du romantisme
anti-capitaliste* (2010)

www.ingramcontent.com/pod-product-compliance
Lightning Source LLC
Chambersburg PA
CBHW030331240426
43661CB00052B/1590